JIM CROW'S
CHILDREN

Also by Peter Irons

THE NEW DEAL LAWYERS

JUSTICE AT WAR
The Story of the Japanese American Internment Cases

THE COURAGE OF THEIR CONVICTIONS
Sixteen Americans Who Fought Their Way to the Supreme Court

JUSTICE DELAYED
The Record of the Japanese American Internment Cases

MAY IT PLEASE THE COURT
The Most Significant Oral Arguments Made Before the Supreme Court Since 1955
(edited with Stephanie Guitton)

BRENNAN VS. REHNQUIST
The Battle for the Constitution

MAY IT PLEASE THE COURT
Arguments on Abortion
(edited with Stephanie Guitton)

MAY IT PLEASE THE COURT
The First Amendment

A PEOPLE'S HISTORY OF THE SUPREME COURT

MAY IT PLEASE THE COURT
Courts, Kids, and the Constitution

JIM CROW'S CHILDREN

The Broken Promise of the
Brown *Decision*

PETER IRONS

VIKING

VIKING

Published by the Penguin Group

Penguin Putnam Inc., 375 Hudson Street, New York, New York 10014, U.S.A.

Penguin Books Ltd, 80 Strand, London WC2R 0RL, England

Penguin Books Australia Ltd, 250 Camberwell Road, Camberwell, Victoria 3124, Australia

Penguin Books Canada Ltd, 10 Alcorn Avenue, Toronto, Ontario, Canada M4V 3B2

Penguin Books India (P) Ltd, 11 Community Centre, Panchsheel Park, New Delhi–110 017, India

Penguin Books (N.Z.) Ltd, Cnr Rosedale and Airborne Roads, Albany, Auckland, New Zealand

Penguin Books (South Africa) (Pty) Ltd, 24 Sturdee Avenue, Rosebank, Johannesburg 2196, South Africa

Penguin Books Ltd, Registered Offices:
Harmondsworth, Middlesex, England

First published in 2002 by Viking Penguin, a member of Penguin Putnam Inc.

10   9   8   7   6   5   4   3   2   1

Copyright © Peter Irons, 2002
All rights reserved
ISBN 0-670-88918-0
CIP data available

This book is printed on acid-free paper.

Printed in the United States of America
Set in Bembo with Michelangelo display
Designed by Carla Bolte

FOR BONNIE,

who knows that teaching begins with love and respect

"Where Are the Buttonwood Kids?"

The story of the legal crusade to abolish Jim Crow schooling in America covers most of the nation's history, and has not yet ended. This book recounts that campaign, beginning in 1849 with a lawsuit filed in Boston by Benjamin Roberts, after his five-year-old daughter, Sarah, was turned away from the primary school nearest her home "on the ground of her being a colored person." This first challenge to racial segregation in public schools ended in defeat, as the Massachusetts Supreme Judicial Court ruled that Sarah's interests "will best be promoted" by forcing her to attend a Jim Crow school. The last case discussed in these pages also ended in defeat for Kalima Jenkins and other black children in Kansas City, Missouri. Ruling in 1995, the United States Supreme Court terminated judicial oversight of a "resegregated" school district in which the vast majority of students were black and conditions so bad that one school principal "stated that he would not send his own child to that facility."

In between the stories of Sarah Roberts and Kalima Jenkins are those of many other black children whose parents joined legal challenges to Jim Crow schools in more than half of the states, across the country from Massachusetts to California. Most of these children remain unknown, their names unrecorded in the history books that students are assigned to read. The only child whose name is now recalled, Linda Carol Brown of Topeka, Kansas, was in third grade when civil rights lawyers placed her father's name first on a suit against the city's practice of segregating its elementary schools. One of five similar cases decided by the Supreme Court in 1954, *Brown v. Board of Education* was hailed by many Americans as a firm judicial statement of the nation's commitment to racial equality.

This book recounts the stories of the five cases that produced the *Brown* decision. We meet the black parents who risked losing their jobs, farms, or homes to join lawsuits against the Jim Crow schools their children were forced to attend. We listen to the lawyers who argued these cases on both sides, attacking and defending school segregation. We sit in the courtrooms of the lower-court judges who first decided these cases, and in the marble-columned chamber of the Supreme Court justices who had the final word in their opinions. And we hear the reactions of politicians, from the states and the Congress to the White House, who praise and denounce the judicial decisions that have shaped and reshaped our nation's schools over the past half-century.

The central figure in these stories is Thurgood Marshall, the tenacious, brilliant lawyer who headed the legal staff of the National Association for the Advancement of Colored People between 1938 and 1961. Marshall argued and won more civil rights cases before the Supreme Court than any other lawyer, and played a major role in shaping civil rights law as a Supreme Court justice, serving from 1967 until his retirement in 1991. It was Marshall who developed the legal strategy that attacked the "separate but equal" doctrine of the *Plessy* case, which stood as precedent in segregation cases since its decision in 1896. Marshall adopted the military tactics of encirclement and attrition in launching the campaign against Jim Crow schooling, first winning Supreme Court orders that graduate and law schools in border states must admit black students, although the justices declined in these cases to overturn the *Plessy* decision. After these skirmishes, Marshall picked the target for the first assault on public school segregation in the Deep South. Clarendon

County, South Carolina, was a rural area in which blacks outnumbered whites three to one but held no public offices. Many black children walked miles on dirt roads to schools in pinewood shacks with no desks or blackboards, while the county's white children rode buses to spacious brick schools with modern facilities. Marshall selected Clarendon County because its Jim Crow schools made a mockery of the "separate but equal" doctrine.

Four more cases, from Virginia, the District of Columbia, Delaware, and Kansas, joined the South Carolina case when the Supreme Court agreed to decide whether school segregation violated the Constitution's promise that every American—black or white—will receive "the equal protection of the laws." In guiding these cases to the High Court, Marshall was aided by a dedicated team of young lawyers, who included Robert Carter, Jack Greenberg, Spottswood Robinson III, and Oliver Hill. The most distinguished lawyer on the other side was John W. Davis, a former presidential candidate who defended the Jim Crow schools of South Carolina in the Supreme Court. The match-up of Marshall and Davis in the oral arguments produced few sparks but much emotion from both lawyers.

There is great drama in the story of the Court's internal struggles over the school cases. Following the first round of oral arguments in 1952, Chief Justice Fred Vinson suffered a fatal heart attack. Vinson had presided ineffectively over a Court that was torn with personal animosities and deeply split on the segregation issue. Earl Warren, who took Vinson's center seat in 1953, wielded his personal charm and political skills to cajole the wavering justices into a unanimous decision in the *Brown* case. Warren's opinion for the Court, short in both length and citation to precedent, was more than a legal document; it was also a promise to America's black children of an education "available to all on equal terms" with that given to whites.

But this was a promise broken within a year of its making. Warren paid a high price for unanimity in the *Brown* case, having agreed to Justice Felix Frankfurter's demand for a third round of arguments, on the "implementation" of the Court's initial ruling. In the second *Brown* decision in 1955, the justices rejected Thurgood Marshall's plea to order the prompt dismantling of the Jim Crow system, and set no deadline for compliance with judicial desegregation orders. Southern officials took advantage of the Court's directive to proceed with "all deliberate speed" by employing every foot-dragging and evasive tactic they could devise. The Court's failure to enforce its decrees spurred calls for "massive resistance" that included shutting down entire school systems. White hostility to integration hardened as southern politicians courted votes by defying court orders. Televised scenes in 1957 of mob violence in Little Rock, Arkansas, shocked many Americans and prompted the Court to warn defiant officials to end their "war against the Constitution." But the warnings went unheeded, as Little Rock's schools were closed and those in most Deep South states remained completely segregated.

During the period between 1968 and 1971, the Court tried in two unanimous decisions to undo the harm it had caused. Ruling in a Virginia case, the justices first directed southern officials to eliminate "root and branch" from their schools every "vestige" of segregation, then upheld a lower-court order that required busing several thousand students to achieve "racial balance" in Charlotte, North Carolina, and the metropolitan school district around the city. But the public reaction to busing quickly turned from denunciations in Congress to dynamiting school buses in Pontiac, Michigan. President Richard Nixon vowed to stop the buses, if necessary by promoting a constitutional amendment. Shortly before Nixon resigned his office in 1974, the Supreme Court attempted to defuse the issue by reversing a lower-court order to bus students from Detroit's largely black schools into 53 lily-white suburban districts. The Court's rejection of this "inter-district" remedy in the *Milliken* case, by a five-to-four vote, turned big-city suburbs into safe havens from busing and increased the "white flight" that had already created black majorities in many urban school districts.

The Court's decision in the *Milliken* case marked the beginning of a long retreat from the *Brown* decision. Over the next two decades, as both the Court and the country turned to the right, the conservative majority led by Chief Justice William Rehnquist began trimming the powers of lower-court judges who had followed the Court's earlier directives to eliminate every "vestige" of school segregation. The issue now was the "resegregation" of urban districts in which residential housing patterns, combined with massive "white flight" to the suburbs and a return to "neighborhood school" policies, had re-created the Jim Crow system of racially separate schools. Between 1990 and 1995, the Supreme Court decided three cases in which the desegregation orders of lower-court judges were "terminated," leaving school officials free to maintain one-race schools without any threat of judicial intervention.

This book tells the stories of two sets of cases, of the people who brought them to the courts, the lawyers who argued them, and the judges who decided them. The stories of the cases that led to the first *Brown* decision are dramatic and inspiring, while those of the cases that followed the "all deliberate speed" ruling are dismal and dispiriting. What adds great poignancy to these stories of lawsuits and legal opinions are the stories of the young men and women, both white and black, who now attend schools in the five communities in which the *Brown* cases began. My recent visits to these schools, and my talks with students, teachers, administrators, and community leaders, have given me insight into the factors that influenced both the making and breaking of the *Brown* promise to black children of an education "available to all on equal terms." I will save for this book's conclusion my thoughts on these factors, except to say here that each reader will most likely reach his or her own conclusions, differing from mine in ways that reflect our individual backgrounds, experiences, politics, and views of the role of race in American society. But I would remind my readers of the prophetic words of W. E. B. DuBois, writing in 1903: "The problem of the Twentieth Century is the problem of the color-line." After completing this book, and visiting the five *Brown* communities, I am convinced that we face the same problem in the twenty-first century.

I want to explain—at greater length than most authors—why I wrote this book, and the perspectives I bring to this project. Its genesis begins in the early 1950s, when I attended Carrie Downie Junior High School in New Castle, Delaware. My family lived in an imposing brick house with a walk-in fireplace in the kitchen. Hidden behind the fireplace was a stairway to a tiny room, which I was told had been a hiding place for escaped slaves on the Underground Railroad. I remember feeling excited about this link with history. I also remember riding my bike down the Wilmington Pike, to watch the construction of the Delaware Memorial Bridge over the river to New Jersey. Along the way, I sometimes turned down the dirt road that went through the hamlet of Buttonwood, whose residents were all black people and whose homes were small and unpainted. The black kids in Buttonwood rode their bikes past mine, checking out the unexpected white kid, but I don't recall stopping to talk or play with them. I enjoyed Carrie Downie, yet I never wondered, or thought to ask anyone, "Where are the Buttonwood kids?" It simply did not occur to me that my school was for white kids only, and that the Buttonwood kids went to a Jim Crow school.

My family moved in early 1954 to the Cincinnati suburb of Wyoming, Ohio. I was in Wyoming High School when the Supreme Court decided the *Brown* case, and we discussed it in my civics class. Wyoming had about a dozen black students out of some three hundred in the school, and several of the boys were stars on the Cowboys football and basketball teams. But I didn't get to know any of the black kids well; they didn't come to Saturday sock hops at the community center, and none of them visited our house. During the Little Rock school crisis in the fall of 1957, I followed the news closely and remember feeling angry at white kids in Wyoming who drove around and yelled, "Faubus for president!" My favorite Sunday school teacher at the Cincinnati Unitarian Church was a wonderful black woman, whose name I have forgotten but whose memory is still vivid. Growing up in the Unitarian church made me sensitive to injustice, and aware of belonging to a religious minority whose early leaders were burned at the stake in Calvinist Geneva and imprisoned in Transylvania.

In the fall of 1958, I entered Antioch College in Yellow Springs, Ohio. I was ripe for social activism, and I quickly joined the campus NAACP chapter, which was led by an articulate black woman, Eleanor Holmes Norton, who greatly influenced me and now represents the District of Columbia in Congress. During my first year at Antioch, I joined a caravan to Washington, D.C., for the NAACP Youth March for Integrated Schools. In early 1960, I held an Antioch "co-op" job near Washington and joined the sit-in movement, picketing movie theaters and restaurants that refused to serve blacks, once getting arrested during a "bowl-in" at a segregated bowling alley. I volunteered my free time in the Washington office of the Student Non-violent Coordinating Committee, and attended the first national SNCC conference in Atlanta in the fall of 1960. Driving to Atlanta with black friends from Howard University in Washington, I experienced the hostile glares of white men who hung around gas stations in the Deep South.

My father had died in 1959 and my mother, who was raising six younger children, couldn't meet Antioch's modest tuition, so I dropped out in 1962 and took a job in the Washington office of the United Auto Workers, helping to edit the UAW's weekly political newsletter. The UAW provided much of the funding and logistical support for the March on Washington for Jobs and Freedom in August 1963, and I helped to coordinate bus rentals and sign printing for the biggest civil rights demonstration in American history. I stood in the sweltering heat at the foot of the Lincoln Memorial and cheered the speeches of SNCC's battle-scarred young chairman,

John Lewis, and the grand old man of the civil rights movement, A. Philip Randolph of the Brotherhood of Sleeping Car Porters. But it was the "I Have a Dream" speech of Martin Luther King, Jr., that stirred me the most at that historic gathering.

I lived for three years in Washington's Adams-Morgan neighborhood, a "transitional" area that became progressively more black as white parents, many of them card-carrying liberals, moved to the suburbs. The District and federal governments poured millions of dollars into the Adams-Morgan schools, but their students—now almost all black and Hispanic—remain near the bottom on achievement tests. I witnessed the early stages of the "white flight" that has left the Adams Elementary School, where black and white children mixed easily in the early 1960s, with only 6 white children out of 316 students in 2001.

I left the UAW in 1965 to complete my last year at Antioch, during which I helped to conduct a study of the fledgling Head Start program in surrounding Greene County, Ohio. Visiting the Head Start centers and interviewing more than a hundred teachers and parents gave me a firsthand exposure to the effects of poor schooling on black parents, many of whom had attended Jim Crow schools in the 1940s and '50s. After graduating from Antioch in 1966, I served a three-year federal prison term for draft refusal. I helped many black and Hispanic fellow inmates—many of them functional illiterates—in writing letters to their families, learning more about the connections between bad schools and "dysfunctional" behavior.

I moved from prison to graduate school at Boston University in 1969, and taught urban sociology after completing my political science doctorate in 1973. Many of my white students at Boston State College, including firemen and police officers, voiced openly racist statements in class discussion. Boston was in turmoil over busing while I lived there, and I recall the beatings of Ted Landsmark and Richard Poleet, one black, the other white, both victims of racial hatred that Boston's cowardly political leaders did nothing to dampen. I left teaching in 1975 to attend Harvard Law School, where I first learned from reading the *Brown* opinions that my Delaware junior high, Carrie Downie, had been one of the segregated schools involved in those cases. I also learned more about the *Brown* cases from Richard Kluger's monumental book *Simple Justice*, to which this book is greatly indebted.

After completing law school in 1978, I spent four years teaching law in Massachusetts before joining the political science department at the University of California, San Diego, where I founded the Law and Society Program and the Earl Warren Bill of Rights Project. My plan for the Warren Project was to involve undergraduates in producing innovative curricular materials for teaching about the Constitution and Bill of Rights in high school and college classes. Beginning in 1993, the Project has produced four sets of edited and narrated audiotapes of Supreme Court oral arguments in the *May It Please the Court* series; the most recent set, *Courts, Kids, and the Constitution*, includes arguments in sixteen cases that involve junior and senior high students and teachers. As part of the Warren Project, I have visited many public schools, playing tapes of Supreme Court arguments and leading discussions about the cases and the issues they raise, from school prayer to drug testing.

Visiting schools across the country, some in urban black and Hispanic areas and some in all-white suburbs, has again exposed me to the glaring disparities in America's schools, both economic and racial. Most recently, in October 2001, I visited T. C. Williams High School in Virginia, the setting for *Remember the Titans*, a movie about the impact of integration on the school's football team. I noticed that about half the students in the school's hallways were black, but they made up only a handful of students in the Advanced Placement government classes in which I talked about Jim Crow schools; segregation within classrooms remains the reality in most "integrated" schools.

All these experiences, over more than forty years, prompted me to write *Jim Crow's Children* and to visit the five communities in which the *Brown* cases began. Another spur to writing this book was being involved with my wife, Bonnie, in educating three children: our two daughters, Haley and Maya, and our godson, Tony Cardenas. Haley is now ten and is mostly Irish in background; Maya, whom we adopted at birth, is six and is African-American; and Tony, who lives in San Diego's Hispanic barrio, is eleven; his parents were born in Mexico and never finished high school. Bonnie is currently homeschooling all three kids through a public charter school, and they are getting a fantastic education. Haley is amazingly bright and would have excelled in any school, public or private. But if Maya had stayed with her birth mother, she would have lived in public housing and probably never have ventured beyond her neighborhood. Tony, a bright and charming boy, was bullied by older kids and ignored by his teachers at the public school where he started first grade. If not for Bonnie's hard work and loving embrace, Tony would now be finishing fifth grade in an overcrowded public school with teachers who do not motivate Hispanic kids to aspire to college. But Tony will be entering the sixth grade this fall in the best charter school in California, the Preuss School at UCSD. It is perfectly obvious to me that most black and Hispanic kids, especially those who live in big-city ghettos and barrios, will not reach the educational and economic levels that middle-class white kids are encouraged by their parents and teachers to attain as a matter of course.

I have put much of myself into this preface, but just as much into the book that follows. From my high school days until now, I have believed strongly that school integration is not only morally and legally right, but also that using every means possible—even busing—to place kids of all racial and ethnic groups in the same classrooms is the best way to promote what Thurgood Marshall called the first goal of education, "learning to live together as fellow citizens." Those readers who think, after completing this book, that I have judged the Supreme Court too harshly, or have ignored or dismissed signs of improvement in the schools that most black children attend, might also think about the last time they visited one of these schools, such as Topeka High, Howard Tech, Shaw Junior High, or Scott's Branch High. Or the public schools in the black areas of Boston, Chicago, Detroit, Philadelphia, or any other American city. There are, to be sure, outstanding schools and excellent teachers in many cities whose stories deserve telling, but they are exceptions to the enduring reality of the Jim Crow schools to which too many black children are consigned, almost fifty years after the *Brown* decision.

Many people have helped me with this book, directly or indirectly, especially the students, teachers, and school officials I talked with in the five *Brown* communities I visited. Let me note that I told the students who talked with me that I would change their names in the book so they could speak frankly. Rather than leave out anyone who helped me, I will single out two for special recognition and give the rest a collective "Thank you!" Mary Stake Hawker, who directs the Deer Creek Foundation in St. Louis, has provided generous support to the Earl Warren Bill of Rights Project for more than a decade. The Foundation made possible my travel and research for this book, and I greatly appreciate its help. Jane von Mehren, who did a great job of editing my recent book, *A People's History of the Supreme Court*, did an even better job with this one. Every page reflects her meticulous and thoughtful editing, and her insistence that legal history and social analysis must focus on real people and their stories. There are more people and fewer numbers in this book than in the manuscript Jane first read, and the book is better for her work. Finally, my thanks and love to Bonnie, Haley, Maya, and Tony, whose homeschooling is happening right outside my study as I write these words. If every kid in this country shared their excitement with learning, this book would not be necessary.

San Diego, California

Contents

JIM CROW'S
CHILDREN

CHAPTER I

"Cut Yer Thumb er Finger Off"

"None of us niggers never knowed nothin' 'bout readin' and writin'. Dere warn't no school for niggers den, and I ain't never been to school a day in my life. Niggers was more skeered of newspapers dan dey is of snakes now, and us never knowed what a Bible was dem days."

These are the words of Georgia Baker about her life as a slave, growing up on a Georgia plantation before the Civil War. Both the land and her body were owned by Alexander H. Stephens, a planter who became vice-president of the Confederate States of America. Like most black people who were born into slavery, Georgia was illiterate, because it was both illegal and dangerous for a slave to learn how to read and write in the days before Emancipation.

Arnold Gragston told of his master in Macon County, Kentucky. "Mr. Tabb was a pretty good man," Arnold said. "He used to beat us, sure; but not nearly so much as others did." When the master suspected that his slaves were learning to read and write, he would call them to the "big house" and grill them. "If we told him we had been learnin' to read," Arnold recounted, "he would near beat the daylights out of us." Sarah Benjamin, who was born on a Louisiana plantation, recalled the fate of fellow slaves whose masters discovered that their "property" had secretly learned to read and write: "If yer learned to write dey would cut yer thumb er finger off."

But some slaves took the risk of beatings or amputations. Mandy Jones described the way that slaves in Mississippi would educate themselves. "Dey would dig pits, and kiver the spot wid bushes an' vines," he said. "Way out in de woods, dey *was* woods den, an' de slaves would slip out of de Quarters at night, an' go to dese pits, an' some niggah dat had some learnin' would have a school." But not all learning took place in "pit schools" in the woods. The children of slave owners sometimes became the teachers of slave children. "De way de cullud folks would learn to read was from de white chillun," Mandy Jones recalled. "De white chilluns thought a heap of de cullud chilluns, an' when dey come out o' school wid deir books in deir han's dey take de cullud chilluns, and slip off somewhere an' learns de cullud chilluns deir lessons, what deir teacher has jes' learned dem."

Too much learning, however, could give a slave the tools to escape from bondage. William Johnson told the story of a "smart slave" on his Virginia plantation, a coachman named Joe Sutherland. "Joe always hung around the courthouse with master," William said. "He went on business trips with him, and through this way, Joe learned to read and write unbeknownst to master. In fact, Joe got so good that he learned how to write passes for the slaves. Master's son, Carter Johnson, was clerk of the county court, and by going around the court every day Joe forged the county seal on these passes and several slaves used them to escape to free states." But Joe was betrayed by another slave, William said, "and Joe was put in shackles until he was sold to a man in Mississippi." Helping another slave to escape was a capital offense in the South, and Joe Sutherland was lucky to survive.

Freedom finally came for the slaves, first announced by the Emancipation Proclamation in 1863. Only a handful of slaves could read that document, but those who could spread the news to others. Mary Bell talked about her father, Spotswood Rice, who supervised his owner's tobacco plantation in Missouri. "His owner's son taught him to read," Mary recalled, "and dat made his owner so mad, because my father read the emancipation for freedom to de other slaves, and it made dem so happy, dey could not work well, and dey got so no one could manage dem, when dey found out dey were to be freed in such a short time."

These stories of former slaves, recorded in the 1930s by interviewers from the Federal Writers' Project, tell in poignant words of the struggle for education of people the Supreme Court described in its *Dred Scott* decision of 1857 as "beings of an inferior order, and altogether unfit to associate with the white race." Perhaps the main reason that blacks were "inferior" to whites, both in the days of slavery and after their emancipation, was that educated blacks were likely to aspire to more than plantation life, an enforced regimen of plowing, planting, weeding, chopping, and picking crops. "They didn't want us to learn nothin'," Annie Perry recalled of her childhood as a slave. "The only thing we had to learn was how to work."

The full impact of depriving blacks of education can only be measured against the historical record of slavery and segregation. From the very first importation of blacks into the British colonies, initially as indentured servants but soon as slaves, education of this servile class was both feared and forbidden. The Virginia legislature enacted a law in 1680 that prohibited gatherings of blacks for any reason, punishable by "Twenty Lashes on the Bare Back well laid on," a law designed to keep slaves from holding clandestine schools as well as meeting to plot rebellion against their masters. In 1695, Maryland imposed a fine of one thousand pounds of tobacco on teachers who instructed blacks. As time passed, other states followed suit. South Carolina made it a crime in 1740 for anyone "who shall hereafter teach, or cause any Slave or Slaves to be taught to write, or shall use or employ any Slave as a Scribe in any manner of writing, whatsoever."

The legal bans on teaching slaves to read and write did not completely prevent all blacks from becoming literate, at least at a basic level. Some masters found it advantageous to have a few slaves who could read instructions and keep records of production. On many plantations, trusted and favored slaves acted as overseers of "field slaves" and needed to keep records of who worked, became ill, or was injured. One former slave recalled that his master had a "special slave" who could "read and write and figger." Other masters believed in converting their slaves to Christianity, and felt that teaching them to read the Bible would not only save their souls but make them more amenable to their state. Christian missionaries sent teachers among the slaves, particularly in cities like Charleston, South Carolina, with support from their owners. And as Mandy Jones recalled of his early life in slavery, white children on plantations often taught the black children of "house slaves" to read and write as they did their lessons.

The successful revolution against British rule, and the adoption of the Constitution by the newly independent states, did nothing to alter the system of slavery. The "Great Compromise" that kept the slave states from bolting the Constitutional Convention included three provisions in the final charter that explicitly recognized the lawfulness of slavery: the clause that counted slaves as "three fifths" of a person in apportioning House seats; the "fugitive slave" clause that required northern states to return escaped slaves to their masters; and the clause that prohibited Congress from banning the further importation of slaves before 1808. But the winds of freedom and independence that blew across the new nation stirred the yearnings of some slaves for their own freedom from bondage. And the most powerful tool they could use to unlock or break their shackles was literacy; slaves who could read and write could also reach other literate slaves with letters and pamphlets.

Frederick Douglass, born on a Maryland plantation in 1817, was separated from his slave mother as an infant and sent by his owner at the age of eight to live in Baltimore as a house servant with the family of Hugh Auld, whose wife defied state law by teaching her young servant to read. When Auld learned of this schooling, he snatched books and newspapers from the boy's hands and ordered his wife to end the lessons. But Frederick snuck from his master's house whenever he could and enlisted white children in the neighborhood to continue his education. After one attempt to escape from slavery was foiled, Douglass finally put on a sailor's uniform and fled from Maryland to New Bedford, Massachusetts, at the age of twenty-one. After his escape from slavery, Douglass spread his knowledge to other blacks, teaching them in Sunday schools, despite the hostility of whites who broke up his classes with rocks and clubs. But he wielded his pen as a powerful weapon against slavery, becoming the most articulate and influential black abolitionist, speaking widely and publishing his own crusading newspaper, the *North Star*, from 1847 to 1860. "He who has endured the pangs of slavery," Douglass wrote in the first issue of his paper, "is the man to advocate liberty," which he did with words that other literate slaves read in secret, from smuggled newspapers and pamphlets.

What many slave owners feared even more than their "property" following the North Star to freedom was the greater danger of slave revolt and insurrection, which might take the lives of their wives and children. The connection between literacy and slave uprisings was not an imaginary one. Nat Turner and Denmark Vesey, who organized slave revolts that failed but that terrified many whites, were both literate; after Turner's bloody rebellion was crushed in 1831, black children were expelled from the white Sunday schools in Washington, D.C., where many had been taught to read the Bible. One prominent defender of slavery asked in 1855:"Is there any great moral reason why we should incur the tremendous risk of having our wives and children slaughtered in consequence of our slaves being taught to read incendiary publications?" Before the Civil War began, the border states of Maryland, Kentucky, and Tennessee were the only slave states that did not prohibit the teaching of slaves.

Opposition to educating blacks was not limited to the South. In 1831, Prudence Crandall, a white Quaker, admitted Sarah Harris, the daughter of a respected black farmer, to her school in Canterbury, Connecticut. Led by a local politician, Andrew Judson, who later served as a federal judge, townspeople objected loudly and passed a resolution that educating black girls would damage "the persons, property, and reputations of our citizens." Judson voiced the sentiments of many northern whites: "The colored people can never rise from their menial condition in our country; they ought not to be permitted to rise here. They are an inferior race of beings, and never can or ought to be recognized as the equals of the whites."

Fueled by Judson's rhetoric, Canterbury's white residents refused to trade with Miss Crandall, threw filth into her well, hurled rocks and rotten eggs at her home, and set fire to her schoolhouse. None of these attacks eroded her determination to keep her school open, and she admitted more black girls. The Connecticut legislature then passed an act making it illegal to teach blacks and whites in the same school, and a defiant Prudence Crandall was arrested, convicted, and jailed, although the state supreme court later quashed her indictment and she returned to her school. Finally, a mob attacked the schoolhouse with iron bars and virtually wrecked the building. Miss Crandall decided not to risk her students' lives and reluctantly closed her school in 1834.

The next year, after the Noyes Academy in New Hampshire opened its doors to black students, "a mob of several hundred men and nearly a hundred yoke of oxen dragged the seminary to a swamp, left it there in ruins, and drove the teacher from town." Also in 1835, white mobs attacked the black schools in Washington, D.C., destroyed several buildings, threatened the white teachers, and ransacked the homes of black students. One of the white teachers, Miss Miner, asked a mob member, "What good will it do to destroy my school-room? I shall only get another and go right on." She continued teaching black children until the eve of the Civil War in 1860, when another mob burned her school to the ground.

The Civil War ended the legal institution of slavery, at the cost of six hundred thousand lives, most of them young men who fought neither to abolish nor defend slavery but simply to survive the carnage of the bloodiest war in American history. The ratification of the Fourteenth Amendment in 1868, three years after the Thirteenth Amendment abolished slavery, conferred state and national citizenship on the former slaves and promised a federal guarantee of "the equal protection of the laws." Firmly in the control of "Radical Republicans" whose Reconstruction policy imposed a military government on the former Confederacy, Congress granted the franchise to the former slaves, who flocked to the ballot boxes and elected delegates to conventions that rewrote the constitutions of the southern states. Several of these constitutions provided for systems of free public education, and black children began attending school in large numbers. In Mississippi, for example, the legislature—controlled by black members and their white Republican allies—established a school system in 1870 that enrolled 127,000 black children the following year, 39 percent of the school-age black population. Even under Reconstruction and black rule, Mississippi's public schools were segregated, because white parents refused to pay taxes for integrated schools. Close to a century passed before the first black child in Mississippi attended school with whites.

The South Carolina constitution, written by black legislators, required that all schools be racially mixed, and black and white children attended classes together in many communities. The state also established an integrated teachers college, which trained many black teachers. Other southern states, however, experienced serious problems with public education, largely because many white voters refused to pay taxes to support black education. Even in states that funded black schools, the lack of qualified black teachers made it difficult to maintain academic standards.

Many of the schools for black children that did exist in the South during the Reconstruction period had been established by the Freedmen's Bureau, the federal agency created by Congress to provide aid and services to former slaves, to help them purchase land, farming equipment, and supplies, and to give them enough schooling

to read, write, and keep books. Bureau agents set up classes for
adults and also provided schools for children, largely staffed by
white teachers from the North, most of whom were young women
who had never been to the South and were treated with scorn and
outright hostility by many whites. One female teacher in northern
Virginia, just across the Potomac River from the nation's capital,
abandoned her job after being shunned by every white person in
the community. "If you are mean enough to teach niggers," one
told her, "you may eat and sleep with them." Male teachers were a
small minority, but they became targets for threats. One teacher in
Alabama received this anonymous and barely literate warning: "You
have set up a nigger school in the settlement which we will not
allow you to teach if you was a full blooded negro we would have
nothing to say but a white skin negro is more than we can stand you
can dismiss the school imediately or prepar yourself to travail we
will give you a chance to save yourself and you had better move in-
stanter." Some white teachers faced greater dangers than threats.
Captain James McCleery, the Freedmen's Bureau superintendent of
education in Texas and northwestern Louisiana, barely escaped a
band of night riders in Louisiana by hiding in a swamp all night.
One of his teachers in Henderson County, Texas, was grabbed by a
white mob, stripped naked, covered with tar and cotton, and given
two minutes to run before he faced a volley of rifle fire.

Teachers who ignored the hostility and threats often lost their
schools to violence. Black schools were burned and pillaged
throughout the South. Seven schools were burned in Georgia in
1866; three schools were burned that year in Texas. A school at
Orangeburg, South Carolina, was fired into; the black school in
Hardinsburg, Kentucky, was blown up on Christmas Eve in 1867.
Despite the efforts to drive them from the South, the vast majority
of the Freedmen's Bureau teachers stuck with their schools and
their black students. By 1870, more than nine thousand teachers
were instructing some two hundred thousand black children, about
12 percent of the school-age population. Northern missionary

groups also sent teachers into southern states, and black churches set up schools for their children. All together, these public and private groups offered schooling to perhaps one of every five black children in the South, which meant that four out of five black children received no education at all during the Reconstruction period and remained illiterate, as their parents had during slavery.

The small minority of black children who did attend school during Reconstruction had an obvious zest for learning. One white teacher in Mississippi reported that when her students turned in their slates or copybooks, "my face was eagerly watched, to find therein approval or disapproval (they were quick to read the human countenance) and if a word of praise fell from my lips, a look of triumph would light up their sable faces as to make even them look beautiful." The condescending tone of this remark, however unintended, reflected the superior attitude and status of the white teacher. But even the most sensitive and understanding teachers encountered problems that stemmed from the reality of black life and culture in the rural South. The learning of black children was clearly hindered by the fact that virtually all came from families with illiterate parents, who could not help their children with lessons. Cut off from the written word, southern blacks had retained the oral traditions of their African roots, which they adapted to their churches and communities, where everyone joins in calling out verses and children's rhymes. Most teachers in Reconstruction schools reported that students in the early grades were quick to learn the alphabet, numbers, spelling of simple words, and the rote memorization of short poems and Bible passages, a reflection of this oral culture. Even in crowded classrooms, children enjoyed chanting in unison as they went through letters, numbers, and verses. One teacher in Virginia wrote that "instruction is necessarily mostly oral, as much time would be lost if we trained pupils singly. The little things gave us almost undivided attention, and are much stimulated by recitations in concert."

Past the primary level, however, teachers expressed frustration at

the inability of black children to master arithmetic and composition. Part of the problem lay in textbooks designed for northern
white students. A black child on a Mississippi farm was unlikely to
associate a picture of Xerxes with the letter *X* or to know that a
"newsboy" was an *n* word. One scholar of black education has
noted this problem of Reconstruction schools: "In the world of the
rural black schoolchild, very little of what was taught and of its presentation had much relationship to daily existence. The drudgery of
manual labor, the lively conversations in the black people's cabins,
and the generally non-literate nature of southern living for both
races had almost nothing to do with what instructors talked about,
once the concrete naming of things had passed."

The most difficult subject for black children was mathematics,
which teachers in the nineteenth century approached from an ab-
stract perspective. Children were not allowed to count on their fin-
gers, or given problems that dealt with real objects like apples,
chickens, or cotton bales. One critic of "mental" arithmetic wrote
that teachers, most of them poorly trained in the subject, were often
"completely nonplussed in any attempt to explain what they have
done, or analyze the principles upon which it is performed." As a
result, the "neglect of mathematics, the single most unmet need of
black education, resulted in mass innumeracy, as tragic as illiteracy, a
deficiency that has received more attention."

There were additional barriers to effective learning that came
from outside the schoolhouse. The need for black children to plant,
hoe, and harvest crops cut weeks and even months from already
short school years; many children lived miles from school and could
not walk on dirt roads when it rained; children got sick or injured
and had no medical care; and because hostile whites sometimes ran
teachers out of town or burned schools, even when children arrived at school, it was not always staffed or even standing. What is
remarkable about the Reconstruction period is not that so few
black children got so little good education, but that teachers and
students alike persevered in the face of such enormous odds. It is

also a testament to their faith in the liberating power of education that black parents—most of them illiterate themselves—worked hard to build schools, raise money for books and teachers, and give their children the desire to learn. One former slave, Charles Whiteside, was told by his master that he would remain in slavery "'cause you got no education, and education is what makes a man free." This remark spurred Whiteside's determination that each of his thirteen children would attend school, no matter how long and hard he would have to work. It was worth all the labor "to make them free," he said.

The modest spread of literacy and learning for the former slaves and their children ended with the return of whites to power in the South, twelve years after their surrender at Appomattox Court House. The official demise of Reconstruction came in 1877, the payoff of a political deal that Republican presidential candidate Rutherford Hayes had made with southern Democrats to win the "Stolen Election" of 1876. Although Hayes had lost the popular vote to Democrat Samuel Tilden, he promised to look with "kind consideration" on southern demands that Reconstruction end, and the sudden resignation of a pro-Tilden member of the commission set up to count the disputed electoral votes gave Hayes a one-vote victory. "I think the policy of the new administration will be to conciliate the white men of the South," one supporter of Reconstruction lamented. "Carpetbaggers to the rear, and niggers take care of yourself." The white "carpetbaggers" who had come south to run the governments of the former Confederate states quickly departed. Blacks were left to fend for themselves, without military protection or federal aid.

With the end of Reconstruction, the white "Redeemers" who returned to power in the South had no desire to give black children an education that would equip them for more than menial labor as sharecroppers or household servants. The Freedmen's Bureau was abolished and its schools closed, and northern churches withdrew their teachers from black schools. Black voters, who had gained representation in every southern legislature, were systematically disenfranchised through a combination of harassment, ballot fraud, and outright violence. During the last two decades of the nineteenth century, the white lawmakers who controlled the South began the process of replacing slavery with segregation, installing the Jim Crow system that separated the races in every aspect of life. The term itself had its origins in the 1830s, beginning with the minstrel show of Thomas "Daddy" Rice, a white man who blackened his face with burnt cork, dressed in rags, and danced and sang in a caricature of blacks. He called this part of his show "Jump Jim Crow," after a crippled black slave who belonged to a white man named Crow. White audiences loved the demeaning portrayal of a grinning, shuffling black man, and the term quickly entered the language. During the 1840s, abolitionist newspapers adopted the term to describe the segregated railroad cars in northern states.

The Jim Crow laws passed by southern legislatures in the 1880s and '90s mandated racial segregation in restaurants, hotels, parks, libraries, theaters, railroads, beauty parlors, and barbershops. With its "WHITES ONLY" and "COLORED ONLY" signs, posted above railroad waiting rooms, bathrooms, and drinking fountains, the Jim Crow system inflicted daily humiliations on blacks of both sexes and all ages. Jim Crow laws were accompanied by a system of southern "customs" that allowed whites to address black men as "boy" and black women as "girl." Blacks who refused to conform to white expectations of deference and grinning servility were considered "uppity" and could lose their jobs or credit if they failed to mend their ways.

The heart of the Jim Crow system, and the institution most central to its functioning, was the segregated public school system. The consignment of black children to separate schools kept them "in their place" and safely away from white children, especially girls, who might not realize that black males—even at the grade-school level—might threaten the "purity" of the young "flowers of southern womanhood." The combined power of racial prejudice and sexual phobia should not be underestimated as a motivating factor in the southern insistence on school segregation. But an equally important reason for maintaining separate schools was to make it simpler to provide a separate curriculum for black children, one that would provide the rudiments of literacy and training for manual labor and domestic service. There was no need to educate blacks in literature, foreign languages, or advanced mathematics, or to encourage them to aspire to higher education. White southerners did recognize the need for "normal schools" to train black teachers, but these postsecondary schools were hardly "colleges" with a full curriculum in the liberal arts and sciences. The governor of Georgia expressed a common attitude toward the efforts of northern philanthropists to establish black colleges: "We can attend to the education of the darkey in the South and give them the education they most need. I do not believe in the higher education of the darkey. He must be taught the trades. When he is taught the fine arts, he is educated above his caste, and it makes him unhappy."

Many blacks, even those with little or no education, were unhappy that their children were forced to attend segregated schools, many of them housed in churches or private homes, and most lacking desks and books for each student. The children sat on benches, crowded together, and shared tattered, hand-me-down books that had been discarded by white schools. These Jim Crow schools were "public" in name only, and often received so little funding from county school boards that hard-strapped parents had to "board" the teachers to supplement their meager salaries. One fact that is little known about black education is that most schools were segregated by law well before the Jim Crow system took hold in the late nineteenth century. Many states had imposed school segregation even before the Civil War, and only a handful of southern states—notably Louisiana and South Carolina—had integrated their schools during the Reconstruction years. Another little-known fact is that Jim Crow schooling actually began in Massachusetts in 1820, and spread to several other northern and western states during the 1860s and '70s. And few people know that black parents in a dozen states mounted legal challenges to segregated public schools during the five decades that preceded the Supreme Court's approval in 1896 of "separate but equal" facilities in the *Plessy* case.

The story of these nineteenth-century school cases offers an illuminating contrast to the twentieth-century legal assault on Jim Crow schools, launched by the National Association for the Advancement of Colored People and commanded by Thurgood Marshall, the best-known and most successful civil rights lawyer in American history. With only one exception, none of the lawyers who argued the earlier school cases had any renown, and none of the cases had the backing of an established, influential organization. What these cases do show, however, is that black parents—with little money or public support—were willing to stand up for their children and fight for integrated schools. They faced a legal system that was virtually all white, judges who displayed no understanding of the harms imposed on black children by enforced segregation, and the hostility of most of their white neighbors and fellow citizens.

The first of these cases came from the capital of the antislavery crusade, Massachusetts, where Horace Mann had pioneered the system of free public schools as the state's commissioner of education. But the free schools had been segregated from the very beginning, even before Mann took his post in 1837. In 1820 the city of Boston had opened the Smith Grammar School for black children. The Boston school board later established two more primary schools for black children, and also adopted a regulation that all children attend the school "nearest their residences." These regulations created a conflict in 1849 for Benjamin Roberts, whose daughter Sarah was five. He first tried to enroll her in the white primary school nearest to her home, but she was "ejected from the school by the teacher, on the ground of her being a colored person." The Smith school was almost half a mile from Sarah's home, while there were five white schools that were closer.

This rebuff to his daughter spurred Benjamin Roberts to file a lawsuit against the city. Roberts enlisted Charles Sumner to argue the challenge to segregated schooling before the Massachusetts Supreme Judicial Court, headed by a renowned judge, Lemuel Shaw. Sumner's eloquent opposition to slavery later propelled him to the Senate, where he served from 1851 to 1874 and headed the abolitionist forces. His argument in *Roberts v. City of Boston* relied on provisions of the Massachusetts constitution that gave every citizen equal rights in civil and political affairs. Confining Boston's black children to segregated schools branded "a whole race with the stigma of inferiority and degradation," Sumner asserted. The city conceded that the Smith school was dilapidated and that its equipment "has been so shattered and neglected that it cannot be used until it has been thoroughly repaired." But Sumner did not base his argument on the physical inequality of the black and white primary schools in Boston. "Admitting that it is an equivalent," he said, "still the colored children cannot be compelled to take it. They have an equal right with the white children to the general public schools." Sumner used words that would be echoed, a century later, by Thurgood Marshall in the United States Supreme Court. "The separation of the schools," Sumner told the Massachusetts judges, "so far from being for the benefit of both races, is an injury to both. It tends to create a feeling of degradation in the blacks, and of prejudice and uncharitableness in the whites."

Chief Justice Shaw did not agree. "The great principle, advanced by the learned and eloquent advocate for the plaintiff," Shaw wrote of Sumner's argument, that "all persons without distinction of age or sex, birth or color, origin or condition, are equal before the law . . . is perfectly sound." But the principle of equal treatment, Shaw added, must yield to the "paternal consideration" of elected lawmakers, whose judgments should not be disturbed so long as their power is "reasonably exercised." The Boston school committee, Shaw wrote, had concluded after "great deliberation" that the interests of the city's children of both races "will best be promoted, by maintaining the separate primary schools for colored and for white children, and we can perceive no ground to doubt, that this is the honest result of their experience and judgment." Shaw noted Sumner's argument that "this maintenance of separate schools tends to deepen and perpetuate the odious distinction of caste, founded in a deep-rooted prejudice in public opinion," but he rejected any judicial responsibility to deal with the impact of white hostility toward blacks. "This prejudice, if it exists, is not created by law, and probably cannot be changed by law," Shaw proclaimed.

The *Roberts* decision, which gave elected officials the power to decide that the interests of black and white children "will best be promoted" by separate schools, became the standard for judges in other states, even after the Fourteenth Amendment—added to the Constitution in 1868—directed the states to guarantee every person "the equal protection of the laws." Ruling in 1871, the Ohio supreme court decided a challenge to a law passed by the state legislature in 1864, permitting local school boards to provide "one or more separate schools for colored children" in districts with more than twenty school-age black children. Those districts with fewer than twenty black children could send them to black schools in an adjoining district. School officials were not required to segregate children by race, but many Ohio districts took advantage of the law that allowed them to establish Jim Crow schools.

John McCann, a black parent with three children, lived in a rural township near the state capital of Columbus, in a school district with fewer than twenty black children. A neighboring district had a black school, but McCann enrolled his children in the nearby white school, where the teacher "wholly neglects and refuses to impart instruction to them," noted the Ohio court in its opinion in *State v. McCann*. The district's lawyer argued that local boards could act "with due regard to the peculiar circumstances, wants, interests, and even *prejudices*, if you please, of each particular locality or neighborhood." The school board in McCann's district could have allowed his children to attend the local school, but ordered the teacher to ignore them. Such an order, the lawyer claimed, lay within the board's "police powers" to determine which students would be admitted to the schools.

The Ohio court upheld the board's power to withhold an education from the three McCann children. During the time McCann "insisted on having his children instructed" in the local white school, the court noted, "an equally good school was open for them in the joint district established for colored children, as provided by law, where they could enjoy the full advantages and privileges of a public common school." The judges agreed that "the real question in this case" was whether the Fourteenth Amendment barred Ohio from allowing local boards to segregate their schools. "We are not aware that this has been as yet judicially settled," they conceded, since the amendment had been ratified just three years earlier. Rather than taking a stand on this question, they fell back on the opinion Chief Justice Shaw had written in the *Roberts* case, twenty years before the Fourteenth Amendment had been ratified. The Ohio judges echoed Shaw in leaving to "the wisdom and discretion of some proper authority" the power to act "in a manner to promote the best interests of all." Ruling that McCann's children enjoyed "equal school advantages" with their white neighbors, the judges ignored the disadvantages of having to travel to another township to attend school, and being forced into separate schools to accommodate the admitted "prejudices, if you please," of the whites in their township. "Equality of rights does not involve the necessity of educating white and colored persons in the same school," the Ohio judges concluded.

Three years after school segregation was upheld in Ohio, the California supreme court faced the issue of Jim Crow schools in San Francisco. The state legislature had directed in 1870 that schools in each district would "be open for the admission of all white children," and that "the education of children of African descent, and Indian children, shall be provided for in separate schools." On July 1, 1872, Harriet Ward took her eleven-year-old daughter, Mary

Frances, to the Broadway Grammar School, the closest public school to their home. In her statement to the court, the black mother said that Noah F. Flood, the school's principal, "at once politely, but firmly and definitively declined" to enroll Mary Frances, solely because "she was a colored person." Flood told Harriet Ward "that he was sorry to be compelled for that reason" to turn away her daughter.

The California supreme court based its ruling in *Ward v. Flood* directly on Chief Justice Shaw's holding in the *Roberts* case, once again brushing aside the fact that it preceded the Fourteenth Amendment by two decades. More than half of the opinion in the *Ward* case, in fact, consisted of lengthy quotations from Shaw's opinion, including his statement that the interests of both races "will best be promoted by maintaining the separate primary schools for colored and for white children." The California judges dealt with the Equal Protection clause with the disingenuous statement that when "the races are separated in the public schools, there is certainly to be found no violation of the constitutional rights of the one race more than of the other, and we see none of either, for each, though separated from the other, is to be educated upon equal terms with the other, and both at the common public expense." The argument that segregation affects both races equally, because white children are barred from attending black schools, could appeal only to judges who deliberately ignored the reality of racial prejudice that created the Jim Crow system. But this argument, however absurd, cropped up in legal briefs and judicial opinions during the eight decades that followed the *Ward* decision.

The first school segregation case to come before federal judges involved the state of Louisiana, whose constitution during the Reconstruction period had prohibited separate schools. The white lawmakers who took control of the legislature in 1877 promptly rescinded this provision and required all districts to segregate their schools. A black parent in New Orleans named Bertonneau—most likely a mixed-race Creole with French ancestry—sued the city's school officials to admit his children to the white school that was closest to their home. William B. Woods, the federal judge who decided the case in 1878, tossed out the complaint without a hearing. His opinion, just three paragraphs long, suggested that the case was too simple for extended discussion. Judge Woods noted that New Orleans provided schools for children of both races, although Bertonneau's children were forced to attend a segregated school. "Is this a deprivation of a right granted by the constitution of the United States?" Woods asked. He found no such right in the Fourteenth Amendment. "Both races are treated precisely alike," he wrote. "White children and colored children are compelled to attend different schools. That is all." Again echoing the words of Chief Justice Shaw in the *Roberts* case, Judge Woods held that Louisiana had "the right to manage its schools in the manner which, in its judgment, will best promote the interest of all."

Although it sits just north of the Mason-Dixon line and did not join the Confederacy, Indiana was distinctly hostile to blacks, before and after the Civil War. The southern part of the state, across the Ohio River from the slave state of Kentucky, harbored many nests of "Copperheads," the Confederate sympathizers named after the poisonous snakes that found camouflage among the mottled leaves in wooded areas. The Indiana legislature revised its constitution in 1851 to prohibit "negroes and mulattoes from coming into or settling in this state," barred those who already resided in the state from voting, and made blacks "a separate and distinct class of inferiors before the law," as the Indiana supreme court stated. Before 1869, Indiana provided no public schools for black children; in that year, the legislature decreed that school officials in each district "shall organize the colored children into separate schools." In 1878, Robert Carter, the father and grandfather of four school-age black children, tried to enroll them in a white school in Marion County, the seat of the state capital, Indianapolis. When school officials refused to admit the black children, Carter filed suit against the school board president, Samuel Cory, and won a ruling from a county judge that local school officials must admit the children to the nearby white school.

Ruling in *Cory v. Carter*, the Indiana supreme court reversed the county judge's decision in an opinion that bristled with hostility toward blacks. Citing the provisions of the 1851 state constitution, the judges found it "very plain and obvious to us, that persons of the African race were not in the minds or contemplation of the wise and thoughtful framers of our constitution" when they drafted that document. The Indiana judges wrote as if the Fourteenth Amendment did not apply to their state, ruling that education was strictly a state and local matter and that the Equal Protection clause posed no barrier to school segregation. The state constitution, they wrote, "was made and adopted by and for the exclusive use and enjoyment of the white race." Because the provisions that consigned blacks to legal inferiority had not been repealed or amended, the judges added, they remained in effect. "A constitution is inflexible and can not bend to circumstances or be modified by public opinion," they stated. In its complete dismissal of the Fourteenth Amendment, the opinion in *Cory v. Carter* ignored the clear wording of Article Six of the federal Constitution, which decrees that its provisions "shall be the supreme law of the land, and the judges in every state shall be bound thereby, any thing in the constitution or laws of any state to the contrary notwithstanding." Robert Carter, however, did not appeal the decision against him to the United States Supreme Court, and the Indiana judges suffered no rebuke for thumbing their noses at the Constitution.

Building on the *Roberts* opinion and the state cases that cited it for authority, New York's highest court ruled in 1883 that Theresa King, a twelve-year-old black girl who lived in Brooklyn, could not attend the public school nearest to her home. John Gallagher, the principal of School No. 5, turned her away, relying on a state law, passed in 1850, that authorized local school boards to "organize and establish schools for colored children." The majority opinion of the

New York Court of Appeals dripped with scorn and condescension. Noting that schools in several cities, including Buffalo and Albany, had been segregated for more than thirty years, the majority of four judges found that the law's "operation and effect have hitherto been found unobjectionable and apparently satisfactory to all parties." Holding that the system of Jim Crow schools "has contributed to the best interests of both classes" of students, the judges added that Theresa King "is receiving the highest educational advantages that the city is capable of giving her," and they chided her for complaining that "she is not receiving those facilities at the precise place which would be the most gratifying to her feelings."

The majority in *King v. Gallagher* felt compelled to decide whether the 1850 state law had been "annulled by the paramount authority" of the Fourteenth Amendment. Their answer was no, because the "privilege" of receiving an education was "created and conferred solely by the laws of the state," and could be "granted or refused to any individual or class at the pleasure of the state." The majority looked to the *Roberts* opinion for support, and deferred to the prejudices of white voters and lawmakers. "The attempt to enforce social intimacy and intercourse between the races, by legal enactments, would probably tend only to embitter the prejudices, if any such there are, which exist between them, and produce an evil instead of a good result," the judges wrote. The state guardian who represented Theresa King, at the court's direction, had conceded that school officials could assign children to different schools on the basis of age, sex, and ability, but had denied that race could be a valid ground for separation. "We think the concession fatal to his argument," the majority replied. If officials could separate children on other grounds, "how can it be argued that they have not the power, in the best interests of education, to cause different races and nationalities, whose requirements are manifestly different, to be educated in separate places." The New York judges cited the decisions of their colleagues in Ohio and Indiana for this dubious proposition. They concluded by advising Theresa King that institutions set aside "for the exclusive benefit of particular races and classes of citizens," like the Jim Crow schools in Brooklyn, "are generally regarded as favors to the races designated instead of marks of inferiority."

Two judges on the court of appeals could not stomach the genteel racism of the majority. They read the Fourteenth Amendment and New York's civil rights law, which protected the right of every citizen to the "equal enjoyment" of public facilities, as barring any discrimination based on race. School segregation, they wrote, "when enforced by law against the wish of the colored race, is directly calculated to keep alive the prejudice against color from which sprung many of the evils for the suppression of which the Fourteenth Amendment and our own civil rights statute were enacted." The dissenters cast scorn on the majority's deference to public sentiment. If lawmakers could segregate the schools, "then with equal plausibility it might be said that the city of Brooklyn could provide parks, streets and sidewalks exclusively for persons of color," they wrote. This was not the exaggeration it seemed to dissenting judges. Many cities and towns in the South, of course, had segregated all their public facilities, even setting aside whole neighborhoods from which blacks were excluded.

State judges decided one more school segregation case in the nineteenth century. This case began in Grundy County, Missouri, a rural area with few black residents. The facts cited in the court's decision were sketchy, but in September 1887, a white parent named Lehew and four others asked a state judge to order the white teachers at the local school to stop instructing the four children of a black parent named Brummell. His were the only school-age black children in the district, and they had attended school without incident until the white parents sued Brummell and the white teachers and board members who had welcomed the black children into their school. The Missouri constitution provided that "separate free public schools shall be established for the education of children of African descent." Ruling on Lehew's petition, the county judge

granted an injunction "restraining Brummell's children from attending the school so established for white children," although the
closest black school to their home was in the next township.

The case of *Lehew v. Brummell* gave the Missouri supreme court no
difficulty. Its unanimous decision in 1890 cited the *Roberts* opinion of
Chief Justice Shaw and the rulings in the Ohio, California, New
York, and Indiana school cases. The Missouri judges borrowed the
reasoning and chunks of writing from these earlier cases, tossing aside
the Fourteenth Amendment as posing a "simple question" with an
easy answer. State lawmakers had found it "expedient and necessary"
to establish Jim Crow schools for black children, and the judges
would not question their "wisdom" in doing so. The judges conceded
that the sole basis for segregating children was color, but "color carries
with it natural race peculiarities which furnish the reason for the
classification," they wrote. "There are differences in races, and between individuals of the same race, not created by human laws, some
of which can never be eradicated. These differences create different
social relations recognized by all well-organized governments. If we
cast aside chimerical theories and look to practical results, it seems to
us it must be conceded that separate schools for colored children is a
regulation to their great advantage."

"Forcibly Ejected from Said Coach"

N one of the judicial decisions upholding Jim Crow
schooling, from the Massachusetts ruling in 1849 to the
Missouri case in 1890, reached the United States
Supreme Court. Consequently, the justices had no occasion to decide whether segregating children by race in public was to the
"great advantage" of black students, or whether this practice violated the Constitution. The Court, in fact, waited until 1896 to decide the constitutionality of Jim Crow laws, in a case that began in a
New Orleans railroad station. The case of *Plessy v. Ferguson* involved
one of the many indignities that blacks endured in the South. The
Louisiana legislature passed a "separate railroad cars" law in 1890,
stating that "no person or persons shall be permitted to occupy seats
in coaches, other than the ones assigned to them on account of the
race they belong to." The law required railroads to provide "equal
but separate" facilities to those of different races, but it did not define "race" and left to conductors the job of assigning passengers to
the proper cars.

A legal challenge to the "separate cars" law began on June 7,
1892, when Homer Plessy entered the New Orleans station of the
East Louisiana Railway and bought a first-class ticket to Covington,
Louisiana, a town about fifty miles away. According to the Supreme
Court's later statement of facts, Plessy "entered a passenger train,

and took possession of a vacant seat in a coach where passengers of the white race were accommodated." The conductor then ordered him "to vacate said coach" and move to one "for persons not of the white race." When Plessy refused to move, "he was, with the aid of a police officer, forcibly ejected from said coach and hurried off to and imprisoned in the parish jail of New Orleans." His stay in jail was brief, and Plessy was released after arraignment in the local court.

Homer Plessy had arranged his arrest to challenge the "separate cars" law, which was especially galling to "Creoles" like him, descendants of the French settlers of Louisiana who often fathered children across the color line. Plessy was an "octoroon," the word then used to describe people with seven white great-grandparents and one who was black. The legal papers filed in his case, which was sponsored by the American Citizens' Equal Rights Association in New Orleans, noted that "the mixture of colored blood was not discernible in him," and Plessy "passed" for white in the racial gumbo of New Orleans. Creoles, many of them well-to-do professionals, were "almost" white, but under state law had no more rights than the darkest black. Plessy and his fellow Creoles wanted to expose the absurdity of a law that made a railroad conductor "the autocrat of Caste, armed with the power of the State" to decide which travelers were white and which were not, using only his eyes to measure racial purity. The prosecutor at Plessy's trial in state court, before Judge John Ferguson, claimed that "the foul odors of blacks in close quarters" made the law a "reasonable" exercise of the state's "police powers" to protect the health, safety, welfare, and morals of the public. Plessy's lawyers argued that the law imposed a "badge of servitude" on him and others with any black ancestry, and deprived him of the "privileges and immunities" of citizenship.

After the Louisiana courts upheld Plessy's conviction for violating the law, the Supreme Court heard arguments on his appeal in April 1896, and decided the case the next month, on May 18. Justice Henry B. Brown wrote for all but one of his colleagues in upholding the Jim Crow law. His opinion displayed the attitudes of educated whites who conceded the "political" equality of blacks but shrank from having any contact with them in such "close quarters" as railroad cars and restaurants. Brown brushed aside the "equal protection" promise of the Fourteenth Amendment with the cavalier statement that "it could not have been intended to abolish distinctions based upon color, or to enforce social, as opposed to political, equality, or a commingling of the two races upon terms unsatisfactory to either." The only question in the case, Brown wrote, was whether the Louisiana law was a "reasonable regulation" of railroads that were licensed by the state. "In determining the question of reasonableness," he stated, state lawmakers were "at liberty to act with reference to the established usages, customs, and traditions of the people, and with a view to the promotion of their comfort, and the preservation of the public peace and good order." The "people" who Justice Brown had in mind, of course, were only the white people of Louisiana who did not want to share railroad cars with blacks, even those as light-skinned as Homer Plessy.

Brown had great difficulty in finding legal precedent for his claim that the "established usages, customs, and traditions of the people" supported the racial segregation of railroad cars in Louisiana. In fact, blacks had not been forced to ride in segregated coaches before the law was enacted in 1890, and the railroad companies did not support the law, which cost them money to maintain separate cars. And a federal court had recently held that Louisiana railroads could not segregate passengers who held tickets for travel across state lines. Instead, Brown looked across the tracks for cases upholding laws that required the separation of whites and blacks "in places where they are liable to be brought into contact" with each other. He found the precedent he needed in the judicial opinions that turned back challenges to Jim Crow schools, citing the cases decided between 1849 and 1890 by courts in eight different states. These cases all dealt, Brown wrote, "with the establishment of separate schools for white and colored children, which have been held to be a valid exercise of the legislative power even by courts of states where the political rights of the colored race have been longest and most earnestly enforced." It was the widespread and long-standing practice of school segregation that gave the Supreme Court a foundation in precedent for the *Plessy* decision.

There were good reasons for the Court to base its endorsement of "separate but equal" public facilities and institutions on the long practice of school segregation, in both North and South. Beginning with the 1849 decision of the Massachusetts supreme court in *Roberts v. City of Boston*, these rulings gave the United States Supreme Court a line of precedent going back almost fifty years. In addition, the state cases involved the institution at the core of the Jim Crow system, the public schools in which white and black children first experienced the reality of segregation. And the opinions in these cases all shared three assumptions: first, that judges should defer to the judgments of elected lawmakers and school officials that segregation was in the "best interests" of all children, black and white alike; second, that the Fourteenth Amendment's guarantee of the "equal protection of the laws" to every person did not apply to education, which was solely a state and local affair; and third, that the "prejudices" of white voters and parents were "not created by law, and cannot be changed by law." The *Plessy* majority easily transferred these assumptions from schools to railroad cars; thus, the long-standing existence of Jim Crow schools in both the South and North became the justification for segregation in virtually every facet of daily life.

In those states in which Jim Crow was not enforced by law, it relied on "custom" to make blacks feel unwelcome and uncomfortable in places where they would encounter whites. By the end of the nineteenth century, whites and blacks in most of the country—especially in the South, where 90 percent of America's black population lived in rural poverty—hardly ever worked, traveled, or went to school together. And, despite the command of the *Plessy* decision that separate public facilities for blacks must be equal to those for whites, the disparities were glaring in virtually every case.

When the Supreme Court decided the *Plessy* case, hardly anyone noticed the momentous ruling. The Court handed down fifty-two opinions that day, and three of these—dealing with the laws of contract, inheritance, and copyright—were reported on the front page of *The New York Times*. The editors relegated the *Plessy* decision to a third-page column on railroad news, between cases on train routes and improvement bonds. Even fewer people noticed the solitary dissent of Justice John Marshall Harlan, which the *Times* did not consider news fit to print. More than a century later, Harlan's harsh critique of the majority opinion seems both prophetic and correct. The product of a slave-owning Kentucky family, Harlan had just one year of legal education, but had served as a county judge and his state's attorney general before President Rutherford Hayes named him to the Supreme Court in 1877. Harlan had organized a Union regiment in the Civil War, but he opposed ratification of the Thirteenth Amendment in 1865 as a violation of the property rights of slave owners. He firmly supported the "civil" rights of black citizens as a justice, having written a sole dissent in 1883 from the Court's invalidation of the federal Civil Rights Act that barred racial segregation in public accommodations in five cases decided together as the *Civil Rights Cases*.

In his *Plessy* dissent, Harlan faulted his colleagues for their dismissal of the Fourteenth Amendment as protection against racial segregation imposed by law. The amendment had "removed the race line from our governmental systems," he wrote, and no longer allowed "any public authority to know the race of those entitled to be protected in the enjoyment" of constitutional rights. All citizens, regardless of race, possessed the same rights. Harlan put this point into a sentence that has become perhaps the most famous, and most quoted, in American constitutional history: "Our Constitution is color-blind, and neither knows nor tolerates classes among citizens." He followed this with another forceful statement: "In respect of civil rights, all citizens are equal before the law."

The notion of a "color-blind" Constitution has enormous appeal as a guiding principle of law. But there are dangers in substituting slogans for hard, realistic analysis. Harlan's famous sentence has been ripped from its historical context by those—including Supreme Court justices—who have wielded it in recent years as a weapon against affirmative action and other "race-conscious" remedial laws and programs. Those who quote the "color-blind" sentence invariably fail to quote the sentences that preceded it in Harlan's opinion. "The white race deems itself to be the dominant race in this country. And so it is, in prestige, in achievements, in education, in wealth, and in power. So, I doubt not, it will continue to be for all time, if it remains true to its great heritage and holds fast to the principles of constitutional liberty."

Harlan stated in these sentences the reality of race in 1896. Whites held the reins of power, which they used to whip blacks into submission. Harlan does not deserve scorn for acknowledging this reality, however much it reflected the "pride of race" that he celebrated. He had no more desire for "social equality" with blacks than Justice Brown. He was, after all, a man of his times, the son of slave owners and a man of superior prestige, education, wealth, and power. Yet he recognized the folly of keeping blacks in subjugation through the Jim Crow system. "In my opinion," Harlan wrote in his *Plessy* dissent, "the judgment this day rendered will, in time, prove to be quite as pernicious as the decision made by this tribunal in the Dred Scott case." He was right, but hardly anyone read his words at the time, or heeded their message.

Although he dissented in the *Plessy* case, Justice Harlan believed in following precedent, and he bowed to that ruling in a case decided three years later, writing for a unanimous Court in upholding the right of a Georgia county to provide a high school education for white students but none for blacks. The school board of Richmond

County argued that it could not afford to maintain grade schools for black children if it also had to build a black high school, although county funds paid the tuition of white students at a private, denominational high school. In his 1899 opinion in *Cumming v. Richmond County*, Harlan rejected the appeal of black parents. He brushed aside the fact that the county had closed a black high school and refused to give its former students the tuition payments to private schools that whites received from tax funds. Harlan held in *Cumming* that "the education of the people in schools maintained by state taxation is a matter belonging to the respective States" and was immune from federal judicial scrutiny "except in the case of a clear and unmistakable disregard of rights secured by the supreme law of the land." Regardless of his own view of these rights, Harlan felt bound by *Plessy* in this case of clear racial discrimination.

At the turn of the twentieth century, the political and racial climate in the country—both north and south—created an insuperable barrier to any challenge to Jim Crow schools. Although the National Association for the Advancement of Colored People was founded in 1909, its leaders focused their limited resources on the most pressing issue confronting blacks: the epidemic of lynchings that exceeded one hundred each year in the first two decades of the twentieth century. And the best-known and most influential black educator in the nation, Booker T. Washington, counseled the black community to accept the Jim Crow system. Washington headed the Tuskegee Institute in Alabama, an institution heavily dependent on funding from white philanthropists and foundations. "We should try," he wrote in 1915, "to keep the young educated Negro from becoming bitter in his attitude toward people and things in general. Therefore, I believe in industrial education, which tends to make the Negro lose himself in his job. He does not then have so much opportunity to become bitter."

Although Washington had critics during his own time and was

later excoriated as an "Uncle Tom" who catered to his white patrons, he set the pattern at Tuskegee for black education across the
South. He also argued that black children should be taught "practical" subjects in primary schools. "We are trying to instill into the
Negro mind," Washington said, "that if education does not make
the Negro humble, simple, and of service to the community, then it
will not be encouraged." He meant that black schools would not be
"encouraged" by whites if their students learned skills that would
allow them to compete with whites for good jobs, or remove them
from the pool of cheap, unskilled black labor. The basic curriculum
of black primary schools reflected the jobs open to black workers.
In 1900, when 90 percent of all blacks lived in the former Confederacy, six of every ten employed blacks labored on farms, with
three-fourths of this number working as sharecroppers, perpetually
in debt to the white landowners to whom they gave a share of their
crop as rent. Almost three in ten blacks, mostly women, worked in
domestic service as cooks, housekeepers, laundresses, and nurse-
maids for white children. More than half of all southern white
families employed a black "girl" to cook and clean. Most of the remaining 10 percent of black workers were laborers in shops and
factories; only 2 percent held professional jobs, serving the black
community as teachers, doctors, and ministers.

Jim Crow schools which taught their students only those skills
needed for agricultural work and domestic service fit the needs of
the white economy and society. Booker T. Washington reflected the
reality of the situation facing southern blacks when he said in 1915
that "white men will vote funds for Negro education just in proportion to their belief in the value of that education." The only
value to a white landowner in educating black children lay in their
ability to pick cotton or wash laundry. Any education beyond the
rudiments of literacy and figuring would not only be wasted on
them, but it might encourage them to seek higher education, which
would make them unfit for working on white-owned farms and in
white homes.

Even the directors of foundations that funded black colleges limited their support to "practical" education. J. L. M. Curry of the Peabody board, which made large donations to the Tuskegee Institute, wrote an article on the "Difficulties, Complications and Limitations Connected with the Education of the Negro." His pessimistic title reflected his dismissive attitude toward black abilities and aspirations. "The hope of the race, in the South," he wrote, "is to be found, not so much in the high courses of University instruction, or in schools of technology, as in handicraft instruction."

By the 1930s, some three decades after the *Plessy* decision, more black children attended school in the Jim Crow states, stayed longer in school, and earned higher scores on achievement tests. Yet they still lagged far behind white children, whose schools were bigger and better and whose teachers had more training than black graduates of second-rate "normal schools." Measured solely in numbers, however, blacks had made substantial educational gains. For example, the federal Census Bureau reported a literacy rate for black adults in 1890 of slightly more than 40 percent. This meant that six out of ten blacks could not read and write at all, at a time when nearly seven out of ten white adults were literate. Forty years later, in 1930, the reported literacy rate for blacks had doubled, to just over 80 percent, while more than nine in ten white adults were literate. In some of the Jim Crow states, the black literacy rate shot up dramatically between 1890 and 1930, from 30 to 74 percent in Georgia, and from 28 to 77 percent in Louisiana. But these seemingly impressive figures masked a serious problem. Asking people if they are literate is not the same as testing their reading and writing skills, and possessing the rudiments of literacy will not prepare anyone for more than manual or domestic work. Among the 80 percent of black adults whom the Bureau reported as literate in 1930, few had stayed in school beyond the primary grades, and virtually all had attended inferior Jim Crow schools.

The obstacles facing black children who thirsted for education in the 1930s—the great-grandparents of today's black students—were enormous. More than three million school-age black children lived in the seventeen states that continued to operate separate schools, along with 81 percent of all the nation's black population. In the Jim Crow states that stretched from Delaware to Texas, local school boards spent almost three times as much on each white student as they did on blacks. The funding disparities in the Deep South states, where blacks outnumbered whites in hundreds of rural counties, were far greater. Alabama spent $37 on each white child in 1930 and just $7 on those who were black; in Georgia the figures were $32 and $7, in Mississippi they were $31 and $6, and those in South Carolina were $53 and $5, a disparity of more than ten to one.

Schools with just one-third as much to spend on each child, or as little as one-tenth of the funds for other schools, can hardly provide as good an education as those with full funding, regardless of the race of their students. The largest chunk of the school budget in every district goes to pay teachers, and the salaries of black teachers during the 1930s were far below those of whites. The monthly salary of black teachers in the South in 1930 was about 60 percent of the white average, $73 for blacks and $118 for whites, with the yearly school term in white schools about two months longer, which added to the salary gap. Poorly paid teachers are not necessarily poorly trained or unable to educate their students, but the meager wages of black teachers in the 1930s did not lure the most promising college graduates into rural Jim Crow schools. Horace Mann Bond, a noted black educator, administered the Stanford Achievement Test—which many college-bound students take in their last year of high school—to a large group of black teachers in Alabama schools in 1931. He discovered that their average score was below that of the national level of ninth-grade students. Almost half of the black teachers had not mastered the material that eighth-graders were expected to know. And many of these teachers were assigned to teach students in grades above their own level of knowledge.

During the late 1930s, the American Council on Education sent a team of investigators into the Deep South to conduct a survey of the schools in which black children were educated. These schools were, of course, segregated by law and long-standing custom. The report of the investigators who visited the black grade school in Dine Hollow, Alabama, reflected the study's findings across the "Black Belt" that stretched from southern Virginia through eastern Texas:

"A typical rural Negro school is at Dine Hollow. It is in a dilapidated building, once whitewashed, standing in a rocky field unfit for cultivation. Dust-covered weeds spread a carpet all around, except for an uneven, bare area on one side which looks like a ball field. Behind the school is a small building with a broken, sagging door. As we approach, a nervous, middle-aged woman comes to the door of the school. She greets us in a discouraged voice marked by a speech impediment. Escorted inside, we observe that the broken benches are crowded to three times their normal capacity. Only a few battered books are in sight, and we look in vain for maps or charts. We learn that four grades are assembled here. The weary teacher agrees to permit us to remain while she proceeds with the instruction. She goes to the blackboard and writes an assignment for the first two grades to do while she conducts spelling and word drills for the third and fourth grades. This is the assignment:

"Write your name ten times.

"Draw an dog, an cat, an rat, an boot."

Elizabeth Moore, who attended the black grade school in Boyle, Mississippi, recalled her math classes: "We had one teacher who didn't know her multiplication tables. She didn't mind telling us that she didn't know. She'd say to us, when we'd ask her what a certain number multiplied by a certain number was, 'Oh, go away, child, I am tired and can't be bothered with you. If I tried to remember all that study and stuff I'd go crazy.' "

The American Council on Education let black parents and students in Jim Crow schools speak for themselves in its report, *Growing Up in the Black Belt*. What they said was both sad and sobering.

Almost without exception, parents wanted their children to learn and succeed. "I believe children ought to get all the education they kin," said a farmer's wife in Coahoma County, Mississippi. "I'd like to see 'em all finish the twelfth grade at least. My daughter is the only one that goes now. The rest have to chop and pick right now, but they be going 'long soon." Almost all black children in the South missed school to do farmwork. A farmer in Johnson County, North Carolina, needed his sons to help with tobacco planting: "Last year I kept my boy out three weeks. I hope he won't have to miss so much this year. Staying out makes him miss so much he ought to have. Farming people don't have much time to spend in books." A tenant farmer in Shelby County, Tennessee, spoke of his vegetable farming: "The children need all the education they can get, but we need them to help on the farm. If you don't make your crop the white man will put somebody else here to do the work. The children go to school when there ain't no work for them in the fields, but when there is work, they has to stay home and do it." White landowners had little interest in educating the children of their black tenants. "It just isn't safe for me to go on a plantation to bring students to school," said a white truant officer in Shelby County. "The landowners show absolutely no concern and they tell me to let the 'niggers' work." The demands of farmwork took a heavy toll on black children in the Deep South states which had the highest rates of sharecropping. In Mississippi, where almost 90 percent of black farmers were tenants in 1930, the average black child spent just 74 days in school, while the average in Virginia, with a tenancy rate of 38 percent, was 128 days in school. Most black children in the Deep South attended school just fifteen or twenty weeks each year in the 1930s.

Those children who did attend school often suffered at the hands of untrained and uncaring teachers. Maggie Cole, a thirteen-year-old girl who was still in grade school, said, "I would be further along in school than I am now, but when I was small I stayed in the Primer three years. I was just scared of my teacher. She used to call on me and I'd know my lesson, but she was so mean that when she'd call on me I'd get scared and couldn't say nothing. Then she'd whip me." Charles King was fourteen and still in fifth grade. "I've failed in the fifth grade twice," he said. "I reckon it was because the teacher was so very mean. All the kids was afraid of her. It seems like every time she'd call on me my head would just go blank, I'd be so scared. I'm getting so I just hate going to school."

Very few of the black children who finished grade school in the 1930s had the chance to attend high school. In 1932, only 14 percent of those between fifteen and nineteen years old were enrolled in public secondary schools in southern states. From Virginia to Texas, only in North Carolina did as many as 20 percent of blacks attend high school; the rates in Mississippi and Georgia were 5 and 8 percent. A report on secondary education for blacks in 1933 showed that between them, the states of Florida, Louisiana, Mississippi, and South Carolina had a total of sixteen black high schools accredited for four-year study. This report also noted that "89 percent of all Negro secondary schools are essentially elementary schools with one or more years of secondary work included at the top—often at the expense of the lower school." Even the four-year high schools had few resources; they averaged just five full-time and two part-time teachers, and most often one of the teachers doubled as principal. Hardly any of these black high schools offered science courses or had laboratories, and very few had courses in foreign languages, music, or art. Their curriculum was limited and their teachers had little training in academic subjects.

The report of the American Council on Education painted a bleak picture of the education of black children in Jim Crow schools at the end of the 1930s: "Present conditions in and around the rural schools are far from conducive to the proper personality development of these youth. The economic inadequacy of all but a few of the rural families and the gross lack of adequate transportation facilities are major factors in limiting school attendance. Poorly prepared instructors, unfit and untrained to cope with rural children and their problems even under normal circumstances, cannot succeed under such conditions. These teachers are expected to give the child an appreciation for a cultural heritage about which they themselves are generally unaware. A traditional, lifeless curriculum; the harsh, unintelligent disciplinary punishment; and the emphasis upon rote learning must share the blame with poverty for excessive retardation, and for the unrest and dissatisfaction of Negro youth."

Perhaps the most distressing aspect of this comprehensive report was its portrayal of the psychological impact of Jim Crow schooling on black children: "The classroom experience has left its mark on these youth. Personal inadequacy is registered in responses on the test [of attitudes about school] which indicate inability to adjust to classroom work, or to understand it at all, and inability to make progress despite individual effort. There is registered also for some an acute consciousness of intellectual inferiority in comparison with certain others, and social inferiority when they feel themselves the object of derision in the classroom. The school experience of youth from culturally backward homes can become a serious and disturbing emotional adventure. In the first place, many of them have little experience in academic procedures, and are doubly confused when confronted with abstractions by poorly prepared teachers who control their pupils more by physical fear than by the interest they can inspire. These children simply go blank, or give indiscriminate answers when called upon to recite in the traditional manner of the rural classroom."

The most important factor that affected the black population in America during the twentieth century was the "Great Migration" from the rural South to the urban North. When the twentieth century began, the nation's black population was just above nine million, with more than 90 percent living in the South, virtually all in rural areas. The serious economic depressions of the late 1890s and early 1900s hit the rural South harder than other places, and many black tenant farmers could not feed their families. Relatively few, however, had left their farms to move north, as jobs were scarce and blacks were unwelcome in many northern cities. The outbreak of war in Europe in 1914 changed the situation, as foreign-born males returned to their homelands to fight or rejoin their families, leaving jobs open during an economic boom. The federal Labor Department noted in 1916 "a disturbing labor condition in the South. A great migratory stream of Negro wage earners was reported as flowing out of southern and into northern states." During the nine-month period between October 1916 and May 1917, almost four hundred thousand blacks left the South. Most of them moved into big cities; Chicago, Detroit, New York, and Philadelphia gained the most black residents between 1910 and 1920. By the end of the 1920s, those four cities all had more than one hundred thousand blacks. The newcomers, mostly poor and unskilled, were forced by economic necessity and white hostility to crowd into run-down tenements.

An article on Harlem, the "Black Mecca" in New York City, published in 1925, described the reaction of whites to the "invasion" of blacks: "They became panic stricken and began fleeing as from a plague. The presence of one colored family in a block no matter how well bred and orderly was sufficient to precipitate a flight. House after house and block after block was actually deserted. It was a great demonstration of human beings running amuck. None of them stopped to reason why they were doing it or what would happen if they didn't." The "white flight" of the 1920s and succeeding decades was largely to other neighborhoods in northern cities; few cities at that time had "suburbs" as we now know them, areas in which working-class and middle-income families could afford to buy homes. In contrast, the "white flight" of the 1960s and '70s, in response to school integration, flew over city boundaries into the suburbs that had sprouted after World War II, financed by mortgage subsidies to returning veterans, and that quickly ringed almost every northern city.

The Great Depression of the 1930s slowed but did not stop the

Great Migration of blacks into northern cities. Without the prospect of decent jobs, many blacks who would have left their farms remained in the South, still poor but at least with a place to live and a source of food in gardens and animals. But World War II created another economic boom, and with eight million young men, most of them white, in the armed forces during the war, jobs in defense factories and other war-related industries and services became available and lured some two million more blacks to the North. Between 1940 and 1950, the black populations of Chicago, Detroit, New York, and Los Angeles each grew by more than one hundred thousand, while cities like Baltimore, Newark, Cleveland, Philadelphia, St. Louis, and Washington, D.C., gained from thirty to ninety thousand black migrants. The black populations of these cities also grew from the birth of children, and by 1950 close to five million of the nation's fifteen million blacks lived outside the Jim Crow states. Yet more than ten million blacks, two-thirds of the total, still chafed under the daily reminders of racial segregation— "WHITES ONLY" signs over water fountains and the crowded rear seats on city buses—that made clear the unwillingness of whites to associate with blacks in public facilities.

During the four decades between 1910 and 1950, about six million blacks joined the Great Migration from southern farms to northern cities. On the whole, these people were younger and better educated than the older blacks who stayed behind. The 1950 census reported that blacks over twenty-five in most northern states had more than eight years of schooling; the figures in New York, Pennsylvania, Ohio, and Illinois ranged from 8.2 to 8.6 years. Black adults in northern states still lagged behind whites in education by about two years, a gap that could be easily measured in dollars. In New York City, for example, black adults earned an average income of $1,707 in 1950, while the income of whites was $2,517 per capita. Blacks in New York earned just 68 cents for every dollar of white income, although this gap was much lower than in southern cities, where black income in Atlanta, Birmingham, and New Orleans was only 47 percent in 1950 of the white level in each of these cities. The black-white income gap has persisted for the past half-century with little change; the national per capita annual income of blacks in 1997 was only 60 percent of the white level.

The educational status of blacks in the Jim Crow states remained abysmally low in 1950, falling below the level of whites in 1930. Black adults in Mississippi had completed an average of 5.1 years in school, while those in Georgia and South Carolina had even lower figures of 4.9 and 4.8 years. For the nation as a whole, just one of every eight black adults had completed high school, while four of ten whites had earned their diploma. While only 9 percent of white adults had attended school for less than five years, 31 percent of blacks fell into this category. At the other end of the educational spectrum, almost 16 percent of white adults in 1950 had attended college and 6 percent had graduated; the figures for blacks were 5 and 2 percent. These numbers should be viewed with awareness of the glaring disparities in quality of the black and white schools in the Jim Crow states; a black student who completed eight years of schooling in one of these states had attended schools that were in session two months less each year, had been instructed by teachers whose own education averaged just ten years, had used out-of-date, hand-me-down textbooks from white schools, and had received little help at home from parents who were most likely illiterate or barely able to read and write. A white student who completed the eighth grade was almost certainly far ahead of the black child at the same grade level.

The black community had no illusions about Jim Crow schools in 1950. In a special mid-century issue, the *Journal of Negro Education* asked leading black educators to assess the educational system. Without exception, these experts laid the blame for inferior black schools on racial segregation. Benjamin E. Mays, president of Morehouse College in Atlanta, wrote "Improving the Morale of Negro Children and Youth" and argued that the "chief cause of the relatively low morale of Negro children is the circumscription imposed upon them by the legal segregation of the Negro in the South and by the traditional segregation of the Negro in the North." Mays asserted that the Jim Crow system "with its inevitable consequences of inequality has warped the minds and spirits of thousands of Negro youths. They either grow to manhood accepting the system, in which case they aspire to limited, racial standards; or they grow up with bitterness in their minds. It is the rare Negro child who comes through perfectly normal and poised under the segregated system." Mays concluded that "the greatest thing that anyone can do to improve the morale of Negro children and youth is to continue to fight to destroy legalized segregation."

Most white Americans in 1950 had some awareness of the nation's "race problem" and the fact that "separate but equal" schools in the Jim Crow states were far from equal. A fair number of northern whites, but just a handful of white southerners, felt strongly that racial segregation was wrong and should be ended. But efforts to repeal Jim Crow laws had no chance in southern legislatures, and liberal members of Congress could not push civil rights bills through committees run by the Dixiecrats who dominated the Democratic party in both the House and Senate, through the power of seniority. Few whites had actually visited one of the Jim Crow schools in which some 2.4 million black children received inferior education. Hardly any of the newspapers and magazines through which most whites viewed the world, in the years before television became the leading source of news, took a critical look at segregated schools. Their limited coverage of racial issues at mid-century most often stressed the "gains" that blacks had made under the Jim Crow system. One good example was the lengthy article on "The New South" in *Life* magazine in October 1949. Under the caption "Still Segregated, Negro Life Is Getting Better," *Life* ran a large photograph of smiling, well-dressed students at George Washington Carver High School in Montgomery, Alabama. The black students at this new school "meet in large, airy classrooms," *Life* told its readers. But even this showcase of the Jim Crow system had serious problems. "Built for 600 pupils, the school has more than 800," the picture caption reported. "It is short on books and as yet has no locker room, auditorium or gym—but is immeasurably better than anything Negro students had before."

Most of the news reports on black education in 1950 focused on the Supreme Court rulings in June of that year, forcing public universities in Oklahoma and Texas to admit black students to graduate programs and law schools. Under the heading "Negro Gains," *Newsweek* reported that "more than 1,000 Negroes are now attending classes with white students" in southern universities. In a short, concluding paragraph, *Newsweek* alerted its readers to a new legal development: "In Clarendon County, South Carolina, last week, the fight to break down segregation entered a new phase. Some 50 Negroes had filed suit, claiming that Negro and white schools did not offer equal facilities, and requesting 'complete integration' of schools. Hearings would probably drag on for some time." For the first time, readers of a major newsmagazine learned of the legal attack on Jim Crow schools in the Deep South, a campaign that had been carefully planned for years by Thurgood Marshall and the young lawyers he directed for the legal arm of the National Association for the Advancement of Colored People.

CHAPTER 3

"We Got a Good Bunch of Nigras Here"

Close to a century after her birth in Clarendon County, South Carolina, Annie Martin Gibson talked with me about her childhood and schooling in the small town of Summerton:

"I was born in Summerton in 1910. My father's name was Hampton Martin and my mother's name was Amanda. My daddy had a one-horse farm. He had a mule and a horse, but the horse was for the buggy, going to church and back. Our farm had cotton, corn, and a garden. There was seven children in my family, two boys and five girls. I'm the third child.

"I started school at Scott's Branch when I was five. It only went to the tenth grade, and there was two rooms for all the grades. We had to build our own fire to keep warm in the winter. Some of the chirren had to go out in the woods around the school and get firewood for the stoves. We had outside toilets, and we didn't have no real desks, just benches to sit on.

"When I was a little girl, we only had school about three months in the year. They would take us out of school to pick cotton. I didn't like that, it was too hard, and we'd cut our hands on the cotton bolls. So I'd put rocks in my bag to weigh more, and I'd lay down in the rows so nobody could see I wasn't picking cotton. I liked school, and I finished the tenth grade. Our teachers were good, but they mostly didn't have no training, they'd only go through the tenth grade themselves. Some of them were just girls."

The Scott's Branch school that Annie Gibson attended was the only school for black children in rural Clarendon County, located on the flat plain between the swampy lowlands of the South Carolina coast and the hilly uplands of the state's western region. This was the domain of King Cotton, ruled by white landlords and populated largely by descendants of African slaves who labored under conditions that had changed very little since the Civil War ended with "freedom" for the slaves and federal promises of a sweeping "Reconstruction" of the rebellious southern states. The federal plan to break up white-owned plantations and distribute land to the former slaves who had toiled in those fields did allow some black farmers to own their land, but far more—most of them unable to read the contracts they signed with an *X*—returned to economic servitude as sharecroppers, perpetually in debt to "Mr. Charlie," who kept the books and the profits. The only hope that succeeding generations of black children could escape from poverty and peonage lay in education, but the efforts of sympathetic white philanthropists and dedicated black teachers and parents fell short under the Jim Crow system of segregated schools.

Annie Gibson became one of the lucky few among the black children of Clarendon County to escape from the illiteracy that consigned many of her generation to lives of poverty, both in the rural South and the urban North. In 1920, when she was in the fifth grade at Scott's Branch school, fewer than one out of ten black children in South Carolina continued in school past the fifth grade. Almost four of every ten black adults in the state were totally illiterate, and few of the remaining 60 percent could read or write beyond a rudimentary level. A federal report on illiteracy, based on data from the 1920 census, concluded that "the chances that a negro child in the rural sections will receive even the rudiments of an education are very small in most of the States of the South."

The Scott's Branch school that became the first target of the twentieth-century legal battle against Jim Crow education in the Deep South was established in the late nineteenth century in the Taw Caw Baptist Church, located three miles east of Summerton. Supported and staffed by church members and ministers, it was the only school for black children in Clarendon County and received no public funds for teachers' salaries or books. A recent history of the county's black schools noted that teachers "were paid by the patrons in the form of farm and garden produce, chickens, eggs, and occasionally, a piece of fresh pork. Most of the children walked to school; hence, on rainy days many of them had to stay home. They also had to go home before the end of the school day on occasions when the church people needed their buildings for funerals, conventions, or other church meetings."

Sharing the Taw Caw church building with its parishioners, and the rural location of the school, created difficulties for both church and school leaders, and black parents decided in the last decade of the nineteenth century to move the school into Summerton. They pooled their meager resources and bought an old "gin house" that had been used for ginning cotton from bolls into bales. Placed on logs and pulled by mules, the gin house was rolled to a vacant lot and refurbished as a schoolhouse. The school was renamed for the Scott's Branch stream that ran behind the building. Several years later, the gin house school burned down and black parents—again with no public funds—raised the money to construct a two-story structure with an upstairs auditorium. This second Scott's Branch school was destroyed by fire in 1937, and black parents again raised money to purchase a larger plot of vacant land near the town center. By this time, the white officials who ruled Clarendon County had established a county board of education that funded and administered the dual system of black and white schools. The board provided funds to erect a white-frame building to which Annie and James Gibson sent their five children in the 1940s. For the first time, black students in Summerton attended a school with running water and electricity, although none of the one-room black schools outside the town limits had these amenities. The white children in Summerton attended classes in an imposing red-brick building with a lunchroom and laboratories, facilities that the Scott's Branch school lacked and that the school board saw no need to provide for "nigra" children.

During the four decades after Annie Gibson's birth in 1910, Clarendon County changed very little. The Great Depression of the 1930s began a decade earlier in the Deep South with the collapse of the cotton economy, and its effects lingered for another decade after the wartime boom created jobs and lifted wages in the northern states. Like most of the "Black Belt" counties that stretched from Virginia to Louisiana, Clarendon County remained largely black, poor, and uneducated. The 1950 census showed a county population of 32,215, with more than 90 percent of the people living in rural areas. Summerton, with a population of 1,419, and the county seat of Manning, with 2,775 residents, were the only "urban" towns in the county. Seven of every ten county residents were black, and of those who were twenty-five years or older, more than 80 percent had not been educated beyond the sixth grade. The average black adult in Clarendon County had completed just 4.2 years of school. Four years of education in Jim Crow schools, with poorly trained teachers, hand-me-down books, and no science labs, would hardly prepare a black student, no matter how bright or ambitious, to succeed and prosper in a society that had already produced nuclear weapons and jet airplanes. At the halfway point of the twentieth century, 80 percent of Clarendon County's black residents worked on farms and more than two-thirds of the black families had incomes of less than $1,000 a year.

Clarendon County *was* changed, however, by a struggle waged thousands of miles from its farms and schools. The world war that raged in Europe and the Pacific, between Allied and Axis forces, pitted the advocates of democracy against totalitarian enemies who preached and practiced the most brutal forms of racial and religious bigotry. Close to a million black Americans, who served in a Jim Crow army and navy, found themselves thinking and quietly talking among themselves about the disparity between American professions of racial tolerance and equality, and the reality of Jim Crow life to which many of these veterans returned. One angry black veteran put his resentment into these words: "The Army jim-crows us. The Navy lets us serve only as messmen. The Red Cross refuses our blood. Employers and unions shut us out. Lynchings continue. We are disenfranchised, jim-crowed, spat upon. What more could Hitler do than that?" Many of these soldiers returned home determined to do something about segregation. They joined the NAACP, boosting its membership and energizing local chapters that had remained dormant for years. In communities across the South, black veterans tried to register to vote, pressed local officials to improve their children's schools, and protested discrimination in jobs and housing.

The southern reaction to black demands for full citizenship was often hostile and sometimes violent. One incident that occurred in South Carolina cast a pall of fear over blacks across the country, and certainly over those in Clarendon County. On February 12, 1946, Isaac Woodward reported to Camp Gordon, Georgia, for his army mustering-out after combat service in the Philippines and New Guinea. Carrying his honorable discharge papers, Woodward headed for home in North Carolina aboard a Greyhound bus. The white driver cursed him for taking too long at a "comfort stop" along the highway and stopped the bus at the police station in Batesburg, South Carolina. White police officers dragged Woodward into the local jail and beat him senseless. During this assault, Chief L. I. Shaw gouged Woodward's eyes with a billy club and left him blind. State officials refused to prosecute Shaw, and an all-white federal jury in Charleston acquitted him of charges that he had violated Woodward's civil rights. The federal attorney who prosecuted Shaw failed to produce any witnesses other than the bus driver who had Woodward arrested. White spectators cheered the jury's verdict, which sickened the federal judge who presided at the trial. "I was shocked by the hypocrisy of my government," Judge J. Waties Waring said later of the prosecutor's failure to call witnesses against the police chief.

Accounts of the Woodward case, and denunciations of the verdict, were prominently reported in the monthly magazine of the NAACP, *The Crisis*, and in the country's most widely circulated black newspaper, the *Afro-American*. One black resident of Clarendon County read the articles about the blinded veteran and shared Judge Waring's sickened feelings. The Reverend Joseph A. DeLaine, born near the county seat of Manning in 1898, had been too old and had too many children to serve in World War II, but he counted several veterans in his congregation at the Pine Grove African Methodist Episcopal Church. To supplement his meager clerical income, both Reverend DeLaine and his wife, Mattie, taught school, he at a rural one-room school several miles from Summerton and she at Scott's Branch school in town.

Reverend DeLaine had no illusions about the indifference of the whites on the Clarendon County school board toward the glaring disparities between the well-maintained schools their children attended and the dilapidated structures into which his parishioners' children were crowded. But he was particularly resentful that his students had to walk to school along dirt roads, their clothes splashed by dust or mud by the shiny yellow school buses that carried white children past them. The school board provided thirty buses for white children, but had never given one—even a hand-me-down—for black children. During the summer of 1947, DeLaine attended an NAACP workshop in Columbia, the state capital, and listened to a rousing speech by the Reverend James Hinton, president of the state's chapters. Hinton told his audience that South Carolina's black schools were a disgrace and would improve only if whites were forced by legal action to make them better. Challenging his listeners, he charged: "No teacher or preacher in South Carolina has the courage to find a plaintiff to challenge the legality of the discriminatory bus-transportation practices of this state."

One person in the audience accepted Hinton's challenge. The

first Sunday after returning to Summerton, Reverend DeLaine visited Levi Pearson, a black farmer with three children at the Scott's Branch high school, nine miles from their home. Pearson owned his farm and was known for standing up to whites. He listened to DeLaine and agreed to stand up for his children. DeLaine then drove back to Columbia and visited Harold Boulware, the state's only black civil rights lawyer. Trained at Howard University Law School in Washington, D.C., Boulware was in his mid-thirties and had been looking for a plaintiff to bring an "equalization" suit against the denial of school buses to black children. Providing thirty buses for white children in Clarendon County and none for blacks could hardly be squared with the "separate but equal" doctrine of the *Plessy* case, in which the separate railroad coaches for blacks were supposedly equal in quality. Forcing the school board to provide buses for black children would not end segregation, but it would at least make it easier for them to attend their separate schools.

All of this legal strategy was lost on Levi Pearson, who simply wanted a bus to take his children nine miles to school and back. He gladly signed the two-page petition to the county school board that Harold Boulware drafted and that Reverend DeLaine brought to his farmhouse. DeLaine then visited another preacher, the Reverend L. B. McCord, a Presbyterian pastor and the county's school superintendent. The two men of the cloth knew each other well. "I was one of McCord's good niggers," DeLaine recalled. But not after their meeting on July 28, 1947. The black teacher handed the white superintendent Pearson's petition, demanding bus transportation "for use of the said children of your Petitioner and other Negro school children similarly situated." McCord read it and curtly told DeLaine the county had no money for buses for black children.

After this rebuff, Harold Boulware wrote the school board that Levi Pearson had retained his legal services and asked for a hearing on his petition. He got no answer to this or subsequent letters. Finally, on March 18, 1948, Boulware filed suit in federal court in Charleston, seeking an injunction to bar Clarendon County officials

from making any "distinction on account of race or color" in busing children to school. But the case was dismissed a month later because the county's white lawyers searched the property records and
discovered that Pearson's farm actually straddled the line between
two school districts; he paid property taxes in one and his children
attended school in another.

Levi Pearson paid for his stand; every white-owned bank and
store cut off his credit and no white farmer would rent him a har-
vester. His crops rotted in the field that fall. Whites told him to forget about buses, and finally gave him credit for next year's crops. Yet
he could not forget his children's inferior schools. The next spring,
in March 1949, Harold Boulware summoned Pearson and DeLaine
to Columbia to meet another civil rights lawyer. Thurgood Marshall had come to South Carolina from New York, looking for
plaintiffs willing to ask for more than buses. Marshall, the general
counsel and chief legal strategist for the NAACP, proposed a new
lawsuit, demanding equal treatment in every area: buildings, teachers, books, and buses. He told Pearson and DeLaine that he wanted
at least twenty plaintiffs, to spread the risk of retaliation. And he
wanted Clarendon County, to expose the myth of "separate but
equal" in South Carolina's most unequal county.

Levi Pearson could not match Thurgood Marshall in education
or eminence. The short, stocky, plainspoken South Carolina
farmer had never finished high school or traveled beyond his native
state, while the tall, imposing, articulate lawyer had argued cases before the courts of a dozen states and had recently won landmark decisions in the United States Supreme Court. But the two men
shared a fierce commitment to equal rights and the courage to stand
up to hostile racists. Marshall had faced death threats and had out-
raced Klansmen in high-speed chases on winding southern roads,
while Pearson kept a shotgun near the door of his farmhouse to
protect his family from hooded nightriders.

Marshall had come to South Carolina looking for a Deep South lawsuit that would put the "separate but equal" doctrine of the *Plessy* case to its hardest test. Civil rights lawyers had been working since 1946 to force local school boards to "equalize" teachers' salaries, school facilities, and textbooks, with the objective of raising the cost of maintaining "separate but equal" systems for black and white students. This legal tactic was part of a long-range strategy to pave the way for the final assault on school segregation in the Deep South. Federal judges in South Carolina and other Jim Crow states had already ordered school boards to begin "equalizing" their separate schools. The NAACP lawyers hoped that local officials, faced with the massive costs of upgrading black schools to make them equal in quality to those for whites, might reluctantly conclude that segregation came with too high a price tag. In Clarendon County, for example, the school board spent $179 for each white student, but only $43 for each black child. With almost four thousand black children in the county's schools, the cost of bringing the spending for blacks up to the level for whites would come to more than half a million dollars each year, far more than the county's total budget. Finding a sympathetic federal judge who would order a county school board to actually equalize the black and white schools in its system would pave the way for a later challenge to racial segregation itself, particularly if the board facing such an order failed or refused to carry out the judge's equalization decree.

Marshall was not ready, however, when he met with Pearson and Boulware, to mount a head-on challenge to Jim Crow education in Clarendon County. He was a bold lawyer, but also one who was realistic about the obstacles—both legal and political—to a frontal assault on the citadel of segregation: elementary schools in the Deep South states. The nation's leading civil rights lawyer was above all a pragmatist, committed to a patient, step-by-step approach to the crusade against segregated schools. Born in Baltimore in 1908, Marshall became a star debater at the city's Colored High School, and then attended Lincoln University in Pennsylvania, an all-black college. After his graduation in 1930, he wanted to apply to the

University of Maryland's all-white law school, but the certainty of rejection because of his race led Marshall to study law instead at Howard University, the "black Harvard," in Washington, D.C. He graduated first in his class in 1933, although the Depression and the lack of jobs for black lawyers had cut his first-year class of thirty-six down to six graduates three years later.

Passing up the offer of a full scholarship for a year of postgraduate study at Harvard Law School, Marshall opened his own law practice in Baltimore, but clients were scarce and he had plenty of spare time for NAACP projects. During the fall of 1933, he answered a call from Charles H. Houston, the dean of Howard's law school and a mentor to Marshall and dozens of young black lawyers. Traveling in Houston's car from Washington through the Deep South to New Orleans, the two black lawyers stopped in small towns to visit schools and document the disparities between those for blacks and whites. "Conditions were much worse than we heard they were," Marshall recalled of the black schools. One incident drove home the isolation of rural black children. Marshall was eating an orange with his lunch while Houston examined a drafty pine-board school in Mississippi, and noticed a young boy staring at him with wide eyes. He offered the boy another orange and watched in amazement. "The kid did not even take the peeling off. He had never seen an orange before. He just bit right through it and enjoyed it."

Marshall won his first civil rights case in 1936, forcing Maryland to admit another black applicant, Donald Murray, to the law school that had rejected him. However, because the state did not appeal to the Supreme Court, the *Murray* case did not establish any precedent on racial segregation outside Maryland. Marshall gave up his law practice in Baltimore and joined the NAACP's national legal staff in 1938 after several years of handling the group's lawsuits in Maryland and Virginia. He quickly rose to the position of general counsel, and commanded a dedicated platoon of young lawyers who fought segregation with a battle plan drafted in 1931 by Nathan Margold, a young Jewish lawyer and protégé of Felix Frankfurter, then a Harvard Law professor. Hired by the NAACP to research Jim Crow laws and recommend a long-range litigation strategy against segregation in public education, Margold had produced a 218-page document that became the master plan for Marshall's troops.

Margold took the Supreme Court's "separate but equal" ruling in *Plessy v. Ferguson* as his starting point, documenting in his report the obvious fact that schools for blacks in southern states were rarely equal to those for whites. He considered two legal strategies to challenge segregation. One would focus on lawsuits designed to force southern officials to make black and white schools truly equal in quality. This strategy had two advantages: it would avoid a direct attack on *Plessy*, which stood firmly in the 1930s as legal precedent; and judicial rulings that ordered equal facilities would impose heavy financial burdens on local school boards. The second legal strategy Margold outlined would assert that separate schools could never be equal because segregation imposed a "badge of servitude" on black children. This approach had many risks, but one virtue: judges could not evade the Equal Protection clause of the Fourteenth Amendment.

Margold urged NAACP lawyers to rely for precedent on *Yick Wo v. Hopkins*, in which the Supreme Court had ruled in 1888 that laws applied by public officials to racial minorities "with an evil eye and an unequal hand" violated the Constitution. The *Yick Wo* decision had struck down a San Francisco ordinance under which every Chinese laundryman in the city was denied a business license under the guise of a supposedly "neutral" fire safety code, while all but one Caucasian applicants were granted licenses. Neither the *Plessy* case nor *Yick Wo* had anything to do with public schools, but the former decision had been cited by the Supreme Court in several cases upholding school segregation, one of which, ironically, had classified Martha Lum, a Chinese girl in Mississippi, as "colored" and forced her to attend an all-black school. Martha's father, Gong Lum, had sued the state education superintendent; his lawyers argued to the Supreme Court that " 'Colored' describes only one race, and that is the Negro." Whites maintained separate schools to protect their children from "the infusion of the blood" from blacks. "The white race may not legally expose the yellow race to a danger that the dominant race recognizes and guards itself against," Gong Lum's lawyers claimed. Ruling in 1927, the Supreme Court held in *Gong Lum v. Rice* that all children who were not white fell into the "colored" category and could be forced by state law to attend separate schools. The Court based its *Gong Lum* decision on the *Plessy* case, making clear that the "separate but equal" doctrine covered not only railroad coaches but schools as well. Nathan Margold admitted that most judges would look first to *Plessy* for precedent, but a sympathetic judge might find *Yick Wo* a more persuasive decision.

Margold had advised NAACP leaders in his report that "it would be a great mistake to fritter away our limited funds on sporadic attempts to force the making of equal divisions of school funds in the few instances where such attempts might be expected to succeed." This approach would force civil rights lawyers to file separate lawsuits in each southern school district, to recruit plaintiffs in each district who had the courage and fortitude to face hostility from whites and delays in courts, and to perform the laborious task of digging out the evidence of school funding disparities in each case. Even if they succeeded, lawsuits to equalize facilities would require judges to act as school superintendents, checking the quality of textbooks, playgrounds, and lavatories in the separate schools for blacks and whites. "And we should be leaving untouched the very essence of the existing evils" of segregation, Margold warned. "On the other hand," he urged, "if we boldly challenge the constitutional validity of segregation if and when accompanied irremediably by discrimination, we can strike directly at the most prolific sources of discrimination."

Thurgood Marshall read the Margold Report with care after he joined the NAACP's legal staff, but he remained skeptical about the proposal to launch a frontal assault on school segregation in the Deep South. Marshall was convinced that such an approach would have sent his legal troops on a suicide mission. The notion of little black boys rubbing knees with little white girls was unthinkable in the 1930s, when black males of any age were considered sexual threats to white girls and women, and a decade in which lynchings—mostly of black men accused of raping white women—approached one hundred each year. Marshall decided instead to mount a flanking attack on the Old Confederacy, beginning with graduate education in border states. This campaign, if successful, would establish legal precedent for a final assault on the citadel of segregation, grade schools in the Deep South.

Marshall based his strategy of encirclement on his victory in 1936 over the University of Maryland Law School, although that ruling was limited to a single state. Two years later, Marshall took another law school case to the U.S. Supreme Court, whose decisions set national precedent. This case began when the University of Missouri denied admission to Lloyd Gaines to its law school, solely because he was black, although state officials offered to pay his tuition if he attended law school in a neighboring state. The NAACP filed suit against the university's registrar, whose last name was Canada, and the case reached the Supreme Court after Missouri's high court ruled against Gaines. Chief Justice Charles Evans Hughes wrote for the Court in *Gaines v. Canada*, holding that Missouri could not give whites a legal education in the state and deny blacks that right. Echoing the Margold Report, Hughes cited *Yick Wo* for support, calling that decision "the pivot upon which the case turns." But he quickly retreated, citing *Plessy* in ruling that states could provide black and white law students with "equal facilities in separate schools" without violating the Constitution. Missouri promptly established a black law school, and the *Plessy* doctrine of "separate but equal" remained the law.

World War II interrupted the NAACP campaign against segregated education, but Marshall returned to court in 1946 with suits against segregated graduate programs in Oklahoma and Texas. In the first case, Ada Lois Sipuel had been turned away from the University of Oklahoma Law School, but was promised that state legislators would create a black law school with "substantially equal" facilities. The lawmakers' foot-dragging prompted Marshall to ask the Supreme Court to put a match to their toes. Faced with a ruling in 1948 that cited the *Gaines* decision for precedent and that ordered the state to provide Ada Sipuel with a legal education "as soon as it does" for white applicants, university officials roped off a section of the state capitol and called it a law school, although the pretend school had no library and no faculty of its own. Ada Sipuel refused to be a pretend student, and Thurgood Marshall returned to the Supreme Court later in 1948 in *Sipuel v. Oklahoma Board of Regents* to argue, for the first time, that segregation was flatly unconstitutional. Even if states provided blacks with better schools than whites, he said, separating them by race imposed a "badge of inferiority" on blacks. But the justices shied away from this divisive issue during a presidential election year and sent the case back to state court for hearings on whether the pretend law school was equal to its real, all-white school. After the voters returned Harry Truman to the White House with a strong civil rights program, Oklahoma officials wearied of legal battles and admitted Ada Sipuel to its real law school.

Another law school case began in 1946 but did not reach the Supreme Court until 1950, along with a second challenge to segregated graduate education in Oklahoma. The first case involved the University of Texas Law School, which denied admission to Heman Sweatt, a black postal worker. After NAACP lawyers filed suit, state judges ordered the university to give Sweatt a legal education "substantially equivalent" to that provided whites. The law school dean offered plans for an all-black school that would occupy four basement rooms in an Austin office building, with no library and three part-time instructors. When Texas judges agreed that four rooms for blacks matched in quality the massive building in which eight hundred and fifty white students attended classes, Marshall filed an appeal with the Supreme Court. In the second Oklahoma case, the university admitted George McLaurin to its graduate education program shortly after Ada Sipuel became the first black law student on the campus. McLaurin, however, was forced to listen to lectures outside the classroom, sitting in a hallway seat marked "RESERVED FOR COLORED." He could study at a "colored" desk in the library's mezzanine, but not in the reading room, and could eat at a "colored" table in the cafeteria, but only after white students finished their meals. NAACP lawyers challenged these demeaning conditions as "badges of slavery" imposed on McLaurin, but they lost the first two rounds in lower federal courts.

The *Sweatt* and *McLaurin* cases reached the Supreme Court for argument in April 1950. The NAACP's briefs in both cases offered the justices a choice: they could order Texas and Oklahoma to provide equal facilities for black students in graduate programs, which would require either full integration or massive spending on schools that were separate but truly equal in quality; or they could overturn *Plessy* and rule that racial segregation violated the Constitution. The Court's decisions would help NAACP lawyers determine their strategy in school cases from the Deep South. Perhaps the time was near for the final assault on Jim Crow education.

Thurgood Marshall argued for Heman Sweatt, and his young NAACP assistant counsel, Robert L. Carter, argued for George McLaurin. Both lawyers urged the Court to abandon the *Plessy* doctrine of "separate but equal." Marshall pointed out the physical inequality of the separate Texas law schools, but he focused on the issue of racial segregation. "They can build an exact duplicate but if it is segregated, it is unequal," he said. The attorneys general of the eleven former Confederate states filed an amicus brief that dropped any pretense of legal argument. Southern whites, they warned the justices, do not "want their women folk in intimate social contact with Negro men." Enforcing this taboo required segregation at every educational level, from kindergarten to graduate school.

The justices declined Marshall's appeal to overrule *Plessy*, and they ignored the southern appeal to sexual fears. In decisions handed down on June 5, 1950, Chief Justice Carl Vinson wrote for a unanimous Court in both cases. His opinion in *Sweatt v. Painter* accepted Marshall's invitation to look closely at the separate Texas law schools. After comparing their facilities, Vinson found it "difficult to believe that one who had a free choice between these law schools would consider the question close." The answer depended not only on factors like books and buildings, he added, but also on "those qualities which are incapable of measurement but which make for greatness in a law school." The black school could not match the "reputation of the faculty" and "influence of the alumni" that added to the "rich traditions and prestige" of the white school. The Court ordered that Heman Sweatt "be admitted to the University of Texas Law School" without delay.

George McLaurin had already been admitted to the University of Oklahoma graduate education school. The only question in his case, Vinson wrote in *McLaurin v. Oklahoma State Regents*, stemmed from his separation from other students in the classroom, library, and cafeteria. "Such restrictions impair and inhibit his ability to study, to engage in discussions and exchange views with other students, and, in general, to learn his profession." McLaurin "must receive the same treatment at the hands of the state as students of other races," the Court instructed his instructors. The "COLORED" signs came down, and McLaurin finally taught the university a lesson.

Even before the Supreme Court decided the *Sweatt* and *McLaurin* cases, black parents in Summerton, South Carolina, had decided the time had come for their own suit against segregation. Reverend J. A. DeLaine and Levi Pearson had worked hard since their meeting with Thurgood Marshall and Harold Boulware to find twenty parents who were willing to become plaintiffs and sign a legal complaint against the white officials of Clarendon County. They reached their goal on November 11, 1949, and took the list of signatures to Boulware's office in Columbia. He drafted a complaint and put names on the caption in alphabetical order. The first was

Harry Briggs, a navy veteran with five children; his oldest boy was Harry Briggs, Jr., whose name appeared first among the black children whose parents brought suit as their "next friend," an archaic legal term that still survives. Harry Sr. pumped gas and fixed cars at H. C. Carrigan's Sinclair station in Summerton. The town's twelve-term mayor, Carrigan expressed a rosy view of race relations between white farm owners and their black sharecroppers. "Colored have made wonderful progress down here," he assured a northern visitor. "I have several farms, and they all have Negroes on them. I sharecrop with them, and they are all as happy as can be." David McClary, who owned the largest feed and livestock business in Summerton, agreed with this "Amos and Andy" sentiment. "We got a good bunch of nigras here," he boasted.

Those good feelings toward Clarendon County's "nigras" abruptly ended when Harold Boulware filed the complaint with the federal court in Charleston. As was common in the Deep South, local whites blamed "outside agitators" from the NAACP for fomenting trouble and stirring up the "happy" blacks whose children attended school in wooden shacks with no desks. The school board's lawyer, S. Emory Rogers, declared that he would not extend credit or rent land to any NAACP member. "Everybody in Summerton feels the same way," he told a reporter. "You would, too, if you had an organization that was trying to destroy everything you believed in. We would like, if they are not satisfied here, for them to go where their ideas are accepted."

The white reaction to the lawsuit was prompt and unforgiving. Mayor Carrigan fired Harry Briggs on Christmas Eve, handing him a carton of cigarettes as severance pay. The motel at which Eliza Briggs cleaned rooms fired her as well. After trying without success to support his family on a small farm, Harry Briggs packed up his children and belongings and moved to New York, where his lack of education kept him in a string of menial jobs. Other plaintiffs suffered reprisals from whites. Bo Stukes lost his garage job; James Brown was fired by a trucking company. John McDonald, a combat veteran of Iwo Jima and Okinawa, lost his credit for farm equipment, and Lee Richardson had his farm mortgage foreclosed. Even Harry Briggs's cow got arrested for stepping on a headstone in a white cemetery. Whites laughed at that little comedy, but blacks in Clarendon County found no humor in the spiteful response to their lawsuit.

The lawsuit that Harold Boulware and Thurgood Marshall filed for the black plaintiffs named Roderick Elliott, the elderly chairman of the county school board, as the first defendant. The complaint in *Briggs v. Elliott* alleged that Summerton's white schools were "superior in plant, equipment, curricula, and in all other material respects to the schools set apart for Negro students." Considering the gross disparities in spending between black and white students, the NAACP lawyers expected the federal judge assigned to the case to order that county officials at least begin the task of equalizing the school funding. Marshall had planned to ask the judge, during a pretrial hearing in November 1950, to order that school officials cooperate in giving his expert witnesses, recruited from Howard University's school of education, full access to school facilities and records. He did not, however, anticipate the first judicial response to the suit. To Marshall's surprise, Judge J. Waties Waring urged him to amend his complaint to include a direct attack on segregated education. Marshall replied that the complaint did challenge the state's segregation laws, but Judge Waring pointed out that the Clarendon County suit asked first for equal facilities for the black and white schools. "It's very easy to decide the case on that issue," he told the assembled lawyers. The school board's lawyers, Emory Rogers of Summerton and Robert M. Figg, a Charleston lawyer with close connections to South Carolina's political leaders, knew exactly how Waring intended to decide the case. In a tone that Marshall took as a directive, Waring suggested that the complaint should charge that South Carolina's segregation laws "are unconstitutional, and that'll raise the issue for all time as to whether a state can segregate by race in its schools."

Facing a determined judge who had clearly signaled his sympathy for the black plaintiffs, Marshall agreed to amend and refile his complaint. Waring's thinly veiled order, however, posed a serious problem for the NAACP lawyers. Congress had passed a law in 1937 requiring all cases in federal court that challenged the constitutionality of state laws to be heard and decided by a three-judge panel headed by a member of a federal appellate court, rather than a single district judge. Marshall did not relish the prospect of arguing the case before two additional judges, neither of them likely to share Judge Waring's rejection of segregation. "We had drafted the pleadings to make an attack on segregation without raising the issue of the constitutionality of the segregation statute in order to escape the necessity of having a three-judge court," Marshall confessed to an NAACP colleague.

Nonetheless, Marshall did not leave Judge Waring's courtroom empty-handed after this initial setback. Although the county's lawyers had been ready to concede the glaring inequalities of the black and white schools, Waring directed them to allow Marshall's expert witnesses free access to school records and facilities before the trial. Waring had driven through the county many times, and had seen "these awful-looking little wooden shacks in the country that were the Negro schools," he later said. "The white schools were really nothing to be enthusiastic about, but they were fairly respectable-looking. In the towns, they were generally of brick and some of them had chimneys, running water, and things of that kind. The Negro schools were just tumbledown, dirty shacks with horrible outdoor toilet facilities." The judge wanted to make sure that his two colleagues, who had not yet been chosen for the panel, would hear live testimony about the conditions in Clarendon County's schools.

CHAPTER 4

"Give Me the Colored Doll"

May 24, 1951, is one of those unremembered dates that marks a significant event in American history. On that hot spring day in Clarendon County, Kenneth B. Clark visited the Scott's Branch school near Summerton and met with sixteen black children between six and nine years old. Armed with Judge Waring's order that county officials allow the NAACP's expert witnesses free access to the schools, Clark had come to Scott's Branch to give tests to black children. But his tests did not ask the children any questions about arithmetic or vocabulary. Clark brought with him a box of four dolls, each about a foot high and dressed in diapers. Two of the dolls were boys and two were girls. They differed in one other way: two were pink and two were brown. One by one, Clark sat down with the children and gave them instructions: "Give me the white doll." "Give me the colored doll." "Give me the Negro doll." Clark then said to each child, "Give me the doll you like to play with." "Give me the doll that is the nice doll." "Give me the doll that looks bad." "Give me the doll that is a nice color."

Clark made notes of each child's responses. When he tallied them, the results closely matched his findings in similar studies he had conducted in New York City, Philadelphia, Boston, and several Arkansas communities. All sixteen of the Clarendon County black children correctly identified both the white and brown dolls. But ten chose the white doll as the one they wanted to play with; eleven said the brown doll looked "bad" to them; and nine picked the white doll as the "nice" one.

What brought Kenneth Clark from New York to Scott's Branch? When Judge Waring had instructed Thurgood Marshall to amend his complaint in the *Briggs* case, he decided to attack school segregation at its roots. What made the enforced separation of black children from whites most damaging, he felt, was not tattered books or untrained teachers, but the stigma of inferiority that segregation inflicted on black children. School officials could buy newer books and hire better teachers for black children, but they could not erase feelings of inferiority from their minds. Marshall had enlisted Clark as an expert witness, hoping that his testimony would make this point. His credentials were impressive. A social psychologist with a doctorate from Columbia University, Clark taught at City College in New York. He and his wife, Mamie, also a psychologist, had devised the doll test more than a decade earlier to study the development of self-images in black children. "We were really disturbed by our findings," Clark later said of his initial studies. "What was surprising was the degree to which the children suffered from self-rejection. I don't think we had quite realized the extent of the cruelty of racism and how hard it hit." The Clarks published an article in 1940 titled "Segregation as a Factor in the Racial Identification of Negro Pre-School Children" and reported on a decade of follow-up studies at a White House conference in 1950. Marshall, who had met Clark and his wife socially and was impressed with their work, hoped that federal judges would listen carefully to this eminent scholar and be equally impressed.

On May 28, 1951, four days after his visit to the Scott's Branch school, Kenneth Clark took a seat at the lawyers' table in the federal courthouse in Charleston, an imposing Victorian structure that had been erected in 1896, the year the Supreme Court had decided in *Plessy* that "separate but equal" public facilities did not violate the

Constitution. Clark had never appeared in court before and felt nervous as he went over the notes from his doll studies. Thurgood Marshall and his young NAACP associate, Robert Carter, chatted amicably with their white opponents across the aisle at the defendants' table. Behind the mahogany railing—the "bar" that separated lawyers and judges from the audience—that stretched across the courtroom, the seats were filling up with black spectators, with those from Clarendon County in the front rows. Annie Gibson and her husband, James, had driven to Charleston with eight people stuffed into their car. Annie remembers that day with vivid clarity. "Judge Waring, he looked so kindly," she recalls. "But the other two judges, they didn't smile or look friendly."

Actually, the judge who sat in the middle of the bench and presided at the hearing, John J. Parker, was considered friendly by NAACP lawyers who had appeared before him in the federal courthouse in Richmond, Virginia, where he sat on the Court of Appeals for the Fourth Circuit. Ironically, the NAACP had vigorously opposed Parker's confirmation to the Supreme Court in 1930, when President Herbert Hoover nominated him, because of remarks Parker had made during his campaign for governor in North Carolina in 1920 on the Republican ticket. "The participation of the Negro in politics is a source of evil and danger to both races," he told white voters. Ten years later, that remark—along with judicial votes that had outraged the union movement—came back to haunt Parker and contributed to his rejection by the Senate. Despite this rebuff, Parker had remained on the federal appellate bench and gained the respect of NAACP lawyers for his fairness, although he rarely strayed from Supreme Court precedent.

The third judge on the panel for the *Briggs* hearing, George B. Timmerman, matched Waties Waring in age—both were seventy, five years older than Parker—and in South Carolina ancestry that stretched back to slaveholders and Confederate officers. Unlike Waring, however, Timmerman was an unabashed, Bible-quoting segregationist and white supremacist. One of many southern racists placed on the federal bench by President Franklin Roosevelt, who bowed to the powerful Dixie senators in filling judicial posts with deserving Democrats, Timmerman made no bones of his belief that God had made whites the superior race. The lawyers on both sides of the aisle had no doubts how Waring and Timmerman would vote in the *Briggs* case, and they knew the outcome—at least in this round—lay with Judge Parker.

The hearing began with a surprise. Normally, lawyers for the plaintiff speak first, and Thurgood Marshall was ready with his opening statement. But as he was rising from his seat to take the podium, Robert Figg jumped to his feet and addressed Judge Parker. "If the Court please," he began, "I wanted to make a statement on behalf of defendants that it is conceded that inequalities in the facilities, opportunities and curricula in the schools of this district do exist." Marshall stood speechless as Parker admonished Figg to wait his turn for an opening statement, but he kept speaking. "I just thought that if we made the record clear and clarified the answer in this case at this time," he continued, "it would serve perhaps to eliminate the necessity of taking a great deal of testimony."

Marshall quickly realized the purpose of Figg's ploy. The county's lawyer hoped that his concession would keep Kenneth Clark and Marshall's other witnesses off the stand, and their damaging testimony out of the case record. Before Marshall could reply, the courtly Judge Parker nodded to Figg, who plowed ahead. South Carolina's legislature, he told the judges, had recently enacted a state sales tax that was earmarked to finance the construction of new schools for black students in rural areas like Clarendon County. The county's school board had already asked the state Educational Finance Commission to help them "formulate and submit to proper authorities a plan to bring about as speedily as possible equality of buildings, equipment, facilities and other physical aspects of the district." Figg asked the judges to give his clients "a reasonable time" to draw up and carry out such a plan.

Well aware that Figg's request for time was a delaying tactic, and

that Judge Parker might well defer to state officials who had promised to upgrade black schools, Marshall was determined to get on
the record the facts he would need for the appeal to the Supreme
Court that both sets of lawyers anticipated, regardless of the ruling
by this judicial panel. When he finally took the podium, Marshall
argued that Figg's statement "has no bearing on this litigation at this
stage. I think it is an effort to prevent the plaintiffs in this case from
developing their case in the only fashion which will enable us to
present a full and complete case." Because the case involved a challenge to the current state of Clarendon County's schools, not to
some future plan that had yet to be designed, Marshall told the
judges that "we must be able to show the inequalities as they actually exist." Figg might get the time he requested, but Marshall
would get the record he wanted. Judge Parker nodded his agreement, and Marshall called his first witness, giving Robert Figg a surprise in turn.

Marshall summoned to the stand a very reluctant and truculent
witness, L. B. McCord, who doubled as Clarendon County's school
superintendent and pastor of the Presbyterian church in the county
seat of Manning. Marshall's purpose in calling McCord as a "hostile" witness was to place oral testimony in the record of the disparities in spending on black and white schools. McCord admitted that
black students outnumbered whites by almost three to one, but the
county spent $282,000 to maintain some sixty black schools and
$395,000 on the dozen white schools. Marshall asked McCord to
explain why the county gave each white student more than four
dollars for each dollar spent to educate black children. "It is not, I
don't think, because of the color" of the children, McCord replied,
suggesting that it was cheaper to run the black schools, most of
them in wooden shacks, than the white schools in brick buildings.
McCord's refusal to admit that the black schools were inferior in
quality rankled Marshall, who asked the superintendent why the
county's schools were segregated. "You would have to ask the children why," McCord responded. "None of them have ever asked me

to go to one school or the other." Marshall finally grew exasperated and turned McCord over to Robert Figg, who posed no questions to the evasive witness.

The next witness, Roderick M. Elliott, proved as obtuse as McCord had been adept at dodging questions. After twenty-five years as chairman of the Clarendon County school board, Elliott could not identify the district's boundaries or name the schools whose affairs he supervised. A sawmill owner who employed many black workers, he displayed no interest in their children's education. Judge Parker finally spared Elliott further embarrassment by excusing him from the stand.

The real case against unequal schools in Clarendon County began with the testimony of Matthew Whitehead, an education professor at Howard University. Robert Carter led Whitehead through a litany of inequalities between the county's black and white schools, which he had visited in the company of Emory Rogers, the Summerton lawyer who shared the school board's defense with Robert Figg. Rogers had tried to impress his unwelcome guest by reciting the county's plans to upgrade the black schools, but Whitehead had nodded politely and kept taking notes as he looked around the schools and questioned principals and teachers. From the witness stand, Whitehead told the judges that none of the black schools he visited had blackboards, maps, globes, an auditorium or music room, facilities the white schools all had.

Whitehead described the outdoor toilet facilities at the black schools in words that brought their stench into the courtroom. Judge Waring asked if there was "any running water for flushing them?" Whitehead recounted his visit to the Scott's Branch school and the "disgust on the part of one who made such a survey, to see 694 students serviced by two toilets for boys and two toilet seats for girls, of the same out-of-door type of construction, no running water, no urinals" and no sinks for washing hands. Carter posed one last question. Considering all his observations, did black children in

Clarendon County receive an education that was equal to that of white children. Whitehead did not hesitate. "Not at all," he firmly replied.

Even though Robert Figg had conceded the inequalities in the county's schools, he knew that Whitehead's detailed testimony would look very damaging in the case record. But the white lawyer's effort to blunt the impact of the black educator's findings on cross-examination only made the record look worse. Figg suggested that the black schools were not as overcrowded as Whitehead reported, because daily attendance was a third less than total enrollment. "I was able to see myself that there were any number of students who should have been in school, being of school age, who were in the fields plowing and working" during school hours, Whitehead replied, adding that county officials made "no enforcement" of attendance laws for black children. Figg then asked if Whitehead knew that none of the homes of black children who lived on farms had indoor toilets or running water, suggesting that they should not mind using the "earth toilets" at their schools. Whitehead replied sharply that "there were certain responsibilities on the Board of Education to insure health and safety" for students in public schools, including protection from raw sewage. Figg next suggested that black schools did not need individual desks for each student, and that rough plank tables were better suited for the "fluctuating attendance" of children who spent much of the school year working in the fields. Noting that the tables in the black schools had holes and cracks in the unfinished wood, Whitehead said they "could not be used anywhere except in a kitchen." All that Figg accomplished in questioning Whitehead was to underscore the county's attitude that black children who lived on farms deserved nothing better than schools that resembled farm sheds and barns.

Professor Whitehead had given the three judges a graduate seminar in the material aspects of educational inequality in Clarendon County. His eyewitness account of the schools he visited, clipboard in hand, left no doubt that black children lacked the minimum facilities and equipment for effective learning. Now it was up to Kenneth Clark to show the judges how these Jim Crow schools affected the black children who sat on their wooden benches. Robert Carter first led Clark through a recitation of his academic credentials and his prior studies of the effects of segregation on the personality development of black children. Clark summarized the findings of the research he had presented the year before at the White House conference: "The essence of this detrimental effect is a confusion in the child's concept of his own self-esteem—basic feelings of inferiority, conflict, confusion in his self-image, resentment, hostility towards himself, hostility towards whites, intensification of . . . a desire to resolve his basic conflict by sometimes escaping or withdrawing."

Clark then described the "doll tests" he had conducted a few days earlier at the Scott's Branch school, telling the judges that eleven of the sixteen black children he examined had chosen the black doll as the "bad" one, and that ten had picked the white doll as the "nice" one. "The conclusion I was forced to reach," Clark went on, "was that these children in Clarendon County, like other human beings who are subjected to an obviously inferior status in the society in which they live, have been definitely harmed in the development of their personalities; that the signs of instability in their personalities are clear, and I think that every psychologist would accept and interpret these signs as such."

Kenneth Clark spent less than an hour in the witness box, and looked and sounded professorial as he testified. Robert Figg had failed to crack the credibility of another professor, Matthew Whitehead, and he only asked Clark a few questions. Did he recognize, Figg asked, "that there is an emotional facet in the problem of two different races living in large numbers together in the same area?" Posed in soft words, the question brought a sharp retort. "I have just given you results which indicate the consequences of that kind of emotional tension," Clark reminded Figg. The school board's lawyer had been a state prosecutor and knew the risks of asking questions on cross-examination to which he did not already know the answer. So he quickly told the judges he had no further questions and let Clark leave the stand. "I was concerned about findings of fact," Figg later explained, "and once we determined that his testimony was based on very few children, that there were no witnesses to the tests, and that this was his own test method and not a well-established one, I didn't press the matter." Figg professed no concern with the impact of Clark's testimony. "Nobody took it seriously," he said.

The only person in the courtroom to whom the seriousness of Clark's testimony really mattered was Judge Parker. Whether the black professor and his "doll studies" had given the judge enough reason to rule that school segregation violated the Constitution—and, in effect, to overrule the *Plessy* decision—remained in doubt for just three weeks, when the decision and opinions in the *Briggs* case were released on June 23, 1951. The decision of the judicial panel had actually been made the day of the hearing, when the three judges met to discuss the case. "It was a long talk," Judge Waring later recalled, "but hardly much discussion. Judge Timmerman is a rigid segregationist. I was and am an equally rigid anti-segregationist. And Judge Parker is an extremely able judge who knows the law, and follows the law, but quite unwillingly, in the Southern country. He just set his feet on *Plessy v. Ferguson* and said, 'We can't overrule.'"

Writing for himself and Judge Timmerman, Parker followed the law without straying from the narrow path of precedent laid down by the *Plessy* case. He first noted Robert Figg's concession that the schools for black children in Clarendon County "are not substantially equal to those afforded for white pupils." But he credited the state's promise to build new schools and upgrade existing ones so that "Negro children will be afforded educational facilities and opportunities in all respects equal to those afforded white children." Parker ordered the Clarendon school board to "file within six months a report showing the action that has been taken by them" to implement the state's equalization program. This was as far as Parker and Timmerman were willing to travel along their judicial path. They dismissed the challenge raised by Thurgood Marshall, for the black children of Clarendon County, to school segregation itself, as a denial of the Fourteenth Amendment's guarantee that every American is entitled to "the equal protection of the laws." "We think," Parker wrote, "that segregation of the races in the public schools, so long as equality of rights is preserved, is a matter of leg-islative policy for the several states, with which the federal courts are powerless to intefere." Parker obviously intended the phrase "equal-ity of rights" to extend no further than "substantially equal" facili-ties in segregated schools.

The bulk of Parker's opinion was devoted to arguing that the segregation in railroad cars upheld by the Supreme Court in *Plessy* was "governed by the same principle as segregation in the schools." That principle, which Parker quoted from the *Plessy* majority opin-ion, was that state lawmakers were "at liberty to act with reference to the established usages, customs, and traditions of the people" in requiring racial segregation in public facilities. Left unsaid in Parker's opinion was his assumption that "the people" to whose cus-toms and traditions he deferred were the white people of South Carolina, not the black parents and children who sought the "equal-ity of rights" promised by the Constitution. Parker buttressed his quote from *Plessy* with citations of eighteen subsequent cases in which federal and state judges had upheld school segregation laws, including courts outside the Deep South in Arizona, Ohio, and New York. "No cases have been cited to us holding that such legis-lation is violative of the Fourteenth Amendment," Parker added. "We know of none, and diligent search of the authorities has failed to reveal any."

With this heavy weight of precedent against them, how could Thurgood Marshall and his legal team budge the judicial boulder that blocked their way around the *Plessy* decision? The testimony of

Kenneth Clark that black children were "definitely harmed" by seg-regation did not impress Judge Parker, nor did Clark's citation of a recent survey of social scientists, 90 percent of whom agreed that segregation had "detrimental effects" on the personalities of black children. Parker pointed instead to the judicial decisions he cited as "overwhelming authority which we are not at liberty to disregard on the basis of theories advanced by a few educators and sociolo-gists." This was Parker's only reference to Clark, whose name and testimony were neither mentioned nor discussed in the opinion. School segregation "has a basis grounded in reason and experience," Parker stated, without any further discussion. His opinion con-cluded with two brief sentences: "Injunction to abolish segregation denied. Injunction to equalize educational facilities granted."

Judge Waring drafted his lengthy dissenting opinion as a valedic-tory address, ending his lifelong ties to Charleston society, the com-fortable legal establishment of which he had been a leading member, and a decade of service on the federal bench. Waring first chided judges Parker and Timmerman for their failure to confront the real issue of the *Briggs* case, the command of the Fourteenth Amendment "to do away with discrimination between our citi-zens." Accusing his colleagues of "judicial evasion" of their duty to decide this issue, Waring contrasted their behavior with the "unex-ampled courage" of the black parents of Clarendon County and their children, "in the face of the long established and age-old pat-tern of the way of life which the State of South Carolina has adopted and practiced and lived in since and as a result of the insti-tution of human slavery." He continued his lecture to Parker and Timmerman by criticizing them for allowing "the mere device of admission that some buildings, blackboards, lighting fixtures and toilet facilities are unequal" to deny the black plaintiffs an "adequate remedy or forum in which to air their wrongs." Waring predicted that "these very infant plaintiffs now pupils in Clarendon County will probably be bringing suits for their children and grandchildren decades or rather generations hence in an effort to get for their descendants what are today denied to them. If they are entitled to any rights as American citizens, they are entitled to have these rights now and not in the future."

Waring devoted the bulk of his opinion to a history lesson, tracing the institution of slavery from biblical times through the Greek city-states and the Roman Empire, noting its widespread adoption in medieval Europe, the Middle East, and Asia. Turning to the American colonies, he lamented that the "moral awakening" against slavery "had not been sufficiently advanced at the time of the adoption of the American Constitution for the institution of slavery to be prohibited." The compromises at the Constitutional Convention in 1787 that recognized the lawfulness of slavery reflected "the insistent demands of those who were engaged in the slave trade and the purchase and use of slaves." Waring left unstated the leading role of his home state's delegates to the Constitutional Convention in forcing this compromise as the price of their agreement to join the federal union. After the Constitution was finally ratified in 1789, he continued, "slavery was perpetuated and eventually became a part of the life and culture of certain of the states of this Union although the rest of the world looked on with shame and abhorrence."

Moving past the "long years of war" that began at Fort Sumpter in South Carolina, just a cannon shot away from the courthouse in which the *Briggs* case was heard, Waring discussed the purpose of the Fourteenth Amendment, a topic his judicial colleagues had avoided in Parker's opinion. He considered it "undeniably true" that the amendment had been adopted "to eliminate not only slavery itself, but all idea of discrimination and difference between American citizens" on the basis of race. Waring heaped scorn on those who insisted on segregation as the way to preserve "Caucasian blood" from dilution by mingling with other races. He noted that South Carolina law "considers a person of one-eighth African ancestry to be a Negro. Why this proportion? Is it based upon any reason: anthropological, historical or ethical?" If the white lawmakers who decided hat it was "dangerous and evil for a white child to be associated with another child, one of whose great-grandparents was of African descent," Waring asked, "is it not equally dangerous for one with a one-sixteenth percentage?"

Waring turned his rhetorical guns on South Carolina's political leaders, who pandered to the bigots at the ballot box. The whole Jim Crow system, he wrote, "is unreasonable, unscientific and based upon unadulterated prejudice. We see the results of all this warped thinking in the poor under-privileged and frightened attitude of so many of the Negroes in the southern states; and in the sadistic insistence of the 'white supremacists' in declaring that their will must be imposed irrespective of the rights of other citizens. This claim of 'white supremacy,' while fantastic and without foundation, is really believed by them for we have had repeated declarations from leading politicians and governors of this state and other states declaring that 'white supremacy' will be endangered by the abolition of segregation. There are present threats, including those of the present Governor of this state, going to the extent of saying that all public education may be abandoned if the courts should grant true equality in education facilities." This judicial assault on the state's elected officials was virtually unprecedented, and reflected Waring's contempt for those, like Governor James Byrnes and Senator Strom Thurmond, whom he considered hypocrites for holding out false promises of real equality for black schools to mask the racism that brought them to political office.

Judge Parker had relied on the *Plessy* case for precedent, and noted in his opinion that the Supreme Court, in its recent *Sweatt* and *McLaurin* decisions, had not expressly overruled *Plessy*. In his dissent, Judge Waring replied to Parker in words that bordered on condescension. "Of course, the Supreme Court did not consider overruling *Plessy*" in those cases, he wrote. "It was not considering railroad matters, had no arguments in regard to it, had no business or concern with railroad accommodations and should not have even been asked to refer to that case since it had no application or business in the consideration of an educational problem before the court. It seems to me that we have already spent too much time and wasted efforts in attempting to show any similarity between traveling in a railroad coach in the confines of a state and furnishing education to the future citizens of this country."

Judge Parker's flick-of-the-wrist dismissal of "the opinion of some sociologists or educators" that segregation harmed the personality development of black children struck Waring as another evasion of the real issue in the case. Citing the "national reputation" of Kenneth Clark and other expert witnesses, Waring pointed to their conclusion that "the mere fact of segregation, itself, had a deleterious and warping effect upon the minds of children." Clark's "doll tests" showed to Waring that "the humiliation and disgrace of being set aside and segregated as unfit to associate with others of different color had an evil and ineradicable effect upon the mental processes of our young which would remain with them and deform their view of life until and throughout their maturity." Waring continued his psychology lecture. "There is absolutely no reasonable explanation for racial prejudice. It is all caused by unreasoning emotional reactions and these are gained in early childhood. Let the little child's mind be poisoned by prejudice of this kind and it is practically impossible to ever remove these impressions however many years he may have of teaching by philosophers, religious leaders or patriotic citizens. If segregation is wrong then the place to stop it is in the first grade and not in graduate colleges."

Kenneth Clark's testimony convinced Judge Waring that "segregation in education can never produce equality and that it is an evil that must be eradicated." He had no patience with promises of eventual equality. "I am of the opinion that all of the legal guideposts, expert testimony, common sense and reason point unerringly to the conclusion that the system of segregation in education adopted and practiced in the State of South Carolina must go and must go now." Waring put his final words in italics to make sure they stood out: *"Segregation is per se inequality."*

However passionate and persuasive in its rhetoric and reasoning, Judge Waring's dissent was just that: a minority opinion in a case that left the "separate but equal" doctrine standing against the determined assault of Thurgood Marshall and his NAACP colleagues. Their loss in this first round of legal combat did not discourage the civil rights lawyers, who began planning a direct appeal to the Supreme Court, which the rules allowed in cases decided by a three-judge panel. The *Briggs* decision was handed down on June 23, 1951, and Marshall filed the appeal on July 20. He noted that the Clarendon County case squarely raised "the question of the constitutionality of the laws requiring segregation of the races in public education." Marshall cited the testimony of Matthew Whitehead and Kenneth Clark as establishing "the fact that the segregation of Negro pupils in these schools would *in and of itself* preclude an equality of education offered to white pupils or pupils in a non-segregated school."

Even after the *Briggs* case left his court, Judge Waring played an active role in pushing the NAACP to press the Supreme Court to overturn the *Plessy* decision. Writing to a New York State judge, Hubert Delaney, who sat on the NAACP's national board, Waring said the appeal "must be handled in a *militant* manner and not in routine pedestrian fashion." He faulted Marshall for filing a brief with the three-judge panel that "was one of those colorless routine affairs reciting the various decisions we all know." Waring urged Delaney to make sure that "some real enthusiasm and fire and imagination is put into the appeal" that Marshall was drafting. The case "has got to be won by an enthusiastic attack upon the citadel of 'white supremacy' and it has got to be won by a determined fight by determined lawyers calling for a reversal" of the *Plessy* case.

Thurgood Marshall was determined to use the *Briggs* case, and its record of glaring educational inequalities, to force the Supreme Court to face the issue of segregation in the citadel of Jim Crow. But the justices did not share his determination. Judge Parker's order that Clarendon County officials report within six months to the three-judge panel on progress toward equalizing their schools gave the Supreme Court an excuse for delay. The justices let the case sit on the docket until the county filed its report with Judge Parker on December 21, 1951. Its authors literally beamed with pride: a contract had been signed to build a new black high school in Summerton for $261,000; the salaries of black and white teachers had been equalized; and bus transportation was now available for black children, more than four years after the Reverend J. A. De-Laine had petitioned the school board for buses and had been curtly rebuffed. Judge Parker promptly forwarded the report to the Supreme Court on January 8, 1952, and the justices promptly sent the case back to the three-judge panel, explaining in a brief, un-signed opinion issued on January 28 that before "consideration of the questions raised on this appeal, we should have the benefit of the views of the District Court upon the additional facts" in the county's report. Since the justices had those facts before them, there seemed no reason for remanding the case except to delay any deci-sion on the constitutionality of school segregation for another year.

The real reason for delay, which the Court left unstated, was that 1952 was an election year, and the justices did not want to issue a decision—sure to inflame an already heated political debate over segregation—before the voters chose a new president and Congress in November. The presidential campaign in 1948 had been roiled by the defection of "States Rights" Democrats, who bolted from the national party convention and ran South Carolina governor Strom Thurmond for president. Thurmond won a million votes, won a majority in five southern states, and almost denied President Harry Truman a full term in the White House. Four years later, Chief Justice Fred Vinson, placed on the Court by Truman in 1946, was determined to keep the Court, and the segregation issue, out of the campaign. Vinson's delaying tactic in the *Briggs* case upset the Court's two most liberal justices, Hugo Black and William Douglas, who dissented from the remand with a statement that "the additional facts contained in the report to the District Court are wholly irrelevant to the constitutional questions presented by the appeal to this Court," but their votes to "set the case down for argument" fell two short of the four votes needed to hear the case before the November elections.

The Supreme Court not only remanded the *Briggs* case to the three-judge panel, it also vacated Judge Parker's earlier order, which left the case without any decision. Parker then set another hearing for March 3, 1952, and asked Robert Figg for a second report on progress toward school equalization. The case literally began all over, with the same lawyers at the same tables for the second hearing in Charleston. One person, however, was absent from the courtroom. Judge Waring had wearied of battling racial prejudice and social ostracism in his native state and city, and he took advantage of his age—he had turned seventy in 1950—and his ten years of service on the federal bench to retire at full pay in February 1952, and moved with his wife to New York City. He died in 1968 at eighty-eight, and returned in death to Charleston. Only a handful of white people attended the funeral services at Magnolia cemetery, but two hundred black mourners came, many from Clarendon County. Annie Gibson and her husband, James, came to pay their respects. "He's dead," James Gibson told a reporter, "but living in the minds of the people here still." At the time of Judge Waring's death, the schools in Clarendon County remained segregated, proving the prescience of Waring's prediction that future generations of black parents and children would be forced to continue the legal battle against segregation.

With Judge Waring gone from the bench at the hearing in March 1952, Thurgood Marshall knew there would be no dissent from Judge Parker's second opinion. Waring's replacement, Judge

Armistead Dobie, had been appointed to the federal appellate court in Richmond after serving as dean of the University of Virginia's law school in his native state. Dobie was known for his abrupt manner, which he displayed after Marshall argued that segregated schools were inherently unequal and that the black children of Clarendon County "are losing rights, for which they cannot be adequately compensated." Dobie shot back from the bench: "Let that alone."

Judge Parker's second opinion, issued ten days after the hearing, praised county officials and Governor Byrnes for moving "as rapidly as was humanly possible" to speed the construction of new black schools, including a Scott's Branch High School to replace a building which had been condemned as unsafe. "There can be no doubt," Parker wrote, "that as a result of the program in which defendants are engaged the educational facilities and opportunities afforded Negroes within the district will, by the beginning of the next school year in 1952, be made equal to those afforded white persons." Speaking for all three judges this time, Parker stated that "we think that the law requiring segregation is valid," a holding that once again offered Thurgood Marshall a direct appeal to the Supreme Court. By the time he filed that appeal on May 10, 1952, judges in four other cases that challenged school segregation had issued decisions that would join the *Briggs* case in the Supreme Court.

CHAPTER 5

"We Are Tired of Tar Paper Shacks"

Barbara Rose Johns recalled a talk in the fall of 1950 with her music teacher, Inez Davenport, at Robert R. Moton High School in Farmville, Virginia, the only secondary school for blacks in rural Prince Edward County. "I told her how sick and tired I was of the inadequate buildings and facilities and how I wished to hell—I know I wasn't this profane in speaking to her, but that's how I felt—something could be done about it. After hearing me out, she asked simply, 'Why don't you do something about it?' I didn't ask her what she meant—I don't know why. Soon the little wheels began turning in my mind. I decided to use the student council."

Barbara Johns was a Moton High junior, a strong-willed girl of sixteen whose parents had twice left Prince Edward County to find better work than farming. They lived in New York City and Washington, D.C., but returned for good when Barbara was in grade school, attending a one-room wooden schoolhouse that housed seven grades. During her first two years at Moton, Barbara plunged into chorus and drama, and was elected to the student council her junior year. She visited other schools for student activities, and became increasingly upset at the bad conditions at Moton.

Shortly after her talk with Inez Davenport, Barbara quietly approached five of her fellow student leaders, including John Stokes and his sister, Carrie, the Moton High student council president.

They met one afternoon on the bleachers at the overgrown athletic field. John recalled Barbara telling the group that the parents of Moton students had been unable to persuade the county's white school board to finance a new high school. "Then she said our parents ask us to follow them," John continued, "but in some instances—and I remember her saying this very vividly—a little child shall lead them. She said we could make a move that would broadcast Prince Edward County all over the world." Barbara did not propose any plan of action at this first meeting, but the group agreed to monitor both the Moton PTA and school board meetings, to see if any firm decisions were made to build a new school. Each member of the group also agreed to enlist a trusted friend, to make planning easier if the time came for action to express their anger at the board's refusal to move ahead.

Prince Edward County is near the top of Virginia's southern tier of counties, a rural area known as the Southside, and lies about sixty miles southwest of Richmond. Its county seat and only sizable town, Farmville, had a population of some five thousand in 1950. Farmville's name accurately describes the town's role as the hub of a farming area, but it is also the home of two small but well-respected colleges: Hampton-Sydney, a private school for men, and Longwood, a state teachers college for women. The faculty and staff of the two colleges have never been part of the county's political and social establishment, but they bring culture—and a more cosmopolitan outlook—to a conservative, rural area.

The countryside in Prince Edward County is mostly pine forest, with hundreds of small farms on cleared land. The major crop is tobacco, but most of the plots are just a few acres and few of the county's farmers—black or white—grew rich from their back-breaking labor. "It's right hard to grow," recalled Mary Croner, a matriarch of the black community. "You got to plow it, replant it, sucker it, top it, and worm it—and there weren't any spraying then. We sold it over in Farmville, mostly for cigars and chewin'." The 1950 census showed that blacks made up 45 percent of Prince Edward

County's residents, and that more than 80 percent of them lived on farms. The average black family in 1950 got by on $852, and almost a third had incomes under $500. Needless to say, the county's black residents were woefully deficient in education. Those who were twenty-five or older had completed an average of 5.5 years of schooling, and more than two-thirds had not gone past the sixth grade.

Not until 1939 did Prince Edward County provide a high school education for black children, in a building named for Robert R. Moton, Farmville's best-known black native. Moton was an educator who had succeeded Booker T. Washington as head of the Tuskegee Institute in Alabama, where black students learned trades and absorbed Washington's "don't fight with whites" message. Moton High had no gymnasium, cafeteria, or science labs, all of which the white students at Farmville High School enjoyed. By 1947, the black high school was jammed with more than twice the number of students it was designed to hold. Faced with a white electorate that refused to raise county taxes to pay for new black schools, the county's white school board decided to ask state officials for money to construct a new building for Moton High. Meanwhile, the board spent $17,000 to put up three temporary classroom buildings to house the overflow at Moton. The new facilities were built of pinewood and covered with tar paper; they had no insulation or electricity, and were heated by woodstoves. During the winter, students who sat near the stoves in "the shacks" were sweltering, while those on the far side of the room were so cold they wore their overcoats. Students complained to their teachers and parents, but all they received were counsels of patience: the white school board had promised that a new Moton High would be built within a few years. Barbara Johns was not a patient girl.

On the morning of April 23, 1951, Moton High's principal, Boyd Jones, received a phone call telling him that two students were at the downtown Greyhound bus station and were in trouble with the police. Jones dashed out of his office without asking who had called or who the students were. Barbara Johns watched him leave, then sent four of her group to each classroom with notices that an assembly for all students would begin immediately in the auditorium. When the 450 Moton students and two dozen teachers gathered in the auditorium, the stage curtains opened to reveal the student group seated around the rostrum. Barbara took the podium and asked the teachers to leave; when a few protested, one was booed off the stage and another was grabbed by the arms and hustled out.

Barbara then told her fellow students they had waited too long for a new school. The school board had announced no plans for building a new high school, and had told the Moton PTA leaders they need not attend any more board meetings; when decisions were made, they would be notified. Barbara told the assembled students that it was time to act, and to act together. "I do not remember exactly what I said that day," she later wrote, "but I do know that I related with heated emphasis the facts they knew to be the truth— such as the leaking roofs, having to keep our coats on all day in winter for warmth, having to have the gymnasium classes in the auditorium, inadequate lunchroom facilities and food, etc." Barbara then told the students the most dramatic action they could take would be to strike, to walk out of school and to stay out until a new building was under construction. But the ultimate goal was more than a new school for blacks. Barbara told her rapt audience, John Stokes recalled, that "we would not come back until we got better schools, but she didn't stop there. She went on to say they wouldn't be better until we went back to school with others of other races." This was truly an audacious plan, the first strike by black students demanding integrated schools in the former Confederacy.

Led by Barbara Johns and the group who helped her plan the strike, the Moton students shouldered picket signs that had been constructed and stored in the carpentry shop classroom and began their march to the county courthouse in downtown Farmville. "WE

WANT A NEW SCHOOL OR NONE AT ALL," one placard read. "WE ARE TIRED OF TAR PAPER SHACKS—WE WANT A NEW SCHOOL," proclaimed another. When the student column reached the courthouse, Barbara and several members of the strike committee entered the office of the school superintendent, T. J. McIlwaine, but he curtly refused to meet with them. The group then marched down Main Street to the office of Maurice Large, the school board chairman who ran a furniture manufacturing company. He met briefly with the Moton delegation and told them, he later said, "that nobody could promise them exactly when they would get a school because we had to promote a bond issue. I said, 'My advice to you is to go back to school; nobody will talk to you about it until you do.'"

Later that day, Barbara and her strike committee met with the Reverend L. Francis Griffin, the young pastor of the First Baptist Church in Farmville, the county's oldest and largest black church. Griffin was a firebrand who had served during the war in an all-black tank corps under General George Patton in Europe. Most black pastors avoided the issue of segregation in their sermons, but Griffin challenged his parishioners to fight the Jim Crow system. He gave the Moton students the name of Spottswood Robinson III, who headed the NAACP legal office in Richmond. Robinson, who had compiled the best academic record in the history of Howard University's law school and who joined the NAACP legal staff in 1948, had won several cases in federal courts, forcing Virginia counties to equalize teacher salaries and school facilities. The day after the Moton students began their strike, Robinson received a letter signed by Barbara Johns and Carrie Stokes:

"Gentlemen, we hate to impose as we are doing, but under the circumstances that we are facing, we have to ask for your help. Due to the fact that the facilities and building in the name of Robert R. Moton High School, are inadequate, we understand that your help is available to us. This morning, April 23, 1951, the students refused to attend classes under the circumstances. You know that this is a very serious matter because we are out of school, there are seniors to be graduated and it can't be done by staying at home. Please we beg you to come down at the first of this week."

The next day, Robinson and his colleague, Oliver Hill, drove into Farmville and met at Reverend Griffin's church with striking Moton students and some of the parents who backed their children's dramatic move. Robinson recalled his questions to the strikers. "I asked one of them what he would do if they didn't get a new school, and he said they would just stay out of school." When the NAACP lawyer reminded the students that school officials could arrest them for violating compulsory attendance laws, one striker replied that "the jail was not big enough for all of us." The students' determination impressed Robinson, who told them the NAACP "would be interested in nothing short of a desegregation suit." He and Oliver Hill had recently met with Thurgood Marshall, who told them about the *Briggs* case in South Carolina and urged them to find a Virginia case to attack segregated education directly. But the Virginia lawyers needed the support of black parents, and the Moton students agreed to gather signatures of parents who would add their names to a lawsuit seeking the end of separate schools in Prince Edward County. Since most of the county's black farmers owned their land, unlike those in Clarendon County, South Carolina, who worked as sharecroppers for white owners, there was less risk of retaliation for signing the list of plaintiffs.

Barbara Johns first approached her grandmother, Mary Croner, who remembered their talk but mixed up the days: "She came up to the house that evening. When she came in, she said, 'Grandma, I walked out of school this morning and carried four hundred and fifty students with me.' Took my breath away. I said, 'You reckon you done the right thing?' 'I believe so,' she say. She say, 'Stick with us.' She say, 'Put your name on this paper,' and mine was the third name on the paper, and I asked her what she was going to do, and she said, 'We're going to carry that paper from home to home, twenty of us.' "

At one of the mass meetings in Reverend Griffin's church to discuss the strike and the lawsuit, Moton High's former principal, J. B.

Pervall, challenged Spottswood Robinson. "I was under the impression that the students were striking for a new building," he said. "You are pulling a heavy load, Mr. Robinson, coming down here to a country town like Farmville and trying to take it over on a non-segregated basis." Robinson turned to the crowd of students and parents that filled the church. "Are non-segregated schools what you want?" he asked. The answer was an outburst of applause. Then Barbara Johns stood up and looked intently at Pervall. "Don't let Mr. Charlie, Mr. Tommy, or Mr. Pervall stop you from backing us," she told the parents. "We are depending on you." The last to speak at the meeting in his church was Reverend Griffin. "Anybody who would not back these children after they stepped out on a limb is not a man," he said. "Anybody who won't fight against racial prejudice is not a man. And to those of you who are here to take the news back to Mr. Charlie, take it—only take it straight."

A small number of Uncle Toms who attended the mass meeting did take the news to the Mr. Charlies who ran the county, and they did not like what they heard. A group of white officials tried to head off the lawsuit with a promise to speed up the construction of a new black high school, but the black leaders they approached refused to budge. The white school board then fired Boyd Jones as Moton's principal, despite a petition supporting him signed by 493 black residents and Jones's sworn statement that he had not instigated and did not support the strike. Barbara Johns later recalled that Jones took her aside one day after the striking students returned to school on May 7 and whispered, "Keep up the good work. I am behind you a hundred percent but I must not publicly acknowledge this."

Another black leader almost lost his job. Fighting a move to fire him by black parishioners who preferred "getting along" with the county's white leaders, Reverend Griffin answered them in a fiery sermon from his pulpit. "When I think of the years of economic exploitation made on my people by the white race," he thundered, "and the hatred thrown against us, I must, in all sincerity, fight against such inhumanity to man with every ounce of energy given to me by God." Griffin spoke of his wartime military service in a Jim Crow army. "I offered my life for a decadent democracy, and I'm willing to die rather than let these children down. No one's going to scare me from my conviction by threatening my job." He paused for a moment. "All who want me to stay as the head of the church, raise your hands." Only a handful of those in the sanctuary did not raise their hands. Reverend Griffin stayed in the pulpit of the First Baptist Church for another two decades, and spoke out forcefully against the continuing effort to keep black students out of the county's schools, or segregated within them after the federal courts finally ordered their integration. After his death in 1980, a plaque was placed in front of his church, inscribed with one of his favorite sayings: "You May Have to Bear It, But You Don't Have to Grin."

Those who did not grin at the prospect of defending Prince Edward County's segregated schools in court included the school board members, who became defendants in *Davis v. Prince Edward County*, the lawsuit filed by Spottswood Robinson and Oliver Hill in federal court in Richmond on May 23, 1951. The first plaintiff was Dorothy Davis, a fifteen-year-old student at Moton High, a quiet, shy girl who had not been among the strike leaders. Ironically, Barbara Johns, whose activism had sparked the lawsuit, was not listed as a plaintiff. Out of concern for her safety, she had been sent by her family to Montgomery, Alabama, where she lived with her uncle, Vernon Johns, the pastor of Dexter Avenue Baptist Church, whose pulpit was later filled by the Reverend Martin Luther King, Jr.

The case of *Davis v. Prince Edward County* came to trial on February 25, 1952, in Richmond's federal courthouse, an imposing building in which both Aaron Burr and Jefferson Davis had been tried for treason. Circuit Judge Armistead Dobie, who would replace Judge Waties Waring in the Clarendon County case a few months later, headed the three-judge panel. Dobie's father had been the school superintendent in Norfolk, and had sent his son to the University of Virginia, where he earned his undergraduate and law degrees and to which he returned, after a year at Harvard Law School for advanced study, to serve for thirty-two years on the Virginia law faculty, including seven as dean. Two federal district judges flanked Dobie on the bench, both native Virginians. Sterling Hutcheson came from Mecklenberg County, a rural area in the state's Southside. Albert V. Bryan had been a state prosecutor in the Washington suburb of Alexandria before he joined the federal bench in 1948. All three judges were stalwart members of the Democratic political machine run by Senator Harry Byrd and dedicated to the preservation of segregation. A caravan of black parents drove to Richmond from Prince Edward County, packing the courtroom during the five-day hearing. "Our people were very enthused," said Reverend Francis Griffin. "They had hopes that this one trial would settle it all." Oliver Hill, who joined Spottswood Robinson at the counsel table, did not share the enthusiasm. "There was never any doubt about the outcome of the trial," Hill recalled. "We were trying to build a record for the Supreme Court."

Robinson and Hill were joined at the counsel table by Robert Carter, who had been dispatched to Richmond by Thurgood Marshall to handle the testimony of the expert witnesses in the case. Carter had lined up an all-star cast of social scientists, each an expert on the harmful effects of segregation on black children. Now that the focus of the NAACP cases had shifted from unequal school facilities to the psychological and social burdens of segregation itself, Marshall wanted the word "stigma," meaning the wounds inflicted on black children by the Jim Crow system that taught them they were inferior to whites, to appear in the case record as often as possible.

Spottswood Robinson opened the hearing by calling T. J. McIlwaine as an "unfriendly witness," hoping to document the poor quality of the county's black schools through the testimony of its white superintendent. Unable to deny the obvious facts, McIlwaine

admitted that Moton High and the other black schools were deficient in books and equipment, but he attributed the lack of academic courses at Moton in physics, geography, and Latin, and
vocational programs in machine shop and shorthand—all offered at
the white high school—to a lack of interest on the part of black
students. They never asked him for these courses, McIlwaine
blandly explained. All the witnesses on this issue agreed that Moton
High was not equal to Farmville High in any tangible respect.

When the NAACP team turned to the intangible effects of Jim
Crow schooling, Kenneth Clark, returning to court a year after his
first appearance in the *Briggs* case, took the witness stand and explained that he had met individually with fourteen Moton High
students. Asked to tell Clark about their school experiences, every
black student said that Moton lacked courses and facilities that were
provided to Farmville High students, and they all expressed feelings
that whites wanted to keep blacks down. Clark testified that the
Moton students considered their school to be "a symbol of some
stigma." He concluded from two decades of studying black children, from elementary grades through high school, that they experienced segregation "like a wall, which society erects, of stone and
steel—psychological stone and steel—constantly telling them that
they are inferior and constantly telling them that they cannot escape
prejudice. Prejudice is something inside people. Segregation is the
objective expression of what these people have inside." Clark told
the judges that the Moton students he interviewed had displayed
"an excessive preoccupation with the race struggle," adding that the
most damaging effect of segregation was that almost every southerner—white and black alike—had become preoccupied with race.

The county's lawyers also looked ahead to the Supreme Court and
fought hard to counter Clark's testimony. Their legal team was
headed by Virginia's attorney general, J. Lindsay Almond, Jr., a former
congressman and future governor. The year before, Almond had
dispatched one of his assistants to observe the *Briggs* hearing in
Charleston, who had reported back that Robert Figg was so sure his

only job was to cite *Plessy* to the judges that he had failed to under-
mine the testimony of Kenneth Clark and the plaintiffs' other expert
witnesses. Archibald Robertson, a prominent Richmond lawyer who
joined Almond in the *Davis* case, outlined a more aggressive strategy.
"Our decision was that up here, we were going to create issues of
fact, not just of law. We were determined to show that segregation
and discrimination were not the same thing."

Justin Moore, the lawyer selected by Almond and Robertson to
conduct the cross-examination of Kenneth Clark, was a partner in a
powerhouse Richmond firm, earning a fortune representing the
Virginia Electric and Power Company and other utility firms.
Moore began by telling Clark that "you appear to be of rather light
color" and asking "what percentage, as near as you can tell us, are
you white and what percentage some other?" Clark bristled at the
question. "I haven't the slightest idea," he replied. "I mean are you
half-white, or half-colored?" Moore demanded. "I still can't understand you," Clark replied. He explained that his parents were both
natives of Jamaica, and that he was born in the Panama Canal Zone.
Moore still wanted to know if Clark was "half Panamanian, or
what?" These exchanges about ancestry had no relevance to the effect of segregation on black children, but none of the judges—who
shared Moore's racial views—stopped this line of questions.

When he moved to Clark's interviews with Moton High students, Moore asked Clark to pose the questions to him and to pretend that Moore was a black student. Clark went along with
Moore's request. "Tell me about your school," he began. "Well, it is
not much good," Moore answered. What could be done to improve
the school, Clark asked. "Well, just work harder," Moore advised.
"Do you think it will get better eventually?" Clark inquired. "Oh
yes," Moore answered, "I think it is getting better all the time." One
of his fellow lawyers recalled that Moore "put on a moronic face
and the accent of a little darkey" during this legal minstrel show,
which apparently entertained the judges. But Clark had the last
laugh, after Moore dropped his pose as a black student and posed his

last question. "Why can't the Negro have pride of race? Why does he want, I suggest, to be in the category of what I believe someone has described as a 'sun-tanned white man'?" Clark took the opening that Moore had given him: "I don't think it is the desire of a Negro to be a 'sun-tanned white man.' I think it is the desire of a Negro to be a human being and to be treated as a human being without re-gard to skin color. He can only have pride in race—and a healthy and mature pride in race—when his own government does not constantly and continuously tell him, 'Have no pride in race,' by constantly segregating him, constantly relegating him to a second-class status."

Moore also displayed his obsession with ancestry in his interroga-tion of Isador Chein, another of the expert witnesses Robert Carter had recruited for the hearing. Chein was the research direc-tor for the American Jewish Congress and had conducted a survey of social scientists on the impact of segregation on both blacks and whites. He reported to the judges that 90 percent of the 517 who responded to the survey agreed that segregation had "detrimental psychological effects" on blacks, and that 83 percent agreed that it also harmed whites, even if "equal facilities" were provided to blacks.

Moore began his cross-examination of Chein by asking for his "racial background."

"I think what you want to know is am I Jewish," Chein replied.

"Are you one hundred percent Jewish?"

"Both of my parents and all of my ancestors, as far back as I know, were Jewish," Chein admitted. Moore's unsubtle appeal to anti-Semitism brought no rebuke from the bench.

The county's lawyers had recruited their own team of social sci-entists, headed by Henry Garrett of Columbia University, a former president of the American Psychological Association who was a Virginia native and who believed that blacks were biologically and mentally inferior to whites. Garrett had also been one of Kenneth Clark's graduate professors and had told colleagues that Clark was "none too bright," but that "he'd rank pretty high for a Negro." In return, Clark called Garrett "a model of mediocrity. He taught me statistics in the most boring and elementary way."

Garrett took the stand as the prize witness for Prince Edward County—and for his home state as well—two days after Kenneth Clark stepped down. Questioned by Justin Moore, Garrett defended school segregation, provided that black and white schools were equal in facilities. "It seems to me that in the state of Virginia today," he said, "taking into account the temper of its people, its mores, and its customs and background, that the Negro student at the high school level will get a better education in a separate school than he will in mixed schools." Garrett had not visited Moton High, or any other school in Virginia since he joined the Columbia faculty thirty years earlier, and his testimony lacked the basis in first-hand studies like those Clark had conducted.

Robert Carter had obtained permission from Judge Dobie to let Clark sit at the counsel table while he cross-examined Garrett. With Clark's prompting, Carter won a surprising admission from Garrett. "Do you consider, Dr. Garrett, that racial segregation, as presently practiced in the United States, and in Virginia, is a social situation which is adverse to the individual?"

Garrett paused for a moment. "It is a large question," he began. "In general, wherever a person is cut off from the main body of society or a group, if he is put in a position that stigmatizes him and makes him feel inferior, I would say yes, it is detrimental and deleterious to him"

This was exactly the point Clark had made, and Carter was delighted that the county's own witness had employed the concept of "stigma" that the NAACP lawyers wanted in the case record. Carter stressed this agreement by the experts on both sides in his closing statement to the three judges who had spent an entire week listening to testimony from more than a dozen witnesses, filling more than a thousand pages of the reporter's transcript.

On March 7, 1952, exactly a week after the hearing ended, the three-judge panel handed down its unanimous decision. Written by Judge Albert Bryan, the panel's opinion covered just three pages in the official report and did not contain a single word of the trial testimony. Bryan first outlined the argument of the NAACP lawyers that school segregation violated the Constitution because it "stigmatizes" black children, that it created "a sense of inferiority as a human being to other human beings," and that the mark it leaves on them "is deeper and more indelible because imposed by law." In one brief paragraph, Bryan dismissed the testimony of the "eminent" social scientists called by the plaintiffs and the "distinguished" witnesses for the county. "Each witness offered cogent and appealing grounds for his conclusion," Bryan wrote, but none of this testimony impressed the judges. In Bryan's words, the case was only about Virginia's "police power," the state's legal right "to legislate with respect to the safety, morals, health and general welfare" of its citizens. The only limit placed by the Fourteenth Amendment on this power, Bryan explained, was "that the regulation be reasonable and uniform." What was the measure of the reasonableness of racial segregation? Bryan found the reason in "the ways of life in Virginia." Echoing the words of Henry Garrett, Bryan wrote that school segregation in Virginia "has for generations been a part of the mores of her people. To have separate schools has been their use and wont." This last word, an archaic term for "custom" or "habit," aptly reflected the pull of the past on judges whose state had first imported black slaves in 1619 and still imposed the Jim Crow system on their descendants.

Speaking for the panel, Bryan wrote that "we cannot say that Virginia's separation of white and colored children in the public schools is without substance in fact or reason. We have found no hurt or harm to either race. This ends our inquiry." Having upheld the constitutionality of segregation, the three judges addressed one final question. Did the black schools in Prince Edward County meet the "separate but equal" standard of the *Plessy* case, which Bryan's opinion relegated to a footnote, citing Judge John Parker's opinion in the *Briggs* case. Canvassing the admitted deficiencies in the facilities and curriculum at Moton High School, the *Davis* opinion ordered county officials "to pursue with diligence and dispatch their present program, now afoot and progressing, to replace the Moton buildings and facilities with a new building and new equipment, or otherwise remove the inequality in them."

Unlike the judicial panel in the *Briggs* case, the Virginia judges did not set any timetable for equalization in Price Edward County, or require any reports on compliance with their order. The NAACP lawyers were free to file an appeal with the Supreme Court, which they promptly did, moving the case onto a growing docket of school segregation cases.

CHAPTER 6

"I Thanked God Right Then and There"

G ardner Bishop had joined the Great Migration from the rural South as a teenager in 1930, but he did not escape the Jim Crow system when he moved from Rocky Mount, North Carolina, to the nation's capital in Washington, D.C. His father owned a barbershop in Rocky Mount, and cut the hair of both white and black customers, who traded jokes and gossip in the small shop. Bishop had grown up playing with white children who came to the swimming hole in the black section of town, but they never invited him to their homes, and he resented the fact that friendships ended at the front door. After his arrival in Washington, Bishop got a job in a barbershop and later opened his own shop in the District's black section, about two miles north of the White House. The crowded neighborhood around his shop, at 15th and U Streets, attracted black prostitutes and street-corner gamblers, and their illegal activities attracted white cops, who swaggered past Bishop's shop with the air of authority that uniforms confer on the ordinary men who wear them.

By the late 1930s, Gardner Bishop was married and had a daughter, Judine. He also had a sharp tongue and an abiding dislike of anyone—black or white—who treated him or his family disrespectfully. One day, when Judine was four years old, he let her enjoy the swings in a park near their home. Bishop saw the "WHITES ONLY" sign at the park's entrance but ignored it. When a white policeman walked by and saw the black child on the swings, he pointed to the sign and told Bishop his daughter must leave the park. Bishop retorted that "she can't read." That "uppity" remark cost Bishop a $10 fine for disorderly conduct after the officer took him to the station-house, where he told the sergeant to "book this nigger."

Ten years after his tongue got him into trouble at the whites-only park, Bishop again spoke out loudly, this time against the District's refusal in 1947 to admit Judine into the whites-only Eliot Junior High School, the nearest school to her home. The Eliot school had a capacity of 918 students, but only 765 were enrolled that year. Judine had been assigned to Browne Junior High, which was designed to hold 783 students but had an enrollment of 1,638. Faced with more than twice the number of students than the school's capacity, the District's board of education had put Browne's students on double shifts, and had refused to shift any black students into the empty seats at the Eliot school.

Gardner Bishop was angry that Judine had to travel farther to school because of her race. He talked with other parents at Browne and organized the Consolidated Parents Group, whose members were mostly poor people who felt out of place at the school's PTA meetings, which were run by middle-class blacks whom Bishop considered snooty and smug. Although PTA leaders had filed a lawsuit in 1947 against the superintendent of schools, seeking an order that would end the double-shifting at Browne, the case languished in federal court and Bishop decided to mobilize his grassroots parents group.

Shortly after the school year began in September 1947, Bishop piled a group of forty black children into taxis and led them into a meeting of the all-white board of education. Without any warning, Bishop demanded to be heard. "These are children from the Browne Junior High School," he told the stunned board members, "and there's not going to be a one of them—or anyone else—at that school tomorrow, so I just wanted to explain who's doin' it and why." After the plainspoken barber had finished, the board president abruptly ended the meeting. Bishop had not been bluffing. The next day, only a handful of the Browne students attended school, while Judine and her classmates hoisted picket signs and stayed outside. The sight of children on strike attracted news reporters and photographers, and sympathetic coverage in the *Washington Post* embarrassed the board, which promised to end the double shifts by the next school year. The striking Browne students returned to their classes, but Gardner Bishop refused to give up his fight against Jim Crow schools in the nation's capital.

The public schools were not the only segregated facilities in the District of Columbia at the midpoint of the twentieth century. Carved out by Congress in 1790 to house the national seat of government, the District hosts the embassies of many foreign countries, including those of Africa. In 1950, the dark-skinned ambassadors and staff from these countries—many of them caught in a tug-of-war between East and West as Cold War tensions mounted—were unwelcome at most of Washington's restaurants, hotels, and theaters. However cosmopolitan and polyglot the city may have looked and sounded, it was then very much a southern town. The Jim Crow practices that kept blacks from most public accommodations were a source of intense embarrassment to the State Department, whose protocol officers were often dispatched to soothe the hurt feelings of foreign visitors who had been turned away—sometimes rudely—from restaurants and hotels, some within a few blocks of the White House.

The reality of segregation in the capital of the world's most powerful and vocal champion of democracy imposed daily humiliations on the native-born black residents of Washington, D.C. They made up more than a third of the District's eight hundred thousand people, and they were squeezed by restrictive covenants and bigoted realtors into the most dilapidated and overcrowded housing in the city's northeast and southeast sections. Even those blacks who worked for the federal government or held professional jobs, and who made up a substantial black middle class, could not escape the ghetto. On the whole, Washington's black residents were more highly educated and earned greater incomes than most whites in states like Virginia and South Carolina. In 1950, the average black adult in Washington had finished 8.8 years of school, and almost 10,000 of the 171,000 black adults had graduated from college. The median income of the city's black residents was $1,906, which put them above the national average for all families, black and white. They still lagged behind Washington's white residents, however, who averaged 12.4 years of school and $2,830 in yearly income. But the city's black population, more than a quarter-million strong, was hardly an illiterate or impoverished group.

In one vital respect, however, the children of Washington's black families shared the same fate as the black children who lived in poverty in the Deep South. The District of Columbia, like a colonial possession, lacked control of its own government and was ruled by Congress. Beginning in the 1860s and continuing without change, Congress had established a dual system in the District's public schools. Segregation was not required by law, but all subsequent legislation recognized separate schools for white and black children, although Congress required that equal amounts be spent for the education of each child, regardless of race. This legislative bow to the "separate but equal" doctrine of the *Plessy* case turned out in practice to shortchange the children in the District's overcrowded black schools. In 1947, more than 40 percent of all classrooms in black elementary schools had more than forty students, while fewer than one of every hundred white classes was that crowded. Despite the congressional mandate of equal funding, the school department spent $160 on each white child that year, but only $120 on each black student.

The disparities between white and black schools in Washington were not as glaring as those in the Deep South states, but they were nonetheless galling to the city's black parents, whose children were often forced to attend schools with double shifts, while classrooms in nearby white schools had plenty of empty seats. In 1947, there were almost two thousand more students in the black junior high buildings than their stated capacity, while there were almost exactly the same number of empty seats at the white junior highs. Given the District's small geographic area, each junior high seat could have been filled with only one student by making minor shifts in school boundaries. But that seemingly commonsense solution to black overcrowding would have required that schools be integrated, and the all-white school board and its congressional overseers had no intention of ending the District's system of Jim Crow schools.

Gardner Bishop was one black parent who refused to put up with overcrowded, run-down Jim Crow schools in Washington. He had attended a speech by Charles Houston, the dean of Howard Law School and the mentor of Thurgood Marshall, shortly after the strike at Browne Junior High had ended. Congress was then being pressured by the District's school board to appropriate funds to construct several new black schools. Bishop was struck by Houston's argument that new schools for black children, no matter how well equipped and staffed, could not erase the stigma of segregation. Bishop sought out Houston and the two men became close friends, working together and planning a legal attack on the District's separate schools.

Congress finally passed a bill in 1949 to build new schools in black neighborhoods, but the crusading barber was still not satisfied. He and Charles Houston kept working on a lawsuit that would directly challenge racial segregation in the District's schools. Their plans hit a legal roadblock in February 1950, when the federal court of appeals in Washington upheld the dismissal by a district court judge of the suit that had been filed in 1947 by the PTA leaders at Browne Junior High. That case, decided as *Carr v. Corning,* had asked the judge for a narrow order that double-shifting be ended in the District's junior high schools, and that—if necessary—students in overcrowded black schools be reassigned to white schools with empty seats.

The district judge had based his dismissal of *Carr v. Corning* on the fact that double-shifting had ended at Browne before the case went to trial. The PTA's lawyers had decided to appeal the ruling that the case was in fact moot, and had repeated in their brief an argument that school segregation violated the Equal Protection clause of the Fourteenth Amendment. The lawyers had not pressed this claim before the district judge, who made no ruling on this issue when he dismissed the case. Indeed, because the provisions of the Fourteenth Amendment apply only to states, and the District of Columbia is not a state, basing a challenge to segregation in the District's schools on that amendment would have been summarily rejected. And while the PTA's lawyers raised the segregation issue in their appeal, they did not stress it in their brief since appellate judges normally limit their review to questions based on the trial record. So the lawyers on both sides in *Carr v. Corning* were surprised when two of the three judges on the appeals court panel stepped outside their self-imposed boundaries to reaffirm the "separate but equal" doctrine of the *Plessy* case.

In his *Carr* opinion for the court's one-vote majority, Judge E. Barrett Prettyman offered a judicial homily to the District's black citizens: "Since the beginnings of human history, no circumstance has given rise to more difficult and delicate problems than has the coexistence of different races in the same area. Centuries of bitter experience in all parts of the world have proved that the problem is insoluble by force of any sort. The same history shows that it is soluble by the patient processes of community experience. Such problems lie naturally in the field of legislation, a method susceptible of experimentation, of development, of adjustment to the current necessities in a variety of community circumstance. We do not believe that the makers of the first ten amendments in 1789 or of the Fourteenth Amendment in 1866 meant to foreclose legislative treatment of the problem in this country."

In response, Judge Henry Edgerton wrote a dissent that covered more than twenty pages and included an appendix with dozens of charts and tables. Edgerton faulted his two colleagues for ignoring a 980-page report to Congress by Professor George Strayer of the Columbia University Teachers College. The Strayer Report had been completed in 1949, after the district judge dismissed the *Carr* case, and Judge Prettyman had ruled that because it "was not before the trial court and is not in the record here," the mass of data about inequalities in the District's schools could not be considered by the appellate panel. Judge Edgerton accused Prettyman of wearing judicial blinders to avoid looking at the Strayer Report and its damning evidence. After quoting extensively from the report's exhaustive comparison of black and white schools, Edgerton distilled its findings in one sentence:"It is plain that pupils represented in these appeals are denied better schooling and given worse because of their color."

Edgerton answered Prettyman with his own judicial sermon about the evils of Jim Crow schooling: "Instead of serving a public purpose, it fosters prejudice and obstructs the education of whites and Negroes by endorsing prejudice and preventing mutual acquaintance." Edgerton noted the unique position of the capital among the nation's cities. "The education required for living in a cosmopolitan community, and especially for living in a humane and democratic country and promoting its ideals, cannot be obtained on either side of a fence that separates a more privileged majority and a less privileged minority." Judge Edgerton issued his own indictment of judicial complicity in Jim Crow education. "School segregation is humiliating to Negroes," he wrote. "Courts have sometimes denied that segregation implies inferiority. This amounts to saying in the face of the obvious fact of racial prejudice, that the whites who impose segregation do not consider Negroes inferior." Judge

Edgerton refused to join the judicial denial of reality. "Both whites and Negroes know that enforced racial segregation in schools exists because the people who impose it consider colored children unfit to associate with white children."

The setback in the *Carr* case did not discourage Gardner Bishop and Charles Houston, who had expected the unfavorable decision. But the courageous lawyer had serious heart problems, and was often hospitalized. In April 1950, two months after the court of appeals upheld the dismissal of the *Carr* case, Houston knew he was dying and called Bishop to his hospital bedside. "He told me that it looked as if he wasn't ever going to practice again," Bishop recalled, "and that the important thing was for us to carry on the fight." Houston urged Bishop to go see James Nabrit, a Howard Law School professor whose former students included Robert Carter and Spottswood Robinson of Thurgood Marshall's legal team. "I explained it all to him," Bishop said of his meeting with Nabrit, "including Charlie's wish that he should take over the lawsuits and continue the fight." Nabrit, who grew up in rural Georgia and had been pelted with stones by white children as he walked to his Jim Crow school, agreed to replace Houston as the lawyer for the Consolidated Parents Group that Bishop headed, with the understanding that any lawsuit against the District school board would directly challenge the constitutionality of segregation. Nabrit had no interest in another equalization case of the kind that NAACP lawyers had filed in Virginia and other states. For him, the legal attack on Jim Crow schools was an all-or-nothing proposition. On April 22, 1950, just days after his bedside visit with Gardner Bishop, Charles Houston died. Five Supreme Court justices attended his funeral, and the lawsuit that James Nabrit filed after his death became a legacy of Houston's dedication to civil rights.

The District's board of education felt vindicated by its victory in the *Carr* case, and continued to build segregated schools. One new school, completed just before classes began in the fall of 1950, was

John Philip Sousa Junior High in southeast Washington. Located across the street from a golf course, Sousa had a spacious auditorium, a double gymnasium, a playground with seven basketball courts and a softball field, and several empty classrooms. On September 11, 1950, the first day of the new school year, Gardner Bishop escorted eleven black children into the building and guided them to the principal's office. The principal of the all-white school refused to enroll the black children, and Bishop left without any verbal fireworks, taking the children to the all-black schools to which the board of education had assigned them. He had taken his charges to the Sousa school knowing full well they would be turned away, but he wanted to have evidence that white schools had plenty of empty seats as ammunition in the lawsuit he was preparing with James Nabrit.

One of the eleven junior high students who had been turned away from Sousa was Spottswood T. Bolling, Jr., a twelve-year-old whose widowed mother worked for the federal government as a bookbinder at $57.60 a week, more than twice the average wage for a black woman in Washington at that time. Young Spottswood, a lanky boy who enjoyed school, had been assigned to Shaw Junior High for the seventh grade. Shaw was located in a run-down and overcrowded building in northwest Washington, just a few blocks from Gardner Bishop's barbershop. The school had no playground and its science room had just one Bunsen burner for several hundred students.

Early in 1951, James Nabrit filed a lawsuit in federal court with Spottswood Bolling as the lead plaintiff and C. Melvin Sharpe, president of the District's board of education, as the first defendant. Nabrit left out of his complaint in *Bolling v. Sharpe* any mention of unequal school facilities or curriculum. He also left out any reference to the Fourteenth Amendment, avoiding the mistake of the lawyers who had prepared—and lost—the *Carr* case. Nabrit looked elsewhere in the Constitution for support. "The educational rights which petitioners assert are fundamental rights protected by the due-process clause of the Fifth Amendment from unreasonable and arbitrary restrictions," he asserted in his complaint. The Fifth Amendment, adopted in 1791, provides that "no person" shall "be deprived of life, liberty, or property, without due process of law," a guarantee binding on Congress, which governed the District of Columbia. The Supreme Court had long employed a relatively lenient test of "reasonableness" in deciding challenges to federal laws under the Due Process clause.

In his *Bolling* complaint, Nabrit conceded that Congress had established separate schools for blacks and whites in the District, beginning in 1862, a policy reaffirmed as recently as 1947. To counter this fact, Nabrit quoted from Judge Edgerton's dissent in *Carr v. Corning* in denying the "reasonableness" of Jim Crow schools: "When the Fifth Amendment was adopted," Edgerton wrote, "Negroes in the District of Columbia were slaves, not entitled to unsegregated schooling or to any schooling. Congress may have been right in thinking Negroes were not entitled to unsegregated schooling when the Fourteenth Amendment was adopted. But the question what schooling was good enough to meet their constitutional rights 160 or 80 years ago is different from the question what schooling meets their rights now."

Nabrit's frontal assault on the "separate but equal" doctrine of the *Plessy* case relied on a dissenting opinion in a recently decided case. However persuasive Judge Edgerton's words might have been, the majority opinion of Judge Prettyman set the law for the district court in Washington, whose judges were bound by that precedent. It would take a daring judge to disregard the *Carr* decision, just one year after it was issued, and District Judge Walter M. Bastian was not willing to take Nabrit's dare. Ruling in April 1951, he dismissed the complaint in *Bolling v. Sharpe* without an opinion. His brief order simply stated that the only issue in the case, the constitutionality of segregated schools in the District, had been decided in *Carr*. Because Nabrit had not alleged any inequality between the Sousa and Shaw junior highs, or any other District schools, there was no need for a hearing in the case, Bastian concluded. Because the *Bolling* case had not challenged the constitutionality of a state law, which would have put it before a three-judge panel and allowed a direct appeal to the Supreme Court, Nabrit was required to file an appeal of Bastian's ruling before the federal court of appeals for the District of Columbia. The distance between the federal courthouse in Washington and the Supreme Court building on Capitol Hill is less than a mile, but it might take a year or more for the *Bolling* case to travel that short distance. And it was just over a mile from the Supreme Court to the run-down Shaw Junior High in whose crowded classrooms Spottswood Bolling would spend another two years while his case moved slowly through the courts. As things turned out, James Nabrit received a telephone call from the Supreme Court's clerk in October 1952; the justices wanted to add the *Bolling* case to their docket, setting it for argument on December 9 with three other cases that challenged Jim Crow schools. Nabrit agreed to file a petition with the Supreme Court to bypass the court of appeals. On November 10, the Court granted his petition; three days later, the attorney general of Delaware asked the justices to add two cases from his state to the list.

The Delaware cases began with two angry black mothers, who lived in two small towns located just two miles from the Pennsylvania border, close to the state's only big city, Wilmington. Sarah Bulah's six-year-old daughter, Shirley, went to first grade in the one-room school for black children in Hockessin, a rural district northwest of Wilmington that provided a bright yellow bus for the white students in its elementary school. The bus went right past Shirley's home, but the bus would not pick her up and her mother had to drive her two miles each way to the black school. Sarah Bulah resented this burden, and wrote a letter to the state Department of Public Instruction, asking that the bus stop for Shirley and take her to school. Her letter went unanswered, so she wrote to Governor Elbert Carvel himself. He sent a personal reply and told Sarah that her letter would be answered by the state superintendent, who finally informed her that, "since the State Constitution requires separate educational facilities for colored and white children, your children may not ride on a bus serving a white school." Shirley could not even sit in the back of the school bus.

In Claymont, a suburban community northeast of Wilmington on the Delaware River, Ethel Belton was upset that her teenage daughter, Ethel Louise, could not attend Claymont High School, located just a mile from her home. Ethel and other black high school students who lived in Claymont were forced to sit on buses for two hours each day to attend all-black Howard High School in downtown Wilmington. Surrounded by factories and run-down tenements, the old school housed more than thirteen hundred students, who had to walk nine blocks to an annex for vocational classes. The only four-year high school for blacks in Delaware, Howard lacked most of the facilities enjoyed by the white students at Claymont High, which occupied a fourteen-acre campus with baseball diamonds and football fields and offered its students courses in Spanish, economics, and trigonometry, none of which Howard students could take.

Although the two mothers did not know each other, Ethel Belton and Sarah Bulah both contacted Louis Redding, the state's only black lawyer who handled civil rights cases, in early 1951. Redding, who had practiced in Wilmington since he became the first black admitted to the Delaware bar in 1929, agreed to help the two women and decided to file separate lawsuits against the two school districts in which they lived. "He said he wouldn't help me get a Jim Crow bus to take my girl to any Jim Crow school," Sarah Bulah recalls, "but if I was interested in sendin' her to an integrated school, why, then maybe he'd help. Well, I thanked God right then and there." Redding named the members of the State Board of Education as defendants in both suits, with Francis B. Gebhart the first in alphabetical order. He filed the complaints in *Belton v. Gebhart* and *Bulah v. Gebhart* in federal court, asking for a three-judge panel to hear the challenge to state law. Much to Redding's surprise and pleasure, the state's attorney general, H. Albert Young, asked the federal judges to transfer the cases to the state's Chancery Court, which handled civil matters.

Delaware proudly boasts on its license plates that it is "The First State," a reference to its role as the first to ratify the Constitution on December 7, 1787, by a vote of thirty to zero in the state's ratification convention. Second only to Rhode Island as the smallest in area, the state's delegates to the Constitutional Convention in Philadelphia ranked last in their support for popular democracy. John Dickinson, Delaware's most notable delegate, opposed the direct election of senators, explaining that "he wished the Senate to consist of the most distinguished characters, distinguished for their rank in life and weight of property, and bearing as strong a likeness to the British House of Lords as possible." Dickinson himself fit that model, and his state became known for the "rank in life and weight of property" of its leading citizens, especially those in the du Pont family, descendants of French nobility who founded one of the most powerful of American industries. The du Ponts set up a gunpowder factory on the Brandywine River in 1802, and within a century their company not only dominated the national chemical industry, it ruled Delaware like a medieval duchy. Headquartered in Wilmington, the state's only sizable city, located in the most northerly of Delaware's three counties, the DuPont corporation turned out chemicals, plastics, fibers such as rayon and nylon, and a vast array of products that were used in virtually every American business and home.

By 1950, more than two-thirds of Delaware's population of 318,000 lived in New Castle County, tucked in the semicircular area just below the Pennsylvania border and the Mason-Dixon line that separated the South and North. Dominated by the city of Wilmington and closely linked to Philadelphia in trade and commerce, the county was urban in outlook and had little in common with the

two southern counties, Kent and Sussex, which were overwhelmingly rural and sleepy. Residents of the downstate counties looked
suspiciously at Wilmington, and held the reins of power in the state
legislature, which spent as little money as possible on public education. With economic control centered in Wilmington and political
power held by the rural counties, Delaware was a divided state.
Many of the more affluent whites in New Castle County had no
love for school segregation, but the downstate members of the legislature, which met in the rural town of Dover, halfway down the
state, had no desire to end the Jim Crow system they had imposed
on all of Delaware's public schools.

One group of Delaware citizens had never held any of the state's
economic or political power. Blacks had lived in slavery before the
Civil War ended, although Delaware had not joined the Confederacy. In most respects, the state was southern in "custom" and attitude. In 1950, blacks made up 14 percent of the state's population,
dispersed fairly evenly between the three counties. Almost 16 percent of Wilmington's residents were black, but they constituted
some 27 percent of the city's public school students. The city
boasted several outstanding private schools, including Friends
Academy and parochial schools, and many white parents sent their
children to them. Despite the more liberal and cosmopolitan atmosphere in Wilmington, the city's public schools remained segregated, like those in the southern counties. The Jim Crow system
kept Wilmington's restaurants, theaters, and hotels segregated, although blacks could mix with whites in libraries, buses, and trains,
and there were no official barriers to keep blacks from voting. In
short, Delaware in 1950 was a true border state, with its northern
city linked to the national economy and its southern counties
rooted in the soil and the past.

The rural stranglehold over the state's education funds, its Jim
Crow schools, and the menial jobs to which the DuPont company
limited blacks kept Delaware's black residents well below whites in
education and income. In 1950, black adults had completed, on

aveage, just 7.2 years of school, more than three years behind whites. More than two-thirds of black adults had not gone beyond the seventh grade, and only 505 in the entire state—most of them teachers in all-black schools—had earned college degrees. More than two-thirds of employed black women worked as "private household workers" for white families, cooking and cleaning, while almost two-thirds of black men held unskilled laboring jobs. The average yearly income of Delaware's black families in 1950 was slightly more than $1,000, barely one-third of white families' earnings.

Very few of Delaware's black residents had the education or income to fight the white establishment on equal terms in the 1950s. Louis Redding, in fact, was the only one with both a law degree and a passion for civil rights. The grandson of a slave, and the son of a mail carrier who became a leader of the Wilmington NAACP chapter, Redding won scholarships to Brown University, where he delivered the student commencement speech in 1923, and to Harvard Law School, from which he graduated in 1929, hardly a propitious year to begin a law practice in a poor community. During these early years, most of Redding's black clients were facing evictions, debt collectors, or jail terms, and often could not pay him, but he gave them legal help equal in quality to the white lawyers who served the DuPont empire and the out-of-state companies which took advantage of Delaware's easygoing incorporation laws.

Louis Redding joined his father as an NAACP leader in Wilmington, and took on a case in 1949 that shocked the state's white leaders. Thirty black students at the Delaware State College for Negroes in Dover, which paid its faculty less than public school teachers and had recently lost its academic accreditation, applied for admission to the University of Delaware in Newark. The state, in fact, had no four-year high school for blacks outside of Wilmington, and the all-black "college" provided little more than vocational training. After the university turned them away, the students turned to Redding, who fired off a letter to the prominent judge, Hugh H. Morris, who headed the university's board of trustees. Redding

asked Morris to call a board meeting to review the segregation policy, which was not mandated by state law and which the board had
the power to reverse. When Morris rejected his request, Redding
wrote another letter, this one threatening legal action if the board
refused to integrate the university.

Redding made good on his threat after the board finally met and
upheld the decision to reject the black applicants. He filed the case
of *Parker v. University of Delaware* in the state's Chancery Court.
Delaware is one of the few states to retain the English system of
chancery courts, whose judges heard and decided "equity" cases,
those civil disputes that ranged from million-dollar corporate wran-
gles to conflicts over child custody. Redding picked the Chancery
Court over the federal court for the *Parker* case because he felt confident about the sympathies of the vice chancellor, Collins Jacques
Seitz. Only thirty-six years old, Seitz had graduated from all-white
Wilmington High School, the University of Delaware, and the
University of Virginia Law School. But he was also a Catholic out-
sider in a largely Protestant state, and took seriously his church's
moral and social rejection of segregation, which he called "the most
pressing domestic issue today in Delaware" in a speech to Catholic
students.

Seitz was also noted as a hardworking judge who dug into the
facts of cases he decided, looking for the human dimension of the
legal conflict. He applied this approach to the *Parker* case, which was
argued by Louis Redding and a young NAACP lawyer from New
York, Jack Greenberg, a fresh graduate of Columbia Law School
who had been dispatched to Wilmington by Thurgood Marshall to
gain some courtroom experience under Redding's tutelage. Chancellor Seitz first listened to legal arguments from Redding and the
state's attorney general, Albert James. Redding urged Seitz to hold
that segregated education at the university level violated the Equal
Protection clause of the Fourteenth Amendment. In his written
opinion, issued in August 1950, Seitz acknowledged that *Plessy v.
Ferguson* was the controlling precedent and noted that just two

months earlier, "the United States Supreme Court applied the separate but equal test in two cases involving graduate and professional schools." In both the *Sweatt* and *McLaurin* cases, he added, "the Supreme Court stated that it found it unnecessary to review the separate but equal doctrine laid down in the *Plessy* case." Feeling himself bound by these decisions, Seitz wrote that "I therefore pass over plaintiff's contention that a segregated school cannot be an equal school."

The remaining question in the *Parker* case was whether "the College is equal to the University within the constitutional requirement that segregated facilities must be equal." To better answer this question, Seitz took the lawyers in tow and visited the white university and the black college to look for himself. "The campus at the University is a thing of beauty," he wrote in his lengthy opinion. Seitz, a graduate of the university, was impressed by "the striking symmetry created by the landscaping and the overall architectural uniformity." In sharp contrast, his visit to the college, whose campus showed "no particular plan" in placing its "inferior" buildings, left him "with the feeling that here was an institution which, even without comparison, was a most inadequate institution for higher learning." Seitz added that he was "also struck by the gross disparity between the richness and variety of particular courses offered at the University and at the College." Ruling that the all-black college was "grossly inferior" to the all-white state university, Seitz ordered university officials to admit the black students, which they did without appealing his decision, making the University of Delaware the first in the nation to desegregate its undergraduate programs by judicial order.

Flushed with victory in the *Parker* case, Louis Redding was delighted that Seitz would decide the two cases he filed in early 1951 to challenge segregation in Delaware's elementary and high schools. Jack Greenberg assumed the task of putting together a panel of experts for the joint hearing on the two cases in October

1951. The fourteen witnesses he presented made up a Who's Who in American social science. Otto Klineberg, a Columbia University social psychologist, testified about the studies he had conducted of more than three thousand black children in Harlem, giving them intelligence tests over a period of several years. Some of the kids had recently migrated to New York from the South; others had lived all their lives in the city. If blacks were less intelligent as a race by their "nature" than whites, as some prominent academics claimed, the test scores of black children should not be affected by their "environment" in the South or North. Klineberg's findings showed, as he reported the study's results, that "the lowest scores are obtained by the groups which have most recently arrived from the South. There is a close, though by no means perfect, relationship between the length of residence in New York and 'intelligence,' either as measured by test score or by school grade. There can be no doubt that an improvement in 'environment,' with everything that this implies, can do a great deal to raise the intelligence-test scores." The black children who had recently moved north, of course, had parents who had attended Jim Crow schools and whose education, by any measure, was greatly inferior to that of black parents who attended northern schools, even if those schools were largely segregated.

Five months after Kenneth Clark had testified about his "doll studies" at the hearing in the *Briggs* case in South Carolina, he took the stand in Wilmington to report on the similar tests he had given to forty-one black children in Delaware schools. He found this group "impaired" in their psychological development. "The nature of that impairment," he testified, "is clearly indicated by the results in which it is seen that three out of every four youngsters who were asked the question, 'Which of these dolls is likely to act bad?' picked the brown doll. Now, when you see that 100 percent of these youngsters correctly identify themselves with the brown doll, I think we have clear-cut evidence of rather deep damage to the self-esteem of these youngsters, a feeling of inferiority, a feeling of inadequacy—evidence which was further supported by the kind of things which the youngsters said: 'I suppose we do act kind of bad. We don't act like white people.' "

The witness whose testimony seemed to impress Chancellor Seitz the most was Frederic Wertham, a noted psychiatrist who had worked with prisoners, alcoholics, and children at Bellevue Hospital in New York City. Wertham and his staff brought thirteen children—eight black and five white—from Delaware to New York, and interviewed each child five times. The children of both races did not hide their feelings about segregated schools and each other. "I travel thirty miles a day to school," one black child said. "The white high school is twelve blocks away." Another said, "When we get on the bus, the white children look at us and laugh." A boy put his feelings in these words: "If I have to go to segregated schools all the time," he said, "I won't know how to react to different people in life." One white girl reported that other white children wanted to tie up black kids: "The boys say that they should work and we should play." Wertham summarized his findings for Chancellor Seitz: "Most of the children we have examined interpret segregation in one way and only one way—and that is they interpret it as punishment. There is no doubt about that. Now, whether that is true, whether the state of Delaware wants to punish these children, has nothing to do with it. I am only testifying about what is in the minds of children."

After the experts called by Louis Redding and Jack Greenberg had completed three days of testimony, Albert Young, who represented the school boards, put just one witness on the stand. George Miller directed the state's Department of Public Instruction and had written the letter to Sarah Bulah, telling her that Shirley could not ride the bus for white children to her black school. Miller's appearance gave Redding the chance to impale the state's leading educator on his own lance. After Miller testified about the strides the state was making in equalizing its black and white schools, Redding picked up a document from his counsel table, paused for dramatic effect, and handed it to Miller. It was a copy of Miller's doctoral thesis at New York University's graduate education school, completed in 1943. Entitled "Adolescent Negro Education in Delaware," the thesis examined the state's black high schools, although Miller had left out the only four-year high school for blacks, the Howard school in Wilmington. Redding asked the obviously surprised witness to read aloud a portion of the thesis to Seitz: "In spite of the progress made in secondary education for Negroes they have a long way to go before the educational chasm between the two races can be bridged. Meanwhile the Negro must continue to face the requirements of American life at a great disadvantage." Redding got Miller to admit that the state legislature had voted to equalize funding of black and white schools just three months before the hearing, and then asked if the schools were still unequal in quality. "Well, I would have to say yes," Miller replied.

After the hearing concluded, Chancellor Seitz conducted his own fact-finding tour, as he had done earlier in the college case. Both sets of lawyers accompanied Seitz on visits to Howard High in Wilmington and Claymont High, and to the two elementary schools in Hockessin. Five months later, in the opinion he issued on April 1, 1952, the chancellor reported what he saw at the schools, first comparing Claymont High with Howard High in Wilmington and its vocational annex, Carver: "Claymont is located on a fourteen-acre site, containing ample room for playground and equipment, as well as for sports of most any character. Aesthetically speaking it is very attractive. The Howard structure is located on a three-and-one-half-acre site with inadequate playing space. The Howard building is flanked by industrial buildings and poor housing. The area surrounding the Carver site is even more congested. There is no land in front, or play space in the rear." After comparing the respective course offerings, teacher qualifications, and student services at the white and black high schools, Seitz wrote that "the cold, hard fact is that the State in this situation discriminates against Negro children."

Seitz also compared the white and black grade schools in Hockessin. The white school, he wrote, "is so beautifully situated that the view immediately catches the eye. The landscaping is also outstanding." The black school "is unlandscaped, and apparently always has been. Its location just cannot compare" with that of the white school. Seitz found "such an obvious superiority" of the white school "as to be depressing." He addressed another factor in the Hockessin schools, the provision of buses only for white students, "because it is a consequence of segregation so outlandish that the Attorney General, with commendable candor, has in effect refused to defend it." Refusing to allow Shirley Bulah and other black children to ride the bus to school, Seitz wrote with scorn, "is only another way of saying that they are not entitled to equal services because they are Negroes. Such an excuse will not do here."

Chancellor Seitz moved on to the trial testimony. "Plaintiffs produced many expert witnesses in the fields of education, sociology, psychology, psychiatry and anthropology," he wrote. "Their qualifications were fully established. No witnesses in opposition were produced." Seitz made special note of Frederic Wertham's testimony: "One of America's foremost psychiatrists testified that State-imposed school segregation produces in Negro children an unsolvable conflict which seriously interferes with the mental health of such children." Seitz rested his conclusion on Wertham's findings. "I conclude from the testimony that in our Delaware society, State-imposed segregation in education itself results in the Negro children, as a class, receiving educational opportunities which are substantially inferior to those available to white children similarly situated."

The chancellor made clear his belief that school segregation was inherently harmful to black children because it "creates a mental health problem in many Negro children with a resulting impediment to their educational progress." It seemed a short step from this conclusion to a holding that segregation was "per se unconstitutional," as Judge Waring wrote in his *Briggs* dissent. And Seitz was the sole judge in the Delaware cases, making his opinion the only one that mattered. But he stepped back from dismissing the *Plessy* decision as precedent, noting that the Supreme Court had not yet overruled that case. "I believe the 'separate but equal' doctrine in education should be rejected," he wrote, "but I also believe its rejection should come from that court."

Seitz agreed with the federal judges who had decided in the earlier school cases that "separate but equal" remained the rule. And he agreed that the black schools in Delaware, as in the other cases, were not equal in quality to those for whites. But he broke with his judicial colleagues in rejecting the promises of state officials to make schools for blacks equal some time later, by spending more to construct new buildings and upgrade old ones, and to improve the curriculum and teaching in black schools. His fellow judges had decided that the constitutional right of black children to "equal" schools—even Jim Crow schools—could be held back for the months or even years it would take to meet the *Plessy* standard. Seitz did not think Delaware's black children should have to wait for their rights. "To do otherwise is to say to such a plaintiff," he wrote, " 'Yes, your constitutional rights are being invaded, but be patient, we will see whether in time they are still being violated.' If, as the Supreme Court has said, such a right is personal, such a plaintiff is entitled to relief immediately, in the only way it is available, namely, by admission to the school with superior facilities."

Chancellor Seitz did something no other judge had ever done: he ordered state officials to admit black children to white public schools. "This is the first real victory in our campaign to destroy segregation of American pupils in elementary and high schools," Thurgood Marshall crowed in a press statement. Five months later, on August 28, 1952, the Delaware Supreme Court upheld Seitz's decision in an opinion that restated most of the evidence he had reviewed of inequalities between the black and white schools. The high court judges, however, offered state officials a chance to return to court if they could show evidence of substantial equality between the schools in the two cases. Whether any motion to "modify" the judicial order to admit black students to white schools would result in the resegregation of Delaware schools was a question the state judges left unanswered. If Ethel Belton was attending Claymont High, and Shirley Bulah was in the formerly white Hockessin elementary school, would they have to return to their former schools? The prospect of school districts going back and forth between segregation and integration, depending on judicial findings of school equality, was hardly appealing to those on either side of the issue. And both sides in the Delaware cases filed appeals with the Supreme Court, the state asking the justices to uphold the Jim Crow system and the NAACP seeking an order to desegregate all the state's public schools.

CHAPTER 7

"Study Hard and Accept the Status Quo"

In 1950, Oliver Brown and his family lived in a small house on First Street in Topeka, Kansas. Their neighborhood, close by the Kansas River, was on the city's north side and was racially diverse, with whites predominating but with black, Indian, and Hispanic families added to the mixture. Brown was thirty-two, the father of three girls and a welder at the Santa Fe railroad shop, where he repaired boxcars. He also served as the part-time assistant pastor at St. John African Methodist Episcopal Church, the city's largest black church. His oldest daughter, Linda Carol, was eight years old and was scheduled to begin third grade at the Monroe School, located about a mile from her home. The previous two years, Linda had walked down the grassy strip between the train tracks that ran past her house, going six blocks to catch a school bus to Monroe, a trip of thirty or forty minutes if the bus was on time.

Shortly before school began in the fall of 1950, Oliver Brown took Linda by the hand and walked with her to the Sumner School, about six blocks from her house. Linda waited outside the principal's office while her father went in to enroll her. Although he knew his daughter would be turned away from the white school closest to home, Linda recalled that her father was nonetheless "quite upset" by the rejection at Sumner, a school ironically named for a leading abolitionist during the crusade against slavery. After that humiliating experience, Oliver Brown agreed to join a lawsuit being prepared by NAACP lawyers, and was selected to be the lead plaintiff in *Brown v. Board of Education of Topeka, Kansas.* Years later, Linda Brown recalled that her father's name appeared first on the complaint not because his last name was first in alphabetical order, but rather because he was the only man among the plaintiffs, and a minister to boot. The lawyers who made this minor decision, and the Supreme Court clerk who later placed the Topeka case first on the Court's docket, both unwittingly put the names of Oliver and Linda Brown into the history books.

On the map of states that separated black and white children in their schools in 1950, Kansas was neither the most northerly nor the farthest west. It was, in fact, the state that imposed the least segregation at that time, with only four elementary schools in one city set aside for black children. That distinction between the schools in Topeka, the state's capital, and those in Deep South states like South Carolina, where every school at every level was completely segregated, did not remove the Jim Crow label from Kansas.

Located smack in the nation's heartland, the territory known as "Bleeding Kansas" had seen bloody warfare between John Brown and his abolitionist followers and the defenders of slavery before the Civil War began in earnest. It became a state in 1861 and remained a racial battleground during the decades that followed the Union victory. By the end of the nineteenth century, the lure of free land and the booming market for wheat and corn had drawn almost one and a half million people to Kansas. But the state's population was overwhelmingly white; fewer than fifty thousand blacks had settled there, most of them in the area just across the Missouri River from Kansas City. Many of these migrants from the South, known as "Exodusters," found work as laborers in railroad and housing construction, and the booming economy drew blacks to cities like Topeka and Wichita. The state's welcome mat stopped, however, at schoolhouse doors. When the first session of the Kansas legislature met in 1861, its members voted to segregate black and white students in all schools, although the power to establish separate schools later was limited to cities and towns with more than one thousand residents. For a brief period of three years, from 1876 to 1879, the Kansas legislature dropped from the state's laws any mention of segregation, and the public schools were opened to students of both races. The school superintendent in Wyandotte County, across from Missouri and the home of about a third of the blacks in Kansas, deplored the end of segregation: "There are a large number of colored pupils in this county," he reported in 1876, "and where they predominate, or attend schools in considerable numbers, these mixed schools are not a success," although he did not elaborate on the ways in which the schools, or their students, had failed.

When the state legislature voted in 1879 to end the short-lived period of school integration, it limited the power to resegregate to "first-class" cities with more than fifteen thousand residents, and only in their elementary schools, although Kansas City, Kansas, was permitted to open a high school for blacks. Of the state's "first-class" cities, only Topeka segregated its elementary students. William Reynolds, a black parent in Topeka, challenged the segregation law in 1903 in state court after his son was turned away from a white grade school. Upholding the segregation law in a unanimous opinion, the Kansas Supreme Court ruled in *Reynolds v. Board of Education of Topeka* that the state legislature had the power to separate grade-school children by race: "Whether, in view of the history of this state, the traditions of its people, the composition and quality of its citizenship, its political and social ideals, and the relations of the white and colored people of large cities to each other, such a law is wise or beneficent this court is forbidden to investigate." The *Reynolds* opinion consisted almost entirely of lengthy quotations from earlier state cases that upheld school segregation, stretching back to *Roberts v. City of Boston*, decided in 1849. The Kansas judges also quoted approvingly from the *Plessy* case, decided just seven years earlier, and dismissed the argument that Jim Crow schools violated the Equal Protection clause of the Fourteenth Amendment in one sentence: "Counsel for plaintiff cites no authority for this position, and none can be found."

Half a century after William Reynolds lost his suit against the Topeka school board, the capital of Kansas had grown to a city of almost eighty thousand residents, just 8 percent of whom were black. With grain elevators within sight of the green-domed capitol building in downtown Topeka, the city linked the state's farmers with its government and served as the hub and headquarters of the Atchison, Topeka, and Santa Fe railroad, which carried freight and passengers across the nation's vast western region. It was less a city than a large town, whose big white houses, wrapped with verandas, sat on spacious green plots along tree-shaded streets. Most of Topeka's six thousand black citizens lived on the city's east side, close to the Kansas River and the railroad yards, but this neighborhood was nothing like the ghettos of other northern cities, and small pockets of blacks lived in widely scattered parts of Topeka. The city's biggest source of jobs in 1950 was the complex of hospitals and clinics, including the famed Menninger Foundation that offered psychiatric care to patients from many states and foreign countries. The Menninger clinics and hospitals brought to Topeka a group of doctors and researchers, many from eastern cities and universities, who added a more liberal and cosmopolitan tone to a solidly conservative and stodgy midwestern city, whose leaders and officials were drawn from the downtown banks and businesses. The elected school board reflected the racial attitudes of a white population that kept the city's blacks out of hotels, restaurants, movie theaters, and even the swimming pool in Gage Park, the site of a well-kept zoo and a well-tended rose garden. Black children were allowed to swim in the Gage pool just once a year, when the park directors invited Topeka's blacks to hold a picnic.

The whites who ran Topeka not only kept blacks out of the municipal pool, they kept them out of state government offices and the city's businesses. In 1950, almost a quarter of Topeka's white males worked in professional or managerial posts, while only 4 percent of black men held such jobs. Topeka had 425 white accountants in 1950, but just one black. There were no blacks among the city's 350 engineers, only 5 black lawyers out of 214, and 14 blacks among 315 doctors. The only occupational category in which black men outnumbered whites was that of "janitors and porters." Black women in Topeka faced a similar exclusion from good jobs. Fewer than 1 percent of the city's female clerical workers were black; just 47 out of 5,740 women in this category. More than half of the 998 black women holding jobs in Topeka were employed as "private household workers" in the homes of white people or as "service workers" in the city's hospitals and nursing homes. These occupational disparities reflected wide gaps between the educational levels of Topeka's residents, with blacks having three years less schooling than whites. In turn, these disparities in education created a wide income gap. The median income of Topeka's white workers in 1950 was $2,068, compared to $1,160 for blacks, a difference of almost two-to-one. Only 15 blacks in Topeka had incomes of more than $5,000 in 1950, while more than 3,000 whites exceeded this level.

Not all of Topeka's black citizens endured the Jim Crow schools without complaint. In 1941, after the school board established an all-white junior high in violation of state law, which limited school segregation to the elementary grades, a group of black parents sued the school board. They won the case and Topeka's junior high schools reopened their doors to black students, although the courtroom victory came at the cost of eight black teachers, who lost their jobs in retaliation. The following year, the school board hired a new superintendent, Kenneth McFarland, who ruled the schools with an iron hand and imposed a form of segregation inside Topeka High, the city's only secondary school at the time. Built in 1931, the school's imposing Gothic towers loomed over the downtown area. Under McFarland's reign, Topeka High fielded two basketball teams, the white Trojans and the black Ramblers, with separate squads of cheerleaders and pep clubs. The school's golf, swimming, wrestling, and tennis teams were limited to whites, and black girls were advised not to take stenography and typing classes, since there were few jobs for black women in these fields. The advice was accurate, since only 16 of the 2,245 stenographers and typists in Topeka were black. Of course, black girls could hardly expect to get jobs for which they were not trained.

With only four elementary schools for Topeka's black children, the school board had drawn attendance district lines that forced many of them, as young as five or six, to travel many blocks to reach their schools. The board did provide buses for black students, but they were often late and children who did not live near a school bus stop had to walk, often across busy streets and railroad tracks. The black schools also lacked some of the facilities and programs in the eighteen grade schools for white children. Few of the black parents complained about the segregated and second-class schools, and those who did were reminded that junior high school integration had cost black teachers their jobs. Teachers and parents also confronted the intimidation of Harrison Caldwell, a hulking black teacher and administrator who enforced the internal segregation at Topeka High and ran the black grade schools under Superintendent McFarland. One black student at Topeka High during the 1940s recalled that Caldwell "would tell us not to rock the boat and how to be as little offensive to whites as possible—to be clean and study hard and accept the status quo—and things were getting better."

Things did not get better enough to satisfy the most outspoken black leader in Topeka, McKinley Burnett, who became president of the city's NAACP chapter in 1948. The son of a slave, he worked for the federal government in a supply depot that served Forbes Air Force Base, a job that protected him from retaliation for his civil rights activism. The NAACP chapter was small, because most black teachers and others who worked for the city or white-owned businesses either worried about being fired or had become comfortable with the racial status quo in Topeka. Burnett, however, began in 1948 to pressure the school board to end segregation in the city's grade schools. The board turned a deaf ear to his appeals, and some board members reacted with insults. One member got so angry when Burnett said that blacks paid taxes just like whites and were entitled to the same rights that he jumped from his seat and said, "Let's go outside and settle this matter right now." Burnett calmly replied, "I don't settle these matters that way. I settle them by legal means."

The NAACP leader did not rush to the courthouse after this rebuff. He continued to show up at school board meetings, repeating his appeals to send all grade-school children to the school nearest their home. But after two years of fruitless effort, Burnett finally lost his patience. In August 1950 he told the board the time had come to end the Jim Crow system in Topeka. One board member shouted at him, "Is that a request or is that an ultimatum?" Burnett responded by turning to legal means to settle the matter. He sent a letter to NAACP headquarters in New York, asking for help in preparing a lawsuit against the Topeka school board and venting his anger at the board's open hostility toward him. "Words will not express the humiliation and disrespect in this matter," he wrote.

Burnett's letter reached Thurgood Marshall, who assigned Robert Carter to help draft a complaint. Four of the five black lawyers in Topeka, all graduates of the local law school at Washburn University, a municipal institution of little distinction, agreed to help Burnett. Three of them belonged to one family. Elisha Scott, born in 1890, had graduated from Washburn's law school in 1916 and became Topeka's first black lawyer. Bombastic and emotional before juries, Scott relied on rhetoric more than careful preparation in his cases; his clients often complained that he missed filing deadlines and court dates, and failed to keep them notified about their cases. Thurgood Marshall had known of Scott's dilatory habits for more than a decade. In 1937, Marshall told the NAACP's national director, Walter White, that Scott had failed to answer two letters about a lawsuit to challenge a segregated swimming pool in Newton, Kansas. The local NAACP branch complained to Marshall that

"Mr. Scott would not tell them anything" about the case. "I wrote Mr. Scott two more letters and I still have heard nothing from him," Marshall griped.

Three of Elisha Scott's sons had become lawyers, and two of them, John and Charles, joined their father's law practice after returning from military service in World War II. Both of the younger Scotts had chafed in the Jim Crow army, and they plunged into NAACP work in Topeka. Along with Charles Bledsoe, the fourth of Topeka's five black lawyers, the Scotts drafted a legal complaint against the city's Jim Crow schools and sent copies to Robert Carter in New York. Carter was shocked by the lack of legal expertise in the draft, particularly on constitutional issues, but he tactfully complimented the Topeka lawyers while he completely revised their work. McKinley Burnett looked for plaintiffs as the complaint took shape. Not a single black teacher in Topeka would join the suit against the school board. Mamie Williams, the leader of the city's black teachers, attended a meeting with Burnett and the NAACP lawyers at the Scotts' law office. "One of the NAACP people was outraged at the situation," she recalled, "saying, 'Imagine, our children have to go right by these white schools and go to separate black schools'—as if that was a dreadful thing." The most dreadful thing Mamie Williams could imagine was losing her job as principal at an all-black school.

Most of the twenty plaintiffs recruited by McKinley Burnett were NAACP members, and all but one were women. Oliver Brown was not a member, although he had once given the opening prayer at an NAACP meeting. Mamie Williams had been one of Brown's teachers at the segregated Buchanan School, and recalled of her former student: "He was an average pupil and a good citizen—he was not a fighter in his manner." But he was willing to join the legal fight against the segregated grade schools his three daughters were forced to attend, leaving the leadership to McKinley Burnett and the NAACP lawyers. The case of *Brown v. Board of Education of Topeka, Kansas* was filed in the U.S. District Court in Topeka on

February 28, 1951. The federal courthouse was about a mile from the all-black Monroe School that Linda Brown attended and a few blocks from the all-white Sumner School that had turned her away. Those were almost exactly the same distances from the Brown family's home to those schools. But this case was not really about which school was closer or farther from Linda's home, but about the reason she was forced to attend the Monroe School and whether that reason—the color of her skin—violated the Constitution's guarantee that every person will receive "the equal protection of the laws."

Thurgood Marshall sent Robert Carter and Jack Greenberg to Topeka for the *Brown* hearing, which began on June 22, 1951. The two NAACP lawyers arrived the day before, to meet the plaintiffs who would testify and to confer with the local lawyers. Because none of the downtown hotels, near the federal courthouse and the state capitol, would admit blacks, Carter and Greenberg spent their first night in Topeka at a "colored" hotel. Their room was dirty, and part of the bathroom ceiling fell on Greenberg's head when he pulled the light cord; they moved the next day to the home of a local NAACP member. This unpleasant welcome to Topeka was matched at the hearing by the abrasive tactics of Lester Goodell, the school board's lawyer and a former county prosecutor, who sounded like Perry Mason in objecting to dozens of questions by the NAACP lawyers as "incompetent, irrelevant, and immaterial." Heading the panel of three federal judges who ruled on Goodell's objections was Walter Huxman, a former Kansas governor and a member of the United States Court of Appeals for the Tenth Circuit. Huxman had been elected governor as a Democrat, during the Great Depression, and had been placed on the bench by President Franklin Roosevelt. But he was hardly a judicial liberal, and he presided over trials and hearings with a firm hand and an intolerance for long-winded argument. He was joined on the panel by district judges Arthur Mellott and Delmas Carl Hill, who were also Democrats of the midwestern, penny-pinching type. None of the three judges had ruled on any case that involved challenges to racial segregation, and all had grown up in parts of Kansas where few blacks lived.

After a pretrial hearing to set the list of witnesses, at which Lester Goodell interjected sarcastic remarks during Robert Carter's answers to questions from the bench, testimony in the *Brown* case began on June 25. No sooner had Robert Carter asked his first witness, a former school board member, why the board had not used its power to end segregation in Topeka, than Goodell jumped up: "Object to that as incompetent, irrelevant, and immaterial and invading the province of the court." Judge Huxman sustained the objection and firmly told Carter that the only issue in the case was whether the board was "furnishing adequate facilities" for black children in separate schools. "If they are doing that, then what they are thinking about is immaterial," Huxman admonished Carter.

Because the black grade schools in Topeka, although older and not as well equipped as most white schools, had "adequate facilities" and more experienced teachers, the NAACP lawyers hammered at the fact that most black children had to travel longer distances to school than white children. The fact that the board provided buses for black students, but not for whites, weakened the claim that the four black grade schools failed to meet the *Plessy* standard of "separate but equal" facilities. Nonetheless, the NAACP lawyers called several witnesses to testify about the burden on their children of spending up to two hours each day on school buses. Robert Carter had asked John Scott to examine the plaintiffs, and he first called Lena Mae Carper, whose ten-year-old daughter, Katherine, had to walk across two busy intersections to catch a bus that would take her twenty-four blocks to school. The bus was often late and overcrowded, Mrs. Carper said, adding that two grade schools for whites were closer to their home than Katherine's school. Scott then called Katherine to the stand, the only child among the plaintiffs to testify. He asked her about the buses. "It is loaded, and there is no place hardly to sit," she answered.

"And are the children sitting on top of each other?" Scott inquired. Lester Goodell promptly objected to "this whole line of leading questions of counsel testifying rather than the child." Judge Huxman overruled the objection but cautioned Scott not to prompt Katherine's answers.

Scott shifted his focus. "Katherine, do you live in a neighborhood with white children?"

"Yes, sir."

"Do you play with them?"

"Yes, sir."

"What schools do they go to?"

Just as Katherine answered, "Randolph," Goodell jumped to his feet. "I object to that as incompetent, irrelevant, and immaterial, outside the issue," he said loudly.

"Objection to this line of questioning will be sustained," Judge Huxman ruled.

Oliver Brown took the stand after Katherine Carper stepped down, although his daughter, Linda, was not in the courtroom to hear her father testify in the case that bore his name. His nervousness showed in speaking so quietly that Judge Huxman asked him to raise his voice, and he stumbled over how many blocks his home was from the Monroe School. But he described how Linda had to walk through the railroad switching yards to the school bus stop, telling the judges the bus, which was due at eight in the morning, was often late and "many times she had to wait through the cold, the rain, and the snow until the bus got there." When the bus was on time, Linda would have to wait outside the school for thirty minutes until the doors were unlocked at nine. Charles Bledsoe, who examined Brown, asked if he would prefer having Linda attend the Sumner School. Goodell jumped up once again, and Judge Huxman again sustained his objection that the question was irrelevant to the case. Oliver Brown left the stand after thirty minutes, the third of ten plaintiffs to testify but the only one whose name is remembered.

Robert Carter and Jack Greenberg had recruited seven expert

witnesses, three of them to document the physical and curricular differences between Topeka's black and white grade schools. This proved a difficult task, since some of the older white schools had no playground space and their classrooms were smaller. The lack of differences, in fact, added strength to the claim that the real harm of segregation was the lesson it gave black children that there was something bad about black skin, something wrong about letting them sit next to white children in school. Three of the NAACP's experts made this point, but the one whose testimony most powerfully affected the outcome of the *Brown* case—not before this panel of judges but in the Supreme Court—was Louisa Holt, an assistant professor of sociology at the University of Kansas in Lawrence, twenty-five miles east of Topeka. Holt was thirty-four and held three degrees from Radcliffe, the "separate and unequal" women's branch of Harvard University. Her main attraction as a witness was her connection with the prestigious Menninger Clinic in Topeka, where she taught part-time in the school of psychiatry. Holt also lived in Topeka and had two children in the public schools.

Robert Carter conducted the examination of Louisa Holt, and his first question was one he had asked of Kenneth Clark in both the South Carolina and Virginia cases: "Does enforced legal separation have any adverse effect upon the personality development of the Negro child?"

"The fact that it is enforced, that it is legal," she replied, "has more importance than the mere fact of segregation by itself does because this gives legal and official sanction to a policy which is inevitably interpreted both by white people and by Negroes as denoting the inferiority of the Negro group. Were it not for the sense that one group is inferior to the other, there would be no basis—and I am not granting that this is a rational basis—for such segregation."

Carter next asked how segregation affected the "learning process" of black children. "A sense of inferiority must always affect one's motivation for learning since it affects the feeling one has of one's self as a person," Holt said. She went on, using the jargon of psychiatry, to assert that a person's "sense of ego-identity is built up on the basis of attitudes that are expressed toward a person by others who are important—first the parents and then teachers and other people in the community, whether they are older or one's peers." Holt continued her lecture to the judges, who leaned forward with attentive looks at the attractive witness. "If these attitudes that are reflected back and then internalized or projected, are unfavorable ones, then one develops a sense of one's self as an inferior being," she said,

Lester Goodell excused Louisa Holt from the witness stand without questioning her testimony, which she based on studies by other social scientists. None of the expert witnesses, in fact, had conducted any studies of students in the Topeka schools, as Kenneth Clark had done in South Carolina and Virginia. Judge Huxman and his colleagues asked few questions from the bench, and seemed eager to end the hearing after Holt's testimony. Goodell cooperated by calling just a handful of witnesses to make the point that Topeka's black and white grade schools were equal in curriculum, teacher salaries, and facilities. The board's lawyer then called Superintendent Kenneth McFarland back to the stand. The man who had ruled the city's schools with an iron hand was now humbled, having been caught in a financial scandal that was front-page news in the *Topeka Daily Capital*. But he was truculent on the stand, unwilling to abandon his support for segregation. Goodell asked McFarland if he believed the superintendent had any duty to shape the "social customs and usage in the community." McFarland disavowed any intention to "dictate the social customs of the people who support the public school system." Goodell then asked if "the separation of the schools that we have is in harmony with the public opinion, weight of public opinion, in this community." The departing superintendent replied in bureaucratic jargon: "We have no objective evidence that the majority sentiment of the public would desire a change in the fundamental structure" of Topeka's schools. McFarland left the stand as the hearing's final witness, and left his job in disgrace a month later. Contrary to his testimony, the most recent school board election, in April 1951, had expressed the "majority sentiment of the public" by shifting control to three new members who opposed the continued segregation of the grade schools. But the new board majority decided to await the final decision of the courts in the *Brown* case before taking any action.

Five weeks after the hearing ended, the three-judge panel issued its opinion on August 3, 1951, upholding the power of the Topeka school board under Kansas law to separate children by race in the city's grade schools. Judge Huxman wrote for all three members in finding that "the physical facilities, the curricula, courses of study, qualification of and quality of teachers, as well as other educational facilities in the two sets of schools are comparable." In fact, Huxman noted, the NAACP lawyers did not give "great emphasis" to this issue, and "relied primarily upon the contention that segregation in and of itself without more violates" the Fourteenth Amendment. Huxman admitted that this claim "poses a question not free from difficulty." As did the judges in the other school segregation cases, he looked to the *Plessy* case for guidance. The Supreme Court had not discarded the "separate but equal" doctrine and *Plessy* still stood as "authority for the maintenance of a segregated school system in the lower grades." But the Supreme Court's recent decisions in the graduate and law school cases troubled Huxman. Looking at the *McLaurin* and *Sweatt* decisions, handed down the year before, he posed two questions: "If segregation within a school as in the *McLaurin* case is a denial of due process, it is difficult to see why segregation in separate schools would not result in the same denial. Or if the denial of the right to commingle with the majority group in higher institutions of learning in the *Sweatt* case and gain the educational advantages resulting therefrom, is a lack of due process, it is difficult to see why such denial would not result in the same lack of due process if practiced in the lower grades."

Judge Huxman clearly hoped the Supreme Court would answer his troubling questions in the *Brown* case. And he offered the justices some help in framing their answers, in the eighth of nine "Findings of Fact" that he appended to his opinion. Restating the testimony of Louisa Holt almost verbatim, Huxman wrote: "Segregation of white and colored children in public schools has a detrimental effect upon the colored children. The impact is greater when it has the sanction of the law; for the policy of separating the races is usually interpreted as denoting the inferiority of the Negro group. A sense of inferiority affects the motivation of a child to learn. Segregation with the sanction of law, therefore, has a tendency to retard the educational and mental development of Negro children and to deprive them of some of the benefits they would receive in a racially integrated school system."

Two decades after he wrote this opinion, upholding the law that allowed school segregation but also finding that segregation harmed black children, Judge Huxman looked back. "We weren't in sympathy with the decision we rendered," he said of the judicial panel he headed in 1951. "If it weren't for *Plessy v. Ferguson*, we surely would have found the law unconstitutional. But there was no way around it—the Supreme Court would have to overrule itself."

CHAPTER 8

"We Only Took a Little Liberty"

W hether the Supreme Court would overrule itself and hold that racial segregation in public schools violated the Constitution was a question presented in the five cases that were set for argument on December 9, 1952, a cool, rainy Tuesday in Washington, D.C. Promptly at 1:30 in the afternoon, following the Court's lunch recess, Chief Justice Fred Vinson led his eight colleagues from behind a velvet curtain to their high-backed leather seats at the bench. The lawyers and spectators in the chamber all stood while the Court's bailiff intoned the words that had opened each session since the very first in 1790: "Oyez! Oyez! Oyez! All persons having business before the honorable, the Supreme Court of the United States, are admonished to draw near and give their attention, for the Court is now sitting. God save the United States and this honorable Court."

Every one of the three hundred seats in the Court's ornate chamber was filled, about half of them with blacks who had begun lining up early that morning outside the Court's marble building, across from the Capitol building. Another four hundred people stood in a long line outside the courtroom and down the broad stairway on which reporters and photographers were clustered beneath umbrellas. Above the massive bronze doors at the Court's entrance, the words "Equal Justice Under Law" were chisled into the stone. Ironically, several of the restaurants on Capitol Hill which were crowded with lawyers and congressional staff members at lunchtime did not serve blacks, a pointed reminder of the Jim Crow system that was imposed on all students in the city's public schools.

Each of the five cases before the justices that afternoon reflected a different piece of the racial mosaic in mid-century America, across a wide arc of the country's geography. Clarendon County in South Carolina was part of the Deep South, more than 70 percent black but governed entirely by whites. Prince Edward County in Virginia was closely balanced in race, with a substantial number of black farmers who owned their land. The District of Columbia was the nation's capital, whose black residents were more educated and affluent than many southern whites. New Castle County in Delaware sat just below the Mason-Dixon line, the most northerly of the seventeen states that imposed the Jim Crow system on its schools. Kansas, with some quarter-million students in public schools, segregated just a few hundred black children in four elementary schools in Topeka, the state's capital.

But the question before the Supreme Court in these cases involved more than the students in five school districts, and more than the Jim Crow schools in seventeen states and the nation's capital. The real question was whether the country that held itself up to the world as the beacon of democracy, during a period of Cold War tensions and anticolonial ferment, could appeal to the "colored" peoples of Africa and Asia while more than a third of its states prevented black and white children from attending school together. It was this question, and the issues of foreign policy it raised, that gave a special urgency and importance to the arguments in the school cases.

Before the lawyers on both sides of these cases stood at the Court's podium that morning, they had prepared—in some cases with great care and deliberation, in others with haste and a cut-and-paste effort—briefs that stated their positions on the questions before the justices. Of all these briefs, which stood almost two feet high when stacked together, the one that most persuasively and powerfully put the issue of segregation in the broadest context had been submitted by the United States government, speaking through the solicitor general as a "friend of the court." Shortly before the school cases were set for argument, both the attorney general and solicitor general had resigned, in the wake of scandals that had tarnished the administration of President Harry Truman. Neither official had been willing to involve the federal government in the cases, particularly during a presidential election year. But their successors, Attorney General James McGranery and Acting Solicitor General Robert Stern, encouraged Philip Elman, who had written the government's briefs in the *McLaurin* and *Sweatt* cases, to prepare one in the *Brown* cases.

Elman dove into his task with zeal and intensity. The result of his labors took a far different approach than the briefs of the parties to the cases, which largely plowed familiar ground, whether supporting or opposing school segregation. Elman was not tied down to a particular state or school district, or to the record in any case, and was free to look at the issue from a national—even international— perspective. He took full advantage of this freedom, pointing the justices to the damaging effects of American segregation from the Court's own neighborhood in Washington to the halls of the United Nations. "The problem of racial discrimination is particularly acute," Elman wrote, "in the District of Columbia, the nation's capital. This city is the window through which the world looks into our house. The embassies, legations, and representatives of all nations are here, at the seat of the Federal Government. Foreign officials and visitors naturally judge this country and our people by their experiences and observations in the nation's capital; and the treatment of colored persons here is taken as the measure of our attitude toward minorities generally."

That attitude, on the part of whites in Washington, was one of exclusion and discrimination. Elman quoted from a 1947 report of the President's Committee on Civil Rights about the treatment a black visitor could expect in the city: "With very few exceptions, he is refused service at downtown restaurants, he may not attend a downtown movie or play, and he has to go into the poorer section of the city to find a night's lodging. The Negro who decides to settle in the District must often find a home in an overcrowded, substandard area. He must often take a job below the level of his ability. He must send his children to the inferior public schools set aside for Negroes and entrust his family's health to medical agencies which give inferior service. In addition, he must endure the countless daily humiliations that the system of segregation imposes upon the one-third of Washington that is Negro."

The report of the presidential committee stressed the harmful effect of segregation in Washington on blacks from other countries, especially those who held diplomatic posts. "Capital custom not only humiliates colored citizens, but is a source of considerable embarrassment" to black diplomats. "Foreign officials are often mistaken for American Negroes and refused food, lodging and entertainment." Elman linked segregation in Washington to the global Cold War with the Soviet bloc. "Racial discrimination furnishes grist for the Communist propaganda mills," he wrote, "and it raises doubts even among friendly nations as to the intensity of our devotion to the democratic faith."

The government's brief also included a letter, written the week before argument of the school cases, from Secretary of State Dean Acheson to Attorney General McGranery, about the effect of racial discrimination on American foreign relations: "As might be expected, Soviet spokesmen regularly exploit this situation in propaganda against the United States, both within the United Nations and through radio broadcasts and the press, which reaches all corners of the world." Acheson pointed to Jim Crow schools: "The segregation of school children on a racial basis is one of the practices in the United States that has been singled out for hostile foreign comment in the United Nations and elsewhere. Other peoples cannot understand how such a practice can exist in a country which professes to be a staunch supporter of freedom, justice, and democracy." Secretary Acheson concluded that racial discrimination "remains a source of constant embarrassment to this Government in the day-to-day conduct of its foreign relations; and it jeopardizes the effective maintenance of our moral leadership of the free and democratic nations of the world."

Even though the Court had politely turned down the solicitor general's request to join the oral argument for one hour, the justices read the final section of the government's brief with care, as it was the only one to suggest a middle path between the all-or-nothing positions of the two sides on the crucial question of implementation, should the Court rule that Jim Crow schools violated the Constitution. "A reasonable period of time will obviously be required to formulate new provisions" to integrate schools that were now segregated, Elman cautioned. He proposed that federal district court judges "could fashion particular orders to meet particular needs" in different communities. The "orderly and progressive transition" to racially mixed schools could best be accomplished, Elman suggested, by requiring school districts to inform judges "at reasonable intervals" of their progress in opening schools to all students. If this sounded like the "all deliberate speed" formula the Court would later adopt, that was Elman's intent. Federal officials feared that any orders to integrate schools immediately—whether from the Supreme Court or lower courts—would lead to disobedience, disorder, and even violence.

Contrary to widespread belief, Thurgood Marshall did not argue the lead-off *Brown* case. Robert Carter spoke for Linda Brown and other black children in Topeka. Jack Greenberg, who had assisted Carter at the hearing before Judge Huxman, recalled that Carter adopted in the Supreme Court "a style typical of mainstream appellate argument—conversational, not terribly loud, not very aggressive, perhaps even a little softer than usual." Despite Huxman's finding that the black and white grade schools in Topeka were equal in quality, Carter tried to point out the inequalities disclosed in the case record, but the justices wanted to hear instead about Carter's position on the *Plessy* case. After all, that was the central issue before the Court, not the number of blocks that Linda Brown traveled to the Monroe School. Carter danced around the question until Justice Felix Frankfurter, who peppered him with questions, forced a direct answer. "I have no hesitancy in saying that the issue of 'separate but equal' should be faced," Carter said, "and should squarely be overruled."

Later in his argument, Carter stated firmly that "we abandon any claim" that the constitutional invalidity of the Kansas law allowing Topeka to operate racially separate grade schools "comes from anything other than the act of segregation itself." Black schools could even be better than white schools, and would still violate the Constitution if segregation was imposed by law. All the evidence about the inequality of black and white schools, in all five cases, would be irrelevant under Carter's bold claim. Even the testimony and studies of social scientists like Kenneth Clark and Louisa Holt would be irrelevant to the basic issue: racial segregation reflected the attitude of whites that blacks were inferior, and using the law to enforce this attitude violated the Equal Protection command of the Fourteenth Amendment. It was the act of racial classification itself, not the quality of black schools or the length of a bus ride, that put into law the notion of black inferiority. Carter was not eager to rest his case on such a bold assertion, and he pointed the justices to the social science testimony in the case record before he left the podium, but his argument put the issue of segregation in its simplest form.

The NAACP brief in the *Brown* case had cited the Court's opinion, handed down in 1943 in the *Hirabayashi* case, in which the justices upheld the wartime curfew imposed on Japanese Americans, the first step in their forced march into "relocation centers" that imprisoned an entire ethnic group without charges or trials. But in that opinion, Justice Harlan Fiske Stone had clearly stated that racial classifications were inherently "suspect" and could only be justified by some compelling "national security" crisis. "Distinctions between citizens solely because of their ancestry," he wrote, "are by their very nature odious to a free people whose institutions are founded upon the doctrine of equality." Robert Carter did not mention the *Hirabayashi* case during his argument, but his statement of its basic principle—that racial classifications are constitutionally suspect—found a receptive audience on the Supreme Court bench. Justice Felix Frankfurter helpfully asked Carter if he agreed that Kansas had "no rational basis for the classification" in its segregation law, and Carter quickly agreed. Frankfurter was the one justice the NAACP lawyers had pitched their briefs to, and his colloquy with Carter gave them hope for a favorable outcome.

Just a few days before this argument, it seemed that Carter would have no opponent at the podium. The Topeka school board, after the April 1951 elections that gave liberals a majority, voted not to defend itself in the *Brown* case and passed the buck to the Kansas attorney general, Harold Fatzer, arguing that the NAACP had attacked the state law under which Topeka segregated its grade schools. Fatzer passed the buck back to the city, responding that Kansas was not even a party to the *Brown* case and refusing to file a brief in the Supreme Court. The justices ended this Alphonse-and-Gaston act with a telegram to Fatzer: "Because of the national importance of the issue presented, we request that the State present its views at oral argument. If the State does not desire to appear, we request the Attorney General to advise whether the State's default shall be construed as concession of invalidity." Faced with this virtual order, Fatzer delegated the distasteful task to Paul Wilson, a young lawyer with no experience in appellate courts. Wilson's hastily written brief clung to the *Plessy* case for support and dismissed the social science testimony that Judge Huxman had cited approvingly in his opinion. None of this testimony, Wilson argued, showed that Linda Brown or any other black child in Topeka had suffered any damage, educational or psychological, from segregation. Without evidence of damage, the black plaintiffs had no basis for challenging the state law.

During his time at the lawyer's podium, Wilson stuck closely to his brief and argued that *Plessy* had stood for more than fifty years without reversal and that seventeen states had relied on the "separate but equal" doctrine in segregating their schools. Wilson also restated his brief's claim that none of Topeka's black children had shown evidence of "some detriment that the rest of the population does not suffer" and thus had no ground to challenge segregated schools. The state's reluctant lawyer faced only a few questions and sat down well before his time expired. If the Jim Crow system had any chance of survival, it needed a lawyer who would defend segregation with more fire and conviction than Wilson.

South Carolina had such a lawyer in John W. Davis, a legendary advocate who had argued more cases before the Supreme Court than any lawyer since Daniel Webster. A senior partner in a powerful Wall Street firm, Davis remained fiercely loyal to the "Southern way of life" and the Jim Crow system he had grown up with and still found more comfortable than the racial and ethnic melting pot of New York City. Of course, the only blacks in his firm's offices and his luxurious apartment building were porters and maids. Davis had willingly accepted the task of defending the Clarendon County school board at the urging of Governor James Byrnes, himself a former Supreme Court justice who had resigned after one unhappy term to return to politics. Still tall and imposing at seventy-nine, Davis had exchanged pleasantries with Thurgood Marshall before their arguments in the *Briggs* case, but privately he had deprecated his opponent as full of "guff" and lacking in legal knowledge, although the NAACP's chief counsel had appeared more than a dozen times before the Court and had an impressive winning record. The match-up between these two lawyers in the *Briggs* case brought everyone in the courtroom to full attention.

Marshall led off and "hovered imposingly over the lectern as he addressed the justices familiarly, but respectfully," recalled Jack Greenberg. He took up where Robert Carter had left off, with an attack on the constitutionality of racial classifications, reminding the justices of the Court's 1927 decision in *Nixon v. Herndon,* which struck down all-white primary elections in Texas: "States may do a good deal of classifying that it is difficult to believe rational," Justice Oliver Wendell Holmes had written, "but there are limits, and it is too clear for extended argument that color cannot be made the basis of a statutory classification" that deprives blacks of rights that whites enjoyed. This decision, and others like the *Hirabayashi* case, Marshall said, showed that the Court "has repeatedly said that these distinctions on a racial basis or on a basis of ancestry are odious and invidious," and were deserving of more weight as precedent than *Plessy* and the segregation cases that relied on it for authority. Marshall followed Carter in directing his argument at Justice Frankfurter, who asked more than fifty questions during Marshall's hour at the podium. His response to Frankfurter's most important question, about the general power of states to make legislative classifications, impressed the professorial justice: "I think that when an attack is made on a statute on the ground that it is an unreasonable classification, and competent, recognized testimony is produced, I think then that the least that the state has to do is to produce something to defend their statutes." Frankfurter beamed. "I follow you when you talk that way," he told the NAACP's lead counsel. Before Marshall left the podium, he brought laughter from the audience by declining Justice Robert Jackson's facetious invitation to file suits for American Indians who were segregated in reservation schools. "I have a full load now, Mr. Justice," Marshall smilingly replied.

The burden was now on John Davis to "produce something" to defend the Jim Crow schools in Clarendon County and the rest of South Carolina. Davis shouldered his load without bending an inch. He spoke with such assurance that only two justices interrupted his argument with questions. But his answers to Justice Harold Burton's questions left an opening through which Frankfurter pounced on Davis, grilling him like a first-year law student. Had social conditions in the South changed in the years since the Fourteenth

Amendment was adopted, Burton asked, "such that what might have been unconstitutional then would not be unconstitutional now?" Davis agreed that "changed conditions may affect policy," but that changing laws to meet these new conditions was a legislative task, not one for the courts. "But the Constitution is a living document that must be interpreted in relation to the facts of the time in which it is interpreted," Burton continued. Davis clearly disagreed with Burton's formulation, but he decided to offer a tactical concession. He assured Burton that "changed conditions may bring things within the scope of the Constitution which were not originally contemplated, and of that perhaps the aptest illustration is the interstate commerce clause."

Justice Frankfurter, who as a Harvard professor had written the definitive book on the changing scope of the commerce clause, leaned forward in his seat. "Mr. Davis," he began, "do you think that 'equal' is a less fluid term than 'commerce between the states'?" The Wall Street lawyer, whose firm represented hundreds of businesses engaged in interstate commerce, seemed rattled by the question.

"I had not compared the two on the point of fluidity," he cautiously replied.

"Suppose you do it now," Frankfurter demanded.

Davis tried to buy time. "I am not sure that I can approach it in just that sense," he said. Still unsure after Frankfurter restated his question, Davis offered his own restatement: "That what is unequal today may be equal tomorrow, or vice versa?"

Frankfurter wanted an answer, not a question. "That is it," he tersely replied.

Davis finally collected his thoughts. "That might be," he conceded. But he refused to retreat another inch from his defense of Jim Crow schools. The lawmakers who adopted the Fourteenth Amendment, Davis argued, had not intended to prevent the states from separating black and white students.

Davis regained his composure after Frankfurter ended his inquisition, and turned his rhetorical guns on Kenneth Clark and the other social scientists who had testified at the *Briggs* hearing that segregation harmed black children. "They find usually," Davis suggested, "what they go out to find." He referred sarcastically to Clark's "doll test" in Clarendon County as "that intensive investigation" of just sixteen black children. Before he left the podium, Davis posed his own question for the justices, asking them to consider whether "the wishes of the parents, both white and colored, should be ascertained before their children are forced into what may be an unwelcome contact." The black parents of Clarendon County, he failed to note, had clearly expressed their wishes by joining and supporting the first lawsuit against Jim Crow schools in the Deep South.

Thurgood Marshall had reserved a few minutes of his time for rebuttal, and he used it to remind the justices that John Davis had failed to "produce something" to defend school segregation, other than the "wishes" of white parents to keep black children from sitting next to theirs in schoolrooms. Davis could heap scorn on Kenneth Clark, but his testimony had gone uncontradicted at the *Briggs* hearing. His opponent could not find a single social scientist, Marshall noted, "who does not admit that segregation harms the child." Davis had ended his argument by asking the justices to look back to 1868, when the Fourteenth Amendment was adopted. Marshall ended his in 1952, asking the justices to walk with him on the dirt roads of Clarendon County, where "you will see white and colored kids going down the road together to school." But they do not stay together. "They separate and go to different schools," Marshall continued, and after their classes end "they come out and they play together." He brushed aside concerns about the effect of a ruling against Jim Crow schools. "I do not see why there would necessarily be any trouble if they went to school together," he said of southern children, black and white. But the NAACP lawyer, who knew that most southern whites supported the Jim Crow system, did not want to forecast any "trouble" from those who would not give up that system without a fight. And the justices, of course, were not supposed to let "troublemakers" outside the Court decide cases for them. Thurgood Marshall and John Davis both knew, however, that Supreme Court justices read the newspapers like other Americans and could hardly be unaware of the volatile nature of the issue they faced.

N one of the eight lawyers who followed Marshall and Davis to the podium, in arguments that spanned three days, matched their oratorical skills or provided the justices with different reasons to strike down or uphold school segregation. Spottswood Robinson, who appeared for the NAACP in *Davis v. Prince Edward County*, argued his case "with the careful, literal precision of the real property lawyer that he was," recalled Jack Greenberg. Robinson re-hashed the evidence in the case record and his brief on the inequal-ities of the county's white and black schools, while his opponent, Justin Moore, went outside the record to attack the NAACP for in-stigating the strike by Moton High students, an assertion for which he offered no proof. Robinson devoted his rebuttal time to the his-torical evidence that the Supreme Court could act on its own to enforce the Fourteenth Amendment, although the amendment's final clause gave Congress the power to enforce its provisions "by appropriate legislation." The Court had never contested Robinson's position on this question, although the justices indulged his lecture.

The lawyers who argued the District of Columbia case, *Bolling v. Sharpe*, shifted the Court's attention from the Equal Protection clause of the Fourteenth Amendment, which applies only to the states, to the Due Process clause of the Fifth Amendment, which protects the "liberty" of every person against deprivation by Con-gress, which governed the District. James Nabrit, who appeared for Spottswood Bolling and the District's other black children, pounded on the distinction between the two clauses. Equality was a concept, he argued, that could be measured to see if separate facili-ties were "substantially equal" in quality. But the concept of liberty could not be measured in the judicial scale. "You either have liberty or you do not," Nabrit said. "When liberty is interfered with by the state, it has to be justified, and you cannot justify it by saying that we only took a little liberty." Nabrit also took advantage of the Court's location in the District of Columbia, in which most of the justices lived, to point out the anomaly of segregation in Washington, the major point in Philip Elman's brief for the federal government. "We submit that in this case," Nabrit declaimed, "in the heart of the nation's capital, in the capital of democracy, in the capital of the free world, there is no place for a segregated school system. This country cannot afford it, and the Constitution does not permit it, and the statutes of Congress do not authorize it."

Nabrit's opponent, Milton Korman of the District's legal office, tried to cast the blame for segregating the schools on congressmen who served almost a century earlier. His otherwise plodding argument created a momentary stir in the courtroom when Korman quoted for support from the 1857 decision in the *Dred Scott* case, in which the Court noted that its rulings should not be "the mere reflex of the popular opinion or passion of the day." Korman did not quote the Court's holding in *Dred Scott* that blacks "had no rights which the white man was bound to respect" and could be bought and sold "whenever a profit could be made by it," but any reliance on the Court's most discredited decision was akin to spitting into the communion cup. Korman seemed oblivious to his blunder, and James Nabrit diplomatically let it pass in his rebuttal argument.

The justices heard last from the lawyers in the Delaware cases, *Gebhart v. Belton* and *Gebhart v. Bulah*, and those on both sides understood that virtually every argument about segregation had already been made. The state's attorney general, H. Albert Young, went first as the losing party in the lower courts. His criticism that Chancellor Collins Seitz had misread the law in his opinion, which Seitz had based on exhaustive legal research and visits to the schools in the lawsuit, prompted a retort from Justice Frankfurter. "If I may say so," he chided Young, "a chancellor who shows as much competence as this opinion shows, probably can read the opinions of this Court with understanding." Louis Redding shared his time with Jack Greenberg, who recalled that he felt "as well prepared as possible" for his first Supreme Court argument. "Even if I did terribly the others already had made many of the points I planned to present," he added. Greenberg simply noted that the black children in both cases had already been admitted to formerly white schools without protest or problem, and that the Supreme Court had no reason to return them to segregated schools.

Greenberg concluded his argument at 3:50 P.M. on December 11, 1952, and Chief Justice Vinson thanked all the lawyers who had spoken during three days of oratory. "Any description of the oral arguments must make clear how dull they were," Greenberg later wrote. More than a dozen lawyers, on both sides, had stood up and sat down without making a single memorable statement or reaching an emotional climax. One of the most divisive issues in American politics, which moved many people to passionate defense or outraged opposition, had been argued in words that were mostly soft and flat. Even the two most noted lawyers, Thurgood Marshall and John W. Davis, had ducked the toughest questions from the bench. Marshall's humor and Davis's eminence were all that distinguished them from their colleagues at the podium. After the Court adjourned, none of the lawyers who spoke with reporters outside the Court was willing to predict the outcome of the cases, although Davis was overheard saying to Justin Moore, "I think we've got it won, five-to-four, or maybe six-to-three."

Neither Davis, nor anyone else, could know how the nine justices would actually line up on the school cases until the Court's clerk released whatever orders and opinions they finally decided to issue. The process of deciding important cases usually takes several months after oral argument has concluded, and all the Court's deliberations before "Decision Day," which at that time was always on a Monday, were conducted behind the closed doors of the justices' conference room. Even if a vote is taken at the first conference on a case, which does not always happen, justices are free to switch their votes up to the time the clerk posts the decisions in the Court's pressroom. More than any other institution of government, the

Supreme Court jealously guards the sanctity and secrecy of its deliberations. Whatever private feelings and intuitions the lawyers who argue cases may have about their outcome, they must wait along with the press and the public for the final decision, the date of which is never announced in advance.

The justices met for the first time to discuss the school cases on December 13, 1952, two days after the arguments ended. Chief Justice Fred Vinson sat at the head of the mahogany table in the Court's conference room, with Justice Hugo Black at the other end, the traditional seat of the senior associate justice. Of the remaining seven justices, four had followed Black to the Court as appointees of President Franklin Roosevelt and three owed their seats to President Harry Truman. All but Justice Harold Burton, a former Ohio Republican senator, were nominal Democrats, and all had experience in the federal government, either in executive or legislative positions. All nine justices had joined the unanimous opinions in the *Sweatt* and *McLaurin* cases, which had undermined but not overruled the *Plessy* case and its "separate but equal" doctrine. But there was no guarantee the justices would rule, unanimously or over the objections of dissenters, that school segregation in public elementary and high schools violated the Constitution. The argument, made by lower-court judges in several of the school cases, that graduate and professional schools could not be compared to public schools, might appeal to justices who hesitated to reshape the school systems of seventeen states and the nation's capital. The Court's decision would affect more than twelve million students in five thousand separate districts, almost all with school boards elected by voters who were overwhelmingly white. No decision the Court had made in the previous century, since the infamous *Dred Scott* case in 1857, held the prospect of unleashing the "passions" of millions of Americans of both races, with the very real dangers of disobedience and even bloodshed.

The outcome of the *Dred Scott* case had been virtually ordained by geography. Five of the seven justices who held that no black person, slave or free, could be a citizen of the United States were southerners, both products and defenders of the slave system. Geography might affect the *Brown* cases as well; four of the justices who would vote on them were from Jim Crow states, although only Hugo Black of Alabama came from a Deep South state. Chief Justice Vinson and Justice Stanley Reed were both from the border state of Kentucky, and Justice Tom Clark was a Texan. Black had even joined the Ku Klux Klan as a young man, although he had won election to the Senate as a populist liberal and supported civil rights in Congress and on the Court. There was nothing in the public records of Vinson, Reed, and Clark to indicate any hostility toward blacks, but they had all grown up in a Jim Crow system in which "nigras" went to separate schools and worked in white homes as maids and yardmen.

By long and firm tradition, the justices keep no record of remarks or votes on cases that are discussed and decided in the conference room. Only the sketchy notes of Justices Harold Burton and Robert Jackson survive, and neither man kept a tally of votes on the *Brown* cases. Between them, however, the notes give some idea of how the justices felt about the issue of school segregation. The Court's unwritten rules provide that the justices speak at conference in order of seniority, with the senior associate following the Chief and the "junior" justice going last. Chief Justice Vinson led off the first conference, and made clear his reluctance to end the Jim Crow system. Jackson noted Vinson's fear that striking down school segregation would mean "complete abolition of public school system in South—serious." Burton indicated Vinson's probable vote on *Brown* as *"Aff?"* The question mark suggested that the Chief Justice had not expressed a firm position on the issue, but was leaning toward affirming the lower-court decision that upheld school segregation in that case.

Justice Hugo Black, then in his sixteenth year of service, spoke next as the senior associate. He agreed with Vinson that Deep

South states like South Carolina might shut down their public schools to avoid integration, but that prospect did not sway his intention to reverse the lower-court decision in the *Brown* case, according to Burton's notes. The next justice to speak, Stanley Reed, was a courtly Kentuckian who had served the New Deal administration of Franklin Roosevelt in several posts, including a stint as solicitor general. His support for segregation was evident in a comment to one of his law clerks after the Court ruled that restaurants in Washington could not refuse service to blacks. Reed, who lived with his wife in the ritzy Mayflower Hotel near the White House, exclaimed, "Why, this means that a nigra can walk into the restaurant at the Mayflower Hotel and sit down to eat at the table right next to Mrs. Reed!" Reed obviously did not relish such an event. It was thus no surprise that Reed expressed his intention to "uphold segregation as constitutional" in the school cases, according to Jackson's notes.

The past record of Justice Felix Frankfurter in civil rights cases left no doubt of his position in the school cases. Although his insistence on judicial deference to the judgments of elected lawmakers often led him to uphold restraints on free speech, he had never wavered in supporting the claims of racial minorities to equal treatment. But Frankfurter was cautious by nature, and wanted to avoid any defiance of judicial orders by local officials. He had always been a compulsive note scribbler, and he reminded himself in one he wrote while the school cases were before the Court of "the psychological truth that change, especially drastic change, takes time" and that changes in "deeply rooted social habits" were "best promoted when firmly designed but not precipitously expressed." Frankfurter urged his colleagues at their first conference on the school cases to order the lawyers on both sides to return to the Court for another round of argument. He clearly hoped that deferring a decision for another year would encourage southern officials to begin planning for a gradual change to integrated schools. To keep the lawyers busy, Frankfurter proposed that they brief and argue questions about the intentions of the Fourteenth Amendment's framers in regard to school segregation and the Court's power to hold it unconstitutional, if the framers had not intended to ban the practice.

Justice William O. Douglas, who grew up in Washington State and preferred its wide-open spaces to the crowded streets of Washington, D.C., did not share Frankfurter's reluctance to decide the school cases. "Very simple for me," he said at the conference, according to Jackson's notes. Burton recorded another Douglas remark: "*State* can't classify by color for education." Douglas also saw no need for further argument. "Can't play factor of time," he replied to Frankfurter. The Court's most liberal member was also its least tolerant of long-winded talk at oral argument and in the conference room; Douglas often worked on his numerous books and articles while he listened to argument with one ear open.

Although they disagreed on how the Court should proceed in the school cases, Frankfurter and Douglas agreed that segregation violated the Constitution. Justice Robert Jackson, in contrast, seemed unable to make up his mind on the issue. A former attorney general under Franklin Roosevelt, Jackson had begun law practice in upstate New York after just one year of legal education; he was more a politician than a jurist, and he knew that southern politicians would denounce the Court if it ruled against Jim Crow schools. Jackson was thus an easy mark for Frankfurter's counsel of delay. Justice Harold Burton, who had befriended Harry Truman in the Senate and was rewarded with the Court's "Republican" seat after Justice Owen Roberts retired in 1945, had a firm civil rights record and was eager to "upset segregation," Jackson recorded. But he also thought integration should proceed in as "easy way as possible" and agreed with Frankfurter's proposal for reargument of the cases.

Justice Tom Clark, another former attorney general, was the Court's first Texan and combined a western twang and southern drawl in his voice. He firmly rejected the Jim Crow system in his native state, but he also knew that most Texans would object to

"Yankee" meddling in their schools. "Have led states on to believe separate but equal OK," Jackson recorded Clark as saying about the Court's long-standing reliance on the *Plessy* decision as precedent. Clark was "inclined to go along with delay" in deciding the school cases. The final justice to speak at the December 13 conference, Sherman Minton, had been a Democratic senator from Indiana and served briefly on the federal appellate bench before his close friend and "poker buddy," Harry Truman, elevated him to the Supreme Court, which proved too high a position for his legal reach. Minton had compiled a mixed record in civil rights cases, voting to uphold "white primaries" that excluded black voters but also writing an opinion that prevented the enforcement of racial covenants in property deeds through damage suits against whites who sold property to blacks. But he took a firm stand at the conference against Jim Crow schools, rejecting Frankfurter's proposal for reargument.

The justices took no formal vote on the school cases at the December 13 conference, although a majority of five had indicated—directly or implicitly—their intention to overrule the *Plessy* case. Only one justice, Stanley Reed, had made clear that he would vote to uphold school segregation. Another three, including Chief Justice Vinson, had not taken a stand at the conference and could join Reed in dissent, assuming the conference majority held firm. Several justices tallied the probable vote after the conference, but they all counted differently. Frankfurter predicted a five-to-four vote to overturn the *Plessy* decision, while Burton saw the vote as six-to-three and Jackson put the votes to strike down Jim Crow schools somewhere between five and seven. None of the justices foresaw a majority vote to uphold separate schools, but none anticipated a unanimous decision against them.

One justice, Felix Frankfurter, was convinced that the Court must speak with a single voice, but he left the initial conference well aware that forging a unanimous decision would take both time and persuasion of the potential dissenters. The only way to buy the necessary time was to order the lawyers to reargue their cases. The former Harvard law professor set himself the task of finding a reason to justify a second round of arguments in the school cases. During the months that followed their first conference in December 1952, the justices continued to discuss and debate the school cases without any formal vote. As the time neared for the Court's term to end in late June of 1953, Frankfurter busied himself in drafting a set of five questions, which sounded very much like a law school exam, for the lawyers to answer in briefs that would read more like research papers. The lawyers who anticipated a decision before the term ended were surprised to receive calls from the Court's clerk on June 8, informing them that the cases had been set for reargument on October 12. Copies of Frankfurter's five questions arrived by mail a few days later.

They first asked the lawyers to provide whatever evidence they could find on whether the Fourteenth Amendment's framers "contemplated or did not contemplate, understood or did not understand, that it would abolish segregation in public schools." If the answer to the first question was negative, the second asked whether the framers understood that either Congress or the federal courts could use their powers to abolish segregation. Frankfurter worded his first two questions to avoid any hint of the correct answers, or of the Court's position on the issues they raised.

The third question on the list, also phrased in neutral terms, assumed that the amendment's framers had not provided any definitive evidence of their intentions regarding school segregation. If that were so, Frankfurter asked, could the Court nonetheless construe the amendment to abolish segregation? The fourth and fifth questions tipped the Court's hand, asking the lawyers to assume that the justices would rule against Jim Crow schools and soliciting their advice on how best to frame judicial orders to implement that ruling. In addition to these questions, the justices also invited the attorney general to file a brief and join the oral arguments, hinting that they wanted to know what steps the federal government—now headed by President Dwight Eisenhower—would take to prevent southern officials from defying court orders to integrate their schools.

Disappointed that the Court had ducked the segregation issue, and dismayed at the massive research job that would consume the summer and scuttle their vacation plans, the NAACP lawyers plunged into their task, recruiting some two hundred sympathetic historians to dig through old newspapers and legislative records for the "evidence" the justices had requested. Jack Greenberg recalled that "I took the five questions as a favorable omen" of the Court's decision to outlaw Jim Crow schools, although he confessed that the act of the Congress that adopted the Fourteenth Amendment in providing funds for segregated schools in the District of Columbia suggested "that it wasn't hell bent on ending segregated education." The NAACP lawyers took solace, however, in the conclusion of leading historians, including C. Vann Woodward, then teaching at Johns Hopkins University and later an eminent Yale professor, that the amendment's framers intended that it "would work a revolutionary change in our state-federal relationship by denying to the states the power to distinguish on the basis of race."

The preparations on both sides were abruptly interrupted on September 8 with the shocking news that Chief Justice Vinson had died in his sleep of a heart attack. Vinson was sixty-one and paunchy, and got his exercise in shuffling cards at the poker table, but there had been no forewarning of his death. Justice Frankfurter had proposed reargument in the school cases because he despaired that Vinson could shape a unanimous court to strike down segregation, and feared that he might even vote to reaffirm *Plessy*, which might well have encouraged defiance of judicial orders by southern officials. Frankfurter's reaction to Vinson's death was characteristically acerbic: "This is the first indication I have ever had that there is a God." His prayers for judicial leadership were quickly answered by President Dwight Eisenhower, who had swept to office in 1952 with the greatest margin in history over his Democratic opponent,

Adlai Stevenson. With his wide grin and disarming manner, "Ike" stayed above the political fray while GOP partisans lambasted the Democrats, who were saddled with the Korean War. During his election campaign and eight months in office, the new president had avoided taking sides on school segregation or the Supreme Court cases. Privately, however, Eisenhower had confessed to friends that he could see why white parents objected to having a "big black buck" sit next to their daughter in school.

In choosing a new Chief Justice, the first Republican president since Herbert Hoover could have elevated the only Republican on the Court, Justice Harold Burton. But the former Ohio senator, although gregarious and well-liked by his colleagues, was a judicial lightweight and was distrusted by many GOP stalwarts for having supported New Deal measures that his party opposed. The most likely candidates from outside the Court included Secretary of State John Foster Dulles, a former Wall Street lawyer, and Thomas Dewey, who had twice been the losing GOP presidential candidate. However, a promise that Eisenhower had made more than a year before Chief Justice Vinson's death resulted in a choice that surprised almost everyone. During the Republican national convention in June 1952, California's governor, Earl Warren, had swung his state's delegates behind Ike at a crucial point in the proceedings. Warren's move scuttled the candidacy of Ohio senator Robert Taft, the party's right-wing favorite and Eisenhower's leading opponent for the nomination (ironically, Taft was far more supportive of civil rights than Eisenhower). In return for Warren's crucial role in securing his nomination, Eisenhower had told Warren he was "definitely inclined" to offer him the next Supreme Court seat. Although he later said his offer did not include the Chief's post, Ike kept his bargain after Warren sent word that he expected the president to follow through. Eisenhower sent his attorney general, Herbert Brownell, to California with instructions to ask Warren if he would be willing to leave his elected post and begin a new job on Monday, October 5, the beginning of the Supreme Court's new term. Warren told Brownell that he would begin packing right away, and Eisenhower announced his choice on September 30. Because the Senate was in recess, Warren did not need formal confirmation, which came the next March.

Born in 1891 to Norwegian parents, the new Chief Justice had received two law degrees from the University of California at Berkeley and practiced briefly before joining the army in World War I, leaving infantry service as a captain. He then spent twenty years in government legal service, rising from deputy district attorney in Alameda County to become California's attorney general in 1939. Warren was a tough prosecutor, sometimes accused of targeting his political enemies. With his eye on the governor's post, he had supported the wartime internment of Japanese Americans, along with every other California politician. As governor in 1943, Warren had warned that "if the Japs are released" from internment camps, "no one will be able to tell a saboteur from any other Jap." But he later repented these insensitive remarks and directed the state's law enforcement officials to protect the Japanese Americans who returned to their homes after the war ended.

Taking his seat as Chief Justice only a week after President Eisenhower announced his appointment, Warren joined a Court that was still in shock from his predecessor's sudden death. The initial reaction by the other justices and the press was not uniformly warm. Felix Frankfurter groused privately that Warren was just a political hack, and several critics noted his lack of prior judicial experience, a deficiency he shared with John Marshall, Charles Evans Hughes, and Harlan Fiske Stone, all of whom served as Chief Justice with distinction. But within a few weeks, the hearty and solicitous Warren won over the justices: he sought Frankfurter's counsel, soothed Robert Jackson's hurt feelings at having been passed over for the post, and asked Hugo Black to preside at the first conference, which pleased the longest-serving justice. And he brightened the Court's dimmer lights—Burton, Clark, and Minton—with his glow.

CHAPTER 9

"We Cannot Turn the Clock Back"

The second round of arguments in the school cases had been rescheduled after Chief Justice Vinson's death, and began on December 7, 1953. Two months after he took the Court's helm, Earl Warren led his colleagues through the red velvet curtain to their seats on the bench, with Hugo Black on his right and Stanley Reed on his left, two southern justices with very different feelings about segregation. Stacked before each justice were briefs that reflected six months of hard labor by lawyers and historians who had struggled to answer the two basic questions Justice Frankfurter had posed: Did the Fourteenth Amendment's framers intend to outlaw school segregation? If not, did the Court have the power to perform that task itself? Each side put its best gloss on the reports of debates in Congress and state legislatures, but in the end they reached similar conclusions: the evidence was equivocal on both issues. How the justices should decide the cases was still an open question.

The arguments stretched over three days and largely rehashed points made a year earlier. Warren had shuffled the Court's docket and the Virginia case now led off, followed by the South Carolina case. The NAACP lawyers in both cases, Spottswood Robinson and Thurgood Marshall, would speak before their respective opponents. Jack Greenberg later described Robinson's argument as "a meticulous, dull, historical presentation" that went on for forty minutes before the first question. In response to Justice Reed's query about the fact that Congress had never acted to prohibit school segregation, Robinson answered that congressional inaction did not limit "the power of the judiciary to enforce the prohibitions of the Fourteenth Amendment."

Marshall followed Robinson to the podium and "was equally uninspiring" in presenting his case, Greenberg said unsparingly of his boss. Richard Kluger wrote in his masterful chronicle of the school cases, *Simple Justice*, that Marshall gave "one of his least creditable performances before the Court." Marshall got stuck in the nineteenth-century segregation cases and stumbled over the *McLaurin* case, in which the Court had ruled just three years earlier that segregating a black graduate student within an otherwise all-white school violated the Equal Protection clause. Marshall sat down without making the obvious point that if Oklahoma could not rope off George McLaurin from his white classmates, how could South Carolina rope off all its white schools from black children?

Now eighty but still erect and imposing, John W. Davis took the podium after Marshall to speak once again for South Carolina. No other lawyer that day "came near matching him for bite, eloquence, or wit," Kluger wrote. Davis first summarized the answers to the Court's historical quiz; the lawyers on both sides differed on the answers, he noted, and the attorney general, speaking for the United States, "says he does not know which is correct." Davis paused for effect. "So Your Honors are afforded a reasonable ground for selection," he said dryly, as the justices chuckled. After the laughter subsided, Davis turned serious. Proclaiming South Carolina's "good faith and intention to produce equality for all of its children of whatever race or color," he choked up as he concluded, "here is equal education, not promised, not prophesied, but present. Shall it be thrown away on some fancied question of racial prestige?" Tears flowed down his cheeks as Davis left the podium for the last time, after 140 arguments that stretched over four decades. Even Thurgood

Marshall was moved by his opponent's emotion. But one lawyer in the courtroom whispered to another, "That sonofabitch cries in every case he argues."

Marshall had reserved some time to answer Davis, and he spoke the next morning. Greenberg recalled that "Thurgood's rebuttal was his best argument ever." Marshall opened with a bow to his aged adversary. "As Mr. Davis said yesterday, the only thing the Negroes are trying to get is prestige," he began. "Exactly correct. Ever since the Emancipation Proclamation, the Negro has been trying to get . . . the same status as anybody else regardless of race." In almost the same words he had used the year before, Marshall took the justices on another verbal tour of Clarendon County, and its black and white children: "They play in the streets together, they play on their farms together, they go down the road together, they separate to go to school, they come out of school and play ball together. They have to be separated in school." Marshall ended by deploring South Carolina's "determination that the people who were formerly in slavery, regardless of anything else, shall be kept as near that state as possible, and now it is the time, we submit, that this Court should make clear that is not what our Constitution stands for."

Virginia's attorney general, Lindsay Almond, defended his state's Jim Crow schools in words that reflected the genteel racism of southerners who looked back with nostalgia to the days when "nigras" knew their place in a segregated society. Almond asked the justices not to "disturb the unfolding evolutionary process of education where from the dark days of the depraved institution of slavery, with the help and the sympathy and the love and respect of the white people of the South, the colored man has risen under that educational process to a place of eminence and respect throughout this nation. It has served him well." Almond did not tell the justices that two-thirds of the black adults in Prince Edward County had not gone beyond the sixth grade in Jim Crow schools that had clearly not served them well.

Arguments in the three other school cases were brief and perfunctory. The Topeka school board had already ended segregation in two of the city's four black grade schools, and Paul Wilson of the Kansas attorney general's office faced a barrage of questions about whether the *Brown* case was now moot. Robert Carter, whose Topeka clients—including Linda Brown—now attended integrated schools, told the justices after ten minutes, "I certainly have no real desire to proceed with an argument," and returned to the counsel table. The lawyers in the Delaware cases had so little to say that Jack Greenberg did not even finish his argument after the Court's lunch break. The NAACP lawyers decided that Thurgood Marshall would take the rest of Greenberg's time to sum up, which he did with a brief review of all five cases.

The only lawyer who had not appeared in the first round of argument was J. Lee Rankin, solicitor general in the Eisenhower administration. The NAACP lawyers had feared that Rankin would back away from the brief written the year before by Philip Elman, which squarely urged the justices to overrule the *Plessy* case. Rankin's new brief took a more equivocal position, but at the podium he declared that "segregation in public schools cannot be maintained under the Fourteenth Amendment." But the solicitor general also urged the justices to allow southern officials to implement judicial orders "with deliberate speed." Rankin did not invent this phrase, but his words stuck in the mind of Felix Frankfurter, who scribbled them down in one of his many notes to himself.

The arguments in the District of Columbia case included both the low and high points of the proceedings. Milton Korman, whose quotation from the *Dred Scott* case the year before had astounded the audience, returned to face questions about whether he still had a client. Eight of the District's nine school board members had been replaced, and the new members had stated their intention to end segregation in Washington's schools. Korman struggled with questions until the day's session ended, and began the next morning with a statement that the board had not officially voted to abolish Jim Crow schools. But the hapless lawyer had little time left to mount a defense of a policy that would soon end. James Nabrit, who followed Korman, concluded his brief argument with a powerful appeal to the nation's conscience: "Our Constitution has no provision across it that all men are equal but that white men are more equal than others. Under this statute and under this country, under this Constitution, and under the protection of this Court, we believe that we, too, are equal."

The second round of arguments concluded on December 10, 1953, but five months passed before the public learned of the Court's decision in the five school cases. During that time, the Court's marble walls concealed from outsiders the politicking that swirled inside. Earl Warren made no pretensions of legal scholarship, but no other justice ever matched the political skills that he brought to the Court after three decades spent winning votes. Even more than Frankfurter, the Chief Justice was determined to forge a unanimous Court around a brief and forceful opinion. Only if the justices spoke with one voice, in words the American people could understand, would the Court be able to help the nation heal its racial wounds.

Warren set himself an ambitious task, and spent months cajoling his colleagues. Three justices required the full Warren treatment. Felix Frankfurter wanted an unequivocal ruling that school segregation violated the Fourteenth Amendment, but he also wanted to give southern districts time to comply with the Court's mandate; he borrowed the phrase that Solicitor General Rankin had used at oral argument and proposed to Warren a judicial decree allowing school officials to proceed with "all deliberate speed" in moving toward integration. Robert Jackson wanted the Court to admit frankly that ending segregation had no explicit constitutional warrant; he drafted a concurring opinion that read like the fable about the emperor with no clothes. Stanley Reed posed the greatest challenge to Warren's unrelenting charm; the courtly Kentuckian had drafted a dissent arguing that the Fourteenth Amendment only provided blacks "an opportunity to obtain facilities substantially equal to his neighbors for himself."

The Chief Justice won over Frankfurter by suggesting that the Court issue the opinion he wanted and also order a third round of argument on methods and timetables for implementing the orders that district judges would frame. The justices would solicit the views of southern officials in this new round, especially those from Deep South states like South Carolina. If the southerners balked at dismantling their Jim Crow schools, the Court would frame a flexible decree ordering compliance with "all deliberate speed," as Frankfurter proposed. Warren's tactic worked like a charm on Frankfurter. "What a pleasure to do business with him," the testy justice gushed to Justice Jackson, who never got back to his concurrence after suffering a heart attack in March 1954. Warren visited Jackson's hospital room and left a copy of his draft opinion. The ailing justice asked his law clerk, Barrett Prettyman, Jr., to read it. Prettyman, whose father had written a judicial opinion upholding segregation in Washington's schools, scanned Warren's opinion and offered Jackson his own: "I said that I wished it had more law in it but I didn't find anything glaringly unacceptable in it." Jackson called Warren and joined his opinion.

Stanley Reed finally succumbed to Warren after more than twenty lunchtime discussions. After Frankfurter and Jackson climbed aboard his bandwagon, Warren offered Reed the last seat: "Stan, you're all by yourself in this now. You've got to decide whether it's the best thing for the country." Reed decided that holding out for segregation was not the best thing for the country, or for the Court.

The Supreme Court's chamber was not crowded on May 17, 1954. Thurgood Marshall had gotten a tip from a friend and took a train to Washington that Monday morning. He entered the chamber as Chief Justice Warren presided over the admission of lawyers to the Court's bar. Justice Tom Clark then read an opinion in an antitrust case, followed by Justice William Douglas, who read two opinions in cases dealing with corporate negligence and labor picketing. Most of the news reporters present that day were lounging in their basement quarters when the Court's press officer stuck his head in the door. "Reading of the segregation decisions is about to begin in the courtroom," he informed them. The reporters dashed up the stairs to witness an historic moment. "I have for announcement," Warren began, "the judgment and opinion of the Court in No. 1,—*Oliver Brown et al. V. Board of Education of Topeka.*" As Warren began reading his opinion, reporters could not tell who had won. "The Court's ruling could not be determined immediately," the Associated Press flashed in its first bulletin.

Reading in a "firm, clear, unemotional voice," Warren reviewed the procedural history of the school cases and the grounds of their challenges to school segregation. He then reviewed the briefs submitted on the Fourteenth Amendment's purpose and reach, stating that "although these sources cast some light, it is not enough to resolve the problem with which we are faced." Warren also found no illumination from precedent, dismissing the *Plessy* case in one sentence as one "involving not education but transportation." Decades of argument, millions of words, and mountains of briefs on *Plessy* had no impact on Warren. In deciding the school cases, he continued, "we cannot turn the clock back" to the nineteenth century, when *Plessy* was decided. Warren was equally unmoved by evidence on "the tangible factors in the Negro and white schools involved in each of the cases." Lower courts had found that school facilities "have been equalized, or are being equalized" in each case. In the end, the school cases had nothing to do with the schools themselves.

What the cases really involved was the psychological impact of enforced separation on black children. Warren stressed "the importance of education to our democratic society." Surprisingly, he said nothing about reading, writing, or arithmetic The primary role of public education lies in fostering "cultural values" and "good citizenship" among children, he stated. Warren asked whether children could absorb these values and become good citizens in segregated schools. He found the answer in the social science data that John W. Davis had dismissed as irrelevant, and that even some NAACP lawyers had doubted. Warren quoted a long paragraph from the "Finding of Facts" that Judge Huxman had appended to his opinion in the *Brown* case, which itself quoted the testimony of Louisa Holt at the Topeka trial. Separation by race denotes "the inferiority of the negro group," she had said, and feelings of inferiority diminish "the motivation of a child to learn." Warren cited in a footnote to his opinion the studies of Kenneth Clark and other social scientists, including Isador Chein, to support Holt's findings. The vice of segregation was not bad schools for black children, but the bad lesson it taught them. "To separate them from others of similar age and qualifications solely because of their race," Warren concluded, "generates a feeling of inferiority as to their status in the community that may affect their hearts and minds in a way unlikely ever to be undone."

Warren finally read the words the reporters had waited for: "We conclude unanimously that in the field of public education the doctrine of 'separate but equal' has no place. Separate educational facilities are inherently unequal." The word "unanimously" was not in the Court's printed opinion, but Warren inserted it during his reading for emphasis. Those who listened, including Thurgood Marshall, were unaware that Warren had worked hard for five months to use this word. He paid the cost of unanimity in the final paragraph. Citing "the great variety of local conditions" in southern states, Warren ordered further argument on implementing the Court's decision.

Most of the reporters hurried from the courtroom to file their stories after Warren finished reading his *Brown* opinion. But the Chief Justice was not done. Because the District of Columbia case, *Bolling v. Sharpe*, had challenged segregation in Washington's schools under the Due Process clause of the Fifth Amendment, Warren read a separate opinion in that case. In view of the *Brown* ruling that the Constitution barred states from segregating their public schools, Warren said, "it would be unthinkable that the Constitution would impose a lesser duty on the Federal Government." Although he was unwilling "to define 'liberty' with any great precision," Warren noted that "it cannot be restricted except for a proper governmental objective." School segregation was not "reasonably related" to any such objective, and "imposes on Negro children of the District of Columbia a burden that constitutes an arbitrary deprivation of their liberty in violation of the Due Process Clause," Warren concluded.

Thurgood Marshall, who sat through Warren's reading of both opinions in the lawyers' section of the courtroom, was elated at the victory he had worked for almost two decades to achieve. "I was so happy I was numb," he recalled of that day. After the justices followed Warren from the chamber, Marshall was surrounded by reporters on the Court's wide plaza. Before he answered any questions, Marshall turned to James Nabrit and George Hayes, who had argued the *Bolling* case, and exulted, "We hit the jackpot." To the reporters, he predicted that southern officials would not "buck the Supreme Court" and would obey its mandate. But the justices had deliberately not ordered any black student admitted to any white school, or directed any district—even those involved in the five cases the Court had decided—to dismantle its system of separate schools. Marshall had dealt with so much delay and foot-dragging by state and university officials in the cases that preceded *Brown* that he knew that integration was not likely to happen anytime soon. Besides, several months would pass before the Court heard argument on implementation of its ruling, and a final opinion might be a year away.

Chief Justice Warren had hoped that a forceful and unanimous opinion would quell any incipient resistance to the Court's ruling, and that compliance might begin even before the implementation question was argued. Southern politicians quickly dashed his hopes; they needed no further argument on this issue. Governors and senators heatedly denounced the decision. Georgia governor Herman Talmadge claimed the Court had made the Constitution "a mere scrap of paper" and promised that his state would "map a program to insure continued and permanent segregation of the races." Governor James Byrnes of South Carolina, a former Supreme Court justice, said he was "shocked" by the Court's action. Senator James Eastland of Mississippi vowed that the South "will not abide by or obey this legislative decision by a political court."

A few voices of moderation rose above the din. Governor Thomas Stanley of Virginia said the decision called for "cool heads, calm study, and sound judgment," although he later backed the advocates of "massive resistance" in his state. The *Atlanta Constitution* urged Georgians to "think clearly" about their response and to ignore those who preached "violence and hatred." The first year after the Court's ruling was relatively calm and peaceful. As no court had actually ordered the admission of black children to white schools, those who counseled disobedience had nothing to disobey. One incident in Delaware, however, gave a preview of the later conflicts over integration. In September 1954, fifteen hundred whites protested the enrollment of eleven black students at the Milford High School in the state's rural south. After local officials closed the school, state officials ordered it reopened and police officers escorted the black students inside, surrounded by hundreds of jeering whites who had been whipped up by an "outside agitator" from the National Association for the Advancement of White People, a racist group that later fomented trouble across the South. After NAACP lawyers filed a complaint against the Milford board in state court, Delaware's supreme court gave a preview of state resistance to federal authority, ruling that Milford officials had not followed proper procedure in admitting the black students and voiding their action.

The Delaware setback did not influence school officials in other border states like Maryland and Kentucky, where integration began slowly but without incident. Schools in Baltimore were opened to both races in the fall of 1954, but only 4 percent of the city's black children attended school with whites. About one in ten of Kentucky's school districts announced plans to integrate their schools within the next year. But the Deep South waited for federal judges to act, and the Supreme Court gave them plenty of time. The final round of argument in the school cases was scheduled to begin on April 11, 1955, and lawyers on both sides hammered out their briefs with two facts in mind: the Court had firmly decided that segregation could not be imposed by law, but the justices had declined to order immediate compliance with their ruling.

The NAACP lawyers focused on the Court's duty to give black children their constitutional rights without delay. Fear of hostile reactions by whites to integration, or claims of logistical problems in shifting children between schools, could not justify foot-dragging and obstructionism. Southern officials who raised these arguments "as a basis for interminable delay in the elimination of segregation in reality are seeking to utilize the product of their own wrongdoing as a justification for continued malfeasance," the NAACP brief said. It also urged the Court to instruct federal district judges, who would actually draft the orders in each case, to set a deadline of September 1955 for the first steps toward integrating schools and the following September for completing the process. Some of the NAACP lawyers, most notably Spottswood Robinson, balked at giving southern districts even this much time. Robinson argued that if integration was "immediately ordered and implemented," obstruction would be hard to organize. William Coleman was among those who counseled a more flexible approach, allowing southern districts to file plans based on a "gradual effective transition" to integration. Thurgood Marshall decided to take a middle-ground position, but his brief did propose a uniform deadline for integrating all Jim Crow schools.

The southern states, not surprisingly, urged the Court to give district judges complete latitude in framing orders. The brief for Virginia appealed for "a now indeterminable period to elapse before requiring integration of the races" in the state's schools. "We do not foresee a complete solution at any future time," Virginia's lawyers added. They based this gloomy prognosis on disparities in "the general level of educational capacity and attainment between the two races" and differing "standards of health and morals" among blacks and whites. Without any hint of awareness, the evidence offered for these claims reflected the damage inflicted on Virginia's black citizens by four centuries of slavery and segregation. Virginia's brief noted that black children in Virginia scored lower than whites on intelligence tests, that tuberculosis was twice as prevalent among blacks, and that blacks in Virginia were four times more likely than whites to contract venereal diseases and ten times more likely to have illegitimate children. The unstated assumption behind the brief was that school integration would put white children at risk of contracting ignorance, disease, and immorality from black children. Virginia's brief proved that racists could dress in white shirts as well as white sheets.

The final round of arguments began on April 11, 1955, with a new face on the Supreme Court bench. Justice Robert Jackson had suffered a final, fatal heart attack in October 1954, and President Eisenhower named a successor with an illustrious judicial name. John Marshall Harlan II was the grandson and namesake of the only justice who dissented in the *Plessy* case. The second Justice Harlan had practiced for twenty years in a prestigious Wall Street firm, and was a thoughtful, principled judicial conservative, unlike the "Four Horsemen of Reaction" who had frustrated the New Deal program of Franklin Roosevelt. Nor did he follow the "judicial restraint" doctrine with the dogmatism of Felix Frankfurter; Harlan would vote to strike down many federal and state laws in free speech cases, and he was the first justice, writing in dissent in 1961, to find a "right of privacy" in the Constitution that later formed the basis of the Court's decision in *Roe v. Wade* to protect the right of abortion from criminal prosecution.

The Court had invited the attorneys general of all the states that maintained Jim Crow schools to file briefs and take part in oral argument, and the justices listened to sixteen lawyers—five for the NAACP and eleven for the southern states—who offered more than thirteen hours of legal oratory that was spread over four days. The lawyers who spoke for the black children in Jim Crow schools all asked the Court to order that integration begin "forthwith" in their districts and not to allow "local hostilities and prejudices and customs" to delay the process. Thurgood Marshall, wrapping up for the NAACP lawyers, told the justices firmly that there was "no local option on the Fourteenth Amendment in the question of rights— that just because there is a Southern area involved, or a border area involved, that is no reason to delay it." As he had in his brief, Marshall urged the Court to set a single, national deadline for the completion of integration in every school district. Allowing district judges to set their own timetables would invite southern officials to offer endless reasons for delay.

Much of what the lawyers for the southern states had to say was repetitive, and several were really giving campaign speeches to their white constituents, promising to defend the "Southern way of life" against judicial meddling. They forecast the effect of integration on their states with terms that evoked disasters, such as "tornado," "man-made cataclysm," and "death blow." Without exception, they claimed that white parents would refuse to send their children to school with blacks, and that public education might not survive in the southern states. The most defiant words came from S. Emory Rogers, who argued for the Clarendon County school board in South Carolina. John W. Davis had died after his last tearful argument, and Rogers had none of his charm or wit. His argument sorely tried Earl Warren's patience. Rogers requested the Court to

issue an "open order" that would impose no time limit or conditions on the county. Warren asked if school officials would "immediately undertake to conform" to the Court's decree.

"I am frank to tell you," Rogers answered, that he doubted
whether "the white people of the district will send their children to
the Negro schools."

Warren pressed him: "You are not willing to say here that there
would be an honest attempt to conform to this decree, if we did
leave it to the district court?"

"No, I am not. Let us get the word 'honest' out of there," Rogers
replied.

"No, leave it in," Warren shot back.

Rogers remained defiant: "No, because I would have to tell you
that right now we would not conform—we would not send our
white children to the Negro schools."

Lawyers saw Warren flush with anger. "We thought he might
charge Rogers with contempt," one recalled.

The federal government's position on implementation of the
Brown decision stuck to the middle ground between the NAACP
and the southern states. Noting that school segregation was "part of
a larger social pattern of racial relationships" and had "existed for a
long time" in much of the nation, the Justice Department's brief
urged the justices to adopt a two-step process: southern districts
should have ninety days to submit plans for ending segregation, but
district court judges would decide how much time school officials
could have to implement these plans. The brief filed by Solicitor
General Simon Sobeloff said that integration should proceed "as
quickly as feasible," which provoked Justice Hugo Black to ask him
at oral argument what "feasible" meant. Sobeloff replied weakly
that it meant "a determination after considering all relevant factors,"
hardly a blueprint for judicial action.

Chief Justice Earl Warren took firm control of the conference
on April 16, 1955. He wanted another unanimous opinion, and he

wanted to keep it short and simple. Justice Burton recorded Warren's formula: "Give District Courts as much latitude as we can but also as much support as we can." This time around the table, none of the justices raised any objections or hinted at dissent. Warren's final opinion, which he read to a packed courtroom on May 31, was just seven paragraphs long. He first said that the "varied local school problems" in different states and districts required local federal judges to exercise "practical flexibility" in shaping decrees. Judges should consider "the physical condition of the school plant, the school transportation system, personnel, revision of school districts and attendance areas into compact units," as well as "revision of local laws and regulations which may be necessary in solving the foregoing problems." The final paragraph remanded the four federal cases—the Delaware courts had already ordered the black children admitted to the formerly segregated schools—to district judges, with instructions to "enter such orders and decrees consistent with this opinion as are necessary and proper to admit to public schools on a racially nondiscriminatory basis with all deliberate speed the parties to these cases."

Two days after Warren read his opinion, Thurgood Marshall called his friend Carl Murphy, who published the influential black newspaper the *Afro-American*. Murphy confessed some disappointment in the decision's lack of timetables, but the language on "good faith, deliberate speed, prompt start" convinced him that "we can go with this." Marshall agreed. Some people "insist on having the whole hog," he said, but "I think it's a damn good decision!" The Court had put the burden of compliance on the southern states. "They've got to yield to the Constitution! And yield means yield! Yield means give up!"

Murphy had a question for his longtime partner in the fight against Jim Crow schools. "What are you going to do, Thurgood?" Marshall's exuberance yielded to a more realistic view of the situation, reflecting his awareness that Warren had limited his opinion to the four cases the Court had decided. He outlined to Murphy "what we're going to do state by state." The NAACP would file suits in every state that refused to abandon school segregation, and march through the courts from Maryland through Georgia, just as Sherman's army had marched through the Confederacy a century ago. "You can say all you want," Marshall assured Murphy, "but those white crackers are going to get tired of having Negro lawyers beating 'em every day in court. They're going to get tired of it."

CHAPTER 10

"War Against the Constitution"

hurgood Marshall completely misread the fierce determination of "white crackers" in the Deep South to maintain the Jim Crow system of segregated schools. One southern politician after another denounced the Court's decision. It was "the most serious blow that has yet been struck against the rights of the states in a matter vitally affecting their authority and welfare," Virginia's powerful Senator Harry Byrd complained. "I shall use every legal means at my command to continue segregated schools in Virginia," echoed Governor Thomas Stanley, a cog in the Byrd machine. "No matter how much the Supreme Court seeks to sugarcoat its bitter pill of tyranny," Governor Marvin Griffin of Georgia railed, "the people of Georgia and the South will not swallow it." In South Carolina, where the first lawsuit against school segregation had been filed in Clarendon County, Governor James Byrnes said that his state "will not now nor for some years to come mix white and colored children in our schools." Governor Fielding Wright of Mississippi, the most intransigent of the Deep South states, proclaimed that "we shall insist upon segregation regardless of consequences." Even politicians considered "moderate" on racial issues, like Governor Luther Hodges of North Carolina, bowed to the "redneck revolt" that he feared would destroy public education; Hodges did not speak out when the state legislature resolved that any "mixing of the races in the public schools . . . cannot be accomplished, and should not be attempted." Newspaper columnists and editorialists joined the critical chorus. "When the Court proposes that its social revolution be imposed on the South 'as soon as practicable,' there are those of us who would respond that 'as soon as practicable' means never at all," the *Richmond News Leader* told its readers.

Many politicians linked the Court's ruling with its recent—and widely criticized—decisions that struck down state and federal efforts to outlaw the Communist party and its leaders. Senator James Eastland, an openly racist Mississippi Democrat who had refused to support his party's candidates in the past two presidential elections, blasted the Court for citing the works of Swedish sociologist Gunnar Myrdahl in the *Brown* decision. Myrdahl, who had written an exhaustive and penetrating book on race relations, *An American Dilemma*, was a leading member of the Swedish socialist party and a firm opponent of communism. Eastland did not see the distinction. "It is evident that the decision of the Supreme Court in the school segregation cases," he growled, "was based on the writings and teaching of pro-communist agitators and other enemies of the American form of government." Eastland's office sent copies of this speech to more than three hundred thousand people, and its charges of subversive influence on the Court were echoed in hundreds of newspaper editorials and columns.

Local officials and school board members heeded these calls for defiance of the Court's ruling. Although most of the border states took the first steps toward integrating their schools in the fall of 1955, after the Supreme Court handed down its "all deliberate speed" ruling, not a single black student attended classes with white children in any southern state from Virginia through Louisiana. Faced with defeat at the polls, school board members in Greensboro, North Carolina, quickly reversed their decision to begin token integration of the city's schools in 1955. Schools in Greensboro, in fact, remained segregated until 1971, when a federal judge finally ran out of patience with delaying tactics.

With racist demagogues leading the charge against the Supreme Court, "moderates" running for cover, and white liberals an impotent handful, most federal district judges read the phrase "all deliberate speed" in the second *Brown* opinion by looking only at the middle word. Even Thurgood Marshall, who had urged the Court to order that integration begin "forthwith" in Jim Crow school districts, took a pragmatic approach to the varied positions of local boards: "If there's a difficult situation and a school board says, 'This will take us six years,' we may well say, 'All right, let's take six years.' But if the board says, 'We'll never sit down and talk our problems over with Nigras,' then we'll say, 'Let's go to court as soon as we can.'" With some six thousand school districts across the South, the outnumbered and overworked NAACP lawyers who worked under Marshall's supervision had to pick and choose their targets with care. It made no sense to file a lawsuit against a school board in federal courts in which the judges had made clear their reluctance to impose any timetables for integration on local officials. Many of the federal district judges in states like Mississippi, Alabama, and Georgia did not conceal their personal belief in segregation and their opposition to the *Brown* decision. Even those who felt themselves bound by their judicial oath to uphold the Supreme Court's rulings had little enthusiasm for ordering any "forthwith" integration in districts where local officials had vowed to close schools rather than allow white and black students to sit in the same classroom.

These reluctant judges took their cue from the opinion of Judge John Parker in the *Briggs* case from Clarendon County, South Carolina. Parker had written the first decision in this case, upholding school segregation and relying on the *Plessy* decision for precedent. As a lower-court judge, he was required to obey the orders of the Supreme Court, but he was still a loyal southerner. On July 15, 1955, six weeks after the Supreme Court had directed the judges in the four cases decided under the *Brown* caption to frame decrees that followed its "all deliberate speed" formula, Parker issued a ruling that kept Harry Briggs, Jr., and rest of Clarendon County's black children in their Jim Crow schools. The setting for his opinion lacked all the drama of the first hearing in the *Briggs* case, at which scores of black parents from Clarendon County packed the courtroom in Charleston. On this occasion, the clerk of the federal court simply announced the decision in an unemotional tone before an almost empty courtroom. Speaking for judges Armistead Dobie and George Timmerman, Parker began his opinion with a bow to the justices in Washington. "Whatever may have been the views of this court as to the law when the case was originally before us," he wrote, "it is our duty now to accept the law as declared by the Supreme Court." Parker put his reading of the Court's decision into a lengthy paragraph:

"Having said this, it is important that we point out exactly what the Supreme Court has decided and what it has not decided in this case. It has not decided that the federal courts are to take over or to regulate the public schools of the states. It has not decided that the states must mix persons of different races in the schools or must require them to attend schools or must deprive them of the right of choosing the schools they attend. What it has decided, and all that it has decided, is that a state may not deny to any person on account of race the right to attend any school that it maintains. This, under the decision of the Supreme Court, the state may not do directly or indirectly; but if the schools which it maintains are open to children of all races, no violation of the Constitution is involved even though the children of different races voluntarily attend different schools, as they attend different churches. Nothing in the Constitution or in the decision of the Supreme Court takes away from the people freedom to choose the schools they attend. The Constitution, in other words, does not require integration. It merely forbids discrimination. It does not forbid such segregation as occurs as a result of voluntary action. It merely forbids the use of governmental power to enforce segregation. The Fourteenth Amendment is a limitation upon the exercise of power by the state or state agencies, not a limitation upon the freedom of individuals."

Underneath the judicial rhetoric of Parker's opinion, its message was simple and crystal clear: federal judges were under no duty to dismantle the system of Jim Crow schools. Parker in effect handed an engraved invitation to school boards to frustrate integration through "freedom of choice" plans, which allowed white parents to pick the "whitest" school in their district for their children. Hundreds of southern boards adopted such plans, most often with provisions that allowed school officials to approve or deny requests for school transfers. Most of the districts with "freedom of choice" plans, in fact, routinely denied the requests of black children for transfer to white schools, usually on grounds that the child's "best interests" would be served by remaining in the black school. The Clarendon County school board adopted such a plan, and no black child was allowed to transfer into a white school before a federal judge struck down the plan in 1965, a decade after Judge Parker issued his initial decree.

Federal judges in dozens of southern districts cited Parker's opinion in the *Briggs* case to justify "go-slow" decrees with no timetables for compliance. He had merely enjoined Clarendon County officials "from refusing on account of race to admit to any school under their supervision any child qualified to enter such school, from and after such time as they may have made the necessary arrangements for admission of children to such school on a nondiscriminatory basis with all deliberate speed as required by the decision of the Supreme Court in this cause." Not only did Parker's decree lack any deadline for compliance, it granted to school officials the power to decide which children were "qualified" to attend any school. In addition to age and residence, the "qualifications" required of black children were set by white officials who followed no standards but their own prejudices.

Judge Parker's opinion was not the evasion of the Supreme Court's ruling in *Brown* that it seemed to many civil rights lawyers and leaders. All he did, in fact, was to translate the Court's "all deliberate speed" phrase into language that other cautious and conservative judges would find appealing. Whether or not the Supreme Court justices had foreseen the invocation of that phrase as the excuse for delay that it became, they could hardly escape responsibility for the foot-dragging judicial decrees that Parker and other judges framed in dozens of school cases. By refusing to set any deadlines for compliance with its decision, the Court had virtually guaranteed that its docket would be clogged for years—four decades, in fact—with cases that reflected the determination of southern officials to delay school integration as long as possible.

During the school year that ended in the spring of 1956, only a handful of black children attended classes with whites in the South, all in border states. Some nine hundred black students were assigned to formerly white schools in Wilmington, Delaware, and 14 of the 20 smaller districts in the rest of New Castle County integrated their schools. Only one district in the state's two southern counties dropped its racial barriers. However, in the neighboring state of Maryland, the city schools in Baltimore had ended segregation in 1954, but only 4 percent of the city's black children attended school with whites. Eight of the remaining 22 Maryland counties integrated their schools in 1955, although the rural Eastern Shore counties refused to abandon their Jim Crow schools. Integration began in 35 of West Virginia's 55 counties in 1955, and in 20 of Kentucky's 224 school districts. Farther west, the states of Missouri and Oklahoma ended segregation in most districts, although pockets of resistance remained in rural areas of both states. Only 60 of the 2,000 school districts in Texas began integration in 1955, including the cities of San Antonio, El Paso, and Austin, while the schools in Dallas and Houston remained segregated. In Virginia and the six Deep South states from South Carolina to Louisiana, not a single black student attended school with whites during the 1955 school year.

As the 1956 school year began, more black children entered formerly all-white schools in border states that had already begun the process of desegregation. But the Deep South refused to bow to "judicial tyranny," and the region's political leaders launched an attack on the Supreme Court with the "Southern Manifesto" in March 1956, a document signed by the vast majority of southern members of Congress. Drafted largely by Senator Strom Thurmond of South Carolina, who had deserted the Democratic party in 1948 to run for president under the States' Rights party banner, this document charged the Court with a "clear abuse of judicial power" in the *Brown* decisions. The manifesto's signers, who included 19 of the 22 southern senators and 77 of the 105 House members, pledged to use "all lawful means to bring about a reversal of this decision which is contrary to the Constitution and to prevent the use of force in its implementation." Among the senators, only Lyndon Johnson of Texas and Albert Gore and Estes Kefauver of Tennessee refused to sign the Manifesto. More than half of the House members who withheld their support were from Texas, where blacks made up just 13 percent of the population.

Whether by design or not, the southern politicians who proclaimed their support for "lawful means" of defending the Jim Crow system gave legitimacy to the rabble-rousers who incited racist mobs to violence. In early September 1956, three small towns became the flash points for white resistance to integration. Clinton, Tennessee, a town of four thousand in the state's eastern hills, was the site of pitched battles over the admission of twelve black students to the local high school. Led by an itinerant agitator named John Kasper, a howling mob of one thousand whites blocked traffic around the courthouse square, battered the cars in which blacks were riding with baseball bats, and overwhelmed the local police. The night after this riot, the police chief enlisted forty citizens into a "peace guard" that met Kasper and his mob with submachine guns. Whipped into a frenzy by Kasper's racist diatribes, the mob stormed through clouds of tear gas with cries of "Let's get the nigger lovers! Let's get their guns and kill them." Just in time to avert a bloodbath, one hundred state highway troopers barreled into Clinton with sirens wailing and searchlights blazing. The troopers dispersed the mob and arrested Kasper, and the next day, Governor Frank Clement dispatched six hundred troops and seven M-41 tanks from the Tennessee National Guard to patrol the town and restore order.

After a federal judge ordered the admission of three black students to the high school in Mansfield, Texas, just south of Fort Worth, a mob of four hundred swarmed onto the school grounds, hung a black dummy above the school entrance, and waved placards that read: "DEAD COONS ARE THE BEST COONS" and "2$ A DOZEN FOR NIGGER EARS." The black students stayed away from the high school in fear of being hung like the dummy. The press reported the comment of Glenda Geyer, a fourteen-year-old white student: "If God wanted us to go to school together, He wouldn't have made them black and us white." That reasoning, of course, would have kept Holstein and Guernsey cows in separate pastures, but Glenda hadn't studied logic at Mansfield High. And in the western Kentucky town of Sturgis, where nine black students enrolled in the high school, armed mobs roamed the streets, yelling for "nigger blood," until National Guard troops forced them back with an M-47 tank. Guardsmen with rifles and bayonets escorted the black students into the school until the white hecklers finally dwindled and then departed.

Most white Americans learned about the mob violence in towns like Clinton, Mansfield, and Sturgis from television news reports, then limited to fifteen minutes of black-and-white film on each network, and from weekly magazines like *Time, Newsweek, Life*, and *Look*. They saw pictures of National Guard troops with fixed bayonets holding back screaming whites, and of tanks rumbling and clanking around the streets of small towns from Kentucky to Texas. For many northern whites, their image of school integration was shaped by these pictures of disorder and defiance. The black students who braved the mobs to enter formerly white schools did not, of course, scream racial epithets, throw rocks, or hang whites in effigy. But it was their presence at the schools that inflamed the southern whites who did all those abusive and unlawful acts, and many people who lived outside the South began to associate school integration with disruption and violence. As the images of protests in 1956 against school integration in three small towns began to fade, the nation's attention turned in the fall of 1957 to the Arkansas state capital, Little Rock, where racist mobs confronted U.S. Army paratroopers in response to a judicial order admitting nine black children to the city's elite school, Central High.

The pitched battles that erupted in the streets around Central High posed the toughest question faced by the Supreme Court in the century since the justices decided the *Dred Scott* case in 1857. What good is the Constitution if government officials refuse to obey its commands? More to the point, what if they defy judicial orders to carry out these commands? The Court handed down an emphatic ruling on those questions in September 1958, but the answers came only after Little Rock had been convulsed for an entire year and the judicial process had struggled to deal with the defiance of a bantam-weight politician with a loud voice, Arkansas governor Orval Faubus. The refusal of Faubus and other state officials to obey judicial orders produced a case, *Cooper v. Aaron*, that tested not only the Court's resolve but also the nation's commitment to the rule of law.

Governor Faubus surprised many people when he emerged as the leader of "massive resistance" to school integration. First elected as a racial "moderate" in 1954, Faubus added black members to state boards and Democratic party committees. He raised no objections when the rural Arkansas town of Hoxie ended its separate school system in June 1955. And he stayed quiet when the Little Rock school board adopted a plan that year, even before the Supreme Court issued its second *Brown* opinion, for "phased" integration, beginning with the admission of black students to Central High in September 1957. Integration of other high schools, then junior highs, and finally grade schools would be "phased in" during a ten-year period. The Little Rock board made no bones that its plan was designed to produce "the least amount of integration spread over the longest period of time." The glacial pace of the Little Rock plan failed to satisfy the Arkansas NAACP, however, and its lawyers filed suit against the board in February 1956. Six months later, federal judge John E. Miller endorsed the ten-year plan as a "good-faith" effort to "ultimately bring about a school system not based on color distinctions." The Eighth Circuit federal appellate court in St. Louis upheld Miller's decision and cleared the path for nine black students to enter Central High on September 3, 1957.

Although most whites in Little Rock supported the school board's "phased integration" plan, news reports of the judicial order inflamed the city's racial bigots, who began waving Confederate battle flags and vowing to block the school's doors to black students. Those who opposed integration lacked a forceful leader, but they flocked to a speech by Governor Marvin Griffin of Georgia, who visited the city a week before schools were set to begin classes. Griffin thundered his denunciation of the Supreme Court in language that used Ku Klux Klan terms, and his audience responded with cheers that reached the ears of Governor Faubus, who quickly shed his "moderate" mask and began railing against federal judges. The night before the "Little Rock Nine" were expected at Central High, Faubus spoke to the state on television. Warning that "blood will run in the streets" if the nine black students entered the school, Faubus announced that he had ordered National Guard troops to surround Central High and keep them out. The next morning, eight of the nine gathered at the home of Daisy Bates, the young president of the state's NAACP chapters. They left in station wagons for the short drive to their new school. Fifteen-year-old Elizabeth Eckford did not show up at Daisy Bates's home. Walking alone, holding her head high, she tried to enter Central High and was turned away by soldiers with bayonets. A menacing crowd surrounded Elizabeth and began yelling, "Get her! Lynch her!" Someone hollered, "Get a rope and drag her over to this tree!" Protected by a white NAACP member, Grace Lorch, Elizabeth finally escaped from the mob on a city bus.

Americans across the country witnessed Elizabeth Eckford's dignity in the face of lynch-mob hysteria on their television screens. Many people had never seen the face of racism so clearly, and calls began mounting for federal intervention to end the Arkansas insurrection, which was led by a governor who was sworn to uphold the Constitution. The public also watched President Dwight Eisenhower playing golf in Newport, Rhode Island, unwilling to interrupt his vacation to deal with the most serious threat to federal authority since the Civil War. Pressure mounted on Eisenhower to intervene, but he took no action. National Guardsmen blocked Central High's doors to the Little Rock Nine until September 20, when a federal judge ordered Governor Faubus to remove the state troops. Little Rock police then escorted the black students into the school, but an unruly mob stormed the building and the nine youngsters barely escaped with their lives through a side door.

Faced with the prospect of televised lynchings, Eisenhower called Faubus and persuaded him to fly to Newport for meetings with the president and his attorney general, Herbert Brownell. After two hours of closed-door talks, Eisenhower and Faubus emerged to face the press. Reading from a prepared statement, the president said the governor had stated "his intention to respect the decisions of the U.S. district court, and to give his full cooperation in carrying out his responsibilities in respect to these decisions." On his part, Faubus sounded cooperative: "The people of Little Rock are law-abiding, and I know that they expect to obey valid court orders. In this they shall have my support." By inserting the qualifying term "valid" in his statement, Faubus had given himself a loophole through which he crawled as soon as he returned to Little Rock. The cocky governor did not consider the Constitution a "valid" document in Arkansas, and he refused to provide the Little Rock Nine with state protection after the local police withdrew in the face of menacing mobs.

After he returned to the White House from his disrupted vacation, President Eisenhower came under growing pressure to deal with the defiant governor. Little Rock's mayor, Woodrow Mann, and the editor of the city's moderate newspaper, Harry Ashmore, appealed for federal troops to restore order. Finally, on September 23, Eisenhower issued a proclamation entitled "Obstruction of Justice in the State of Arkansas" that commanded "all persons engaged in such obstruction to cease and desist therefrom, and to disperse forthwith." The president also directed the secretary of defense to "use such of the armed forces of the United States as he may deem necessary." The next day, one thousand paratroopers of the 101st Airborne Division arrived in Little Rock from Fort Campbell, Kentucky, and quickly ringed Central High with troops. The city's racists lacked the guts to battle paratroopers, and the Little Rock Nine finally began their classes. During the remainder of the school year, a band of white students harassed them unmercifully while school officials turned their heads. After a white boy dumped a bowl of soup on the head of Minniejean Brown during a lunch period, the principal suspended both of them for the remainder of the year. Unwilling to endure further abuse, Minniejean left Little Rock and took refuge in New York City, where she lived with Kenneth Clark and his family and attended a prestigious private school. It was a hard year for the remaining eight black students at Central High, but they finished the year, and on May 27, 1958, Ernest Green became the school's first black graduate. Two decades later, he became one of Central High's most distinguished alumni in his post as assistant labor secretary under President Jimmy Carter.

Shortly before the Central High graduation ceremony in May 1958, the Little Rock school board asked federal judge Harry Lemley to delay any further integration until January 1961. The board's lawyers argued that school integration "runs counter to the ingrained attitudes" of many Little Rock whites. They also pointed to Governor Faubus, who had persuaded the Arkansas legislature to pass laws authorizing him to take over local school boards that admitted any black students to white schools. Faubus had also issued statements that the *Brown* decisions had no force in Arkansas, which the board's lawyers presented to Judge Lemley to support their request for delay. Lemley held a three-day hearing, at which school officials—all white—testified about the "chaos, bedlam, and turmoil" at Central High. The judge did not ask who had caused the chaos, but he granted the board's petition on June 20, 1958, resegregating all Little Rock schools for more than two years.

Judge Lemley's move precipitated a legal storm, as NAACP lawyers rushed between St. Louis, Little Rock, and Washington. They sought and obtained a stay of the judge's order from the Eighth Circuit appellate court, which reversed his ruling on August 18 after a hearing before all seven of the circuit judges. All but one signed an order that rebuked both Judge Lemley and the Arkansas officials who refused to obey judicial orders, putting into italics their admonition that *"the time has not yet come in these United States when an order of a federal court may be whittled away, watered down, or shamefully withdrawn in the face of violent and unlawful acts of individual citizens in opposition thereto."* Despite this stern language, NAACP lawyers were stunned when the Eighth Circuit judges abruptly, and without explanation, reversed themselves on August 21 and stayed their own order until the Little Rock school board could file an appeal with the Supreme Court. The NAACP lawyers then asked the Supreme Court to step in and end the legal chaos. Although the justices had scattered around the country during their summer recess, Chief Justice Warren summoned them back to Washington for a "special term" on August 28, more than a month before the Court's traditional opening session on the first Monday in October. Little Rock schools were scheduled to open on September 15, and Warren wanted to decide this momentous case before the class bells rang.

William Cooper, the Little Rock school board president, and John Aaron, first in alphabetical order of the black plaintiffs, gave their names to the case of *Cooper v. Aaron*. But the real parties were Orval Faubus and Earl Warren, for this case was really a contest for supremacy between the defiant governor and the determined Chief Justice. All nine justices had answered Warren's call and returned to Washington for the oral arguments. Despite the short notice for this early session, the courtroom was packed with spectators, lawyers, and reporters. Richard Butler, the board's lawyer, began his argument with an appeal for delay. "All we're asking," he said, "is for time to work this thing out in a climate of calm rather than a climate of hysteria." Chief Justice Warren listened politely to Butler's assurance that he was not speaking for the "law defiers" in Little Rock. "I know you're not," Warren soothingly replied.

The Chief's smile quickly faded when Butler spoke for the chief law defier in Arkansas. "The point I'm making is this," Butler said, "that if the governor of any state says that a United States Supreme Court decision is not the law of the land, the people of that state, until it is really resolved, have a doubt in their mind and a right to have a doubt."

"I have never heard such an argument made in a court of justice before," Warren shot back, "and I've tried many a case, over many a year. I never heard a lawyer say that the statement of a governor, as to what was legal or illegal, should control the action of any court." The former California governor now wore a black robe, and he would not tolerate this challenge to judicial authority, especially from a governor who thumbed his nose at the Supreme Court.

Russell Baker, who covered the hearing for the New York Times, reported that Thurgood Marshall took the podium for the black plaintiffs with "the hint of a scowl on his face, looking like Othello in a tan business suit." Marshall was just as angry as the Chief Justice, and his voice rose as he spoke for Little Rock's black children. "I think we need to think about these children and their parents," he said, "these Negro children that went through this every day, and their parents that stayed at home wondering what was happening to their children, listening to the radio about the bomb threats and all that business." Marshall's voice filled the chamber with outrage. "I don't know how anybody under the sun could say, that after all those children and those families went through for a year, to tell them: All you have done is gone. You fought for what you considered to be democracy and you lost. And you go back to the segregated school from which you came. I just don't believe it."

The justices did not believe it either, and they scolded Governor Faubus with a single voice. On September 12, the day after the Court held a second round of argument that largely rehashed the issues, the Court issued an unsigned order reversing Judge Lemley's two-year delay of integration. Central High could now begin classes, with two thousand white and nine black students, the same number as those who entered the year before. On September 29, the Court handed down its written opinion in *Cooper v. Aaron*. Never before—or since—has every justice personally signed an opinion. Richard Butler had argued that Governor Faubus's claim that *Brown* had no effect in Arkansas left its citizens "in actual doubt as to what the law is." Warren proposed the collective opinion to remove any doubt.

The justices professed astonishment that Faubus and Arkansas lawmakers would claim "that they are not bound by our holding in the *Brown* case." The Court's opinion treated the defiant officials like schoolroom dunces. It was their "determination to resist this Court's decision in the *Brown* case" which had "brought about violent resistance to that decision in Arkansas," the justices stated. Had the Arkansas officials not read the Constitution? Article Six "makes the Constitution the 'supreme law of the land.'" Had they not all taken oaths "to support this Constitution?" The justices took out their paddles: "No state legislator or executive or judicial officer can wage war against the Constitution without violating his undertaking to support it." And who had the power to interpret and enforce the Constitution? "It follows that the interpretation of the Fourteenth Amendment enunciated in the *Brown* case is the supreme law of the land," the justices told the Arkansas officials. Looking beyond Little Rock to politicians in other states who might be tempted to emulate Governor Faubus, the Court demanded "the obedience of the States" to "the command of the Constitution" that federal court orders must be obeyed.

Despite this stern judicial lecture, the Arkansas officials did not learn their lesson. Defying the Court once again, Governor Faubus and the state legislature closed down Little Rock's schools for an entire year. Going back to federal court, NAACP lawyers won a ruling in 1959 that reopened the schools. By spring 1960, Central High had fifteen hundred white students and just five blacks. Under the "pupil placement" laws that allowed school officials to assign students under such vague criteria as the "suitability" of the child for a particular school, the Little Rock school board granted just six of the sixty applications from black children who asked for transfers to white elementary schools, and allowed sixty-eight white students to transfer from schools slated for integration to all-white schools. Litigation over the Little Rock schools dragged on for years, raising the question once again: What good is the Constitution if government officials refuse to obey its commands? What the Arkansas politicians finally obeyed was not the Supreme Court, but the commands of public opinion. Little Rock's voters finally tired in 1960 of chaos and turmoil in their schools and elected a new school board that moved toward compliance with court orders. But the images of the violent mobs in the streets around Central High, and of the army troops who pushed back rioters at bayonet point, lingered in the minds of millions of white Americans, and convinced many that school integration might expose their children to danger. Even before federal judges turned to busing as a remedy to overcome the effects of residential segregation, many white parents recalled the images of Little Rock and recoiled at the prospect of sending their children to schools with large numbers of black students. In that respect, the Supreme Court's invitation to proceed with "all deliberate speed" in dismantling Jim Crow schools had produced the deliberate obstruction and delay that blocked any effort to bring about the meaningful integration of America's schools.

CHAPTER II

"Too Much Deliberation and
Not Enough Speed"

The Supreme Court's unanimous and emphatic decision in the Little Rock case sent important messages to three different groups. First, the Court reminded those southern politicians who might think of emulating Governor Orval Faubus that any effort to "wage war against the Constitution" would be met with firm judicial action. Next, officials in every school district that still refused to begin the process of desegregation received notice that the Court's rulings in *Brown* were "the supreme law of the land" and must be obeyed. Finally, the American people—except for diehard defenders of segregation—gained a new respect for the Court, which made clear that violent resistance to its orders would not keep black children out of white schools. The decision in *Cooper v. Aaron* did not prevent Faubus and the Arkansas legislature from closing the schools in Little Rock for another year, nor did the recalcitrant governor face any real danger of going to jail for his contemptuous behavior. But the Little Rock decision did move the battles over school integration from noisy streets to the quieter chambers of legislatures, school boards, and courtrooms.

During the two years that followed the *Cooper* decision, dozens of challenges to southern foot-dragging and outright refusal to dismantle Jim Crow school systems clogged the dockets of federal district judges and the circuit courts of appeals that reviewed their decisions.

Most of these cases involved the evasive stratagems that school boards devised to keep integration to a bare minimum. By June 1960, fewer than fifteen of the sixty cases filed by NAACP lawyers had been decided by federal judges, while forty-six unresolved cases were pending in thirteen states from Delaware to Texas. Clearly, the Supreme Court's directive to proceed with "all deliberate speed" had not prompted either southern officials or cautious judges to step on the gas pedal. For example, L. B. McCord, the school superintendent in Clarendon County, South Carolina, continued to speak in words of defiance: "Our way of life calls for separation of the races, and come hell or high water we plan to keep it that way." District Judge T. Whitfield Davidson, who presided over an integration case in Dallas, Texas, declared that blacks must recognize that "the white man has a right to maintain his racial purity and it can't be done so easily in integrated schools."

Southern officials devised a number of ploys to avoid or limit integration. Many districts adopted "pupil placement" laws that permitted school boards to use criteria such as "suitability" in assigning students to schools; others employed "freedom of choice" plans that allowed white parents to choose the "whitest" school for their children. Another popular way to keep integration to a bare minimum was through "minority-to-majority" plans that allowed parents to move their children from schools in which they were in a racial minority to those in which their race formed a majority. Needless to say, all these plans were designed to frustrate the Supreme Court's ruling in *Brown* that assignments to public schools must be made "on a racially nondiscriminatory basis."

Federal judges took different approaches to the varied plans that perpetuated the Jim Crow system. Surprisingly, considering the growing number of school cases in the lower federal courts, and the vagueness of the "all deliberate speed" directive, the Supreme Court declined to provide more definite guidance for almost a decade after the original *Brown* decision. Despite the often contradictory rulings in the lower courts, the Supreme Court decided just a handful of school cases between 1955 and 1964, during which period the number of black students attending school with whites in the states of the former Confederacy rose from zero to 2 percent. At this pace, full integration would not be achieved for another five centuries. Clearly, this glacial pace had to change, but the Court seemed unwilling to raise the judicial speed limit.

The Supreme Court finally abandoned its "hands-off" position in a case that posed the greatest challenge to the institution of public education. Faced with a court order to dismantle its Jim Crow system, the school board in Prince Edward County, Virginia, made its contribution to the state's "massive resistance" program by shutting down its public schools, black and white. The NAACP had sued the Prince Edward board in one of the cases decided with *Brown* in 1954, and board members and local white leaders had been infuriated by their judicial rebuff. Led by J. Barrye Wall, the pugnacious editor of the *Farmville Herald*, and Maurice Large, a former school board chairman, white residents of Prince Edward County dug in their heels against integration. In May 1956, they gathered 4,184 signatures on a statement that vowed their intention "to abandon public schools and educate our children in some other way if that be necessary to preserve the separation of the races."

That same year, the Virginia legislature passed a law requiring the closure of any public schools where black and white children attended classes together and authorizing the payment of tuition grants to students who attended private schools in districts where public schools had been closed. The Virginia supreme court struck down the school-closing law in 1959, and a federal appeals court ordered Prince Edward officials to begin the integration of its two high schools in September 1959. In response, the county board of supervisors voted to close the public schools, and virtually all of the county's white students enrolled in the Prince Edward Academy, which was staffed by sixty-seven teachers, all but two from the now-closed public schools. The board also voted to provide tuition grants from public funds for the white students in the private academy, adding to the grants offered by the state.

The county's black children had no schools between 1959 and 1964, although the National Council of Negro Women brought together a coalition of groups that set up "activity centers" for them. The centers did not pretend to replace the black schools the county had closed. The largest, in the basement of the First Baptist Church in Farmville, had "two blackboards, a couple of worktables, and a variety of books for its ninety-four 'pupils,'" one reporter noted. Black children who lived in rural areas crowded into abandoned tenant farmers' shacks with no plumbing and wood-burning stoves. "We are operating activity centers to help maintain the morale of children," said Dorothy Croner, who directed the project. "The centers are not in any respect offered as a substitute for schools." Many of the black children who did not attend the centers simply wandered the streets of Farmville or helped out on rural farms. Some two thousand black children in Prince Edward County had no formal education for at least four years, and they clearly suffered from this deprivation. A team of researchers from Michigan State University visited the county in 1963 and found that the average IQ of children with no schooling over the past four years was just 65, a level within the range of the "mentally defective."

Led by the Reverend L. Francis Griffin, the firebrand black minister who had supported Barbara Johns and the other black students whose strike at Moton High School in Farmville had sparked the NAACP lawsuit that went to the Supreme Court with the *Brown* case, a group of black parents went back to federal court in 1961 and filed an amended complaint to the original case. Under the caption of *Griffin v. Prince Edward County*, the first plaintiff in the revived suit was Leslie Francis Griffin, the thirteen-year-old son of Reverend Griffin. District Judge Oren Lewis struck down the county's tuition grants for private schools, but declined to decide whether closing the schools violated the federal Constitution, pending a ruling by the Virginia courts on that question under the state constitution. After the Virginia judges decided that the state's counties were authorized but not required to operate and fund public schools, thereby ducking the issue of whether Prince Edward County could shut down its schools, Judge Lewis reopened the *Griffin* case and ruled that one county could not close its schools "while the Commonwealth of Virginia permits other public schools to remain open at the expense of the taxpayers." The Fourth Circuit Court of Appeals reversed Judge Lewis, however, ruling that public schools "must be made available to all citizens without regard to race, but what public schools a state provides is not the subject of constitutional command." In other words, Prince Edward County had no obligation to operate any public schools.

During the months in which the *Griffin* case shuttled between the lower courts, both chambers of Congress were filled with debate over the Civil Rights Act of 1964, the most sweeping proposal to strike down Jim Crow laws since the *Plessy* decision upheld them in 1896. The legislative package was sent to Congress by President Lyndon Johnson, whose nationally televised speech urging its passage ended with the words of the civil rights hymn "We Shall Overcome." Johnson acted in response to national outrage at the Klan-directed violence that included the bombing deaths of four young black girls at a church service in Birmingham, Alabama, the assassination of Medgar Evers, who directed the NAACP's field-work in Mississippi, and the murders of three young civil rights workers—two white and one black—in Mississippi's Neshoba County. The centerpiece of the Civil Rights Act, prompted by the "sit-in" movement against lunch-counter segregation and the "Freedom Rides" that challenged segregation on interstate buses, was a section that prohibited racial discrimination in such "public accommodations" as restaurants, theaters, hotels, and transportation. Another provision of the law, spurred by southern resistance to school integration, allowed the federal government to withhold funds for educational programs from districts that failed to comply with judicial orders to dismantle their Jim Crow schools.

Against this backdrop of debate over civil rights, the Supreme Court scheduled argument in *Griffin v. Prince Edward County* for March 1964. Across the street from the Capitol, where lawmakers filled their chambers with rhetoric, the Court's chamber was quiet but crowded with spectators for the most important school case since the *Brown* decisions. Robert Carter, the NAACP lawyer who had argued the *Brown* case before the Supreme Court, returned to the podium and warned the justices that other southern districts would follow suit if the Court allowed Prince Edward County to avoid integration by closing its public schools and funding private segregated schools. The county's lawyer, J. Segar Gravatt, stood firmly behind states' rights and asserted that "education and the methods by which its is provided is a state matter—not a federal matter," prompting Chief Justice Earl Warren to reply that Prince Edward County had given black children the "freedom to go through life without an education."

The Supreme Court handed down its ruling in the *Griffin* case on May 25, 1964, ten years and one week after the *Brown* decision. Justice Hugo Black expressed the Court's frustration with the slow pace of school integration in his majority opinion. The issues before the Court "imperatively call for decision now," he wrote. "There has been entirely too much deliberation and not enough speed in enforcing the constitutional rights which we held in *Brown v. Board of Education* had been denied" the black children in Prince Edward County. Black denounced the county's "continued, persistent efforts to circumvent our 1955 holding" that Jim Crow schools violate the Constitution. Like the Virginia state courts and the Fourth Circuit judges, Black ducked the question of whether counties were required to operate public schools at all, but he found it clear "that Prince Edward's public schools were closed and private schools operated in their place with state and county assistance, for one reason, and *one* reason only: to ensure . . . that white and colored children in Prince Edward County would not, under any circumstances, go to the same school. Whatever nonracial grounds might support a State's allowing a county to abandon public schools, the object must be a constitutional one, and grounds of race and opposition to desegregation do not qualify as constitutional."

Although he sidestepped one sticky constitutional issue, Justice Black showed no hesitation in forcing Prince Edward officials to reopen their public schools. Indeed, he went much further, giving Judge Lewis the authority to "require the Supervisors to exercise the power that is theirs to levy taxes to raise funds adequate to reopen, operate, and maintain without racial discrimination a public school system in Prince Edward County like that operated in other counties in Virginia." The notion that federal courts could order local or state officials to raise taxes for any purpose struck many commentators as judicial overreaching. Even the liberal *New Republic* wrote that "some eyebrows were raised" by Black's ruling on the tax issue. Among those with raised eyebrows were justices Tom Clark and John Marshall Harlan, who appended to Black's opinion a one-sentence statement that they "disagree with the holding that the federal courts are empowered to order the reopening of the public schools in Prince Edward County, but otherwise join in the Court's opinion." County officials could not reopen the schools, of course, without obtaining the funds, from local or state taxes, to operate them.

The Court's ruling in the *Griffin* case put an end to the "massive resistance" campaign that had closed the public schools in Prince Edward County and threatened to shut down schools in other die-hard districts in Deep South states. But the justices had still not expressed their opinion of less drastic efforts to block or limit integration, such as "pupil placement" laws and "freedom of choice" plans. There was no dearth of cases in the lower federal courts, many of them ripe for review by the Supreme Court. In the Fifth Circuit of the federal court system, which covered the Deep South from Georgia to Texas, the district courts handled 128 school cases between 1956 and 1966; during the same period, the Circuit Court of Appeals reviewed 42 cases, many of them more than once. Four of the judges on the Fifth Circuit—Richard T. Rives, John R. Brown, Elbert P. Tuttle, and John Minor Wisdom—formed a judicial phalanx that held firm against the obstructionism, foot-dragging, and outright refusal to begin the process of school integration that characterized virtually every district official in Georgia, Alabama, Mississippi, and Louisiana. These four judges, all native southerners, endured more abuse and displayed more courage than the nine members of the Supreme Court, insulated and protected in their marble palace in Washington.

It was, in fact, an opinion by Judge Wisdom that provided the Supreme Court with every judicial tool it needed to strike down the "freedom of choice" laws that deterred all but the most determined black parents from sending their children to "white" schools in which they would most likely be shunned or harassed. A native of New Orleans who had been active in Louisiana's tiny Republican party, Wisdom owed his judicial post to President Dwight Eisenhower, who reportedly vowed—after Wisdom became the South's leading judicial advocate of integration—that his nominee would never be elevated to the Supreme Court. Sitting on a three-judge panel with Circuit Judge Homer Thornberry of Texas and District Judge William H. Cox of Mississippi, Wisdom labored for a year in writing a thirty-thousand-word opinion in a set of school cases from Alabama and Louisiana. His opinion in *United States v. Jefferson County Board of Education*, issued on December 29, 1966, decided seven cases from these two states, neither of which had allowed a single black child to attend school with whites before 1965. The first of the seven cases involved the public schools of Birmingham, Alabama, a city in which police commissioner "Bull" Conner had used police dogs and fire hoses against civil rights activists, and

Klansmen used dynamite to kill black children in their churches. The school boards in all seven cases were composed of white segregationists who had defied every lower court order to integrate their schools.

Judge Wisdom noted in his *Jefferson County* opinion that the school districts before his court had a total of some 96,000 white and 59,000 black students. Of this number, only 110 black children attended school with whites, in districts that had grudgingly begun the process of integration to avoid the cutoff of federal education funds under the Civil Rights Act of 1964, which poured more than a billion dollars each year into local schools. Schools with large numbers of students from low-income families qualified for the greatest amount of federal aid, and many districts in the Deep South were eligible for badly needed funding. But the tempting carrot of federal money came with the stick of mandated integration, enforceable by the federal courts. Wisdom pointed out that in each of the seven cases, the first step toward integration "was a consequence of a court order obtained only after vigorous opposition by school officials." He clearly felt the time for any further delay had ended. "The dead hand of the old past and the closed fist of the recent past account for some of the slow progress," Wisdom wrote, casting much of the blame on the "local loyalties" that had "compelled school officials and elected officials to make a public record of their unwillingness to act."

Wisdom then turned his guns on a fellow judge, John Parker of the neighboring Fourth Circuit, who had written in 1955 that the Constitution "does not require integration," but merely an end to segregation imposed by law. Parker's ruling in the *Briggs* case from Clarendon County, South Carolina, had given ammunition to local officials and lower-court judges who took no affirmative steps to place black and white children in the same classrooms. Wisdom blasted Parker's statement about integration as "pure dictum," a term for comments in a judicial opinion that are not relevant to the case and have no binding force as precedent. Wisdom conceded that his own court and other federal judges "have often paraphrased or quoted with approval the *Briggs* dictum." He did not fault local school officials who had "the *Briggs* dictum dinned into their ears for a decade" and who relied on Parker's opinion to support evasive tactics like "pupil placement" and "freedom of choice" plans. He did fault Parker for limiting his *Briggs* ruling to the individual black children whose parents had the courage and fortitude to join a lawsuit against Jim Crow schools. Federal judges with little sympathy for integration had followed Parker's lead, making it difficult for black students who were not parties to integration suits to escape from Jim Crow schools, and making it easier for recalcitrant school officials to frustrate court rulings. "What is wrong about *Briggs* is that it drains out of *Brown* that decision's significance as a class action to secure equal educational opportunities for Negroes by compelling the states to reorganize their public school systems," Wisdom complained.

Judge Wisdom understood the reasons why meaningful integration had proven so difficult to achieve, listing five in his opinion: "(1) Some determined opponents of desegregation would scuttle public education rather than send their children to schools with Negro children. These men flee to the suburbs, reinforcing urban neighborhood school patterns. (2) Private schools, aided by state grants, have mushroomed in some states in this circuit. The flight of white children to these new schools and to established private and parochial schools promotes resegregation. (3) Many white teachers prefer not to teach in integrated public schools. They are tempted to seek employment at white private schools or to retire. (4) Many Negro children, for various reasons, prefer to finish school where they started. These are children who will probably have to settle for unskilled occupations. (5) The gap between white and Negro scholastic achievements causes all sorts of difficulties. There is no consolation in the fact that the gap depends on the socioeconomic status of Negroes at least as much as it depends on inferior Negro schools."

Having outlined the reasons for the persistence of Jim Crow schooling, Wisdom moved to the question of "establishing fair, workable standards for undoing de jure school segregation in the South." He acknowledged the difficulties in his judicial task, but was undaunted: "We grasp the nettle," he wrote firmly. The remedy he ordered left no room for doubt or delay. "The position we take in these consolidated cases," Wisdom wrote for himself and Judge Thornberry, "is that *the only adequate redress for a previously overt system-wide policy of segregation directed against Negroes as a collective entity is a system-wide policy of integration.*" The italics in this sentence added emphasis to Judge Wisdom's determination to enforce his order. Integration to him meant that every school in a district would have both black and white students, teachers, and staffs. Devices such as "pupil placement" laws and "freedom of choice" plans were no longer lawful. His order required "conversion of the dual zones into a single system. Faculties, facilities, and activities as well as student bodies must be integrated." Wisdom included in his opinion a lengthy list of criteria, forms, and procedures that school officials were required to follow. From the Supreme Court on down, judges had given local and state officials little guidance in moving from segregation to integration; Wisdom's opinion spelled out their duties in minute detail. Those who criticized judges like Wisdom for taking over the functions of school officials failed to acknowledge that they had failed—and in many cases, flatly refused—to carry out their duties.

Widely admired as a judicial scholar, Judge Wisdom addressed the famous statement of Justice John Marshall Harlan, in his *Plessy* dissent, that "our Constitution is color-blind, and neither knows nor tolerates classes among citizens." Wisdom amended Harlan's sentence and explained his reasons. "The Constitution is both color blind and color conscious. To avoid conflict with the Equal Protection clause, a classification that denies a benefit, causes harm, or imposes a burden must not be based on race. In that sense, the Constitution is color blind. But the Constitution is color conscious to prevent discrimination being perpetuated and to undo the effects of past discrimination. The criterion is the relevance of color to a legitimate governmental purpose." Wisdom turned to the cases before him. "Here race is relevant, because the governmental purpose is to offer Negroes equal educational opportunities. The means to that end, such as disestablishing segregation among students, distributing the better teachers equitably, equalizing facilities, selecting appropriate locations for schools, and avoiding resegregation, must necessarily be based on race. School officials have to know the racial composition of their school populations and the racial distribution within the school district." The courts and federal agencies, Wisdom concluded, "cannot measure good faith or progress without taking race into account." His words were echoed twelve years later in Justice Harry Blackmun's concurring opinion in the *Bakke* case, in which the Court wrestled with the divisive issue of affirmative action in medical school admissions. "In order to get beyond racism," Blackmun wrote in 1978, "we must first take account of race. There is no other way." Judge Wisdom saw no other way in 1966 to deal with the persistence of school segregation than to take into account the race of each student in a segregated district.

The Supreme Court declined to hear the appeals of the seven districts involved in the *Jefferson County* case, leaving Wisdom's ruling intact and implicitly approving his opinion. In May 1968, the justices took his blueprint and applied it to three cases that were consolidated under the caption of *Green v. New Kent County, Virginia*. All three involved "freedom of choice" plans that had resulted in the token integration of schools in rural areas of Virginia, Tennessee, and Arkansas. The lead case began in 1965 in New Kent County, some ten miles east of Richmond, Virginia. There was no residential segregation in the county, and its black and white residents lived mostly on small farms and in small towns. Before the 1964–65 school year, the county maintained two schools, each combining elementary and high school grades. Every one of the 552 white children attended the New Kent School on the county's eastern side, and all 739 black children were in the George W. Watkins School on the western side. Under pressure from federal education officials, the county school board reluctantly adopted in 1965 a "freedom of choice" plan that brought 111 black students into the New Kent School in 1966, but left the Watkins School with an all-black enrollment of 628 students. Not a single white child, even those who lived within walking distance of the Watkins School, had chosen to attend the county's "black" school. Charles C. Green, a black parent, had joined an NAACP lawsuit that urged the federal court to order the county the "freedom to choose" one of two integration plans: send all elementary students to one school and high school students to the other; or draw a line across the county that would send all children to the school on their side.

After a federal judge in Richmond, John Butzner, Jr., rejected both plans submitted by the NAACP and approved the county's "freedom of choice" plan, and the Fourth Circuit Court of Appeals upheld his ruling, the Supreme Court agreed to hear the NAACP's appeal. The justices also took appeals from black parents in Jackson, Tennessee, and Gould, Arkansas. In the city of Jackson, 80 percent of the black children attended all-black schools, while every white child had utilized the "freedom of choice" plan to pick schools in which blacks were a small minority. The town of Gould, Arkansas, operated two school complexes, each with an elementary and high school, just a few blocks apart. Under the district's "freedom of choice" plan, the formerly all-white Gould School had 300 white and 70 black students, while the Field School remained entirely black.

Lawyers in all three cases presented oral argument to the Supreme Court on April 3, 1968. Only four of the nine justices who had decided the second *Brown* case in 1955 took their seats on the bench that morning. Justice Stanley Reed, the last holdout in the *Brown* case, had retired in 1957; Harold Burton followed Reed into retirement the next year; Felix Frankfurter stepped down in

1962 and died three years later; and Tom Clark left the bench in 1967 to avoid any conflicts of interest after his son, Ramsey, became attorney general under President Lyndon Johnson. Their replacements moved the Court, under the genial but firm control of Chief Justice Warren, much closer to the positions of the NAACP and other civil rights groups. In fact, Thurgood Marshall, who left his job as the NAACP's general counsel in 1961 to sit on the Second Circuit Court of Appeals, and gave up that lifetime post in 1965 to serve as solicitor general, had been placed on the Supreme Court by President Johnson just six months before arguments in the *Green* cases.

The four other new members of the "Warren Court" included two nominees of President Dwight Eisenhower. William Brennan, Jr., who joined the Court in 1956, had served on the New Jersey supreme court and used his political skills and personal charm to become—during his thirty-four years on the bench—the leader of the Court's liberal bloc and the most influential justice of the twentieth century. Eisenhower once groused that placing Warren and Brennan on the Court were the two biggest mistakes he ever made. Potter Stewart, who became Eisenhower's final justice in 1958, stayed as close to the judicial center as he could, but never wavered in supporting civil rights claims. President John F. Kennedy placed Byron White on the Court in 1962; the former all-star college and professional football player had tackled civil rights crises in the Deep South as a Justice Department official and lined up with Warren and Brennan on segregation cases as a justice. Lyndon Johnson persuaded his old friend and political advisor, Abe Fortas, to leave a lucrative law practice for the Supreme Court in 1965; despite his fervent support of civil rights, Fortas resigned in disgrace in 1969 after reporters discovered that he had accepted legal payments from a convicted swindler with cases before the Supreme Court, and had been paid hefty fees for lightweight college lectures.

With these nine justices on the bench, lawyers for the school boards in the *Green* cases had virtually no chance of preserving their "freedom of choice" plans. At the beginning of oral arguments in the lead case from Virginia, the lawyer who represented New Kent County, Frederick T. Gray, quickly encountered skepticism from Chief Justice Warren:

"Has there ever been a white child admitted to the colored school?" Warren asked Gray.

"No white child has applied to go to the colored school, no sir," Gray replied. He boldly suggested that under the "freedom of choice" plan, no student in New Kent County could "stand before the bar of this Court and say: 'I am being denied my equal rights.'"

"If I was a Negro in Kent County, I would say so," Warren said, looking down at the white lawyer from a big Richmond firm.

"But, sir, by signing this piece of paper, you may go to either school that the County offers," Gray assured Warren, holding up a copy of the county's school-choice form.

"But the social and cultural influences, and the prejudices that have existed for centuries there, are by themselves written into that piece of paper," the Chief replied.

Gray's later response to a question from Justice White about the reasons black parents choose to keep their children in the black school pointed up the insight of Warren's remark. They make that choice, Gray asserted, "because in a rural Virginia county the colored school is the community center of colored activity. It's the hub of their social life. They don't want to lose that school. This is the heart of their social life and their community center; they go to that school because they want to go there." Gray ended with a rosy claim: "Race relations in New Kent County, Virginia, are excellent."

The lawyer for the Jackson, Tennessee, school board painted a similar picture of his city. "We're not a racist town," said Russell Rice. "We've had no trouble. We are not fighting the problem." Asked to explain why most black parents kept their children in the all-black school, Rice said that "in Jackson, Tennessee, we have a considerable group who have great pride in their race and in things that are Negro. And I think it's an erroneous conclusion to conclude that anything that is 'all-Negro,' per se, is bad." Rice offered his own rosy claim: "We now live together, play together, work together, go to school together, and we do extremely well in our community, in view of the uncontrolled forces that are now loose in this country." Justice Brennan was skeptical of Rice's portrayal of his town as a peaceful shelter from the racial storms that battered much of the South. If the Court approved a plan that divided Jackson into school zones, Brennan asked, would white parents whose children were assigned to the black school "move out rather than have their children go to that school?" Rice gave an honest answer. "I don't think there is any question about it, Your Honor."

Robert V. Light, who practiced in a prominent Little Rock firm, spoke for the school board of Gould, Arkansas, a town with a two-to-one black majority. He addressed the NAACP's proposal that Gould designate one of its two schools for elementary grades and the other for high school students. Under this plan, Light said, "you've got approximately two Negro students to one white student, in each of those schools. And I think that if we examine that situation with candor—and the time, I believe, has come for candor—that we know from experience that the white students will not continue to attend those schools." Light told the justices that "when the predominant culture becomes that of the Negro people in the community, the white people will flee from it. It's not acceptable to them. As I say, this is a difficult thing to speak about with candor, but I feel obligated to speak about it with candor."

Robert Light's candor did his case no more good than Frederick Gray's sugarcoated words. The Supreme Court handed down its decision in *Green v. New Kent County* on May 27, 1968, during a presidential campaign in which the Republican candidate, Richard Nixon, adopted a "southern strategy" of appealing to white voters who objected to the "meddling" of federal judges and officials in "their" schools. Nixon found that playing on white fears of school integration could become a winning electoral hand. The Supreme Court justices, well aware of the political currents swirling outside their chamber, did not trim their sails in striking down "freedom of choice" plans that had proved their "ineffectiveness as a tool of desegregation." Justice William Brennan wrote for a unanimous Court that school districts were "clearly charged with the affirmative duty to take whatever steps may be necessary to convert to a unitary system in which racial discrimination would be eliminated root and branch." The justices ordered New Kent County officials to "fashion steps which promise realistically to convert promptly to a system without a 'white' school and a 'Negro' school, but just schools." Conceding that a "freedom of choice" plan might pass constitutional muster, Brennan noted that "if there are reasonably available other ways, such as zoning, promising speedier and more effective conversion to a unitary, nonracial school system, 'freedom of choice' must be held unacceptable."

The Court directed its *Green* opinion to the federal judges across the South whose dockets were clogged with school cases. "The obligation of the district courts," Brennan wrote, "is to assess the effectiveness of a proposed plan in achieving desegregation." A school district must "establish that its proposed plan promises meaningful and immediate progress toward disestablishing state-imposed segregation," and judges "should retain jurisdiction until it is clear that state-imposed segregation has been completely removed." Brennan drove the final judicial nail into the coffin of "deliberate speed" as a delaying tactic. "The burden on a school board today," he wrote, "is to come forward with a plan that promises realistically to work, and promises realistically to work *now*."

Jack Greenberg, who argued for the black plaintiffs in the Arkansas case, later wrote that the *Green* decision was a "smashing victory" for the NAACP lawyers, who promptly filed motions in dozens of pending cases, asking judges to force foot-dragging school boards to eliminate segregation "root and branch." During the year that followed the *New Kent County* ruling, NAACP lawyers took on the toughest state in the Union, Mississippi, in which more than a dozen civil rights workers had been murdered by Klansmen and racist police officers. The federal district judges in Mississippi made no secret of their intense hostility toward integration, but the Fifth Circuit judges overruled their go-slow rulings and directly ordered compliance with the *Green* mandate of "integration now!"

During the summer of 1969, a judicial crisis erupted when the Fifth Circuit ordered the integration of thirty-three Mississippi school districts, beginning with the opening of schools in September. Senator John Stennis, the political baron who chaired the Armed Services Committee, reportedly threatened to hold up the Nixon administration's antiballistic missile system unless federal education officials persuaded the Fifth Circuit judges to delay the implementation of their orders for another year. Robert Finch, the secretary of health, education, and welfare, took the unprecedented step of sending a hand-delivered letter to the home of the Fifth Circuit's chief judge, John R. Brown, requesting that the Mississippi districts be granted a delay until December 1 in order to avoid "chaos, confusion, and a catastrophic educational setback." Justice Department lawyers appeared in court on August 25 to support the delay, and the Fifth Circuit granted the request on August 28.

Schools in the thirty-three Mississippi districts began classes in early September, still segregated, and NAACP lawyers asked the Supreme Court to hold an early hearing on their appeal of the Fifth Circuit order. The justices set the case, *Alexander v. Holmes County Board of Education*, for argument on October 23, and for the first time, Justice Department and NAACP lawyers sat on opposite sides of the courtroom. Jerris Leonard, who headed the Justice Department's civil rights division, argued that compliance with orders to begin "massive integration" in the middle of a school year would create serious administrative and logistical problems. Justice Hugo Black shot back: "Why not put [the plans] into effect and make arrangements afterward?" Leonard simply repeated Secretary Finch's predictions of chaos and confusion. Jack Greenberg, who argued for the NAACP, warned the justices that granting further delay would encourage southern districts to replace "segregation forever" with "litigation forever." Greenberg also reminded the justices that Medgar Evers had been a plaintiff in the case from Jackson, Mississippi, before his assassination. "The question in these cases," Greenberg concluded, "is whether the children in these districts, and indeed, the children in any school districts throughout our beloved land, are at last to learn that there is a supreme law of the land, binding upon children and parents, binding upon school boards, binding upon the states, binding upon the United States."

Six days after this argument, on October 29, 1969, the Supreme Court unanimously reversed the Fifth Circuit's delay order, remanding the case with a directive to issue new orders "effective immediately, declaring that each of the school districts here involved may no longer operate a dual school system based on race or color, and directing that they begin immediately to operate as unitary school systems within which no person is to be effectively excluded from any school because of race or color." The justices prefaced their order with a one-paragraph opinion that extended the *New Kent County* ruling to every remaining Jim Crow system in the South. The Fifth Circuit "should have denied all motions for additional time because continued operation of segregated schools under a standard of allowing 'all deliberate sped' for desegregation is no longer constitutionally permissible," the Court stated in an unsigned per curiam opinion.

Amazingly, not even the Supreme Court's clear and firm order budged the Fifth Circuit judges, who directed the Mississippi districts to integrate their faculties, staff, and activities by February 1, 1970, but allowed them to delay student integration until the following September. Once again, this time without oral argument, the Court slapped the wrists of the Fifth Circuit judges. Ruling on January 14, 1970, the Court directed that all school districts within the circuit must integrate their student bodies by February 1. Another one-paragraph, unsigned opinion, in cases from five states decided under the caption of *Carter v. West Feliciana Parish School Board*, chided the Fifth Circuit for having "misconstrued our holding" in the *Alexander* case.

The *Carter* decision exposed the growing rift within the Supreme Court over the issue of "integration now!" For the first time since the *Brown* cases were decided, fifteen years earlier, the justices did not all join a single opinion. The main reason for the division was that Chief Justice Earl Warren no longer headed the Court and herded his colleagues into line. Five months after Richard Nixon became president in January 1969, Warren retired. His successor, Warren Earl Burger, was a Minnesota native and Republican activist who had been named to the District of Columbia Circuit Court of Appeals in 1955. Burger staked out a "law and order" position in criminal cases, and President Nixon picked him as Chief Justice with the expectation that he would lead the Court to the right, cutting back if not toppling the Warren Court's expansion of individual rights. While Burger had little sympathy for federal power over state officials, he had no judicial record of hostility toward school integration.

Joined by Justice Potter Stewart, Burger wrote a "Memorandum" in the *Carter* case that read like a dissent to the unanimous opinion he had joined. Burger's objection to the Court's ruling was its "summary reversal without argument" of the Fifth Circuit's one-year delay of full integration in the Deep South districts. "That court is far more familiar than we with the various situations of these several school districts, some large, some small, some rural, and some metropolitan, and has exhibited responsibility and fidelity to the objectives of our holdings in school desegregation cases," Burger wrote. Although his memorandum did not generate any news coverage, NAACP lawyers and other civil rights activists who read it were now aware that the justices no longer formed ranks in the solid judicial phalanx that Earl Warren had commanded. Whether the Court would stand firm against segregation under Burger's leadership remained to be seen.

The Supreme Court's decisions in the *Alexander* and *Carter* cases, and its directives to the Fifth Circuit judges that school officials in Deep South districts must integrate their schools without any further delay, turned the "deliberate speed" formula into "full speed ahead." Nonetheless, the Court's rulings did not break the back of southern resistance to integrated schools, and Jack Greenberg's prediction that "litigation forever" would replace cries of "segregation forever" proved a good forecast. During the six months between September 1969 and February 1970, the Fifth Circuit handed down 166 orders in school cases, with scores of cases still pending on the court's docket. Legislators in southern states within the Fourth and Fifth appellate circuits, from Virginia through Texas, began passing laws designed to block or slow down school integration. Challenges to these laws added to the congestion of the district and circuit court dockets, and hearings in these cases dragged on for years.

As the number of "die-hard" school districts began to dwindle, many local officials accepted the inevitability of integration and began devising plans to dismantle their Jim Crow systems. Most of the plans adopted in larger districts, however, assigned students to their "neighborhood" school and mirrored in classrooms the residential segregation that divided most southern cities into separate black and white areas. In most cities, the vast majority of students would attend schools in which few, if any, children of other races sat beside them. Confronted with continued segregation, even without the help of such devices as "freedom of choice" plans, federal judges began considering other ways to accomplish the judicial goal of real integration. One of these remedies, designed to reduce the school segregation that resulted from the division of most cities into residential areas that were largely black or white, involved reassigning students from their "neighborhood" schools to those in other parts of the district, sometimes to schools that were miles away from their homes. The only feasible way in many districts to transport students to their new schools was to put them on buses. As the 1960s ended, federal judges began ordering school officials in both southern and northern cities to implement busing programs. And in many of these cities, white parents objected, loudly and sometimes violently. By the early 1970s, the yellow school bus had become a symbol to many whites of judicial "tyranny," and busing became the most volatile political issue of the decade.

CHAPTER 12

—

"Do Two Wrongs Make a Right?"

The case that made busing a heated national issue was filed in 1964 and was decided by the Supreme Court in 1971 under the caption of *Swann v. Charlotte-Mecklenburg Board of Education*. But it really began in September 1957, when a fifteen-year-old black girl named Dorothy Counts started classes at Harding High School in Charlotte, North Carolina. The state's largest city and its commercial hub, Charlotte is home to four-fifths of the residents of Mecklenburg County, which sits on the state's border with South Carolina. The county covers some five hundred square miles, and the suburban and rural areas that surround the city of Charlotte are virtually all white.

Dorothy Counts was one of four black students whose parents had decided to send them to formerly all-white schools, after Charlotte officials announced that students of either race could attend the school closest to their homes. Blacks made up about one-quarter of Charlotte's population in 1957, and most lived in the city's northeast section. Very few black students lived closer to an all-white school than to the black schools they formerly attended, and Dorothy's parents were among the few who took advantage of the "neighborhood school" policy to make their children pioneers in Charlotte's small first step toward integration. This new policy was initiated by Superintendent Elmer Garinger, who gathered his principals in the spring of 1957 and told them firmly that "desegregation is not only the law, it is also right."

Not all whites in Charlotte agreed with Garinger, and some four hundred of them—including many students at Harding High—clogged the street outside the school on the morning of September 4, 1957. Walking beside a family friend, Dorothy Counts was quickly surrounded by shouting protesters who spat on her and screamed racial epithets. Once she entered the school, Dorothy was pushed and baited by white students in the hallways and cafeteria. The next day, newspapers across the country and around the world carried photographs of Dorothy, in a black-and-white checkered dress with a long white bow and crinoline petticoats, looking straight ahead with grim determination as grinning whites, most of them boys in white T-shirts with their sleeves rolled up, swarmed around her.

After one week in Harding High, Dorothy gave up. Her locker had been ransacked, white teachers pointedly ignored her, racial slurs followed her down the hallways, a blackboard eraser hit her in the back, and several boys threw trash on her plate in the cafeteria. When her older brother came to pick Dorothy up, his windshield was shattered by a heavy mock orange, thrown at his car by a group of white boys who laughed and made obscene gestures. That night, after a meeting at Dorothy's home with Charlotte's black leaders, her father said, "Dot, I really don't think it's worth it." The next day, Herman Counts, a philosophy professor at all-black Johnson C. Smith University in Charlotte, read a statement to a press conference: "It is with compassion for our native land and love for our daughter Dorothy that we withdraw her as a student at Harding High School. As long as we felt she could be protected from bodily injury and insults within the school's walls and upon the school premises, we were willing to grant her desire to study at Harding. . . . Contrary to this optimistic view, her experiences at school on Wednesday disillusioned our faith and left us no alternative." Dorothy spent the rest of the school year in Philadelphia, living with family friends and attending a largely white high school. The other three black students at Harding also endured taunts and abuse, but they completed the school year. It was Dorothy's decision to leave the school, however, that dominated the news accounts of integration in Charlotte.

One of the people who read about Dorothy's ordeal in 1957 and saw the photograph of the gauntlet she faced at Harding High was Darius Swann, a Presbyterian missionary in Allabahad, India. Those images made a lasting impression on Swann, who had studied under Herman Counts in college and greatly admired his former professor. Swann and his wife, Vera, returned to Charlotte in 1964 with their two young children. That fall, they took their six-year-old son, James, to the school nearest their home. Seversville Elementary had several black children in its first-grade classroom, and the Swanns were pleased that James would be attending an integrated school. But they discovered, through a note James brought home after his first day at Seversville, that he had been assigned to an all-black school, Biddleville Elementary. The Swanns learned that their home was located in an attendance district carved out to keep all but a few black children out of Seversville. Darius wrote a letter to the Charlotte-Mecklenburg board of education: "James attended Seversville briefly on August 31 and he liked the school and its atmosphere. We did also and feel that this is where we would like him to be." Swann reminded the board that white students were allowed to transfer out of integrated schools, but that black students could not transfer into these schools. "We hold that the law should be equally binding on both races," Swann wrote. "Otherwise the law is discriminatory."

After the school board rejected their request to transfer James back to the Seversville school, the Swanns contacted Julius Chambers, a young black lawyer who had come to Charlotte in 1964 after completing law school at the University of North Carolina. Chambers had then spent a year in New York with the NAACP Legal Defense Fund, working under the tutelage of Jack Greenberg, who had succeeded Thurgood Marshall as its chief counsel in 1961, when President John F. Kennedy nominated Marshall to the federal Court of Appeals for the Second Circuit, which sat in New York City and was considered second only to the Supreme Court in power and prestige. After leaving New York, Chambers began a practice in Charlotte and immediately began looking for plaintiffs to challenge the "minority-to-majority" transfer policy of the Charlotte-Mecklenburg school district. The city and the surrounding county had merged their districts in 1960, and the combined district in 1964 had more than a hundred schools that housed 84,000 students, about 24,000 of them black.

Julius Chambers filed a lawsuit in federal court in January 1965, claiming that the "minority-to-majority" transfer policy was designed to allow white students who lived closest to a formerly all-black school to escape from integration. The lead plaintiff in the suit was Darius Swann, who had been outraged by the ordeal suffered by Dorothy Counts when integration first began in Charlotte. The complaint that Chambers drafted noted that 88 of the district's 109 schools remained segregated after seven years of token integration—57 had only white students and 31 were all black. Only 6 of the 21 "integrated" schools had more than a dozen black students, and just 11 white children attended a largely black school.

The *Swann* case first came before District Judge Braxton Craven in 1965. Although most lawyers considered him thoughtful and fair, Craven displayed little interest in the case, and held just one brief hearing before he issued a ruling on July 14, the day after the school board's lawyer told the judge that the board was committed to the "ultimate" ending of segregation in the district's schools. Yet, the board had adopted a desegregation plan that retained neighborhood school zoning, and allowed "freedom of choice" transfers for parents who wanted their children out of schools in which their race was the minority. During the hearing, Julius Chambers noted that the board's plan left more than 90 percent of the district's black children in all-black schools. In his brief order, Judge Craven approved the board's plan without change, except for ordering a quicker pace for faculty and staff desegregation. "As a general proposition," Craven wrote, "it is undoubtedly true that one could sit down with the purpose in mind to change [district] lines in order to increase the mixing of the races and accomplish that with some degree of success. I know of no such duty upon either the school board or the district court." The board's plan, of course, did virtually nothing to "increase the mixing of the races" in schools that kept the Jim Crow system intact.

Julius Chambers filed an appeal from Judge Craven's decision, arguing that his decision was "patently erroneous." The Fourth Circuit Court of Appeals upheld the ruling in October 1966, and Chambers decided that a further appeal to the Supreme Court would be futile. Shortly after the Court struck down "freedom of choice" plans in the *Green v. New Kent County* case in 1968, however, Chambers went back to federal court and asked for "further relief" to bring about the "root and branch" elimination of segregation the Supreme Court had ordered in that case. Judge Craven had been elevated to the Fourth Circuit bench in 1968, and Chambers was encouraged that the revived *Swann* case was now before James McMillan, a Harvard Law School graduate who had voted against the exclusion of black lawyers from the North Carolina bar association and served on the board of the Charlotte legal aid society.

Judge McMillan took the case seriously and held extensive hearings in March 1969. His first opinion, issued on April 23, noted that segregation in the Charlotte-Mecklenburg schools had declined since Judge Craven's ruling in 1965, but "approximately 14,000 of the 24,000 Negro students still attend schools that are all black, or very nearly all black, and most of the 24,000 have no white teachers." The board's "neighborhood" zoning plan, McMillan wrote, "superimposed on an urban population where Negro residents have become concentrated almost entirely in one quadrant of a city of 270,000, is racially discriminatory." Most of Charlotte's black residents lived in the city's northeast section, and the school board had drawn its attendance zones precisely on the boundaries of the black residential area. McMillan ordered the board to submit a "positive plan" to integrate the schools, adding that it was "free to consider all known ways of desegregation, including busing." He pointedly noted that white parents had not objected when buses were used to maintain segregation. "There is no reason except emotion," he wrote, "why school buses can not be used by the Board to provide the flexibility and economy necessary to desegregate the schools."

Judge McMillan had underestimated the emotion his decision would unleash among whites in Charlotte. William E. Poe, the school board chairman, declared that he was "unequivocally" opposed to busing, and his speeches at civic-group meetings around the city spurred the listeners to organize the Concerned Parents Association, which plastered NO FORCED BUSING bumper stickers on thousands of cars and gathered 67,355 signatures on an antibusing petition that was delivered to the White House. Busing opponents picketed McMillan's home, and he received death threats over the phone and in the mail. Critics overlooked the fact that McMillan had not actually ordered any busing, pending the school board's submission of a plan to accomplish real integration. But the board, led by Poe, dragged its feet until McMillan appointed an expert, Dr. Robert Finger of Rhode Island College, to fashion an integration plan that would produce as closely as possible in each school the district-wide percentages of 79 white and 21 black students. The "Finger Plan" did not substantially change the board's revision of junior and senior high attendance zones, which put black and white students in every school, but kept the black enrollment below 40 percent in each one. An unspoken assumption behind this plan was that few white parents would send their children to a majority-black school, and that a "tipping point" of 40 percent black students became the upper limit of white tolerance.

The Finger Plan departed substantially from the board's proposal for integrating the district's seventy-six elementary schools, which largely retained neighborhood school zoning. His plan "grouped" inner-city black schools with outlying white schools, producing student bodies that ranged from 9 to 38 percent black. The district already bused 23,000 children, about a third of all students; under the Finger Plan, black students in grades one through four would be bused to outlying white schools, and white students in the fifth and sixth grades would ride buses to the inner-city black schools. The Finger Plan would put an additional 13,000 children, most from the grade schools, onto buses. Ruling on February 5, 1970, Judge McMillan rejected the board's neighborhood school proposal and adopted the Finger Plan. Citing the Supreme Court ruling in *Alexander v. Holmes County,* McMillan ordered the board to implement the Finger Plan by April 1, a deadline that sent shock waves through the white community. Leaders of the Concerned Parents Association stepped up their protests, and the board's lawyers filed an appeal with the Fourth Circuit Court of Appeals in Richmond. One of the NAACP lawyers received a blunt message from Judge Braxton Craven, who now sat on the appellate court but recused himself from further proceedings in the *Swann* case. Speaking for his fellow judges, Craven said: "You guys have led your friend McMillan out on a limb. And we're about to cut it off behind him."

Craven was right. The Fourth Circuit issued a stay of McMillan's order, directing him to hold new hearings and apply a "test of reasonableness" to the busing of grade school children. McMillan conducted the hearings and allowed school board members to vent their hostility to busing, but he refused to budge from the Finger Plan and reinstated his original order on August 7, 1970, with a new deadline of September 9, when schools were scheduled to open in the Charlotte-Mecklenburg district. Reeling from shock, the board's lawyers flew to Washington and asked Chief Justice Warren Burger for a stay of McMillan's order. But he refused to intervene, setting the *Swann* case for argument on October 12. On the morning of September 9, some 525 school buses—including almost 200 that had been hurriedly borrowed from other districts across the state—began rolling along their new routes, carrying thousands of black and white children to new schools. At 8:10 that morning, a bomb scare forced the early dismissal of South Mecklenburg High School. It was the first of six that day, and the bomb scares continued for three months. The Concerned Parents Association had called for a boycott, and more than three thousand white children left the public schools for good, swelling the enrollment of private schools that had few, if any, black students. Community leaders appealed for calm, but tension remained high as lawyers on both sides prepared for a showdown in the Supreme Court.

Seven of the justices who heard the oral arguments in the *Swann* case had joined the Court after its *Brown* decisions. The Court's junior member, Justice Harry Blackmun, had been President Nixon's third choice for the seat vacated by Abe Fortas, who had resigned in disgrace in 1969. Blackmun had been tapped for the Court after the Senate rejected Nixon's first two nominees, both federal judges from the South whom the president had lauded as "strict constructionists." The first candidate, Harrold Carswell, had defended "white supremacy" in political speeches, while the second, Clement Haynesworth, had failed to disclose stock holdings in companies with cases before his court. Nixon reluctantly abandoned his "southern strategy" and named Blackmun, a Minnesota native who served on the federal appellate bench, to the Court as a way of placating Republican moderates who had voted against Carswell and Haynesworth. Most observers predicted that Blackmun, a boyhood friend of Warren Burger, would join his "Minnesota twin" in hewing to the conservative line that Nixon expected the Court to follow.

The oral arguments in *Swann* began on a sour note for the school board's lawyer, William Waggoner, who told the justices he would discuss the issue of racial balance in the district's schools, leaving the question of busing to his colleague, Benjamin Horack. Justice Thurgood Marshall quickly knocked Waggoner off balance, demanding to know if Charlotte had bused "children of tender age" before the 1970 school year. Marshall explained to a puzzled Waggoner that he meant children in grade schools.

"They were busing children of tender age," Waggoner conceded.

"For the purpose of maintaining segregation?" Marshall continued.

"No, sir."

"For what other reason?" Marshall pressed.

"They were bused to get them to school," Waggoner answered, trying to duck the question..

"Did they ever pass a colored school on the way?" Marshall asked.

"We bused white children past black schools, and black children past white schools," Wagonner admitted. "This is incontrovertible."

Marshall landed the punch he had set up with his previous jabs. "So what is wrong with busing them for the purpose of integrating?"

Waggoner countered weakly. "Do two wrongs make a right?"

"Is that the only answer?" Marshall asked.

The board's lawyer could not find a better answer. "I think so, yes, sir," he concluded lamely.

In contrast to Waggoner, who seemed unnerved by Marshall's interrogation, Julius Chambers "was absolutely unflappable; brilliant," one reporter later wrote, "as if he had rehearsed his answers before he ever came in the room—which in fact he had." Chambers, facing the justices for the first time at the age of thirty-four, had endured two "woodshed" sessions before his argument, at both Howard and Columbia law schools. His major point was that the Charlotte school board had for years drawn the boundaries of school attendance zones to match precisely the segregated housing patterns in the city, patterns which had been shaped by decades of "state action" in zoning laws, urban renewal programs, and the placement of public housing in the city's black section. Because of these factors, Chambers argued, the Jim Crow schools that existed in Charlotte before the *Brown* decision were perpetuated by the neighborhood school policy and "freedom of choice" plan that the school board adopted to keep black and white children in separate schools. "It would be a rejection of the faith that black children and parents have had in *Brown*, the hope of eventually obtaining a desegregated education, for this Court now to reverse the decision of the District Court and now adopt, sixteen years after *Brown*, a test that would sanction the continued operation of racially segregated schools."

The justices gathered in their conference room to discuss the *Swann* case on October 17, 1970. They all recognized that their decision might have the greatest impact on America's schools since *Brown*, largely because the connection between "state action" in creating and maintaining segregated residential patterns and the segregation that resulted from "neighborhood school" policies was not limited to southern cities like Charlotte. All of the Court's earlier school cases had come from states in which schools had been segregated by law, known to lawyers as "de jure" segregation. But if the Court accepted the argument of Julius Chambers, northern cities in which black ghettos had been created by "state action" in zoning, public housing placement, and urban renewal programs could be challenged for the "de facto" segregation of their schools. Cities like Chicago, Philadelphia, Detroit, and scores of smaller northern cities might become targets for lawsuits and demands that students be bused to achieve the racial balance that Judge McMillan had ordered in Charlotte.

Faced with the prospect of "litigation everywhere," to paraphrase Jack Greenberg, the justices at first voted six-to-three to reverse McMillan and send the *Swann* case back for another round of hearings. After lengthy debate and this initial vote, however, the justices agreed that each would draft an opinion and circulate it to the others. Nina Totenberg, the enterprising reporter who uncovered the backstage maneuvers that preceded the Court's final decision, described the shifting events. "Justice Harlan's was said to have been the toughest pro-busing opinion," she wrote of the first round of drafts. "Then several justices had second thoughts and shifted their votes. Soon the vote was six to three for busing, with Burger, Blackmun, and Black dissenting." But the votes kept shifting as the justices read each other's draft opinions. "Eventually, the three capitulated—Black being the last holdout," Totenberg wrote. "And Burger, who had envisioned himself writing the opinion against busing, ended up writing the opinion for it and incorporating much of the language from the drafts of the more liberal justices." Totenberg's sources told her that Burger decided that he wanted to be seen as leading the Court on this controversial issue, rather than wasting his breath in dissent.

The Chief Justice looked and sounded like the man in charge when he announced the Court's unanimous decision on April 20, 1971, six months after the oral arguments and the judicial politicking that had followed. Burger opened his opinion with language that approvingly quoted the Court's "liberal" decisions in the *Alexander, Griffin,* and *Green* cases. "If school authorities fail in their affirmative obligations under these holdings," Burger stated, "judicial authority may be invoked. Once a right and a violation have been shown, the scope of a district court's equitable powers to remedy past wrongs is broad, for breadth and flexibility are inherent in equitable remedies." This bow to Judge McMillan and his lower-court colleagues, however, was all the deference the Chief Justice felt inclined to show. Three times in the pages that followed, Burger pointedly noted that "judicial powers may be exercised only on the basis of a constitutional violation." Without directly addressing the argument of Julius Chambers that "state action" in creating residential segregation justified the use of busing to achieve greater racial balance in schools, Burger reminded district judges to keep their focus on the actions of school officials. "We do not reach in this case the question whether a showing that school segregation is a consequence of other types of state action, without any discriminatory action by the school authorities, is a constitutional violation requiring remedial action by a school desegregation decree," Burger wrote. "Our objective in dealing with the issues presented by these cases is to see that school authorities exclude no pupil of a racial minority from any school, directly or indirectly, on account of race," he continued; "it does not and cannot embrace all the problems of racial prejudice, even when those problems contribute to disproportionate racial concentrations in some schools."

Burger followed these cautionary words with even more limiting language. It was "clear" to him that "the existence of some small number of one-race, or virtually one-race, schools within a district is not in and of itself the mark of a system that still practices segregation by law." District judges should "scrutinize such schools," Burger added, but districts could retain one-race schools if they met "the burden of showing that such school assignments are genuinely nondiscriminatory."

When he reached the volatile issue of busing, the Chief Justice tried hard to minimize the impact of Judge McMillan's order. "Bus transportation has been an integral part of the public education system for years," Burger wrote, adding that in 1969–70, some eighteen million children across the country were bused to school, some 39 percent of the total. He stressed that under McMillan's decree, children would be picked up at schools near their homes and bused directly to their new schools. The trips for grade-school children would average seven miles and take no longer than thirty-five minutes. "This system compares favorably with the transportation plan previously operated in Charlotte under which each day 23,600 students on all grade levels were transported an average of 15 miles one way for an average trip requiring over an hour," Burger wrote. "In these circumstances, we find no basis for holding that the local school authorities may not be required to employ bus transportation as one tool of school desegregation."

Once a school district has achieved "full compliance" with the Court's decisions and has become a "unitary" system, Burger continued, the federal courts should withdraw from their supervisory roles. "Neither school authorities nor district courts are constitutionally required to make year-by-year adjustments of the racial composition of student bodies once the affirmative duty to desegregate has been accomplished and racial discrimination through officials action is eliminated from the system." Absent "a showing that either school authorities or some other agency of the State has deliberately attempted to fix or alter demographic patterns to affect the racial composition of the schools," Burger concluded, "further intervention by a district court should not be necessary."

The Chief Justice wrote his opinion for a small audience of federal district judges, placing them on notice that all-black schools were not necessarily unlawful and that districts in "full compliance" with judicial orders could escape further supervision, even if their schools became resegregated through "white flight" to the suburbs. Burger's words offered some hope to those southerners who found its approval of busing an "appalling" development. The conservative Richmond *Times-Dispatch*, which had defended the "massive resistance" campaign in Virginia, was relieved that the *Swann* decision "may not be as harsh and unyielding as a first reading indicated. Here and there, one can find a phrase that lifts the spirits, that kindles hope for a restoration of sanity and stability to the pupil assignment systems of the South's public schools."

It was hardly surprising that the *Swann* decision found little support among white southerners, who had long resented the "meddling" of federal courts in their schools. Southern politicians, from race-baiting demagogues like Governor George Wallace of Alabama to racial "moderates" like Senator Sam Ervin, had long courted white voters by denouncing the Supreme Court. Allowing black students into formerly all-white schools was bad enough for segregationists, but the remedy of busing went too far, evoking fears of terrified white children being shoved into buses and driven miles from their homes, unloaded in crime-ridden black ghettos and marched into decaying black schools. The word "busing" soon became an epithet in the American political lexicon, hardly ever used without the adjective "forced" to make the concept even more forbidding and frightening.. However unrealistic such fears may have struck those who supported busing, they were real to many white parents, in both the North and South. Mrs. Millie Hobbs of Mobile, Alabama, where more than forty thousand students were scheduled to ride buses to school in September 1971, told a reporter of a niece who had been assigned to a school in the black ghetto: "We work all our life trying to get children out of that, into a decent area. Then about the time we think we've got it made— wham!—they stick you right back into it."

Millie Hobbs was one of millions of white parents—and more important, white voters, many of them lifelong Democrats—whose opposition to "forced busing" was echoed from the "bully pulpit" of the White House. Ten days after the Court handed down its *Swann* decision, President Richard Nixon gave his reaction at a press conference. "I do not believe that busing to achieve racial balance is in the interests of better education," he said. But the president tempered his criticism of busing with assurances that his administration would "comply with the Court" in carrying out orders that affected federal agencies. He reminded the nation that "nobody, including the President of the United States, is above the law as it is finally determined by the Supreme Court of the United States."

President Nixon tried hard to avoid the kind of Court-bashing that George Wallace had exploited so effectively in courting white voters. At his first White House press conference in February 1969, Nixon had stood firmly behind the Court: "As far as school segregation is concerned, I support the law of the land. I believe that funds should be denied to those districts that continue to perpetuate segregation." He later expressed "my personal belief" that the Court's decision in the *Brown* case "was right in both constitutional and human terms." However sincere his professions, Nixon nonetheless understood the partisan benefits of taking a "go-slow" position on school desegregation. After initially backing the federal government's power to cut off education funds to southern districts that resisted court orders, he shifted his position in September 1969 and ordered that funds be withheld only when "absolutely necessary" to force compliance. When a reporter bluntly asked him if his new position "amounts to an effort to build a party base for the Republicans in the South," Nixon sidestepped the question, but took the opening to distance himself from both sides on this volatile issue. "There are those who want instant integration and those who want segregation forever," he replied. "I believe that we need to have a middle course between those two extremes."

Even before the *Swann* case reached the Supreme Court, Nixon spoke out repeatedly against busing. In March 1970, he warned in a public statement on "Desegregation of Elementary and Secondary Schools" that "several recent decisions of lower courts have raised widespread fears that the Nation might face a massive disruption of public education: that wholesale compulsory busing may be ordered and the neighborhood school virtually doomed." One of the decisions that prompted Nixon's statement was Judge McMillan's order of February 1970 that busing would begin that fall in the Charlotte-Mecklenburg district. That same month, District Judge Damon Keith ruled that school officials in Pontiac, Michigan, had intentionally segregated the city's schools and ordered that a third of the district's 24,000 students be bused to schools outside their neighborhoods to integrate Pontiac's elementary and junior high schools. This ruling by a black judge in Detroit inflamed many white residents of Pontiac, a blue-collar city of 70,000 in which most of the nation's school buses were built. Pontiac was one of the working-class northern cities in which the Ku Klux Klan had tried but failed in the 1920s to keep blacks who moved north to seek factory jobs from living and working, but racial hostility remained a half-century later.

In response to these and other busing orders from federal judges, President Nixon directed that "transportation of pupils beyond normal geographic school zones for the purpose of achieving racial balance will not be required" by any federal program. While stumping for Republican candidates in the November 1970 elections, Nixon visited North Carolina to restate his opposition to "the use of busing solely for the purpose of achieving racial balance" in the schools. "That is our position," he assured Tarheel voters. "We will continue to hold to that position until or unless there is any other finding by the courts."

The Supreme Court's April 1971 ruling in *Swann* gave federal district judges a green light to order busing in school districts across the country, subject to Chief Justice Burger's cautionary words about finding a "constitutional violation" by school officials in maintaining a segregated system. Lawyers for the NAACP had previously filed lawsuits against several northern districts, claiming that school board members and other public officials had taken actions that resulted in de jure segregation, even though state laws prohibited racial separation of students. President Nixon, himself a lawyer, had argued in 1970 that there was a "fundamental distinction between so-called de jure and de facto segregation," and that "de facto segregation results from residential housing patterns and does not violate the Constitution." What the NAACP lawyers showed through school board records and those of other public agencies, in several northern cases, was that segregated housing and segregated schools both resulted from official actions and were part of the same discriminatory pattern in most cities. The distinction between de facto and de jure segregation struck many federal judges as artificial, and they issued a spate of busing orders in the months after the *Swann* decision. When the new school year began in September 1971, more than half a million students in dozens of cities were assigned to schools outside their neighborhoods, as "busing for racial balance" threatened to unbalance American society.

Even before the fleets of yellow buses were scheduled to begin their daily trips, violence erupted. In Pontiac, Michigan, ten buses went up in flames when dynamite bombs shattered their gas tanks. On Labor Day, thousands of whites marched through downtown Pontiac in a "funeral procession" for a cardboard school bus. When schools opened the next day, police arrested nine white mothers who had chained themselves to the gates of the school bus yard. Other whites screamed "Niggers go home" to black children who were escorted by state troopers from the buses into their new schools. The violence over school integration in Pontiac was the worst in any American city since screaming mobs filled the streets around Central High in Little Rock, Arkansas, in 1957. FBI agents arrested Robert Miles, a former Grand Dragon of the Michigan Klan, and five other men for bombing the city's school buses, and the violence in Pontiac subsided, although tension remained high in the city's schools..

Pontiac was just one of several dozen cities in which the opening of schools in 1971 provoked resistance to busing. Protesters poured sand into the gas tanks of nineteen buses in Wilmington, North Carolina. White parents organized boycotts of integrated schools in Jacksonville, Florida, and several other southern communities. Fights between black and white students broke out in Austin, Texas. Yet, within a month of the violence in Pontiac and the picketing and boycotts in other communities, school buses were picking up and dropping off children who had been assigned to ride them by court orders with little disruption. As schools quieted down and protests in the streets ended, the political upheaval over busing grew more heated, however. Politicians in both parties got an earful at town meetings, and the offices in the Capitol were inundated by letters from outraged white voters. A national Gallup poll, taken a month after the Pontiac bus bombings in 1971, showed that opposition to busing was not limited to the South. Some 82 percent of southern respondents opposed "the busing of Negro and white children from one school district to another," while the percentages of those in the East, Midwest, and West who opposed busing ranged from 71 to 77. Overall, more than three-fourths of those polled across the nation stated their opposition to busing.

The political impact of constituent pressure could be seen in the sudden conversion of northern liberal Democrats in Congress from staunch supporters of desegregation into anti-busing crusaders. Perhaps the most notable convert was Representative James G. O'Hara, whose district in the Detroit suburbs had so few Republicans that he had never faced a serious challenge at the polls. O'Hara had served for years as a House floor leader in fights against efforts to put anti-busing provisions in appropriations bills. But in September 1971, two weeks after the Pontiac uproar, a federal district judge in Detroit, Stephen Roth, issued an order that parts of O'Hara's district be included in a three-county, "metropolitan" plan to desegregate schools in Detroit. Judge Roth had only ordered that Detroit and suburban school officials submit plans to bring about racial balance between largely black Detroit schools and virtually all-white suburban districts. Many whites, however, feared that Roth would later order busing that would send white children into Detroit and blacks into suburban schools. Representative O'Hara promptly assured his constituents that he would "do whatever is necessary by way of further legislation or a constitutional amendment to prevent implementation of [desegregation orders] by cross-district busing."

Delighted that O'Hara and other northern liberals had joined their camp, anti-busing leaders in Congress won their first victory in November 1971, when the House overwhelmingly approved an amendment to a higher education bill, offered by Michigan Republican William Broomfield, which would postpone the implementation of any federal court order requiring busing until all judicial appeals had been exhausted. Not only did Broomfield's amendment pass by a 235-to-126 margin, but more than fifty northern Democrats voted in favor, including such liberals as Otis Pike and James Scheuer of New York, Spark Matsunaga of Hawaii, and Edith Green of Oregon.

James O'Hara and Edith Green, in fact, became the leaders of House efforts to block all judicial busing orders, putting them in the company of conservative Republicans and die-hard Southern Democratic segregationists. For this act of political apostasy, O'Hara and Green were excoriated by fellow Democrats who supported busing as a remedy for entrenched school segregation. Ronald V. Dellums, a black House member from Berkeley, California, heaped scorn on those who feared they would lose their seats if they failed to oppose busing. Dellums accused those who voted for anti-busing measures of "following the paranoia, irrationality, and racism of millions of people in this country." The angry congressman pointed his finger at O'Hara, Green, and those other liberal Democrats who had deserted the civil rights coalition: "We do not need you if you cannot come through in the clutch." Dellums addressed those of his colleagues who privately confessed their fears that racist challengers would replace them if they supported busing. "Send us some real racists and then we will know what we are dealing with," Dellums challenged. The schism within the Democratic party over busing came just a year before the presidential and congressional elections in November 1972, and no politician looked forward to exploiting the busing issue with more anticipation than Richard Nixon.

The House vote to block judicial busing orders was, in truth, more of a symbolic gesture of defiance than a real threat to stop buses from running. Even with substantial margins for such "court-curbing" bills in the House, there were enough senators who opposed the anti-busing bills to block them with filibusters. But the prospect of Senate defeat did not deter President Nixon from sending Congress two bills in March 1972. The first, with the appealing title of the Equal Educational Opportunities Act, would have barred any busing except to the closest or next closest schools to a student's home. The other, more honestly titled the Student Transportation Moratorium Act, would have blocked any new judicial busing orders until July 1973 or passage of the Equal Educational Opportunities Act, whichever came first.

The president made a nationally televised speech on March 16, 1972, to announce and promote his anti-busing bills. "My own position is well known," he began. "I am opposed to busing for the purpose of achieving racial balance in our schools. I have spoken out against busing scores of times over many years." The problem was urgent, Nixon went on, because "recent decisions of the lower federal courts have gone too far in ordering massive busing to achieve racial balance." Those rulings "have left in their wake confusion and contradiction in the law; anger, fear, and turmoil in local communities; and, worst of all, agonized concern among hundreds of thousands of parents for the education and the safety of their children who have been forced by court order to be bused miles away from their neighborhood schools." He spoke directly to parents who were "burdened with new worries about their children's safety on the road and in the neighborhoods far from home." Nixon did not have to say that the neighborhoods he meant were those in black ghettos, but his white audience understood him clearly. Stoking the fears of white parents for their children's safety verged on playing the race card in this high-stakes political game, but Nixon disavowed any appeal to "the extremists on the one side who oppose busing for the wrong reasons," those of racial animus. His targets, he said, were "the extreme social planners on the other side who insist on more busing, even at the cost of better education."

Hearings on the Nixon administration's anti-busing bills began in March 1972, with Elliot Richardson, secretary of health, education, and welfare, as the lead witness before both Senate and House committees. Coming from the liberal wing of the GOP, the patrician Richardson had little stomach for the more strident anti-busing members of his party, and he chose his words carefully in supporting the Nixon bills, using the loaded term "busing" as little as possible. "We must downgrade our reliance on the transportation of students between schools or school systems as our primary tool to achieve equal educational opportunity," he told the Senate panel. "Transportation can never do the whole job. It can never reach the core areas of our cities where educational deprivation is the greatest."

One of the witnesses who followed Richardson was Mrs. James Farrell, a housewife from Pine Bluff, Arkansas. Her blunt testimony showed no deference to the senators: "The elite, such as yourselves, can sit back and say, 'I can afford the best for my child so I will send him to a private school and so to hell with busing.' But gentlemen, it is because of the sweat off our backs that pay your salaries that you can speak such grand phrases; but I want you to know that John Q. Citizen is sick and tired of being taken for granted. We pay taxes to support our schools and we are entitled to say what takes place in them." Mrs. Farrell was just the kind of person that President Nixon hoped would take out their anger at the "limousine liberals" who supported busing when they voted in November.

Several witnesses before the congressional panels, including busing opponents, warned that bills designed to curb the remedial powers of federal courts—even if they passed both houses of Congress by wide margins—ran the risk of being declared unconstitutional by judges who resented any intrusion on their turf. Earlier efforts to limit the jurisdiction of federal courts over cases involving legislative reapportionment and school prayer through constitutional amendment had died in Congress because of concerns over the separation of powers, which the courts jealously guarded from congressional incursion. The only sure way to stop further busing was through a constitutional amendment, although this route took longer and required the approval of two-thirds of each house of Congress and three-fourths of the state legislatures. Earlier that year, the Equal Rights Amendment to ban discrimination against women had been passed by Congress after years of acrimonious debate and sent to the states, where it later died, two states short of ratification. In contrast, an amendment to lower the voting age to eighteen had sailed through Congress in 1971 and had been ratified within months.

Not all congressional busing foes supported a constitutional amendment, but more than fifty House members introduced proposed amendments. The version with the most sponsors had been drafted by Representative Norman Lent, an upstate New York Republican. His resolution stated: "No public school student shall, because of his race, creed or color, be assigned to or required to attend a particular school." Lent's proposal did not include the word *busing*, and could be read broadly to bar any pupil assignment plan based on race, even if students were not bused. Hearings on the various anti-busing amendments by the House Judiciary Committee began in March 1972 and stretched through August. Lent admitted in his testimony that his amendment was designed to "reverse the *Swann* decision" of the Supreme Court. "If it was wrong in 1954 to assign a black child to a particular school on the basis of race, it is just as wrong to do the same thing to other children in 1972. "This is 'Jim Crowism' in reverse, as practiced by our courts." Lent argued.

Even committee members of his own party expressed doubts about Lent's proposal. Robert McClory of Illinois asked Lent if his bill would "modify the Fourteenth Amendment." Lent conceded the point: "Yes. It would alter its effect. It would balance the Equal Protection clause against the student's right to attend the neighborhood school." McClory asked Lent why he opposed legislative efforts to limit or prohibit busing. Lent replied that "the federal courts will ignore statutes that come into conflict with the Fourteenth Amendment. Only a further amendment of the Constitution will do what is needed."

The political maneuvering over the anti-busing amendment grew intense as the November elections approached. Judiciary chairman Emanuel Celler, a New York City Democrat, made no bones of his opposition to any amendment, and he refused to schedule a committee vote on Lent's proposal. The only way around Celler's committee was for the amendment's supporters to persuade a majority of House members—218 of the 435 representatives—to sign a "discharge petition" that would remove the amendment from Celler's grasp and bring it directly to the House floor. Busing foes came up short, however, gathering only 164 signatures on their petition. This setback did not deter them, and persuaded the southern-dominated Rules Committee, chaired by William Colmer of Mississippi, to send the amendment to the House floor. Celler responded by employing his mastery of House rules to keep the proposed amendment from a vote before the November elections. While this congressional chess game was being played out, President Nixon turned Celler's parliamentary moves against the Democrats, painting them as the "busing party" in campaign speeches across the country.

Just before the Republican National Convention, Judge Stephen Roth in Detroit handed Nixon ammunition for his anti-busing crusade, ruling in June 1972 that school segregation in Detroit must be remedied by a "metropolitan" plan under which white students in fifty-three suburban school districts in the three-county area around Detroit would be bused into largely black city schools, with black students riding buses to the suburbs. "The Detroit case," Nixon complained, "is perhaps the most flagrant example that we have of all the busing decisions. . . . It completely rejects the neighborhood school concept. It requires massive busing among fifty-three different school districts, including the busing of kindergarten children, up to an hour and a half a day." The president urged Congress to "deal with problems like the one in Detroit" by passing his anti-busing bills.

The House of Representatives heeded Nixon's call to action. On August 18, an amended version of his Equal Educational Opportunities Act was adopted by a lopsided vote of 283 to 103, although the companion Student Transportation Moratorium Act died in both the House and Senate committees. The House adopted an amendment offered by Edith Green of Oregon, barring the busing of students to schools other than the one closest or next closest to their homes, rejecting an amendment by James O'Hara of Michigan to limit busing to the closest school. Busing opponents ran into a red light, however, in the Senate, where the Nixon bill never came to a vote. The president expressed his frustration at a press conference on October 5: "If we cannot get Congress to act on the legislative front, then we would have to move on the constitutional amendment front." But the Congress, despite the rounds of hearings and torrents of rhetoric about constitutional amendments, was not willing to move at all before the election. Nixon's frustration at congressional inaction was tempered by his huge lead in the polls, which turned into a forty-nine-state rout of his hapless Democratic opponent, Senator George McGovern of South Dakota, who evaded the busing issue during his campaign. After the election, the battle over busing moved from the Capitol to the courtroom, as judges in the trenches of federal district courts struggled to define the limits of the Supreme Court's ruling in the *Swann* case.

CHAPTER 13

"Two Cities—One White, the Other Black"

he Supreme Court's approval of busing as a remedy for
school segregation lit a fuse that led to protests—most of
them noisy and some of them violent—in cities across the
country. Resistance to busing by white parents had first emerged in
medium-sized cities like Pontiac, Michigan, and Knoxville, Tennessee, in which black students were a minority in the school population. Whether the busing conflict would spread to big cities in
which the schools were heavily black was a question that troubled
many Americans, including civil rights activists who had not anticipated the explosive reaction in Pontiac. The Supreme Court's decision in the *Swann* case had not addressed the issue of whether
federal district judges could order busing across school district lines,
as the only feasible method of creating greater "racial balance" in
the metropolitan areas around big cities. This was a question most
likely to arise in a northern city, in which the growth of black ghettos during the 1950s and '60s had created largely black school districts, surrounded by lily-white schools in the suburbs. The case that
brought this question to the Supreme Court came from a city with
a long history of racial conflict and violence, just twenty miles from
Pontiac.

Detroit, the "Motor City" and the hub of the nation's auto industry, had seen its black population grow rapidly as Henry Ford's

sprawling factories, and those of his competitors, offered better jobs and bigger paychecks than most blacks could hope for in the rural South. Beginning in 1910, when blacks comprised just 1.2 percent of the city's population, the Great Migration from the South brought new black residents on every train and bus. By 1940, the black population in Detroit had grown to 9 percent, and that figure increased to 16 percent in 1950.

Even though blacks made up a relatively small minority of Detroit's population until the 1960s, the growth of the city's ghetto areas caused friction as blacks moved into previously all-white neighborhoods. Conflicts over housing had sparked a race riot in 1943, as blacks poured into the city to fill defense jobs during World War II. Bands of armed whites roamed the streets, beating and shooting blacks and burning their homes and shops. When the gunfire ended and the smoke cleared, the human toll was 34 dead and 675 seriously injured. Yet, despite the overt hostility that blacks encountered in many areas of Detroit, the lure of jobs swelled their numbers after the war. By 1960, the black population of Detroit reached 487,000, some 29 percent of the city's residents.

Not surprisingly, Detroit was not spared from the death and destruction that swept across the country, from Newark to Los Angeles, during the urban riots of the mid-'60s. When that decade began, close to half of the nation's black citizens lived below the federal poverty line, and black unemployment more than doubled the white rate, with more than a third of all young black men jobless and idle in big-city ghettos. Angry and frustrated, urban blacks lashed out at the white police who pushed them off their stoops and street corners and goaded them with racial epithets. Between 1964 and 1967, more than twenty urban ghettos blew up and burned. The Watts riots in Los Angeles, the most violent since World War II, began on a hot August night in 1965 with white cops dragging a young black driver from his car and clubbing a young black woman who objected. Within hours, hundreds of cops in riot gear confronted a noisy crowd that showered the police with rocks and bottles. Over the following week, hundreds of stores were looted and firebombed, thirty-four people were killed, and hundreds were injured. One journalist wrote that "in Los Angeles the Negro was going on record that he would no longer turn the other cheek. That, frustrated and goaded, he would strike back, whether the response of violence was an appropriate one or no."

The Watts riots shocked the American people, but they were not the most deadly of the urban insurrections of the 1960s. Detroit erupted in 1967 after the police raided an after-hours bar whose patrons were black; the rioting that followed culminated in 43 deaths, $50 million in property damage, and the occupation of the city by seventeen thousand U.S. army and national guard troops. In the wake of the Detroit riot, white residents fled from the city in droves. By 1970, the city's black population grew to 660,000, some 44 percent of the total. During the preceding decade, the white population within the city limits had declined by 350,000, while the suburban white population swelled by just that number. These were not all the same white people, of course, as some left the state and others moved directly into the suburbs, but the trend was clear: Detroit was becoming a black city surrounded by a ring—or noose—of white suburbs in the surrounding three counties. Most of these suburbs, including two of the largest, Dearborn and Warren, had just a handful of black residents in 1970. Just 13 of Dearborn's 104,000 residents were black, as were only 132 of Warren's population of 179,000. Hardly any blacks lived in such upper-income suburbs as Sterling Heights, Birmingham, and Madison Heights; in fact, just 71 of the 125,000 residents of these three cities were black. Some 86 percent of all blacks in the Detroit metropolitan area lived within the city in 1970, and most of the remainder lived in working-class suburbs like Inkster and Pontiac and labored in the auto plants in those towns.

The segregation of Detroit and its suburbs was even more pronounced in schools. Although blacks and whites lived within the city limits in roughly equal numbers in 1970, the city's neighborhoods were clearly separated by race. The vast majority of Detroit's census tracts were more than 90 percent white or black, and the city's public schools mirrored this residential segregation. In 1970, more than 70 percent of the schools were virtually all-white or all-black, with more than 90 percent of their students in the majority race. The phenomenon of "white flight" had already begun in Detroit, as white families with school-age children either moved to the suburbs or sent their children to private and parochial schools. The steady flow of whites from the city to the suburbs became a virtual stampede after the 1967 riot.

Given the segregation in Detroit's schools, it was hardly surprising that NAACP lawyers filed a lawsuit in August 1970 on behalf of "all school children in the City of Detroit, Michigan, and all Detroit resident parents who have children of school age." Ronald and Verda Bradley were the black parents whose names appeared first on the caption, but some of the plaintiffs were sympathetic white parents who felt their children were being denied an integrated education. Michigan's Republican governor, William Milliken, headed the list of defendants, which included the Detroit and Michigan boards of education. The case—decided by the Supreme Court under the caption of *Milliken v. Bradley*—fell on the docket of District Judge Stephen J. Roth, who was born in Hungary in 1908 and whose parents had brought him to Detroit at the age of five. Roth had been a prosecuting attorney, state court judge, and attorney general of Michigan before his nomination to the federal bench in 1962 by President John F. Kennedy.

Judge Roth held several rounds of hearings in the *Milliken* case and considered desegregation plans from both sides before he ruled in June 1972 that Detroit officials had intentionally segregated the city's schools by building new schools well inside neighborhood boundaries, to keep black and white students in separate schools, rather than placing new schools in areas that would draw students of both races. Roth also found that school officials had allowed transfers from schools in racially "transitional" areas, allowing white students to escape from largely black schools. The judge's finding that Detroit had practiced de jure segregation did not surprise anyone, given the clear evidence in the testimony and records at the hearings. But one aspect of Roth's decision shocked the white residents of the white suburbs that ringed Detroit. He ordered a "multi-district" remedy that would include fifty-three suburban districts in a desegregation plan under which 310,000 students would be bused across district lines to new schools. White children would ride buses from their suburban homes into city schools, and black children would sit in suburban classrooms that had never had black students. Judge Roth made clear in his opinion that "no school, grade, or classroom" in the Detroit metropolitan area would have a racial balance "substantially disproportionate to the overall pupil racial composition" of the three-county area covered by his order.

Roth noted in his *Milliken* opinion that school district boundaries in Michigan—like those in most states—were drawn by the state legislature. "School district lines," he wrote, "are simply matters of political convenience and may not be used to deny constitutional rights." Roth found nothing sacrosanct about school district boundaries, pointing out that state lawmakers had often redrawn district lines to consolidate rural schools, and that several districts covered by his order included two or three towns. He placed the blame on state officials for allowing the Detroit school board to build schools and draw attendance zones in ways that produced the segregation he found to be an "official" policy.

Public reaction to Roth's decision flooded the area's newspapers and radio shows with outrage from whites. One parent objected to sending his children to school in "dirty, violent, undesirable Detroit." The fact that some three hundred thousand children in the three-county area were already bused to school did not change many minds. "No kid of mine is going to get on a bus," one white mother said. "I'd go to jail first." Some parents admitted they had joined the "white flight" to the suburbs because "my kids weren't going to go to that school down there" in Detroit, as one put it.

School officials in forty-four of the fifty-three suburban districts that had been included in Judge Roth's busing order filed appeals with the Sixth Circuit Court of Appeals, claiming there was no evidence they had done anything to segregate any school in their district, and that they bore no responsibility for the segregation in Detroit's schools. Lawyers for the suburban districts complained that they had not even been parties to the NAACP lawsuit until Roth dragged them in by judicial order. The appellate judges upheld his order in 1973, however, finding that the Michigan board of education had adopted policies that "fostered segregation throughout the Detroit Metropolitan area."

When the appeal from the Sixth Circuit decision reached the Supreme Court in 1973, interest groups from around the country took sides in "friend of the court" briefs that were often unfriendly in tone. Not surprisingly, the National Suburban League asked the Court to reverse Judge Roth, while the Mexican American Legal Defense and Education Fund lined up behind his order. The stakes in *Milliken* were high, potentially greater than those in the *Swann* case. Busing children within a single district, even one as large as Charlotte-Mecklenburg, did not frighten white suburbanites as much as the prospect of sending their children to schools in "dirty, violent" cities that were largely black. There were many northern cities whose school boards had juggled attendance zones to separate black and white students, and NAACP lawyers would certainly follow up a victory in *Milliken* with similar cases in Kansas City, St. Louis, Chicago, Cleveland, Philadelphia, Boston, and other cities with largely black schools and lily-white suburbs. If the Supreme Court upheld Judge Roth's order, suburbs would no longer be safe havens for whites

Oral argument in *Milliken v. Bradley* began on February 27, 1974. Frank Kelley, Michigan's Democratic attorney general, defended the state's Republican governor and other state officials. He quoted Judge Roth's comment at the initial hearings: "This lawsuit is limited to the city of Detroit and the school system; so that we are only concerned with the city itself, and we are not talking about the metropolitan area." Months later, Kelley said, Roth had "candidly revealed" his real goal in the case: "The task that we are called upon to perform is a social one—which the society has been unable to accomplish—to attain a social goal through the education system by using law as a lever." Kelley urged the justices not to hold Governor Milliken responsible for the long-ago acts of the Detroit school board.

William Saxton, a partner in one of Detroit's most prestigious law firms, argued for the forty-four suburban districts that had appealed from Judge Roth's order. He did not contest Roth's findings that Detroit officials had deliberately segregated their schools, "aided and abetted by acts of certain officials of the state government." But the suburbs had done nothing to deserve judicial fingerpointing. "You will search this record in vain to find one whit, one jot, of evidentiary material that any suburban school district committed any de jure act of segregation, either by itself, in complicity with the state, or complicity with anyone else," Saxton claimed.

J. Harold Flannery, a partner in another of Detroit's leading firms and himself a suburban resident, followed Saxton to the podium to argue for the NAACP in the *Milliken* case. He stressed Judge Roth's findings that the acts of state and local officials had "caused housing segregation and school segregation to be mutually supportive, mutually interlocking devices, with the result that black families and black children were confined to a small portion of the tri-county area," unable to escape from Detroit's black ghetto. Flannery shared his time with Nathaniel Jones, the NAACP's general counsel and a future Sixth Circuit judge. Given the residential segregation in Detroit and its origins in official acts, Jones argued, any "Detroit-only" remedy for school segregation would result in "the perpetuation of a black school district surrounded by a ring of white schools." Judge Roth had ample grounds for including all three metropolitan counties in his remedial order, Jones added, since "they are bound together by economic interests, recreation interests, social concerns and interests, governmental interests of various sorts, and a transportation network."

Three years before the *Milliken* case reached the Supreme Court, Chief Justice Warren Burger had warned in his *Swann* opinion that only proof of a "constitutional violation" could justify remedies such as busing, even within a single district. Burger was upset that district judges like Stephen Roth had not heeded his warning, and he exercised his prerogative as Chief to assign the *Milliken* opinion to himself. But he did not write for a unanimous Court. For the first time since the *Brown* decision in 1954, the justices were split in a school case, voting by a five-to-four margin to reverse Judge Roth. Their single-vote division reflected the right-wing stamp that Richard Nixon placed on the Court during his first term as president.

Nixon, who had denounced advocates of "instant integration" as "extremists" during his 1968 presidential campaign, followed his appointments of Warren Burger and Harry Blackmun to the Supreme Court with two justices to fill the seats of Hugo Black and John Harlan, who both resigned from the Court in September 1971 and died of cancer before the year ended. Their replacements, Lewis F. Powell, Jr., and William H. Rehnquist, joined the Court in January 1972 and cast their first votes on school integration in the *Milliken* case.

Nixon could not have picked two justices more hostile to Judge Roth's order. Their clear opposition to judicial orders in school cases had been instrumental in Nixon's decision to add Powell and Rehnquist to the Court. Powell's roots in his native state of Virginia went back to 1607, three centuries before his birth. A graduate of Washington and Lee University's law school, he spent forty years in corporate practice in Richmond and had served as chairman of both the Richmond and Virginia school boards. Powell had not supported Virginia's "massive resistance" to school integration, but the Richmond school board under his leadership had done nothing to integrate the city's schools. When he stepped down as chairman in 1961, exactly two black children attended classes with white students in Richmond.

William Rehnquist, who was born in Milwaukee in 1924, attended Stanford Law School and served as law clerk to Justice Robert Jackson during the Supreme Court's deliberations on the *Brown* case. During his Senate confirmation hearings in 1971, a memo he wrote to Jackson in 1953 surfaced. "I think *Plessy v. Ferguson* was right and should be reaffirmed," Rehnquist had stated, arguing that states should be able to operate segregated public schools. Confronted with this memo, he told skeptical senators that it represented Jackson's view, not his, but Rehnquist's self-serving disavowal prompted outrage among those who had worked closely with Jackson. After his Supreme Court clerkship, Rehnquist had practiced real estate law and Republican politics in Phoenix, Arizona, working in Barry Goldwater's presidential campaign in 1964. That same year, he opposed the city's public accommodations law, defending in a letter to the *Arizona Republic* "the historic right of the owner of a drug store, lunch counter, or theater to choose his own customers." Three years later, he opposed a Phoenix school integration plan, writing that "we are no more dedicated to an 'integrated' society than we are to a 'segregated' society." These opinions helped Rehnquist land a job in the Nixon administration, as director of the Justice Department's Office of Legal Counsel. Just one senator voted against Powell's confirmation, but twenty-six opposed Rehnquist, arguing that his conservative record on civil rights issues made him a poor choice for the Court.

Along with Powell and Rehnquist, Justices Blackmun and Stewart lined up with Chief Justice Burger in the *Milliken* case. Burger's opinion for this narrow majority, handed down on July 25, 1974, stopped the school buses at the Detroit city limits. He conceded that school district boundaries "may be bridged where there has been a constitutional violation calling for interdistrict relief," but he deplored "the notion that school district lines may be casually ignored or treated as a mere administrative convenience" by lower-court judges. Burger sounded like a Rotary Club speaker: "No single tradition in public education is more deeply rooted than local control over the operation of schools; local autonomy has long been thought essential both to the maintenance of community concern and support for public schools and to the quality of the educational process." Three times on one page, Burger praised "local control" over education, and three times on the next page he warned that only a "constitutional violation" by school district officials could justify any judicial directive to those officials. "Before the boundaries of separate and autonomous school districts may be set aside by consolidating the separate units for remedial purposes or by imposing a cross-district remedy," Burger wrote, "it must first be shown that there has been a constitutional violation within one district that produces a significant segregative effect in another district."

Burger dismissed the findings in Judge Roth's opinion. "The record before us," he wrote, "voluminous as it is, contains evidence of de jure segregated conditions only in the Detroit schools; indeed, that was the theory on which the litigation was initially based and on which the District Court took evidence." As Burger read the trial record, "Disparate treatment of white and Negro students occurred within the Detroit school system, and not elsewhere, and on this record the remedy must be limited to that system." He professed dismay at the consequences of Judge Roth's order. "The metropolitan remedy would require," he wrote, "consolidation of fifty-four independent school districts historically administered as separate units into a vast new super school district," and would turn Roth into "the 'school superintendent' for the entire area." The Chief Justice agreed, however, that Roth could frame "a decree directed to eliminating the segregation found to exist in Detroit city schools," and sent the *Milliken* case back to him for that limited task.

The four dissenters in the *Milliken* case had never been on the losing side of a school case. Thurgood Marshall, in particular, felt betrayed by the majority and answered Burger's thirty-page opinion with one that was longer, more detailed, and undertook to review Judge Roth's order "for what it is, rather than to criticize it for what it manifestly is not." Speaking for Justices Douglas, Brennan, and White, Marshall took the unusual step of reading portions of his opinion from the bench, his tone both sad and scornful as he answered Burger point by point. He began with the *Brown* decision, two decades earlier. "This Court recognized then that remedying decades of segregation in public education would not be an easy task," Marshall said. "Subsequent events, unfortunately, have seen that prediction bear bitter fruit. But however imbedded old ways, however ingrained old prejudices, this Court has not been diverted from its task of making 'a living truth' of our constitutional ideal of equal justice under law." Marshall quoted in this sentence from the Court's unanimous opinion in *Cooper v. Aaron*, the Little Rock case in which the justices demanded "the obedience of the States" to the Constitution's guarantee of "the equal protection of the laws" for every citizen, regardless of race. "After twenty years of small, often difficult steps toward that great end, the Court today takes a giant step backwards," wrote the Court's first black justice.

After this pointed rebuke, Marshall began his dissection of Burger's majority opinion. He first noted that Michigan, unlike many states, kept a tight state rein on local school districts. Marshall wrote that Burger's praise for "local autonomy of school districts in Michigan will come as a surprise to those with any familiarity with that State's system of education." He cited a dozen rulings of the Michigan supreme court, including this statement: "We have repeatedly held that education in this State is not a matter of local concern, but belongs to the State at large." Marshall noted that school district lines did not follow the boundaries of cities and towns; of the eighty-five districts in the Detroit metropolitan area, "seventeen districts lie in two counties, two in three counties. One district serves five municipalities; other suburban municipalities are fragmented into as many as six school districts." Not only had the state taken actions that created and maintained segregated schools in Detroit, a point Burger had conceded, "it was well within the State's powers to require those districts surrounding the Detroit school district to participate in a metropolitan remedy," Marshall wrote.

The heart of Marshall's argument was that the state of Michigan had "engaged in widespread purposeful acts of racial segregation in the Detroit School District" with the result that "Negro children had been intentionally confined to an expanding core of virtually all-Negro schools immediately surrounded by a receding band of all-white schools." Because of the "rapidly increasing percentage of Negro students in the Detroit system, as well as the prospect of white flight, a Detroit-only plan simply has no hope of achieving actual desegregation," Marshall continued. The Court's ruling, Marshall predicted, would increase segregation in Detroit as "white parents withdraw their children from the Detroit city schools and move to the suburbs in order to continue them in all-white schools." The reversal of Judge Roth's order would guarantee "that Negro children in Detroit will receive the same separate and inherently unequal education in the future as they have been unconstitutionally afforded in the past."

Marshall ended his dissent with a paragraph that expressed his dismay at the Court's capitulation to the growing white backlash to school integration: "Desegregation is not and was never expected to be an easy task," he reminded the majority. "Racial attitudes ingrained in our Nation's childhood and adolescence are not quickly thrown aside in its middle years. But just as the inconvenience of some cannot be allowed to stand in the way of the rights of others, so public opposition, no matter how strident, cannot be permitted to divert this Court from the enforcement of the constitutional principles at issue in this case. Today's holding, I fear, is more a reflection of a perceived public mood that we have gone far enough in enforcing the Constitution's guarantee of equal justice than it is the product of neutral principles of law. In the short run, it may seem to be the easier course to allow our great metropolitan areas to be divided up each into two cities—one white, the other black—but it is a course, I predict, our people will ultimately regret. I dissent."

Justice Marshall's prediction that white parents would "react to a Detroit-only decree by fleeing to the suburbs to avoid integration" turned out to be correct. Between 1970 and 1980, the number of white school-age children in Detroit dropped by more than half, from 194,000 to 80,000, while the number of black children increased to 230,000, three-quarters of the school-age population. The 1990 census reported another sharp drop to 35,000 in the white school-age population, while black children made up 85 percent of this age group. The impact of white flight on Detroit's public schools turned them into virtually all-black institutions. By 1999, black children made up 91 percent of the city's public school students, with whites just 4 percent of the total enrollment. Meanwhile, schools in Detroit's white suburbs remained virtually all-white. The 1990 census reported that black children made up less than 1 percent of the students in the upper-income suburbs of Grosse Point, Farmington Hills, Livonia, and Rochester Hills. The middle-class suburbs of Dearborn and Warren, just over the Detroit city line, also had less than 1 percent black enrollment.

One result of these racial disparities, which can be traced directly to the "white flight" that followed the *Milliken* decision, can be seen in the huge gap between the scores of Detroit and suburban students on Michigan's state academic tests. The "culture of failure" that pervades Detroit's schools, in which black students have little incentive to aspire to college, let alone to finish high school, has crippled their academic skills. To illustrate, in 1999 the Michigan Educational Assessment Program (MEAP) administered tests in mathematics, science, reading, and writing to eleventh-grade students in all of the state's public schools. The test separated students into four categories: those in Level 1 "exceeded" Michigan standards; those in Level 2 "met" those standards; those in Level 3 tested at a "basic" level; while students in Level 4 fell below the standard and were "not endorsed" for promotion in the subject. On the eleventh-grade math test, just 18 percent of Detroit's black students scored at Levels 1 and 2, while 63 percent dropped into Level 4 at the bottom of the scale. On the same test, 43 percent of Dearborn students and 61 percent of those in Warren schools met or exceeded the state standard. Some 88 percent of Detroit's black students fell below the standard in science, compared to just 50 percent of the suburban students. The reading and writing scores of black students in Detroit were higher, although 69 percent failed to meet the state standard in reading and 70 percent fell below the standard in writing. More than half of the students in Dearborn and Warren met or exceeded the standard in these areas.

The gaps in test scores were most pronounced in Detroit's high schools, but even in the elementary and middle schools, the city's students fell below those in the suburbs. For example, 58 percent of fourth-graders in Detroit schools made "satisfactory" scores in math, and 45 percent met that standard in reading. But in the upper-income suburb of Rochester, with just 147 black students among 10,801 whites, 94 percent of fourth-graders had "satisfactory" scores in math and 82 percent in reading. One consequence of these dismal test results is that many of Detroit's students just give up on school. The 1999 Michigan school report shows a dropout rate of 26 percent in each year of high school, with just 30 percent of those who enter the ninth grade receiving a diploma.

By any standard, Detroit's public schools are failing their students. The reasons for this educational disaster are complex, but they can be traced back to one primary factor: the legacy of Jim Crow schooling that Detroit's black residents brought with them during the Great Migration from rural southern areas to the Motor City. Black adults in Detroit have lagged behind whites in education in every census, and the percentage of blacks with high school diplomas in the most heavily black parts of the city remains below half. In areas with more than 99 percent black residents, just 42 percent of adults had high school diplomas in 1990, and only 2 percent had earned college degrees. This lack of education hampers ghetto residents in finding good jobs, with more than 80 percent of those in the labor force holding unskilled service and manufacturing jobs, and fewer than one in a hundred in Detroit's all-black areas in professional or executive jobs. Not surprisingly, blacks with poor education and low-skill jobs are also low in income. The per capita income of whites in the Detroit metropolitan area in 1990 was slightly more than $24,000, with those in suburbs like Rochester and Grosse Point earning more than $40,000 per capita and more than $90,000 for each family, while residents of Detroit's all-black areas had a per capita income of just $5,300, well below the federal poverty line.

Perhaps the most telling statistic in the city's "blackest" areas is that 75 percent of all family units in 1990 were headed by females, compared to just 13 percent of the city's white families. Black women who are single mothers are by far the least educated and lowest in income of any family group in American society. Three-quarters of all the children in Detroit's all-black neighborhoods and schools live in "female-headed households," with mothers who most often work long hours at low-paying, exhausting jobs, and who have neither the time nor the skills to help their children with homework and school assignments. These black children enter kindergarten with serious handicaps, and fewer than half of them graduate from high school. Both the dropouts and the graduates are thrown into a job market that relegates them to low-wage, dead-end jobs. Only the small minority of black graduates of inner-city schools who go on to community and state colleges have any chance of escaping the ghetto. Another consequence of life in the black ghetto is that many of the young men—those between twenty and thirty-four—are not even there. In Detroit, the 1990 census counted 106,000 black women and only 82,000 black men in that age group, a shortfall of almost 25,000. Most of these "missing" black men were serving time in jail or prison, many of them the absent fathers of children who grow up and attend school in high-crime areas, ridden with drug use and violence.

The serious problems that face Detroit's black residents did not begin with the *Milliken* decision, nor would they have been solved if the Supreme Court had upheld Judge Roth's "metropolitan" remedy for the state's deliberate segregation of the city's schools. Nonetheless, had the cross-district busing order been implemented, it would have given several thousand black children access to suburban schools with better teachers and facilities, and their skills and test scores would most likely have improved, along with their chances of completing high school. But the Supreme Court's decision in *Milliken* had a broader impact than on the black children in Detroit's failing schools. It told blacks who lived in urban ghettos across the country that their children could not sit in classrooms with any significant number of white children, and conveyed a clear message that suburban whites did not want their children in classrooms with any significant number of black students.

The *Milliken* decision created a dilemma for many federal judges. Barred from requiring that students be bused across district lines to desegregate the schools in metropolitan areas, they found themselves forced to order busing within cities, which often required more busing to achieve a "racial balance" that reflected the city's ratio of black and white students. These busing orders had their greatest impact on working-class white parents who lived in cities and were unable to afford private schools or to join the "white flight" to more expensive suburbs, and who reacted to busing with ferocious anger. Other whites, who could have moved but were attached to their neighborhoods and simply refused to move, also lashed out at the black children who "invaded" their schools.

The furor over busing did not die down after the *Milliken* ruling; in fact, it flared up in several northern cities, none with more turmoil and violence than Boston, a city of ethnic and racial enclaves, a city that rivaled Belfast and Beirut as a powder keg in the 1970s.

Back in 1849, the Massachusetts supreme court had ruled in *Roberts v. City of Boston* that racial segregation in the city's public schools was warranted because the "deep-rooted prejudice in public opinion" against blacks in Boston "probably cannot be changed by law." More than a century later, NAACP lawyers cited the prejudice of white Bostonians in filing a lawsuit in Boston's federal court on behalf of Tallulah Morgan and other black parents against the city's elected school committee. The committee was an entirely Irish-Catholic group whose members included chairman James Hennigan, Paul Ellison, John McDonough, Kathleen Sullivan, and Paul Tierney; the suit also named school superintendent William Leary as a defendant. Ironically, Irish Catholics had themselves been the victims of "deep-rooted prejudice" by Yankee Protestants during much of the nineteenth century. Signs reading "No Irish Need Apply" had been replaced with invisible but real signs that read "No Blacks Can Live Here."

The case of *Morgan v. Hennigan* came before District Judge W. Arthur Garrity, who was himself an Irish Catholic, born in 1920 in nearby Worcester; he attended Holy Cross College in Worcester before his graduation in 1946 from Harvard Law School. After serving as the United States attorney for Massachusetts under Presidents John Kennedy and Lyndon Johnson, Garrity joined the federal district bench in 1966. Lawyers praised Garrity for his fairness and integrity, but he became the symbol of judicial "tyranny" for many white Bostonians.

One factor distinguished Massachusetts from every other state, and complicated the task facing Judge Garrity. In 1965, the state legislature had passed the Racial Imbalance Act, which prohibited any school district from operating any schools with more than 50 percent minority students. In effect, the law required that every school in Massachusetts have a majority of white students. Under the "neighborhood school" system in Boston, most students were assigned to the school closest to their home; the exceptions were the city's prestigious "examination schools" like Boston Latin School, and several vocational schools that drew students on a citywide basis. The majority of Boston's black residents lived in the Roxbury neighborhood, and dispersing their children to majority-white schools would have required busing hundreds of black students into white neighborhoods such as Roslindale, and sending white children into Roxbury's schools.

Judge Garrity conducted lengthy hearings before he ruled on *Morgan v. Hennigan* in June 1974, one month before the Supreme Court decided the *Milliken* case. His opinion first canvassed the composition of Boston's public schools. During the 1971–72 school year, when the *Morgan* case was filed, 61 percent of the 94,000 students in Boston's public schools were white and 32 percent were black. Fewer than one school in five, however, came within 10 percent of matching the city's overall ratio of black and white students. Garrity found that 84 percent of Boston's white students attended schools that were more than 80 percent white, while 62 percent of black students attended schools that were more than 70 percent black. These figures, of course, meant that Boston's school committee had failed to comply with the Racial Imbalance Act. The committee had simply ignored the law, Garrity charged, holding that its actions over the preceding decade had "intentionally brought about and maintained a dual school system" in Boston. "Racial segregation permeates schools in all areas of the city, all grade levels, and all types of schools," Garrity noted, holding that "the entire school system of Boston is unconstitutionally segregated."

The blame for creating and maintaining a segregated educational system fell squarely on the Boston school committee, whose members had campaigned for years with pledges to protect "our neighborhood schools" against legislative and judicial interference. But this was an empty promise and a misleading slogan. "The neighborhood school has been a reality only in areas of the city where residential segregation is firmly entrenched," Judge Garrity wrote. Looking at the district map for elementary schools, he noted that it was not "consistent with a neighborhood school policy: schools are not located near the center of regular, compact districts, but rather near the edges of irregular districts requiring some students to attend a relatively distant school when there is another school within one or two blocks" of their homes. With some two hundred schools serving a total student population of 94,000, the school committee had "pursued a pattern of building relatively small schools to serve defined racial groups," Garrity added.

In his initial ruling, Garrity did not issue orders of his own, but adopted the integration plan framed by the state's education officials to comply with the Racial Imbalance Act. This plan changed the school assignments of 45,000 students from the previous year, almost half the school population, changing the racial composition of eighty of the city's two hundred schools by more than 10 percent. Making matters worse, in the opinion of most white parents, the state plan required the busing of 18,235 students, including 8,510 white children. As was true in many other cities in which busing sparked white protests, sending children to school on buses was not the real issue. Judge Garrity noted that about one-third of Boston's students, most in high school but some three thousand in elementary grades, were already bused or took public transportation to school. What inflamed whites in Boston was that the state plan, which Garrity adopted as an interim measure, would bus 797 black children into South Boston, a working-class Irish neighborhood, and send the same number of white children from "Southie" into Roxbury, the city's blackest area. The plan affected schools in other Boston neighborhoods, including heavily Irish Charlestown and mostly Italian East Boston, but resistance centered in South Boston, where hostility to blacks was deep-rooted and vocally expressed.

Even though Judge Garrity had adopted the state's desegregation plan and not issued his own busing order, most of the busing opponents in Boston blamed him for sending black children into "their" schools. Several hundred members of ROAR—an acronym for the militant anti-busing group called "Restore Our Alienated Rights"—formed a motorcade one evening and drove to Garrity's home in the affluent suburb of Wellesley. The town's entire police force lined up shoulder-to-shoulder in front of the judge's house. Under the bright lights of the TV cameras, the protesters waved signs and sang loudly: "Over there, over there, we won't send our kids, over there." The judge did not appear, and the ROAR group finally went back to Boston, honking and flashing their headlights as they left.

Another protest of Garrity's ruling came from the White House. President Gerald Ford told a news conference that he would not send federal marshals to Boston to enforce a federal judicial order. He added his own, dissenting opinion to Garrity's: "The court decision, in that case, in my judgment was not the best solution to quality education in Boston. I have consistently opposed forced busing to achieve racial balance as a solution to quality education. And, therefore, I respectfully disagree with the judge's order." With this statement—an echo of his predecessor, Richard Nixon—Ford gave the ROAR protesters his assurance that the federal government would not help the Boston police keep order when the buses rolled into South Boston from Roxbury.

What happened when Boston's schools opened in September 1974 was reported in *Time* magazine under the headline "Echoes of Little Rock." When the first bus arrived at South Boston High School with twenty black teenagers from Roxbury, "it touched off an eruption of ugly passion that made South Boston look like Little Rock in the bad old days," *Time* reported. "An angry mob of white parents and truant students greeted the newcomers with the school fight song. A rock arced through the air, crunching into the bus. 'Nigger go home,' bellowed someone in the mob. And as a phalanx of police pushed the crowd back, a Jesuit priest said gloomily: 'If what I've been seeing isn't hate, then I don't know what hatred is.' " Eight black students were cut by flying glass from rocks that shattered their bus windows. Boston police finally cleared the streets around South Boston High, but the school was almost empty as white students joined a boycott organized by ROAR. The group's leader was an unlikely agitator, a pudgy South Boston mother of two, Louise Day Hicks. Her rise to political prominence was fueled entirely by opposition to busing, which propelled her from the Boston school committee to the city council and later to Congress. A classic single-issue politician, Hicks had led some twenty thousand whites on a protest march to the Massachusetts capitol on Beacon Hill, pressuring Governor Francis Sargent to sign a bill that limited busing to children whose parents voluntarily chose it. Judge Garrity quickly ruled the law unconstitutional, but Louise Day Hicks had emerged from the protest march as the undisputed leader of Boston's busing foes.

As the South Boston school boycott dragged into its second month, violence spread across the city. Black students in Roxbury responded to repeated stonings of buses by rampaging through the streets, dragging whites from their cars and beating them. The anger of whites who opposed busing even turned on Senator Edward Kennedy, who had won virtually every vote in South Boston since his first campaign in 1962. When he appeared at a ROAR rally on the Boston city hall plaza and asked to speak, Kennedy was drowned out by hecklers: "Why don't you put your one-legged son on a bus for Roxbury!" one protester yelled. "Yeah, let your daughter get bused there so she can get raped!" another shouted. Pelted with eggs and tomatoes, a shaken Kennedy finally gave up and fled to the safety of his office in the nearby federal building, pursued by protesters who pounded on the plate-glass windows and shattered a panel before the police dispersed them.

The turmoil in Boston did not subside over the next year. In fact, the situation got worse after Judge Garrity issued his own order in June 1975, replacing the plan of the state education department, which he had adopted on an interim basis while he conducted additional hearings in the *Morgan* case. Garrity's order required even more busing to meet the demands of the Racial Imbalance Act. His written opinion was unusual in its frank discussion of the political fallout in Boston from his prior order: "The court has heard members of the school committee in testimony and others speak against 'forced busing' and has received hundreds of letters protesting its use in connection with the state court plan currently in operation." But he placed the blame for the city's turmoil on its politicians, from the mayor to the school committee. "This is an election year in Boston and candidates are already campaigning for municipal offices," Garrity noted. "Many of them are proclaiming that they are for school desegregation but are against forced busing." He accused Boston's politicians of posturing on this issue. "They tell the parents that they will take steps to bring about an amendment to the federal Constitution that will ban forced busing, neglecting to add that it takes several years to adopt even a relatively noncontroversial amendment. Meanwhile the children suffer." The bottom line, Garrity wrote, was that "Boston is simply not a city that can provide its black school children with a desegregated education absent considerable mandatory transportation."

The buses continued to roll into South Boston after schools opened in September 1975, but the turmoil and violence did not subside. Fights broke out between black and white students inside the schools and on the sidewalks around them. Boston police cruisers raced around the city, stamping out the sparks of racial conflict that landed in every neighborhood. Violence did not subside during the school year, either. In January 1976, a group of white students walked out of Charlestown High School, located in a neighborhood in which blacks were routinely subjected to racial epithets. As the students marched toward City Hall, they chased a black man and knocked down and beat a white passerby who protested. When the group arrived at City Hall, they were greeted by Louise Day Hicks, who told reporters the "boys and girls" from Charlestown had shown good behavior in their busing protest.

On April 5, 1976, students from Charlestown and South Boston high schools again marched to City Hall, where their leader, Edward Irvin of the Charlestown High student council, read a statement to the press, saying that white students "refused to be sacrificial lambs and sacrifice our education for a black and white numbers game." The group then left City Hall and headed for the nearby federal courthouse, where they planned to picket with signs denouncing Judge Garrity. As they crossed the City Hall plaza, a group of students, including Edward Irvin, encountered Theodore Landsmark, a black lawyer and executive director of the Contractor's Association of Boston, who was on his way to a City Hall meeting. Led by Irvin, a group of white students tried to impale Landsmark with the sharp end of a flagpole on which an American flag waved its message of "liberty and justice for all." After knocking Landsmark down with the pole, the white youths clubbed their victim with it, breaking his nose and leaving him bleeding and bruised. Landsmark was rescued by Boston police, who arrested Irvin and three other students for assault and battery with a dangerous weapon. The next day, newspapers across the country ran front-page photographs of the students charging at Landsmark with the flagpole as a lance, exposing Boston's ugly racial wounds to the nation. Boston's mayor, Kevin White, who witnessed the attack from his office, called it "racism, pure and simple." Louise Day Hicks, who had welcomed the students to City Hall, chided the "boys and girls" who attacked Landsmark in soft words: "What started out as a peaceful demonstration turned into this sort of thing that none of us approves of." Landsmark put his own reaction into harder words: "To say the least, I resent being beat up."

Two weeks after the attack on Landsmark, a white auto mechanic named Richard Poleet, who was driving through Roxbury at night, stopped at a red light. "There goes whitey," someone yelled from a crowd of black youths on the corner. A dozen members of the group surrounded Poleet's car, dragged him out, smashed his face with chunks of pavement, stole his wallet, and left him unconscious. As police arrived, more than one hundred blacks surrounded Poleet's body, some of them shouting, "Let him die!" After the police cleared the way for an ambulance, Poleet was taken to Boston City Hospital, where he was treated for a fractured skull, blood clots, and extensive facial injuries. Six black youths were arrested the next day and charged with assault and battery with a deadly weapon. Louise Day Hicks turned up her rhetoric in blaming the attack on Poleet to "forced busing, which has made this city fertile ground for such brutality." Landsmark and Poleet both survived their attacks, but Boston's image was badly injured by the national publicity of the violence on its streets.

The long series of explosions over busing in Boston did not end for several years, and the reverberations still echo through the city until the present. One measure of the damage inflicted on the city's public schools can be seen in the precipitous decline in the number of students in the two decades after 1970, when the case of *Morgan v. Hennigan* was filed. In 1970, the Boston public schools enrolled some 96,000 students; by 1990, that number had fallen to 58,000, a drop of 40 percent. The 59,000 white students in 1970 had declined by 1990 to 14,000, an enormous fall-off of 76 percent. The enrollment decline was reversed by the year 2000, when the number of students reached 64,000, with increases of more than 5,000 black and 6,000 Hispanic students offsetting a further decline of 5,000 white students. At the start of the twenty-first century, only 9,300 white students, some 15 percent of the total, attended Boston's public schools. Almost half—some 48 percent—of all white students in Boston attended private or parochial schools.

The city's schools are once again segregated. Black students made up 48 percent of the school enrollment in 2001, with the city's rapidly growing Hispanic population adding another 27 percent, and Asian students 9 percent. More than two-thirds of Boston's black students attend heavily black schools, while the white students are clustered in largely white neighborhoods. Perhaps the most dramatic change in the Boston schools can be seen in the composition of the school committee, which had been an all-Irish group of professional politicians when the busing controversy began. In 2001, three of the seven members were black, including the vice-chair, and one was Hispanic. The school committee chair, Elizabeth

Reilinger, earned a Ph.D. in public policy and management from Cornell and was president and CEO of one of Boston's oldest social service agencies. Boston's school superintendent in 2001, Thomas Payzant, came to the post from San Diego, where he won praise for building racial and ethnic bridges to the black and Hispanic communities. Judge Garrity bowed out of the Boston case in 1987, and judicial oversight of the city's schools ended in 1990, on the heels of the Supreme Court's decision in *Oklahoma City v. Dowell*, which prodded federal judges to free hundreds of school districts from orders that had sparked conflict over "forced busing" as a remedy for racial segregation. Ironically, most of these districts were more segregated in the 1990s than they had been when lawsuits were first brought to integrate their schools. The schools in most large cities had become "resegregated" by 1990, a consequence of racially divided housing patterns and the return of many districts to the "neighborhood school" policy. Whether these developments would allow school boards to escape from judicial desegregation orders was a question the Supreme Court faced as many Americans— a growing number of blacks among them—began to waver in their support for school integration.

CHAPTER 14

"Too Swift and Too Soon"

On July 20, 1990, a steamy Friday in Washington, Justice William Brennan sat alone in his chambers and composed a brief letter to President George Bush. "The strenuous demand of court work and its related duties required or expected of a justice," he wrote, "appear at this time to be incompatible with my advancing age and medical condition. I therefore retire immediately as an associate justice of the Supreme Court of the United States." A gallbladder operation had weakened Brennan, and a recent stroke had produced episodes of confusion. After thirty-four years on the Court, Brennan knew he could no longer function at full capacity. He was determined to leave the bench with the dignity that he consistently urged his colleagues to give every American.

Brennan's retirement did more than give a Republican president the chance to replace one of the most liberal justices in the Court's history. It also removed the justice who had been the intellectual leader of the Warren Court, and whose personal charm and persuasive abilities had protected that Court's landmark decisions from reversal by the Burger and Rehnquist courts. Significantly, Brennan had never once voted to deny, cut back, or limit the powers of federal judges to issue sweeping remedial orders in school cases. And he had been one of four dissenters in the *Milliken* case in 1974. In the years after *Milliken*, dozens of federal judges had been asked by school officials to free them from desegregation orders that had been imposed fifteen or twenty years earlier. In most cases, the judges had refused to vacate those orders. The Supreme Court now faced, in 1990, the task of deciding whether districts that had achieved "unitary" status by eliminating the "vestiges" of segregation could run their schools without further judicial oversight. The question was complicated by the claims of lawyers for black parents and children that the "resegregation" of urban schools, which followed the return of the "neighborhood school" policy, required additional remedies to bring about greater racial balance in the schools. Many cities now had substantial numbers of "one-race" schools, a distressing return to the Jim Crow era. To many observers and activists, the very notion of school integration and the unfulfilled promise of the *Brown* decision hung on the Court's decisions in cases that asked for the lifting of desegregation orders.

The first of these cases, *Oklahoma City v. Dowell*, reached the Court in October 1990, four months after Justice Brennan's departure. His seat was still empty as the eight remaining justices entered the chamber for oral argument. The Oklahoma City case had begun in 1961 with a lawsuit to integrate the city's Jim Crow schools, which had been segregated by law since Oklahoma joined the Union in 1907 with a constitution that mandated segregation in the state's public schools. Robert L. Dowell and other black students and parents, represented by NAACP lawyers, sued the Oklahoma City school board and won a federal court ruling from Judge Luther L. Bohanon in 1963 that ordered school officials to dismantle their "dual" system. In 1965, Bohanon issued another order, based on his finding that the "neighborhood zoning" plan adopted by the board had not produced any real integration, because the city's residential segregation—which had once been imposed by law—had resulted in the perpetuation of one-race schools. While the city's black population was less than 20 percent, it was tightly clustered in the northeast quadrant. In 1972, still dissatisfied with the board's foot-dragging,

Judge Bohanon adopted a plan drafted by Dr. John Finger of Rhode Island College, who had previously designed the integration plan imposed by judicial order in Charlotte, North Carolina. Under the "Finger Plan," black children in the first four grades would be bused to formerly white schools, white fifth-graders would be bused to black schools, and students in upper grades would be bused to schools around the city to achieve racial balance.

The Oklahoma City board asked Bohanon to close the case in 1977, and he complied with an "Order Terminating Case" in which he professed his confidence that "the present members and their successors on the Board will now and in the future continue to follow the constitutional desegregation requirements." Robert Dowell and the other black plaintiffs did not appeal this order. But in 1985, after the board adopted a Student Reassignment Plan that returned to the "neighborhood school" policy of the 1960s, the plaintiffs asked the court to reopen the case, charging that under the new plan, thirty-three of the city's sixty-four elementary schools would have more than 90 percent of their students from one race. The revived *Dowell* case bounced back and forth between the district and appellate courts until 1989, when the Tenth Circuit Court of Appeals, holding that Judge Bohanon had not specifically dissolved his 1972 order "terminating" the case, reinstated the original decree with instructions to require the Oklahoma City board to draft a new integration plan.

The school board's appeal from the Tenth Circuit's ruling came before a Supreme Court with five new members since the *Milliken* decision in 1974. William O. Douglas, a prickly loner who never tried to cajole his fellow justices into joining his liberal opinions, retired in 1975 after thirty-six years of service, the longest tenure in the Court's history. Potter Stewart, who stayed as close as possible to the judicial center, left the Court in 1981, without having written a single landmark opinion. After seventeen years in the Court's center seat, Chief Justice Burger retired in 1986, ostensibly to oversee preparations for the Constitution's bicentennial celebrations, although observers thought he had tired of the judicial bickering that he seemed incapable of quelling. Burger enjoyed the ceremonial trappings of his office and relished the details of judicial administration, but his colleagues never looked to him for leadership. Justice Lewis Powell stepped down in 1987, having served until a few months before his eightieth birthday. Brennan's retirement in 1990 created a fifth opening to be filled by Republican presidents, who created a new majority with their appointments.

President Gerald Ford, a moderate conservative who backed into the White House after the Watergate scandal forced Richard Nixon to leave office in disgrace in 1974, picked John Paul Stevens to replace William O. Douglas. Stevens, a well-respected federal appellate judge from Chicago, staked out an independent position on the Court and moved steadily from the center to the liberal side of the bench after his first few terms. Ronald Reagan, who swept into the presidency in 1980 on a wave of conservative sentiment, had pledged to name the first woman to the Court, and he chose Sandra Day O'Connor in 1981 to succeed Potter Stewart. An honors graduate of Stanford Law School in 1952, O'Connor discovered that corporate firms hired women only as secretaries; she finally landed a job in a California county attorney's office and later moved to Arizona, where she practiced small-town law and Republican politics. She served in the Arizona senate for six years and in state judicial office for another six years before Reagan honored his campaign promise and placed her on the Supreme Court. During ten years on the Court before the *Dowell* case landed on the docket, Justice O'Connor had generally sided with state and local officials in contests with federal judges, but she also sympathized with discrimination claims by racial minorities and women. Her vote in *Dowell* remained in doubt before the Court's decision.

No doubt surrounded the position of Justice Antonin Scalia, who joined the Court after President Reagan opened a seat by elevating William Rehnquist to the post of Chief Justice in 1986, replacing Warren Burger. Scalia, a fifty-year-old judge on the District of Columbia appellate court, was a Harvard Law School graduate who had taught at the Virginia and Chicago law schools and served in the Justice Department post that Rehnquist had once held. The two lawyers were equally partisan in their conservative views, although Scalia was more combative in legal debate. Both in law review articles and judicial opinions, Scalia had forcefully argued that the Equal Protection clause mandated a "color-blind" Constitution, and he rarely sided with plaintiffs in civil rights cases.

The retirement of the soft-spoken and courtly Lewis Powell, who shunned ideological conflict in his centrist opinions, set off one of the most bruising confirmation battles in Supreme Court history, with President Reagan's nomination of the gruff, glowering, and highly ideological Robert Bork. One year after the Senate had confirmed the equally conservative Antonin Scalia without dissent, fifty-eight senators voted against Bork after a ferocious campaign by liberal groups, spurred by fears that Bork would become the fifth vote to overturn the *Roe* decision and give back to state lawmakers the power to make abortion a criminal act. A second effort to place a hard-line conservative on the Court ended when reporters discovered that Judge Douglas Ginsburg, who taught at Harvard Law School before joining the District of Columbia appellate court, had smoked marijuana at law school parties. Reagan's third candidate was a squeaky-clean judge from the Ninth Circuit appellate court on the West Coast. Anthony Kennedy had an altarboy image and was a devout Catholic whose friends considered him totally square. Reagan's far-right supporters harbored doubts about Kennedy's devotion to conservative dogma, but the president was convinced he would vote "right" on overturning the *Roe* decision, and the Senate confirmed him with a sigh of relief.

The fifth new justice, David Souter, was the first nominee of President George Bush and took the seat vacated by William Brennan. A quiet, unassuming man who lived with his mother in a small New Hampshire town, Souter was the third straight Harvard Law graduate to join the Court and had served the Granite State as attorney general and supreme court judge before Bush placed him on the First Circuit appellate court in 1990, just seven months before the president named him to replace Brennan. During his earlier years as a judge, Souter had not voted or written an opinion in a federal civil rights case, and his views on constitutional issues remained unknown.

Oral argument on the Oklahoma City school board's appeal from the Tenth Circuit ruling took place on the first day of the Supreme Court's new term on October 2, 1990, a week before Souter took his seat. Only eight justices sat behind the bench as Ronald L. Day, who represented the board, led off with the claim that Jim Crow schools in his city were history. "Today, in Oklahoma City, no child is compelled to attend school by virtue of his race," he stated. "The important thing today is that parents of all races have a choice." Day was referring to the board's "majority-to-minority" policy, allowing parents to transfer their children from neighborhood schools in which they were in the majority race to schools where they would be in the minority. Few parents of either race had chosen this option, and school attendance boundaries had not been revised to create more racially balanced schools.

Justice Thurgood Marshall had first visited Oklahoma City in 1941 as an NAACP lawyer, after local blacks begged him to defend an illiterate black man who was charged with killing a white couple and one of their children, and who had been savagely beaten by police to extract a confession. As soon as his train from New York pulled into the Oklahoma City station, the black men who met him pushed Marshall into the backseat of a car and sped away, fearful that Klansmen would try to kill him. Marshall was shuttled from one house to another every few hours, with armed blacks keeping watch. He lost the case, after a circus-atmosphere trial before an all-white jury, But he never lost his memories of Oklahoma City, and Marshall grilled Ronald Day in his gruff, raspy voice.

"How is the school board injured by being required to continue to operate the schools in conformity to the United States Constitution?" Marshall asked.

"They weren't harmed that much," Day replied, "not as much as the black schoolchildren, who the district court found were adversely affected by busing."

"What assurance is there that the school board will continue to comply with the Constitution absent a court order?" Marshall continued.

"The board must comply with the Constitution's Equal Protection requirements," Day answered.

"But you'll have to file a new suit to assure that," Marshall retorted.

Day focused his argument on Judge Bohanon's finding that the Oklahoma City schools had achieved "unitary" status after dismantling the "dual" system of segregated schools. He claimed the district had complied with the Court's demand in *Green v. New Kent County*, the Virginia case decided in 1968, that school officials eliminate "every vestige of segregation" before any judicial finding of "unitary" status. The "*Green* standard," defined in Justice William Brennan's opinion, had become the judicial test of compliance with desegregation orders. Justice Anthony Kennedy questioned Day on this issue, citing the number of "one-race" schools in Oklahoma City.

"Does the fact that some neighborhood schools remain black mean that the desegregation plan didn't work?" Kennedy asked.

"No, Your Honor," Day replied. "The fact that some neighborhood schools are not integrated is not under the school board's control."

"But didn't an early district court order find that residential segregation resulted in part from school segregation?" Kennedy inquired.

"That finding related only to segregated schools, not neighborhoods," Day responded.

Kennedy seemed satisfied by Day's answers. "You're operating in an environment in which any family, assuming economic ability, can move to any neighborhood," he concluded.

The Reagan administration had entered the *Dowell* case as a "friend of the court" on the city's side, and Solicitor General Kenneth Starr followed Ronald Day to the podium. His argument that "good faith compliance" with desegregation orders justified termination of judicial oversight of school officials prompted a question from Justice O'Connor: "How does a school system eliminate the last vestiges of discrimination when residential segregation remains a reality, and segregated schools may have contributed to that pattern?" Starr replied that under the *Green* standard, "residential segregation is not considered a vestige of discrimination once there has been good faith compliance with a desegregation plan over a substantial period of time." Justice Marshall, himself a former solicitor general, looked down at Starr.

"But the poor Afro-American kid is still in the same school," Marshall said. "Then it is still a segregated school and you don't think segregation is unconstitutional."

"With all respect, Justice Marshall, that is emphatically not our position," Starr protested. "The schools that are majority black are not so by virtue of any 'state action' assigning children on the basis of race, but as a result of citizens' decisions on their residence. The school board has no realistic control over where people live."

Julius Chambers, who had argued the *Swann* case that led to the Court's approval of busing, argued for the Oklahoma City black children who no longer rode buses to schools outside their all-black neighborhoods. The *Swann* decision, he said, "demands that where there is a segregated system as in Oklahoma City, the school board must take affirmative steps to desegregate." Those steps included busing students to eliminate "one-race" schools. Justice Scalia, the Court's most active and aggressive questioner, grilled Chambers about his claim that residential segregation was a "vestige" of segregated schools.

"You're using 'segregated' in an unusual way," Scalia began.

"Oklahoma City is a segregated community," Chambers replied. "No one expects whites to move to the black residential area."

"But 'segregated' means blacks aren't allowed to move to white areas," Scalia countered, noting that residential segregation was no longer imposed by law in Oklahoma City. Scalia's own definition of the term "segregated" seemed more unusual than Chambers's use of the word.

Chambers then faced a question from Justice O'Connor. "What if the same residential pattern exists one hundred years from now?" she asked. "Would the school board still be subject to the busing order?"

"The order should remain and must remain in force until all vestiges of discrimination have been eliminated," Chambers doggedly replied.

"So the answer is 'Yes,'" O'Connor said.

Along with Thurgood Marshall, Justice Byron White was the last remaining member of the Warren Court. White had vigorously enforced civil rights laws as a Justice Department official under President Kennedy, and had written a pointed dissent in the *Milliken* case, lamenting that "deliberate acts of segregation and their consequences will go unremedied" by the Court's rejection of busing across school district lines. He now posed a skeptical question to Chambers.

"It is not against the law for blacks and whites to go to school anymore in Oklahoma City," White began. "You're saying that they're back to their same old tricks," he said of the school board. "That isn't so, is it?"

"They have gone back to the same geographic zones," Chambers replied. "However unitariness is defined, it should not permit a city to reinstate the same pupil assignment practices that caused segregation in the past. The neighborhood school plan perpetuates black segregated schools in the same black residential area as before the district court's decree."

lthough he joined the Court a week after oral argument in the *Dowell* case, Justice Souter could have voted on the basis of the written briefs and the argument transcripts. But he decided not to participate, leaving the decision in the hands of eight justices. A four-to-four split would have left the Tenth Circuit decision in place, ordering Oklahoma City officials to take all "feasible" steps to reduce the number of one-race schools and to draft another desegregation plan. Some observers thought that Jusice Byron White's past record in civil rights cases might produce an equally divided Court, despite his skeptical questions to Julius Chambers. But any doubts about the outcome disappeared when Chief Justice Rehnquist began reading his summary of the Court's decision on January 15, 1991. For the first time since he took his seat in 1972, Rehnquist wrote for the majority in a school integration case. The five-to-three vote in *Dowell* reflected White's switch from the *Milliken* case. White joined Rehnquist's opinion and did not reveal his reasons for changing sides, although he had become increasingly conservative in civil rights cases. Along with White, three of the four post-*Milliken* justices—Sandra O'Connor, Antonin Scalia, and Anthony Kennedy—joined Rehnquist in reversing the Tenth Circuit decision.

Mindful of his narrow majority, and perhaps as the price for White's vote, Rehnquist wrote the narrowest possible opinion in the *Dowell* case, seeming eager to hand both sides a partial victory. The Oklahoma City school board was assured that judicial decrees "are not intended to operate in perpetuity," and that local control of education "allows citizens to participate in decision making, and allows innovation so that school programs can fit local needs." Rehnquist faulted the Tenth Circuit judges for a ruling that "would condemn a school district, once governed by a board which intentionally discriminated, to judicial tutelage for the indefinite future." Neither the principles of judicial power, nor the Constitution itself, "require any such Draconian result."

Having praised the "good faith" of the Oklahoma City board, Rehnquist declined to let its members off the hook. The Court sent the case back to Judge Bohanon, who had by now presided over the *Dowell* case for thirty years, with instructions to decide "whether the Board had complied in good faith with the desegregation decree since it was entered, and whether the vestiges of past discrimination had been eliminated to the extent practicable." Compounding the confusion about the "good faith" of the board, Rehnquist told Bohanon not to treat its adoption of the neighborhood school plan at issue in the case "as a breach of good faith" by the board. The Supreme Court majority gave Bohanon two assignments. He was directed first to decide whether the original decree should be terminated, based on the school board's "good faith" compliance with that decree. Hinting that Bohanon should make that finding, the Court then instructed the judge to evaluate the board's adoption of the neighborhood school plan, which resulted in thirty-three one-race grade schools in Oklahoma City, "under appropriate equal protection principles."

Confronted with the judicial burial of the *Brown* decisions, Justice Thurgood Marshall replied to Rehnquist with a blistering dissent, joined by Harry Blackmun and John Stevens. With a tone of bitterness, Marshall asked whether, after thirteen years of judicial supervision, the Oklahoma City schools should be "allowed to return many of its elementary schools to their former one-race status." He castigated the Court's majority for suggesting "that thirteen years of desegregation was enough." Chief Justice Rehnquist had barely touched the fact that Oklahoma City's schools had been segregated by law, and wrote nothing about the history of its Jim Crow schools. Not only had Oklahoma "mandated separation of Afro-American children from all other races in the public school system" in its first constitution, Marshall reminded the majority, but "racially restrictive covenants, supported by state and local law, established a segregated residential pattern in Oklahoma City." Even after the *Brown* decisions, the record in the *Dowell* case "reveals nearly unflagging resistance by the Board to judicial efforts to dismantle the city's dual education system." Marshall noted that some 44 percent of the city's black children in kindergarten and the first four grades had been assigned under the neighborhood school policy to schools that were more than 95 percent black. Any decision to terminate Judge Bohanon's decree, Marshall argued, "must take into account the unique harm associated with a system of racially identifiable schools and must expressly demand the elimination of such schools."

Marshall returned to the concept of "stigma" that underlay the arguments he and other NAACP lawyers had made forty years earlier in the *Brown* cases. The focus in those cases "upon the stigmatic injury caused by segregated schools explains our unflagging insistence that formerly de jure segregated school districts extinguish all vestiges of school segregation." Black children suffered a "stigmatizing injury" when they were relegated to all-black schools, Marshall stated. "Against the background of former state sponsorship of one-race schools, the persistence of racially identifiable schools perpetuates the message of racial inferiority associated with segregation," he added. "Therefore, such schools must be eliminated whenever feasible." The most feasible means of eliminating one-race schools in Oklahoma City was to bus students from their one-race neighborhoods to integrated schools, but the Supreme Court was no longer willing to poke the hornet's nest of public hostility to busing. Marshall ended his dissent with a reference to the "separate but equal" doctrine of the *Plessy* case: "In a district with a history of state-sponsored school segregation, racial separation, in my view, remains inherently unequal."

The *Dowell* case finally ended in 1993 with an order of the Tenth Circuit Court of Appeals: "After more than thirty years, this case is closed. Any further complaints of racial discrimination in the Oklahoma City school system will have to be brought by new litigation." The appellate judges expressed dismay and sorrow about their decision, noting the "ugly history" of racial segregation in Oklahoma City. "This case was primarily about busing," they added, obviously distressed that the remedy of busing was no longer a "feasible" alternative to one-race schools. With student assignments now based on the "neighborhood school" policy, Oklahoma City's schools have become even more racially separated. In the 2000 school year, black students were the largest racial group, comprising 39 percent of public school enrollment, more than twice the citywide black population of 16 percent. White students made up 33 percent in 2000, while Hispanic students had become a growing minority at 20 percent. Substantially more than half of the city's black children now attend majority-black schools, with more than half of the white children in majority-white schools. The outcome of the *Dowell* case seemed to justify the gloomy prediction of Thurgood Marshall in his *Milliken* dissent, seventeen years earlier, that the Court's abandonment of the *Brown* decisions would result in America's urban areas being "divided up each into two cities— one white, the other black," with the children in each divided city attending schools in which few of their classmates belong to a different race.

One year after the Supreme Court decided the *Dowell* case, the justices handed down a ruling in another "termination" case, this one from DeKalb County, Georgia, which lies due east of Atlanta. In 1968, lawyers for the American Civil Liberties Union filed a lawsuit in federal court on behalf of Willie Eugene Pitts and his sister Vivian, and other black children in DeKalb County, naming Superintendent Robert Freeman as the lead defendant. Fourteen years after the *Brown* decision, the county still maintained segregated schools. When the suit was filed, black students made up just 6 percent of the DeKalb County school population. In 1969, the district judge who presided over *Pitts v. Freeman* ordered the closing of the all-black schools and the assignment of students to the closest neighborhood school. These modest steps put only a handful of black students into formerly all-white schools.

Until the 1970s, DeKalb County had a rural character and very few black residents. But the rapid expansion of Atlanta's economy produced a growing black middle class, and many blacks moved into the bedroom communities that spread across DeKalb County. Between 1975 and 1980, some 64,000 blacks moved into the southern half of the county, while 37,000 white residents moved out, mostly to surrounding counties with many fewer blacks. The northern half of DeKalb County remained largely white, with just 15,000 blacks among some 200,000 whites.

By 1986, after several rounds of court hearings and judicial decrees, 47 percent of the county's students were black, but they were not evenly spread throughout the schools. More than half of the black students attended schools that were more than 90 percent black, while the vast majority of white children were in schools with few black students. Despite these racial disparities, District Judge William C. O'Kelley granted the school board's motion to declare that the county's schools had achieved "unitary status" with respect to student assignments, and withdrew the court's supervision over that area. O'Kelley ruled, however, that "vestiges" of segregation remained in the assignment of teachers and principals, and in the poor "quality of education" in the county's schools; he ordered the board to address those problems before any termination of judicial oversight. The black plaintiffs felt the judge had not considered more effective remedies, such as revising attendance zones, to achieve greater racial balance in the county's schools.

Both sides in *Pitts v. Freeman* appealed to the Eleventh Circuit Court of Appeals, which included the states of Georgia, Alabama, and Florida. The opinion of the three-judge panel which decided the case in 1989 was written by Judge Joseph W. Hatchett, a former NAACP lawyer who had been named to the bench by President Jimmy Carter and was the first black circuit judge in the Deep South. Judge Hatchett wrote a stinging rebuke to the DeKalb County school board. Despite two decades of judicial oversight, the county's schools remained segregated and the board "refuses to take affirmative action and seeks to justify its inaction with frivolous and long-rejected arguments." Hatchett reversed Judge O'Kelley's finding that the DeKalb schools had achieved "unitary" status in student assignments and his termination of supervision in that area. "We hold that a school system does not achieve unitary status until it maintains at least three years of racial equality in six categories: student assignment, faculty, staff, transportation, extracurricular activities, and facilities." These were the "*Green* standards," taken from the Supreme Court's 1968 opinion in the Virginia case that struck down "freedom of choice" plans. Hatchett also directed the DeKalb school board to "consider pairing and clustering of schools, drastic gerrymandering of school zones, and grade reorganization." He also told the board and Judge O'Kelley to "consider busing" as a remedy for racial imbalance, "regardless of whether the plaintiffs support such a proposal." Hatchett's opinion was remarkable in proposing remedies that went beyond those requested by the black plaintiffs.

The Supreme Court could have summarily reversed the Eleventh Circuit's ruling in *Freeman v. Pitts*, leaving Judge O'Kelley's order in place. The Court's conservative majority read Judge Hatchett's opinion with alarm, however. His directive to "consider busing" in DeKalb County, and his order that all six *Green* standards be met for three years before judicial oversight could end, went far beyond the remedies imposed on the Oklahoma City schools in the *Dowell* case. The Supreme Court granted the DeKalb County board's petition for review and set the case for argument on October 15, 1991.

Once again, as when the Court heard arguments the year before in *Oklahoma City v. Dowell*, there was one vacant seat on the bench when arguments began in the *Freeman* case. Three months earlier, Justice Thurgood Marshall had finally given up as the Court swung to the right under Chief Justice Rehnquist. Justice Brennan's retirement the year before had left Marshall feeling lonely and isolated, and his lungs wheezed from years of smoking. On June 27, 1991,

the last day of the Court's term, Marshall sat grimly next to Rehnquist as the Chief read an opinion upholding a death penalty imposed on a black man convicted of killing a white woman and her
two-year-old daughter. Marshall had consistently opposed capital
punishment, and Rehnquist's eagerness to speed up executions of-
fended his sense of fairness. In a scathing dissent to the majority
opinion, which overruled decisions just two and four years old,
Marshall indicted the conservative majority for its disregard of precedent. "Power, not reason, is the new currency of this Court's decisions," he wrote. The Constitution had not changed in four years,
"only the personnel of this Court did." He warned that "today's
majority ominously suggests that an even more extensive upheaval
of this Court's precedents may be in store. The majority today sends
a clear signal that scores of established constitutional liberties are
now ripe for reconsideration." When the justices returned to their
conference room, Marshall informed his colleagues that he was re-
tiring after twenty-four years on the Court. "I'm old and I'm coming apart," he told reporters the next day.

Four days after Marshall announced his retirement, Clarence
Thomas, a forty-three-year-old judge on the District of Columbia
circuit court, stood next to President George Bush at a press conference at Bush's summer home in Maine and heard himself lauded as
"the best qualified" person to replace the first black justice. Born
into poverty in Georgia, Thomas was raised by his grandfather after
both parents abandoned him. After being educated in Catholic
schools, Thomas won a scholarship to Yale Law School, and wound
up in Washington in 1979 after five years of law practice in Missouri. He moved into the Reagan administration in 1981, heading
the federal Equal Employment Opportunity Commission and becoming the highest-ranking black lawyer in government. As an
outspoken black conservative, Thomas underwent grilling by liberal
senators at his confirmation hearings, which focused on his views
on affirmative action and abortion. Despite his evasive answers and
poor grasp of constitutional law, he seemed headed for the Court

by a wide margin until Anita Hill, a University of Oklahoma law professor and former Thomas aide, charged that her former boss had propositioned her and made crude sexual remarks. Thomas heatedly denied the accusations and won the "she-said-he-said" battle when the Senate narrowly confirmed him by a vote of 52 to 48 on October 15, 1991, one week after the Court heard oral arguments in *Freeman v. Pitts.*

Rex E. Lee, a former solicitor general in the Reagan administration who now taught law at Brigham Young University in Utah, argued for the DeKalb County school board. He conceded that the county's schools were racially unbalanced, but attributed this to the rapid growth of the black population, which was concentrated in the county's southern half. Justice Byron White, who had cast the deciding vote in the *Dowell* case, asked Lee if the county's schools had ever been racially balanced. After the initial 1969 district court order, Lee replied, the county had a "clean record" on desegregation. But the current "resegregation" was caused by housing patterns and not by actions of the school board. "We're only asking for relief from expanded jurisdiction aimed at factors we have no control over," Lee said.

Once again, Solicitor General Kenneth Starr appeared as a "friend of the court" on behalf of the school board, echoing the arguments of his friend and predecessor, Rex Lee. "The school board acted in good faith," Starr claimed. "If the demographics change, the situation cannot be landed at the feet of the school board." Christopher Hansen, the American Civil Liberties Union lawyer who spoke for Willie Pitts and the other black children in DeKalb County, took issue with Lee and Starr. "It is the obligation of the Board to break the pattern of segregation," Hansen argued, provoking a barrage of skeptical questions.

"Did the school board ever fix its segregation problems after the first district court order?" Justice White asked.

"No, Justice White, even after the plan was enacted, disproportionately black schools existed," Hansen replied.

"Didn't you concede that the system was desegregated at one point?" Chief Justice Rehnquist pressed.

"No, the system has always been segregated," Hansen stated. "What we conceded was that all the totally black schools had been closed. The schools today are both separate and unequal." He urged the justices to affirm the Eleventh Circuit's decision, ordering the DeKalb County school board to draft a desegregation plan that included all "feasible" means to achieve racial balance. "The school board should not be rewarded for requiring blacks to have a segregated education," Hansen concluded.

Chief Justice Rehnquist announced the Court's decision in the *Freeman* case on March 31, 1992. While Justice Thomas did not vote, the other eight justices were unanimous in reversing Judge Hatchett's decision and remanding the case to the Court of Appeals. This outcome was misleading, however, as three justices filed an opinion "concurring in the judgment" but in effect dissenting from the majority's treatment of the Eleventh Circuit opinion. Justice Anthony Kennedy wrote for a majority of five, which included Justice David Souter, who had not voted in the *Dowell* case. Justice Sandra O'Connor, however, switched from the *Dowell* majority to the "concurring" dissenters, along with John Stevens and Harry Blackmun. The shifting alignments in these cases reflected the difficulty of defining the judicial standards for the termination of desegregation orders. Justice Kennedy stated the majority's view that "in the course of supervising desegregation plans, federal courts have the authority to relinquish supervision and control of school districts in incremental stages, before full compliance has been achieved in every area of school operations. While retaining jurisdiction over the case, the court may determine that it will not order further remedies in areas where the school district is in compliance with the decree."

Kennedy addressed the growing problem of resegregation, which lay at the root of the increasing racial imbalance in districts like Oklahoma City and DeKalb County. "Racial balance is not to be achieved for its own sake. It is to be pursued when racial imbalance has been caused by a constitutional violation. Once the racial imbalance due to the de jure violation has been remedied, the school district is under no duty to remedy imbalance that is caused by demographic factors." Citing academic studies that "show a high correlation between residential segregation and school segregation," Kennedy noted the expert testimony in the *Freeman* case that "racially stable neighborhoods are not likely to emerge because whites prefer a racial mix of 80 percent white and 20 percent black, while blacks prefer a 50-50 mix." Despite the frank recognition that white flight is the usual consequence of blacks moving into neighborhoods past the "tipping point" of 20 percent, Kennedy disclaimed any judicial responsibility for the resulting school resegregation. "Where resegregation is a product not of state action but of private choices," he wrote, "it does not have constitutional implications. It is beyond the authority and beyond the practical ability of the federal courts to try to counteract these kinds of continuous and massive demographic shifts." The busing in DeKalb County that Judge Hatchett ordered the school board and district court to "consider" as a remedy for resegregation was clearly outside the majority's boundaries, and the Supreme Court reversed that aspect of his opinion.

Harry Blackmun wrote for the three justices who concurred with the judgment to send the *Freeman* case back for further proceedings. Agreeing that both lower courts had been "in error" in their divergent rulings, he felt the Court should direct the district judge to give "close examination" to whether neighborhood segregation in DeKalb County "may in fact have been created, in part, by actions of the school district." Blackmun identified some of the ways in which boards had created racial imbalance, noting that the "placement of new schools and closure of old schools and programs such as magnet classrooms and majority-to-minority transfer policies affect the racial composition of the schools." School board policies "can identify a school as 'black' or 'white' in a variety of ways," Blackmun wrote, and such racial labels affected the choices of many parents on where to live. "This interactive effect between schools and housing choices may occur because many families are concerned about the racial composition of a prospective school and will make residential decisions accordingly." Blackmun felt that Judge O'Kelley, whose "termination order" the Eleventh Circuit had reversed, had failed to examine the history of school board actions in DeKalb County to see how they had affected the racial balance in its schools. The Court's majority did not order such an examination in remanding the *Freeman* case, effectively approving the growing racial imbalance in the county's schools.

Blackmun noted in his opinion that the *Brown* case had been decided thirty-eight years earlier. "In those thirty-eight years," he wrote, "the students in DeKalb County, Georgia, never have attended a desegregated school system even for one day." They still have not, as the DeKalb schools have become increasingly segregated. In 1999, black children made up 77 percent of the county's public school students, while only 14 percent were white. Only six of the nation's fifty largest districts—DeKalb is thirty-ninth in size—had a greater percentage of black students.

A third case testing the power of district judges to continue their oversight of school desegregation came before the Supreme Court in 1995. The line-up of parties in this case, *Missouri v. Jenkins*, was unusual. Eighteen years earlier, in 1977, the school board of Kansas City, Missouri, filed a lawsuit in federal court against the state and several school districts in the Kansas City suburbs. The complaint was filed in the name of Kalima Jenkins, the daughter of a black Kansas City school board member, and it alleged that both the state and the virtually all-white school districts in the Kansas City suburbs had created the segregation of the city's schools. Although whites made up 51 percent and blacks 42 percent of the city's population when the suit was filed, 71 percent of the

33,000 public school students were black. Almost half of the city's white children attended private schools.

The complaint in the *Jenkins* case charged that the state's failure to give Kansas City adequate funds to improve the quality of the city's schools had resulted in "white flight" to the suburbs and to private schools. Kansas City is surrounded by largely white, upper-income suburbs on both sides of the state boundary separating Missouri and Kansas. Lees Summit and Liberty in Missouri, and Leawood and Overland Park in Kansas, all have fewer than 2 percent black residents and students in their public schools. The suit also noted that all schools in Missouri had been segregated by state law before the *Brown* decision in 1954, a law the state legislature did not repeal until 1976.

The *Jenkins* case proceeded at a crawl until 1984, when District Judge Russell G. Clark presided over a trial that lasted more than seven months. Clark's first order after the trial held that the suburban districts had not contributed to the racial imbalance in Kansas City's schools, but he also found that both the state and the city's school board had caused the continuing segregation of the city's schools. Clark exerted his judicial power by switching the school board from plaintiff to defendant in the case it had filed against the state, which was now a fellow defendant. In 1985, Clark issued a remedial order, holding the state responsible for "a system-wide reduction in student achievement" in Kansas City's schools during the years since the *Brown* decision. He attributed this persisting decline in test scores and skills to the Jim Crow system the state had mandated by law before *Brown* and perpetuated since that decision. Clark ordered the state to fund and the Kansas City board to implement a wide range of remedial programs to improve the "quality" of the city's schools. These programs included a reduction of class sizes, full-day kindergartens, expanded summer school and tutoring programs, and an early childhood development program.

In many ways, Kansas City had escaped the crumbling and razing of its black neighborhoods that afflicted cities like Chicago and De-troit, but its schools were literally rotting. Judge Clark found that the city's schools had "numerous health and safety hazards," including "inadequate lighting; peeling paint and crumbling plaster on ceil-ings, walls, and corridors; loose tiles, torn floor coverings; odors re-sulting from unventilated restrooms with rotted, corroded toilet fixtures," and a host of other physical and educational deficiencies. "The conditions at Paseo High School are such that even the prin-cipal stated that he would not send his own child to that facility," Clark wrote. In response to these conditions, he issued a spate of orders that forced the state of Missouri to spend close to a billion dollars to upgrade the Kansas City schools, including $540 million in capital improvements, $200 million in salary increases for the city's teachers, and $200 million in school programs. The Supreme Court later called Judge Clark's orders "the most ambitious and ex-pensive remedial program in the history of school desegregation."

Clark stated frankly in his opinions that the purpose of these costly programs was to lure white students from the suburbs into Kansas City's public schools, and to entice white children from pri-vate schools back into public schools. His orders had financed "high schools in which every classroom will have air conditioning, an alarm system, and 15 microcomputers; a 2,000-square-foot plane-tarium; greenhouses and vivariums; a 25-acre farm with an air-conditioned meeting room for 104 people; a Model United Nations wired for language translation," and elementary schools with "animal rooms for use in a zoo project; swimming pools; and numerous other facilities." As the Supreme Court noted, Judge Clark's orders "have converted every senior high school, every mid-dle school, and one-half of the elementary schools" in Kansas City into "magnet" schools. The district itself had been transformed into a magnet, designed to pull white students into the totally rebuilt and refurbished schools.

Saddled with a huge financial burden, Missouri officials appealed for relief to the Eighth Circuit Court of Appeals, arguing that the

Kansas City school district should be granted "partial unitary status," relieving the state from having to fund expensive programs in areas where the district had complied with earlier judicial orders. But the appellate judges stood behind Judge Clark, ruling in 1993 that both the salary increases for Kansas City teachers and programs to provide "quality education" had been designed to improve the "desegregative attractiveness" of the city's schools and to reverse "white flight" to the suburbs. Until the schools met the goal set by Judge Clark of raising student test scores to meet "national norms," the district would be required to continue funding the Kansas City schools.

The Supreme Court set oral argument in the state's appeal from the Eighth Circuit ruling for January 11, 1995. Two new justices sat behind the bench as Chief Justice Rehnquist opened the session. Byron White had retired in June 1993 after thirty-one years of service, having never joined any of the Court's ideological factions. His successor, Ruth Bader Ginsburg, had joined Sandra O'Connor as the Court's second female member. After graduating at the top of her class at Columbia Law School in 1956, where she served as a law review editor, Ginsburg found—like Sandra O'Connor—that her credentials did not impress any prestigious law firms, which were still hiring women only as secretaries. She taught law at Rutgers and Columbia before President Jimmy Carter named her to the District of Columbia appellate bench in 1980. During her teaching years, Ginsburg created and directed the ACLU's Women's Rights Project and argued six gender discrimination cases before the Supreme Court, winning five. President Bill Clinton pleased the abortion rights movement by placing her on the Supreme Court, a sure vote against overturning the *Roe* case.

Assured by Ginsburg's confirmation that the *Roe* decision would survive his departure, Justice Harry Blackmun, who had written the historic abortion opinion, retired in June 1994. President Clinton named Judge Stephen Breyer of the First Circuit Court of Appeals to fill Blackmun's seat. Born in 1938, Breyer graduated from Harvard Law School, worked closely with Senator Ted Kennedy on issues such as airline deregulation, and taught administrative law at Harvard before President Carter placed him on the federal appellate bench in 1980. Known as cautious liberals, both Ginsburg and Breyer wrote careful, precise opinions as appellate judges that stuck to precedent whenever possible and broke no new constitutional ground.

Missouri's chief counsel for litigation, John R. Munich, opened the oral arguments on January 11, 1995. He attacked Judge Clark's orders as thinly disguised efforts to get around *Milliken* by not ordering busing outside the Kansas City school district, but trying to achieve the goal of moving suburban white students into the city's schools by improving their "desegregative attractiveness." Not only had Clark imposed "a remedy of unprecedented breadth and unparalleled expense," Munich complained, but his goal of reaching "suburban comparability" for the city's schools through state funding went far beyond the state's "constitutional violation" of having once maintained a Jim Crow school system. Justice David Souter reminded Munich that students in Kansas City's schools, most of them black, were still well behind suburban white students in standardized test scores. Forcing the state to spend money on the city's schools would help reduce the racial achievement gap, Souter suggested.

"Why is it irrelevant to look at whether resources are having any effect?" Souter asked.

"How a student performs is a different matter," Munich replied. "The inputs that the school board introduces are filtered through individual students with individual talents."

Justice Stephen Breyer, the Court's junior member, pointed out that many black children lack basic academic skills and that racial "attitudes" might affect their performance. "You're honestly saying you can't look at whether they can read now?" Breyer asked.

Munich restated the answer he had given Justice Souter. "Schools have no control over many factors that contribute to performance, including that individuals learn at different paces."

Justice Anthony Kennedy joined the debate. "Isn't substandard academic performance one of the original evils identified in school segregation?" he asked.

Justice Antonin Scalia jumped in before Munich could answer Kennedy's question. "But if the state provides nondiscriminatory inputs for a period of time, after which student achievement drops, the latter event couldn't be a vestige of discrimination, could it?"

"That's right," Munich gratefully replied to Scalia, yielding the podium to Theodore M. Shaw, who argued for the black plaintiffs. Scalia quickly returned to his questioning.

"How is the average test score of the whole district relevant?" he asked. "That average is going to include non-minority students' scores, won't it?"

"The district court did find that the effects of segregation eventually overtook the entire district," Shaw responded, "causing all students to suffer as a result."

Justice Anthony Kennedy asked Shaw when Judge Clark intended to terminate his supervision of the Kansas City schools. "I just see no end to this," Kennedy said.

"There is no doubt that there will be an end to the order in this case," Shaw assured Kennedy. "The first goal is to remedy the violation, and then to return control to local authorities."

The addition of Justices Ginsburg and Breyer to the Supreme Court did not block the conservative majority from striking down Judge Clark's orders in *Missouri v. Jenkins*, in an opinion issued on June 12, 1995. Chief Justice Rehnquist wrote for the majority in a five-to-four decision, joined by Justices O'Connor, Scalia, Kennedy, and Thomas. Rehnquist noted that the new schools and programs in Kansas City, funded by Missouri taxpayers under Clark's orders, had provided the city's students with "facilities and opportunities not available anywhere else in the country" and had literally turned the city "into a magnet district." This effect of Clark's orders met with Rehnquist's approval. "Magnet schools have the advantage of encouraging voluntary movement of students within a school district in a pattern that aids desegregation on a voluntary basis, without requiring extensive busing and redrawing of district boundary lines." The virtue of magnet schools was that "they promote desegregation while limiting the withdrawal of white student enrollment that may result from mandatory student reassignment."

Despite this laudable goal, Rehnquist explained the vice of Judge Clark's orders: "The District Court's remedial plan in this case, however, is not designed solely to redistribute students within the KCMSD [Kansas City district] in order to eliminate racially identifiable schools within the KCMSD. Instead, its purpose is to attract non-minority students from outside the KCMSD schools. But this *inter*district goal is beyond the scope of the *intra*district violation identified by the District Court. In effect, the District Court has devised a remedy to accomplish indirectly what it admittedly lacks the remedial authority to mandate directly: the interdistrict transfer of students." Even though Clark had not ordered school officials in any other Missouri district to take any action, Rehnquist nonetheless faulted his "goal" of transforming Kansas City's schools into "magnets" for suburban white students. Clark had exceeded the scope of his judicial authority, which was limited to ordering school programs "tailored to remedy the injuries suffered by the victims of prior de jure segregation" in Kansas City's schools. Rehnquist cited for authority the Court's decision in the *Milliken* case, striking down a judicial order that would have required the busing of children from Detroit's white suburbs into the city's largely black schools. Judge Clark had expressly noted that "any *mandatory* plan which would go beyond the boundary lines of KCMSD goes far beyond the nature and extent of the constitutional violation" he had found in the Kansas City schools, but Rehnquist obviously considered this statement a fig leaf for Clark's real purpose of enticing suburban white students to cross district lines into Kansas City schools.

The Court's decision left Kansas City with at least twenty-five "all-black" schools, an outcome that did not faze Justice Clarence Thomas, who issued a lengthy concurring opinion in the *Freeman* case. During his first term on the Court in 1992, Thomas had joined a majority that ordered Mississippi to remove barriers that kept black and white students in separate state colleges and universities, but he had written a separate opinion in that case, *United States v. Fordice*, to express his view that maintaining "historically black institutions" should not be ruled unlawful. "It would be ironic," he wrote, "if the institutions that sustained blacks during segregation were themselves destroyed in an effort to combat its vestiges."

Thomas went beyond this statement in his *Jenkins* concurrence to launch a surprise attack on the very basis of the *Brown* case, four decades after that historic decision. "It never ceases to amaze me," he began, "that the courts are so willing to assume that anything that is predominantly black must be inferior." Without citing the *Brown* decision, Thomas expressed his disdain for "the theory that black students suffer an unspecified psychological harm from segregation that retards their mental and educational development. This approach not only relies upon questionable social science research rather than constitutional principle, but it also rests on an assumption of black inferiority." There are studies that have questioned the social science research, such as Kenneth Clark's "doll tests," on which the *Brown* decision relied, although Thomas did not cite any. But it was not Clark's research that rested on assumptions of black inferiority, as Thomas suggested, it was the Jim Crow system imposed by whites who considered blacks unfit to attend school with their children. Thomas drew a line between de jure and de facto segregation, arguing that school segregation caused by housing patterns "does not constitute a continuing harm after the end of de jure segregation."

Thomas did not view the existence of all-black schools as a deplorable legacy of Jim Crow education. On the contrary, he wrote, "black schools can function as the center and symbol of black communities, and provide examples of independent black leadership, success, and achievement." The "racial isolation" of blacks, Thomas argued, "is not a harm; only state-enforced segregation is." The links between the Jim Crow schools of the past and those of the present did not interest or concern him. Thomas directed his scorn at those, like Thurgood Marshall, who argued that school integration was good for black and white children alike. "After all," he wrote in rebuttal, "if separation itself is a harm, and if integration therefore is the only way that blacks can receive a proper education, then there must be something inferior about blacks. Under this theory, segregation injures blacks because blacks, when left on their own, cannot achieve. To my way of thinking, that conclusion is the result of a jurisprudence based upon a theory of black inferiority." This had certainly not been Marshall's theory, and Thomas did not identify anyone, black or white, who espoused such a notion. But his concurrence in the *Jenkins* case did illustrate the ideological chasm that separated him from his predecessor on the Court.

Justice David Souter wrote for the *Jenkins* dissenters, who included Justices John Stevens, Stephen Breyer, and Ruth Ginsburg. He faulted the majority for the "unreality" of their assertion that "white flight" from Kansas City to the suburbs had no link to the prior de jure segregation of the city's schools. The majority opinion of Chief Justice Rehnquist argued that, once segregation imposed by law had ended, the decisions of white parents to leave the city were "private choices" and "do not figure in the remedial calculus." In Rehnquist's view, the resegregation of Kansas City's schools was largely a result of the "white flight" that followed Judge Clark's initial orders to "eliminate the vestiges" of the Jim Crow system, and was not a consequence of the segregation that had required those remedial orders.

What might have seemed a semantic exercise to some was highly relevant to the proper decision in the case, Souter argued in rebuttal. "There would be no desegregation orders and no remedial plans without prior unconstitutional segregation as the occasion for issuing and adopting them," Souter wrote, "and an adverse reaction to a desegregation order is traceable in fact to the segregation that is subject to the remedy." In other words, "segregation had caused the flight" of whites from the city because of white resistance to judicial orders to remedy the effects of segregation. Consequently, programs designed to "eliminate the vestiges" of that segregation fell within the allowable scope of judicial power. And because the state of Missouri had imposed the Jim Crow system on Kansas City, the state was responsible for funding the programs ordered by Judge Clark.

Justice Souter also took issue with the majority's reliance on the *Milliken* decision to strike down Clark's orders as a barely disguised interdistrict remedy. Since that ruling, Souter noted, the Court had approved several "metropolitan area" judicial orders that "would not consolidate or in any way restructure local governmental units." One such order had required busing across school district lines in Wilmington, Delaware, and suburban districts that surrounded the city. This busing plan, in fact, differed very little from the interdistrict plan the Supreme Court had struck down in *Milliken*. The only real difference was that the number of students bused would be much smaller than in the massive three-county area around Detroit. Although the state of Delaware had appealed the district court's busing order to the Supreme Court in 1975, the justices refused a hearing and simply issued a one-word opinion, "Affirmed."

Justice Ruth Ginsburg added a final, emphatic note to Souter's "illuminating dissent" in a brief opinion of her own. The majority, she wrote, stressed the fact that Judge Clark's remedial orders "have been in place for seven years" and had presumably achieved their original purpose of eliminating the "vestiges" of the Jim Crow system in Kansas City. "But compared to more than two centuries of firmly entrenched official discrimination," she wrote, "the experience with the desegregation remedies ordered by the District Court has been evanescent." Ginsburg cited the Code Noir of 1724, the first slave code for the French-ruled colony of Louisiana, which included present-day Missouri. When Missouri joined the Union in 1821, it entered as a slave state. Before the Civil War, Missouri law barred "the instruction of negroes or mulattoes, in reading or writing, in this State." Jim Crow schools had been imposed by the Missouri constitution since 1865, and that provision was not repealed until 1976. Ginsburg offered her view of this record:"Given the deep, in-glorious history of segregation in Missouri, to curtail desegregation at this time and in this manner is an action at once too swift and too soon."

CHAPTER 15

"Doing the White Man's Thing"

The Supreme Court's trio of rulings between 1991 and 1995 in the *Dowell, Freeman,* and *Jenkins* cases effectively closed the doors of federal courts to black parents whose children were now consigned to "separate and unequal" schools. To be blunt, the Jim Crow system has returned to America's schools, with virtually complete racial segregation in the cities—both north and south—in which more than two-thirds of the nation's black children live. The effect of the Court's directives to lower-court judges to "terminate" their oversight of school integration can be seen across the country. Over the past quarter-century, since the Court approved a large-scale busing plan in the *Swann* case, more than ten million white families have moved from big cities to the suburbs, or have enrolled their children in private schools. The most dramatic figure in the plethora of educational statistics is this: In the year 2001, not a single one of the nation's twenty-five largest central city school districts—all with total enrollments of more than sixty thousand students—had a majority of white students. In eighteen of these districts, in fact, fewer than 20 percent of students were white, and the only two with more than 40 percent white enrollment were Albuquerque, New Mexico, and Tucson, Arizona. Significantly, every one of the metropolitan areas in which these school districts are located has a white majority in total population.

Another measure of the resegregation of America's public schools is that every one of the twenty largest cities with a black population of at least 25 percent has a much greater percentage of black students than of black residents. For example, 40 percent of Philadelphia's residents are black, while 65 percent of public school students are black. In thirteen of these twenty cities, the gap between the percentage of black residents and black students in the public schools is at least 20 percent. Only in New York City and Dallas is this gap less than 10 percent. The reasons for these disparities in the racial composition of big cities and their public schools reflect demographic differences between the races. White residents of big cities tend to be older than blacks and to have fewer school-age children; more of the whites under forty are young singles and childless couples; and the birthrate of black women is higher than that of whites. In addition, more than half of the white parents in most big cities have opted to send their children to private or parochial schools. The phenomenon of "white flight" to the suburbs to avoid school integration, however, has been the leading factor in the resegregation of big-city schools, and the continuing segregation of suburban schools.

In July 2001, the Civil Rights Project at Harvard University released a 54-page report entitled *Schools More Separate: Consequences of a Decade of Resegregation*. Prepared by the project's director, Gary Orfield, this report incorporates data from the 2000 census and offers the most comprehensive study of this important topic. Orfield, the leading scholar in this field for the past two decades, summarized his findings in these words: "The United States has the most diverse group of students in its history, and all the basic trends indicate the diversity will become even greater. Among our school age population we have only a generation before the entire country becomes majority non-white or non-European in origin. . . . Yet our schools remain largely segregated and are becoming more so. Segregated schools are still highly unequal. Segregation by race relates to segregation by poverty and to many forms of inequality for African

American and Latino students; few whites experience impoverished schools. Efforts to overcome the effects of segregation through special programs have had some success, but there is no evidence that they have equalized systems of segregated schools. Americans believe that their children benefit from integrated education, and there is substantial evidence that those beliefs are correct. Segregated schools, particularly those in big cities, have stunningly high levels of high school dropouts and very poor records of preparing students for higher education. Segregation has not been a successful educational or social policy. Yet we are experiencing a continuing expansion of segregation for both blacks and Latinos and serious backward movement in the South."

The Harvard report notes that black students made the greatest strides toward integration in the South, which had been totally segregated before the *Brown* decisions. Even a decade after that ruling, in 1964, just 2 percent of southern black children attended majority white schools. But after passage of the Civil Rights Act of 1964, and judicial enforcement of its provisions, that number steadily increased, reaching a peak of 44 percent in 1988. This figure means, of course, that more than half of all southern black children have always attended largely black schools. Between 1988 to 1998, most of the progress toward integration of the previous two decades had disappeared. Since that peak, the percentage of southern black students in majority-white schools has steadily declined as federal judges have lifted desegregation orders and as residential segregation has increased. Orfield reports that in the 1998 school year slightly fewer than 33 percent of southern black students were in majority-white schools, leaving two-thirds in largely black schools. This level of integration was below that of 1970, meaning that all the progress of the past three decades, however modest, had been wiped out.

On a national level, the Harvard study reports that in 1999 more than 70 percent of all black students attended schools that were predominantly black. Segregation was even more pronounced in schools outside the South. In the Northeast, Midwest, and West, the number of black students in majority-black schools ranged from 74 to 78 percent. The number of black children in schools that were between 90 and 100 percent black—and could properly be called Jim Crow schools—has also increased during the past decade. In 1999, more than a third of the nation's black students, 37 percent, attended virtually all-black schools, most of them in northern and midwestern cities. In the Northeast, 51 percent of black students were in Jim Crow schools, along with 46 percent of those in the Midwest. The four states with the lowest percentages of black students in majority-white schools were all outside the South: New York, California, Michigan, and Illinois, with percentages ranging from 14 in New York to 19 in Illinois. Similarly, the states with the highest percentages of black students in Jim Crow schools with more than 90 percent black enrollment were in the North: Michigan, Illinois, New York, and New Jersey, with percentages ranging from 64 in Michigan to 51 in New Jersey. More than half the black students in these large, urbanized states attended virtually all-black schools.

Segregation runs both ways, of course, and affects students of all races. The Harvard study reports that "white students are by far the most segregated in schools dominated by their own group. Whites on average attend schools where less than a fifth of the students are from all other groups combined." Orfield's data shows that, on a national level, the average white student attends a school where the percentages of black, Latino, and Asian students are 9, 7, and 3, respectively. These national averages conceal the fact, of course, that the vast majority of white children attend schools with few or no students of any other race.

Racially separate education has spread from the cities to the suburbs over the past two decades. Middle-class black families are increasingly moving to the suburbs, but in most metropolitan areas they tend to become clustered in largely black areas. An earlier study of the Harvard project, entitled *Resegregation in American Schools* and published in 1997, reported that slightly more than a quarter of black students across the country attend suburban schools, and that the "population growth of minority students is going to be overwhelmingly suburban if the existing trends continue." In 1997, the average black student in the big-city suburbs attended a school with a 60 percent nonwhite enrollment. Only in the suburbs of smaller cities, those with populations under 250,000, did most black students attend schools that were largely white, although this percentage was just 56, slightly more than half. With blacks still a small minority in most suburban areas, white students attended schools with an average of 7 percent black enrollment.

The most significant aspect of the Harvard report of 1997 is the linkage it shows between racial segregation and poverty in America's schools. "Concentrated poverty is strongly linked to many forms of educational inequality," it stated. The report shows that in schools attended by white children in 1996, 19 percent of their fellow students were classified as "poor," because their low family income qualified them for free or reduced-price lunches. In contrast, 43 percent of students in schools attended by blacks were "poor" under this standard. The data also showed that in schools that are more than 90 percent minority, 88 percent of the children were poor. "In other words," the Harvard report stated, "the students in the segregated minority schools were 11 times more likely to be in schools with concentrated poverty and 92 percent of white schools did not face this problem. This relationship is absolutely central to explaining the different educational experiences and outcomes of the schools. A great many of the educational characteristics of schools attributed to race are actually related to poverty but the impacts are easily confused since in most metropolitan areas there are few if any concentrated poverty white schools while the vast majority of segregated black or Latino schools experience such poverty and all the educational differences that are associated with it."

The Harvard study of 2001 reported that "segregated white minority schools had concentrated poverty nine times out of ten.

Since there is a strong relationship between a school's poverty level and the quality of its teachers, the nature of its instruction, and its achievement test scores, and since poverty is known to affect schools in many other important ways, it is often easy to confuse the impact of poverty as if it were an impact of race." Poverty and race are not only highly correlated, but they interact in so many ways—both inside schools and in the neighborhoods and homes in which poor black children live—that the damaging impact of both factors on the educational achievement of black children is more than doubled.

The Harvard report places much of the responsibility for increasing resegregation at the door of the Supreme Court. Orfield writes in *Schools More Separate* that "new statistics from the 1998–1999 school year show that segregation continued to intensify throughout the 1990s, a period in which there were three major Supreme Court decisions authorizing a return to segregated neighborhood schools and limiting the reach and duration of desegregation orders. . . . The Supreme Court's resegregation decisions took place at the very time there was a turn toward increased segregation for black students. After an increase in integration for black students for a third of a century, segregation began to intensify again."

The growing resegregation of America's schools, and the concentrated poverty of the students in largely black schools, places the futures of millions of black children at great risk. The magnitude of this problem can hardly be measured in dry statistics, but they provide a frame within which the faces of individual children can better be seen. In the year 2000, blacks made up slightly more than 35 million of the country's total population of 270 million, just under 13 percent of the American people. Of the 52 million school-age children of all races, those between five and eighteen years old, some 9 million were black. Because the black population is younger than whites, black children made up 17 percent of the school-age population, one in six children in this age group.

If we place an "average" black child in a group with five "average" white children, we find enormous differences between the black child and his or her white companions. One difference is that the family income of the black child is far lower than those of the whites. The gap between black and white family income has remained almost unchanged since 1970, although the booming economy of recent years has helped black families draw slightly closer to whites: in 1970, black family income was 61 percent of the white level, and rose to 64 percent in 1997, the highest level in the past fifty years. In other words, black families have less than two-thirds of the income of white families, and are forced to spend proportionately more on such essentials as housing, food, health care, and transportation. This leaves black parents with less to spend on "nonessentials" such as books, computers, visits to museums, and cultural events. Some parents, of course, scrimp on essentials in order to broaden their children's horizons, but many do not have the "cultural capital" that middle-class and upper-income parents invest in their children.

The most encouraging development for black families over the past three decades is the growth of a solid middle class. Between 1970 and 1997, the number of black families with incomes above $50,000 (measured in "constant dollars") rose from 12 to 21 percent; for white families the percentages were 28 and 39. At the bottom end of the income scale, however, almost twice as many black families had incomes below $15,000 as whites. In 1970, 37 percent of black families and 19 percent of whites were below the poverty line; those figures in 1997—after a decade of booming economic growth—had dropped slightly for both races, to 32 percent for blacks and 17 percent for whites. Today, almost one-third of black families have incomes below the poverty line, while one-fifth have reached the solidly middle-class level. The remaining half of the black families are in the working-class category, although they are less likely than whites to hold steady, full-time jobs, and their average family income is almost $10,000 lower than that of whites.

The substantial and persisting income gap between whites and blacks is reflected in the number of children who live in poverty, as defined by federal standards. In 1970, 11 percent of white children and 42 percent of black children lived under the poverty line; by 1997, the percentage for white children increased to 15, while the percentage of black children under this level had declined to 37, meaning that about half a million black children no longer live in poverty, a significant number but less than one-eighth of the four million who remain in poor families.

Family income is closely related to educational levels, which have always been lower for blacks than whites. The gap between the two races has narrowed considerably during the past forty years, a reflection of the widespread requirement of a high school diploma or its equivalent for steady, well-paying jobs in the service and manufacturing sectors. In 1960, 43 percent of white adults had finished high school, in contrast to just 20 percent of black adults. By 1996, this educational gap had almost disappeared. The percentage of white adults who completed high school had risen to 84 percent, with blacks close behind at 76 percent. The gap between the races in completion of college narrowed even more during the years since 1960. In that year, 8 percent of white adults had college degrees, compared to just 3 percent of blacks. Those figures increased by 1996 to 25 percent for whites and 15 percent of blacks. By these two measures, the educational level of blacks has improved dramatically. The rapid growth of the black middle class is a direct result of the increasing number who have college degrees; and the children whose parents attended college are highly likely to follow them into higher education.

But the years of schooling completed by blacks and whites are often not comparable in terms of academic and job-related abilities. Many black high school graduates, after sitting in classrooms for twelve years, have not mastered an eighth-grade level in reading and math skills. Black students who enter college are more likely than whites to drop out, and those who complete their degrees receive lower grades. There is no doubt that even the children in black middle-class families suffer from the legacy of the Jim Crow schools in which their grandparents and earlier generations of blacks received inferior education. Very few studies have explored the impact of schooling during the Jim Crow era on later generations of black children, but a 1998 report on the black-white test score gap, published by the Brookings Institution, concluded that "parenting practices" such as giving children learning experiences within and outside the home—reading to them, visiting libraries and museums, providing books and magazines—have a significant effect on children's test scores. Based on self-reported data about the education of parents and grandparents, this report suggests that "changes in families' class position take more than one generation to alter parenting practices. It could therefore take several generations for educational or economic changes to exert their full effect on the black-white test score gap."

The most damaging impact of Jim Crow schooling falls on the black students who attend highly segregated schools in America's big cities. Close to a third of school-age black children, some 2.8 million out of 8.6 million, live in the fifty largest cities. These are children at great risk of receiving such an inferior education that they leave school, whether as dropouts or graduates, barely able to read, write, or do simple calculations. The factors that contribute to the poor academic performance of these urban black children are complex and interrelated. But the vast majority share three characteristics: they live in female-headed households; their mothers have low educational levels; and their family income is well below the poverty level. Data from the 2000 census provide graphic examples of the disparities in these areas between blacks and whites in big cities and their suburbs. For example, in ten big cities from Boston to Kansas City, the percentage of female-headed households with children under eighteen in heavily black neighborhoods ranged from 61 in New York City to 84 in Cleveland. In most of those cities, including Chicago, Philadelphia, Detroit, Baltimore, and St. Louis, more than 70 percent of households in the "blackest" areas were female headed. In contrast, the percentage of female-headed households in the "whitest" suburbs of these cities ranged from 9 in New York City to 14 in Kansas City.

The disparities between the "blackest" urban neighborhoods and the "whitest" suburbs in these big cities are equally striking in levels of income and education. For example, the per capita income level in the virtually all-black areas of Chicago, Detroit, Washington, D.C., St. Louis, and Cleveland was less than 30 percent of the level in white suburbs. The percentage of high school graduates in the big-city black areas ranged from 47 in Chicago to 63 in Boston, compared to 84 percent in Philadelphia's white suburbs and 95 percent in the suburbs around Washington, D.C. The percentages of college graduates in the "blackest" city areas are far below those in the "whitest" suburbs. In the black areas they range from 2 percent in blue-collar Cleveland to 12 percent in Boston, with the nation's largest number of colleges. In contrast, the percentages of college graduates in white suburbs ranged from 30 in Kansas City to 61 in Washington, D.C.

Boiled down from reams of census data, these figures show that most children in the heavily black areas of northern cities—and the figures are highly similar in southern cities like New Orleans, Atlanta, Birmingham, and Richmond—live with their mothers, who have very low levels of education and income. Virtually all of these urban black children attend schools that have few white students. The children in the heavily white suburbs of big cities, both north and south, live with both parents, who have very high levels of education and income. Virtually all of these suburban white children attend schools that have few black students. These "social facts" show the truth of Justice Thurgood Marshall's prophecy in 1991 that America's metropolitan areas were becoming "divided up each into two cities—one white, the other black."

Every year, more than 600,000 black children begin school, most of them in kindergarten classes at the age of five. Close to 250,000 of these children, about 40 percent of those across the country, will attend schools in big cities, with heavily black enrollments. Even at this young age, most of these children enter school with serious handicaps. For example, a 1996 report of the *National Household Education Survey* showed that the parents of black children from three to five years old are less likely than white parents to read to their children, to tell them a story, or to visit a library. The report also shows that black parents with no high school diploma engage in these activities much less frequently than those with more education. For example, 91 percent of parents of both races with college degrees read to their preschool children three times or more each week, compared to 59 percent of those without high school diplomas. While 52 percent of parents with college degrees visit a library with their children at least once a month, only 19 percent of those who did not finish high school do so. Although the report does not provide figures for these activities by income or family structure, it seems likely that single black mothers with low income engage in literacy activities with their preschool children at much lower rates. It should be kept in mind that 92 percent of all black children in households with yearly incomes below $15,000 live in female-headed homes. These children, some three million in number, are those at greatest risk of doing poorly in school, from kindergarten to high school.

The most common method of measuring the performance of students across the country is through standardized tests, some of which are used on a national basis while others are designed for individual states. The most widely used tests have all been criticized as racially biased, since black students receive lower scores than whites.

Virtually all reputable scholars reject claims, most recently leveled by Richard Herrnstein and Charles Murray in their 1994 book *The Bell Curve*, that the lower scores of blacks on intelligence tests have a genetic cause. In a thorough review of all the studies cited by Herrnstein and Murray, who conducted no research of their own, and of many studies their book did not discuss, Richard Nisbett of the University of Michigan concluded in 1998 that the evidence "provides almost no support for genetic explanations of the IQ difference between blacks and whites." Nisbett also reviewed studies of the impact of family structure and other "home" factors on IQ scores and noted that "all of the studies that examine home environment indicate strong environmental effects on the IQ of blacks," with those in female-headed households receiving lower scores than children in two-parent homes. The substantially greater number of black children who live only with their mothers explains much of the IQ gap between black and white children, largely because these mothers have less time and money to provide their children with the "enrichment activities" that are highly related to higher test scores.

The most widely used test in America's high schools, the Scholastic Assessment Test, is given annually to more than a million high school students, most of them headed for college. About 9 percent of students taking the SAT are black, some 119,000 out of 1.3 million in 1999. The SAT is scored on a scale of 200 to 800, with separate verbal and math tests; the highest possible score is 1600. In 1999, the average scores for black students were 432 on the verbal test and 434 on the math test, a combined average of 866. White students had average scores of 531 on the verbal test and 548 on the math test, a combined average of 1068. The SAT gap between black and white students in 1999 was 202 points, and has steadily increased after shrinking to an all-time low of 189 points in 1988. Significantly, 1988 was also the year in which the percentage of black students in majority-white schools reached its highest level, from which it has steadily declined. This growing disparity in test scores raises questions about why black students have been unable to catch up, despite the growth of a substantial black middle class and more blacks completing high school and attending college. There is no simple answer to this perplexing question. If family income was the best predictor of SAT scores, then black students should have scores equal to those of whites at the same income level. Yet blacks from families with incomes between $80,000 and $100,000 actually have lower scores on average than white students whose families earn less than $10,000, a figure below the federal poverty level. Factors other than family income obviously exert a downward push on the SAT scores of black students.

Efforts to explain why black students have lower scores on standardized tests and lower grades in school courses require an examination of three sets of factors: those within the schools they attend, those within their homes, and those within their neighborhoods. These factors cannot easily be separated and studied in isolation. Such "objective" factors as living in a female-headed household, having low family income, or having parents without high school diplomas, are related to "subjective" factors such as low self-esteem, having an "attitude" that alienates teachers, and approaching standardized tests with crippling fear and anxiety. Many white children share one or more of these factors with blacks, but not at such high levels and not within environments that continue to impose a "stigma" on black children.

It is essential to understand that all of these related factors operate for many black children, particularly those who live in urban black ghettos, within a larger environment than the school and the home. This "total environment" includes the black child's neighborhood, which most likely has high rates of crime, drug use, alcoholism, and decaying buildings. These ghetto areas rarely have attractive parks, well-stocked libraries, and accessible health care facilities. Black children also live within a broader cultural environment which glorifies violence, entices poor children with expensive clothing, shoes, and electronic gadgets, and holds out sports stars and "gangsta rappers" as role models. Not all black children, of course, are damaged by living in this total environment and the values it embodies. Many live in families that offer them love, strength, and the values of self-esteem and service to others. Black churches, extended families, community groups, and dedicated teachers can do much to counteract the corrosive impact of urban decay and generations of Jim Crow schools. Yet too many of the black children who enter kindergarten every year begin with handicaps that become more damaging during their high school years.

The one factor most closely associated with black children in big-city schools is living in a female-headed household. More than two-thirds of all black children who attend urban schools are raised by single mothers, and more than 90 percent with family incomes below $15,000 live with their mothers. There is nothing about being a single mother, of course, that causes their children to do poorly in school. Black single mothers, however, find it difficult to give their children the time, support, guidance, and "cultural capital" they need to do well in school. A recent study of this group by Shirley A. Hill noted "strong positive correlations among single-mother families, poverty, welfare dependency, and an array of adverse social, psychological, and health factors for children." Even during their pregnancies, poor black women "have more chronic health problems and less access to medical care," and are "less likely than white mothers to receive early prenatal care." Single black mothers "live in more stressful environments, have a more limited diet, and experience more psychological distress and depression" than white mothers. More than twice as many poor black mothers, Hill reports, have low-weight infants than whites, and these children have more health problems and do more poorly in school than normal-weight infants.

Hill documents the impact of single parenting and poverty on children, who "experience high levels of depression, dependence, unhappiness, and anxiety, and low levels of self-confidence and social adaptation. They are also more likely than affluent children to have impairments in their cognitive development, to engage in problem behaviors, and to perform less well in school. Children in single-mother families have lower academic test scores, have poorer attendance, and are about twice as likely to drop out of high school than are those in dual-parent families." Despite these problems, a large majority of single black mothers told Hill they expected their children to attend college, and "had already begun to instill in their children that college was a necessity" in gaining the economic status they lacked. But these hopes and expectations are highly unrealistic for many black children, who experience the reality of bad schools and uncaring teachers and whose school performance and test scores suffer from the internalized conflict between expectations and reality.

Another recent study of one hundred single black women in Springfield, Illinois, underscores the gap between expectations for their children and the reality of ghetto life. Prohanda Nanti and Hugh Harris reported in 1999 that only half of these young women had finished high school and just 15 percent were employed. Nonetheless, most of those who had no high school diploma expressed a desire to get an equivalency diploma, and more than half of the high school graduates said they wanted to attend college. "The overwhelming majority mentioned that they wanted their children to become educated," Nanti and Harris wrote. But these women live in a crime-ridden public housing development in a largely black area "with no medical facilities, movie theaters or parks. Typical civic facilities are virtually absent. Residents seem to be constantly under stress." The public schools that serve this neighborhood are largely black, in a school district that is two-thirds white. Nanti and Harris did not report on the school performance of the single black women they interviewed, but a look at the Lee Elementary School, closest to the housing development they studied, is revealing. Some 62 percent of the Lee students in 2000 were black, and 81 percent of all the school's students came from low-income families. Scores on the Illinois Standards Achievement Test for Lee's third-graders in 1999 were very low, with 75 percent falling "below standards," compared to 39 percent in this category for the Springfield district and 32 percent in the state. Given these scores, any hopes of the single black women in Springfield's public housing project that their children would attend college would seem highly unrealistic.

Single mothers who live in poverty and face daily threats of crime are not the only blacks who are "constantly under stress." Virtually everyone, of course, experiences stress in various situations, regardless of race. Stress can be a normal reaction to environmental factors such as unemployment, lack of health care, and unsafe streets. It can also be a response to internal factors such as the fear of failure in school or work, of falling short of the expectations of teachers and employers. These latter factors are not limited to poor blacks; in fact, their impact on performance may be greater on those from middle-class black families, who face the added pressure of "representing their race" in unfamiliar settings. Only a handful of middle-class blacks—probably not more than 10 percent of those with family incomes above $50,000—have parents and grandparents whose incomes and social status exceeded the white average. Two or three generations ago, the families of most of todays's upper-income blacks, even those with professional jobs and graduate degrees, most likely lived in the rural South and attended inferior Jim Crow schools. The psychic legacy of this family background, however distant in time and location, cannot be ignored as a contributing factor in the lower performance of today's black students in grades and test scores.

The field studies of John Ogbu, an anthropologist at the University of California, Berkeley, provide evidence of the connection of structural racism in American society—of which Jim Crow education was the bedrock institution—and the "adaptive strategies" of blacks who perceive that hard work in school will not pay off in good jobs. The "oppositional culture" of young blacks, expressed by some in truancy, disruptive behavior in school, "tuning out" in class, and denigrating their black classmates who "act white," has an impact even on those black students who work hard, follow instructions, and aspire to college and economic success. Between 1968 and 1970, Ogbu conducted ethnographic studies in Stockton, California, a middle-sized, middle-income city in the state's agricultural center. During the late 1960s the city's black children were concentrated in schools in low-income areas. About half of Stockton's thirty-two elementary schools had a white majority, and half were predominantly minority in enrollment. In 1969, first-graders in ten of the eighteen largely white schools scored at or above the district average in reading skills on statewide proficiency tests, while students in only three of the fourteen largely minority schools met that level. Third-graders in twelve of the white schools met or exceeded the district average in reading, compared to only one of the minority schools. Sixth-graders in fifteen of the eighteen white schools met or exceeded district averages in both reading and math, with just one minority school at these levels.

Ogbu reported that Stockton's black parents and children both "say that they desire education and school credentials for the same reasons that whites and others gave in my interviews with them: to get a good job with good pay." But they learn at an early age about the "job ceiling" that prevents blacks from rising above the levels set by whites in the most desirable and well-paying jobs. Ogbu notes that "even very young black children begin to realize that for black people in Stockton the connection between school success and one's ability to get ahead is weak, or at least not as strong as whites." As they grow older, black children develop "survival strategies" that focus on "making it without working," both in school and jobs. "School curriculum is equated with white culture and doing schoolwork is interpreted by some as 'doing the white man's thing' or as obeying white people's orders," Ogbu writes. "It is believed by some that school knowledge is white man's knowledge, not black people's knowledge, so that although it is necessary to learn school knowledge to get credentials for employment, black people cannot really identify with it." Ogbu makes clear that not all black children adopt the "oppositional culture" that leads to the devaluation of schooling, but those who do make it hard for blacks who "act white" to fully escape the pressure to work just hard enough to get the diploma that white employers demand.

In more recent studies, Ogbu has refined his analysis of the reasons why black students, even those in elite high schools with demanding courses, still perform well below the levels of white and Asian classmates. He finds that racial stratification in American society, in which blacks at the same educational level of whites continue to encounter barriers in employment and advancement, better explains the lower performance of black students than class stratification that looks primarily at income and considers blacks at the same level of whites to have achieved "equality." Ogbu notes that "while all minorities may start lower than their white peers in the early grades, Asian students improve and even surpass their white peers eventually; for black students, on the other hand, the progression is in the opposite direction. The gap widens between them and their white peers in subsequent years." As black students grow older and begin to think about a career after completing school, they "compare themselves *unfavorably* with whites and usually conclude that, in spite of their education and ability, they are worse off than they should be because of racial barriers, rather than lack of education or qualification." Not all black students reach such negative conclusions, of course, but enough do to depress the average grades and test scores of blacks.

Based on his fieldwork in California schools, Ogbu writes that black students "verbally assert that making good grades and obtaining school credentials are important. They also say that in order to make good grades, one must pay attention in class, do what teacher says, answer questions in class, and do homework. However, from our observations in the classroom, in the family, and in the community I must conclude that many do not do these things." Ogbu suggests that "the reason for this lack of adequate and persevering effort is that, historically, blacks were not adequately rewarded for their educational achievement. So they may not have developed a widespread effort optimism or a strong cultural ethic of hard work and perseverance in pursuit of academic work." Black students who fail to exert their best efforts in school are not inherently lazy, contrary to the Jim Crow stereotype that still persists among many whites. Rather, they make a realistic calculation of the anticipated rewards for their effort and conclude that "working harder than whites" is not worth the effort.

John Ogbu looks at black high school students who literally "give up" in the race for credentials that are passports to prestigious colleges and well-paying jobs. Claude Steele, a black social psychologist at Stanford University, has studied a much different group of black students who worked hard, did well in high school, and received SAT scores high enough to gain admission to Stanford, one of the nation's most prestigious universities. Steele has conducted sophisticated experiments, using black and white Stanford students as subjects, designed to measure the effect of what he calls "stereotype threats" on test performance. Steele notes that, at the college level, "only 38 percent of black entrants graduate within six years, compared with 58 percent of white entrants. Those African Americans who do graduate typically earn grade point averages two-thirds of a letter grade below those of white graduates." The reasons he identifies for these disparities "reflect the effect of historic and ongoing socioeconomic disadvantages, segregation, and discrimination." Racial discrimination, going back to the Jim Crow era, itself reflects negative stereotypes about the intelligence and abilities of blacks as a group. For those in college, the prospect of being judged on a racial basis triggers a "stereotype threat" that adversely affects test performance.

Steele conducted experiments in which difficult tests were administered to black and white students. Some in both groups were told the test was designed to measure "intellectual ability," while other subjects of both races were told the test was merely "a laboratory problem-solving task," with no mention of intellectual ability. Steele hypothesized that black students who believed their intellectual abilities were being tested would feel the pressure of stereotypes that blacks are intellectually inferior to whites, and that such internalized pressure would adversely affect their test-taking abilities. In contrast, a "problem-solving task" would not elicit pressures based on racial stereotypes of black intelligence. The experimental results were striking. Steele reported that blacks performed worse than whites when the test was presented as a measure of their intellectual ability. Their performance improved dramatically and matched that of whites when the test was presented simply as a problem-solving task.

Steele summarized his results: "Our experiments show that making African Americans more conscious of negative stereotypes about their intellectual ability as a group can depress their test performance relative to that of whites. Conditions designed to alleviate stereotype threat, in turn, can improve the performance of blacks." Steele also reported that "stereotype threat may be an under-appreciated source of blacks' poor performance on IQ tests." The fact that IQ scores for black children decline as they grow older may reflect the pressures they feel in the test situation as blacks, more conscious in their teens of being judged in comparison to children of other races, particularly whites, on a "white man's" test. However subtle and unconscious these pressures may be, their impact on test performance—whether in the classroom, on the SAT, or on IQ tests—cannot be dismissed on the ground that test taking creates anxiety for many children in all racial and ethnic groups. Steele's research, adding a psychological dimension to Ogbu's anthropological field studies, suggests that being black in America—and being aware of the Jim Crow legacy of "separate and unequal" education—imposes on many black children an added measure of anxiety as they fill in the blanks on a test sheet.

One question raised by Steele's research is whether the impact of "stereotype threat" on black students is related to racially biased attitudes and expectations on the part of public school teachers. A recent study by Lee Jussim, Jacquelynne Eccles, and Stephanie Madon of the University of Michigan has shown a measurable effect of that bias on the grades of black students. They picked a racially mixed group of sixth-graders in math classes and measured the correlation between teacher assessments of their students' abilities in October and the math grades and scores of these students on the statewide math competency test the following May. The Michigan study concluded that the "impact of teacher perceptions is almost three times as great for African American students as for whites." The study also reported that black children from low-income families experienced the double impact of negative perceptions by teachers of their students' race and their poverty. The authors concluded: "Evidence that teacher perceptions affect subsequent performance more for blacks than for whites suggests either that black students respond differently than whites to similar treatment from teachers, or that teachers treat black and white students differently, or both." It seems likely that "both" is correct: many black students perceive their teachers, whether black or white, as authority figures much like police officers; and many teachers expect less of black students than of whites, and treat them differently in ways that range from overt to subtle.

The interaction between teachers and students is affected by a host of factors, some of which are difficult to observe in classroom settings, and difficult to measure separately. Nonetheless, Susan Gross explored the effect on black students of differential treatment by teachers in a study of high-achieving students in a racially integrated suburb of Washington, D.C. She talked with fourth-graders who scored above grade level in math, and reported "a deep commitment on the part of high-achieving black students to do well in mathematics so that they could move on to good colleges and professional careers." But these students expressed "deep frustration at the incidents of racism they had experienced in the lower expectations they had perceived from teachers and other students." And the teachers in these classes told Gross that "black students were over-represented among students who were 'least studious' and 'did not come to their classes prepared to work or in the proper frame of mind to attend fully to instruction.'"

How can we best assess the large-scale and long-term impact of Jim Crow schooling on black Americans? By any objective measure, generations of "separate and unequal" education have kept, and continue to keep, most blacks from achieving real equality with the white majority. Writing in 1896, Justice John Marshall Harlan stated in his *Plessy* dissent that the white race "deems itself to be the dominant race in this country. And so it is, in prestige, in achievements, in education, in wealth, and in power." More than a century later, blacks continue to lag well behind whites on each of these measures. Hardly anyone can deny that real progress has been made: "Whites Only" signs have come down from drinking fountains and lunch counters; blacks now vote freely and in record numbers; a substantial black middle class has spilled out of urban ghettos into the suburbs; blacks like Bill Cosby and Michael Jordan have become icons of popular culture and professional sports; and legal barriers to interracial marriage, home ownership, and access to public facilities have been dismantled. But this progress is often more symbolic than real. Whites still control 99 percent of the nation's total wealth; the blacks who become stars in films and television do not own the studios and networks that profit from their popularity; and not one of the one hundred largest American corporations is headed by a black president.

The key to this persisting inequality is education. A hardworking person of any race can achieve financial success without a college degree, or even a high school diploma. But it has become virtually impossible, in a postindustrial and high-technology economy, to move from the ghetto into the suburbs without the credentials of diplomas and degrees. And, more important, not every diploma or degree has equal weight and value in the "human resources" offices in which employment decisions are made in both the private and public sectors. Particularly for job applicants who must take some kind of standardized test of reading and math abilities, two people who have both completed twelve years of schooling will often have widely differing scores on these tests. Scores of studies have reported that blacks score below whites at the same level of education on all kinds of tests, from the elementary grades through high school and college, with the racial gap increasing with age. The main reason for this disparity, it seems clear, lies with the continuing legacy of Jim Crow schooling.

Perhaps the best way to view this legacy is to look at two "composite" five-year-old children, both entering kindergarten in 2002. One child is white, the other black. The white child, Kaitlin, and the black child, Keisha, both attend school in a large northern metropolitan area. In Kaitlin's school, 82 percent of her fellow students are white and 9 percent are black, with Hispanic and Asian children making up about 10 percent. Keisha's school has a majority of black students at 55 percent, with 33 percent white students and slightly more than 10 percent being Hispanic and Asian. These are the racial and ethnic compositions of the "typical" American public school. If Kaitlin lives in a middle-class suburb, her school is likely to have fewer than 2 percent black students, and if Keisha lives in an inner-city neighborhood, whites will make up fewer than 10 percent of the students in her school. Some 19 percent of the children in Kaitlin's "typical" school are considered "poor" under federal standards, while 43 percent in Keisha's school live in poverty.

Kaitlin lives with her mother and father, as do 77 percent of her classmates. Keisha lives with her mother, who has never been married; more than half of the black children in her school, 53 percent, also live with their mothers in single-parent homes. Kaitlin's parents have an income of $45,347, while Keisha's mother earns $14,624. Both of Kaitlin's parents graduated from high school, and her father has a college degree, while her mother has picked up two years of college credits. Keisha's mother dropped out of high school in the eleventh grade, but has since completed a General Education Diploma.

The parents of both girls were born in 1970. Kaitlin's grandparents, who were born in 1945 in the Midwest, both graduated from high school in 1963, although neither went on to college. Keisha's grandparents, also born in 1945, moved to the Midwest in 1965 from Alabama, where they attended Jim Crow schools. Her grandfather dropped out of school after seventh grade, but he can only read at a third-grade level. Keisha's grandmother completed the ninth grade, and reads at a seventh-grade level. Going back another generation, Kaitlin's great-grandparents were born in Pennsylvania in 1920; her great-grandfather finished the tenth grade and her great-grandmother finished high school. Neither of Keisha's great-grandparents, who both lived in sharecropper's cabins as youngsters, went past the fourth grade in a one-room school with a wood-burning stove and two outdoor privies. Their teacher, whose forty students went from first through sixth grade, had herself only completed tenth grade in a Jim Crow school.

While both Kaitlin and Keisha are "composite" children, they are fairly typical of white and black children at their age level. The educational levels of their parents, grandparents, and great-grandparents are representative of whites and blacks of those generations and birth years. A report of the National Adult Literacy Survey, funded by the U.S. Department of Education and published in 1992, helps us understand the even greater differences in actual literacy skills of the three generations that preceded these composite children. The survey administered tests of prose reading, document interpretation, and computational skills to a national sample of 26,000 adults. Scores on each test were separated into five proficiency levels, from Level I at the bottom to Level V at the top. Of the entire national group, some 21 percent—projected to 40 million of the nation's 191 million adults—scored at Level I in prose literacy, able to read simple, short passages of text and locate a single piece of information in it, matching a fourth-grade level of proficiency. Going up the prose ladder, 27 percent of adults scored at Level II (about an eighth-grade level), 32 percent at Level III (roughly the level of high school graduates), 17 percent at Level IV (roughly the level of college graduates), and 3 percent at Level V (the level of those with graduate degrees). The racial disparities in prose literacy are striking: 39 percent of whites and 75 percent of blacks scored at Levels I and II. At the other end, 25 percent of whites and just 4 percent of blacks scored at Levels IV and V.

The document proficiency test showed 43 percent of whites and 79 percent of blacks at Levels I and II. Twenty-two percent of whites but only 3 percent of blacks scored at Levels IV and V on this test. On the test of quantitative skills, 28 percent of whites scored at Levels I and II, compared to 80 percent of blacks. Twenty-six percent of whites and just 3 percent of blacks scored at Levels IV and V. Even at the same levels of education, white adults scored at much higher levels than blacks on all three literacy tests. And for adults over sixty, the gap between whites and blacks was substantial, with more than 90 percent of older blacks (like Keisha's "composite" grandparents and great-grandparents) scoring at Level I, the most rudimentary level of literacy.

How do these figures affect the prospects of Kaitlin and Keisha as they move through their separate public schools? It would be impossible, of course, to forecast the educational success of any individual student, based solely on her race. What we can say with some certainty, however, is that the Keishas in our society—that is, the six hundred thousand black children who will enter school this year—will be less likely than the Kaitlins to score above the median on standardized tests, from third grade through high school, to score in the upper half on the SAT test, or to graduate from college. Unless the "opportunity structure" changes significantly in the next quarter-century, Keisha will earn less than Kaitlin, more likely become a single mother, live in a less desirable neighborhood, and face greater danger of crime, drug abuse, and mental illness. Even if we project the gains made by blacks in education and income over the past four decades into the future, it will take at least another century—some experts say two or even three centuries—to erase the disparities between blacks and whites in America. This is the legacy of Jim Crow schooling, and the reason that African Americans of all ages can be considered, in a very real sense, Jim Crow's children.

CHAPTER 16

"The Court's Ruling
Remains Unfulfilled"

Linda Brown was eight years old and in the third grade at Monroe Elementary School in Topeka, Kansas, when the case bearing her name was filed on February 28, 1951. This two-story brick building had thirteen classrooms and served black students from kindergarten through eighth grade. Directly across the street from the school was a playground area, where the older students played softball. Younger children used smaller playgrounds on the north and south ends of the building.

Today, the Monroe school has been transformed into a museum, where visitors can troop through the renovated classrooms, look at photo displays, and watch a video about the history of the *Brown* case. The weed-covered playground across from the school has been spruced up, and friendly, helpful guides from the National Park Service are ready to answer questions about the school and the historic case that challenged the segregation imposed on Linda Brown and other black children in Topeka's elementary schools. One question, however, lies beyond their ability to answer. Have things improved for Topeka's black students in the years since the Supreme Court decided in 1954 that Jim Crow schools violated the Constitution? One person with an answer to that question is Linda Brown, who still lives in Topeka and whose children and grandchildren attended integrated schools. "Sometimes I wonder if we really did the children and the nation a favor by taking this case to the Supreme Court," she told a reporter in 1994, who visited Topeka on the fortieth anniversary of the *Brown* decision. "I knew it was the right thing for my father and others to do then," she said. "But after nearly forty years, we find the court's ruling remains unfulfilled."

One way of measuring the extent to which the *Brown* decision has been fulfilled is to look at the racial composition of Topeka's schools, nearly five decades after the Court's ruling. In 1999, some 14,232 children attended twenty-one elementary schools, six middle schools, and three high schools in Topeka. Overall, 24 percent of these students were black, 59 percent were white, and the remaining 16 percent were Hispanic, Native American, or Asian. The racial disparities among the elementary schools remain high; three schools have fewer than 10 percent black students, with the Lundgren school in the city's largely white west side having the lowest number at 4 percent. At the other extreme, black students make up more than 40 percent of the enrollment at three elementary schools, all located near the center of Topeka's black population. One of these schools, Quinton Heights, has a black majority of 59 percent, the highest of any school in Topeka.

In the city's six middle schools, the percentage of black students ranges from 16 at the French school to 40 at Eisenhower. Of Topeka's three high schools, Highland Park on the east side has the greatest number of black students at 40 percent, while Topeka High in the city's central area has 21 percent, and black students make up just 13 percent at the city's newest high school, Topeka West. Numbers can illustrate the continuing racial disparities in Topeka's schools, but they cannot speak about the atmosphere in the hallways and classrooms of the schools, and the interactions between students and teachers.

I recently visited Topeka High School, whose two thousand students occupy an imposing building with twin towers, constructed in 1931. The hallways are lined with old-fashioned lockers built into the walls, and corridors and stairways are festooned with placards and notices for school activities. During breaks between classes, students throng the building and spill out onto the tree-shaded grounds that occupy two city blocks. About one in five Topeka High students is black, and most of the school's black students stick together in the hallways, cafeteria, and in the groups that leave the school after classes end. There are some racially mixed groups in the swirl of students, and even a few couples of different races, holding hands and hugging. But most of Topeka High's students stay with their own racial group inside and outside the school.

I got some idea of the school's racial divide in the current events class of Richard Bolejack, a young white teacher who graduated from Washburn University, whose campus sits just a few blocks from Topeka High. On a hot fall morning, twenty students amble into the second-floor classroom and slouch into their seats. Four of the five black students in Mr. Bolejack's class sit together in one corner of the room and the fifth, a stocky young woman, takes a seat across from them. Four or five Hispanic students are scattered around the room, while the ten white students are clustered near the teacher's desk. My visit had been hastily arranged and Mr. Bolejack explained that I teach constitutional law and would like to discuss the *Brown* case and its impact on Topeka High with the class. The students quickly burst into spirited and often contentious debate.

I toss out a broad question. "What do you think about the *Brown* case?"

Sandy, a talkative white girl with a small silver ring in her left eyebrow, jumps right in: "It was the right thing back then, because it wasn't right to keep all the black kids in another school, which wasn't nearly as good as this school. And Linda Brown graduated from Topeka High, I know that. If you come in here and look around for the first time, like you are, everything looks cool, you know. Lots of black kids and white kids talk, you know, and do stuff together."

Sandy pauses and looks directly at Mariana, the Hispanic girl sitting next to her, before she addresses me. "But there's something wrong here, and the school won't do anything about it. Did you know that everything here has to be racially balanced, like there have to be so many white kids on the cheerleading squad, and so many blacks, and so many Hispanics? And it's like that in most of the activities here. I think that's against the law," Sandy concludes, shooting another sharp look at Mariana.

Mariana takes the bait. "Yeah, but if we didn't have a rule like that, you know there wouldn't be hardly any black or Hispanic kids on any of those squads. A lot of the teachers and coaches here, you know, they're going to pick white kids for everything. So if we don't have some kind of rule about it, everything in the school is going to be mostly white."

"So what happens," Sandy demands of Mariana. "You get some fat cheerleaders who are just there, you know, because there's a rule about minorities. That's really not fair, and it makes our school look bad when other schools have better squads."

Mariana shoots back. "So what you're saying, you know, is you want our school to look white when we go play schools that are all white."

Both girls are getting heated, and I try to cool things down, posing a question to Tanisha, the stocky black girl who sits across from Sandy and Mariana.

"What do you think about that?" I ask. "Is that really what they do here?" Tanisha nods her head up and down, but does not speak. I try again. "How do the black kids here think about that?"

Tanisha looks at the four black kids sitting in the corner, all with their heads on their desks. "I don't know," she finally replies. "It's like, if they voted on everything here, the white kids would always win." She pauses. "But it's not that bad. Black kids and Latin kids get on everything, and they all do good."

After the buzzer sounds to end the class, I ask Tanisha if we could talk some more during the next period, which is her lunch break. She agrees, and we move outside to a concrete bench, with cans of soda and chips from a lunchroom machine. "You seemed a little uncomfortable in class," I begin. "Do you ever feel that you can't say what you think about something?"

Tanisha nods her agreement. "It's not really the teachers," she says. "I mean, Mr. Bolejack is good, and he lets everybody talk. But me and the other black kids, we know if we say what we really think about things like race, kids like Sandy are going to jump on us. They keep talking about how the black kids run everything at Highland Park, even though there are more white kids in that school. And they talk about how we're loud, you know, in the halls. Which we are, but that's just a black thing."

Tanisha has a final word about the racial situation at Topeka High. "This is a good school, you know, and I know I'm going to college, but it's really like two schools, like they used to have here. I mean, if you look at the honors classes here, they're almost all white, and if you look at what kids get suspended or expelled, they're mostly black. That's real." Why is this so? I ask. "Well, a lot of the teachers don't like kids who are loud, you know, and they send you out of class if you're loud, or use bad language. And the white kids who get in the AP classes, they just hang with each other."

After I thank Tanisha for talking with me, I walk down the street toward the state capitol and pass a dozen groups of Topeka High students, heading back to school after lunch period. Only two of these groups are racially mixed. Almost five decades after the *Brown* decision, Topeka High appears to be integrated, but a closer look shows two schools in one. The racial divisions are not complete, but most black and white kids seem unwilling or unable to bridge the gap that still separates them.

Back in 1951, Ethel Louise Belton sat on a school bus for almost two hours every day. She had been refused admission to the all-white high school in suburban Claymont, Delaware, where her family lived, and was forced to attend the all-black Howard High School in downtown Wilmington. Howard was then housed in a dilapidated building in an area of warehouses, factories, and run-down brick row houses. Many of its students had to walk nine blocks to classes in the Carver vocational school, an adjunct to Howard for teaching "trades and skills to Black students." The trades and skills were largely those needed for jobs in the factories and plants of the DuPont chemical company, which dominated Delaware's economy.

Today, the school is known as the Howard High School of Technology, with about eight hundred students, and boasts of its "state-of-the-art computer technology lab which makes available to all students a variety of programs ranging from skill reinforcement and SAT preparation to word processing and desktop publishing." Howard "is a designated site for school-to-work transition programs, with an emphasis on training students not only at school, but also at businesses in the community." Among the vocation programs offered at Howard are culinary arts and medical assistance. "Howard is a school well prepared to meet the educational demands for the twenty-first century," it assures the Wilmington community.

This rosy picture of Howard Tech, and the exhortations its faculty and staff give to students—almost all black—"to affirm that all students can learn," is belied by the reality of low test scores and the few graduates who gain admission to prestigious colleges and universities. Howard enrolled 765 students in 2000, with blacks a majority of 53 percent, whites at 40 percent, and Hispanics at 6 percent. Although the scores of Howard students on the Delaware State Testing Program are not broken down by race, the national percentile ranking of the school's tenth-graders in math was 32 and in reading was 28. In fact, only 10 percent of this group met or exceeded the state standard in all three subjects of reading, math, and writing. Howard students also scored well below state and national averages on the SAT, with scores of 377 in math and 381 on the verbal test for the class of 2000.

Test results on a statewide level raise more concerns about the performance of Delaware's public school students of all races.

Scores on the SAT lagged well behind national levels in 1999; the average score for all Delaware students of 484 on the verbal test was 18 points behind the national average, and the math score of 481 was 27 points lower. Black students in Delaware did even more poorly on the 1999 SAT tests, with average scores of 421 on the verbal portion and 411 in math. Scores at this low level make it virtually impossible for black students to clear the admissions hurdle at good colleges, and only a handful of Howard Tech graduates are admitted to the University of Delaware each year.

One Howard Tech student, however, is determined to attend the state university and major in electrical engineering. Robert is sixteen and in the eleventh grade; he lives with his mother and sister in a largely black neighborhood in Wilmington, about two miles from Howard. He looks eager and studious, with round wire-rimmed glasses and a button-down white shirt, as he talks with me about his hopes. He volunteered to talk with me over Cokes and pizza in a lunch counter near the school.

"My mom, she's an admission clerk at the VA hospital, and she graduated from Wilmington High and went to business college for a couple of years. She and my dad got divorced about ten years ago, and he moved to New York. My sister and me, she's twelve, visit him two or three times a year. He's got two more kids now, they're both boys and they're about six and four."

Robert likes his teachers and classes at Howard Tech, but he confesses that English and social studies give him trouble. "It's not like I can't read the stuff in English class, but it's boring. They give us a lot of poems and stories by African American people, but I just don't relate to it, you know. And we get all these quizzes, and I just guess a lot on them. Mostly what I like is computers, and Howard has really great computer labs. I can read all the computer manuals and instructions, that's no problem, but grammar and literature just don't work for me. And I really don't care what the main product of some country in South America is. I probably won't go there anyway."

Robert's mother pushes him to complete all his homework, and puts their computer off-limits from seven to nine every night. "My mom, she's like, if you don't get this done, you don't touch that computer for two days. She don't talk like that with my sister, but she gets her homework done in school and she just talks all the time on the phone with her girlfriends."

I asked Robert if he reads any books outside of school. "Well, if you mean books like in English class, no. But I read a lot of stuff about computers and stuff you can do with them, like space missions and making robots." He senses that I think he should be reading "good" books, and adds with a smile, "I was in this program in ninth grade where if you read like a book every week, and write a book report, you get movie tickets. So I read like three books every week, science fiction and stuff like that, and I take all my friends to the movies. So I figure I don't have to read more books like that until I'm in college, you know what I mean." Robert has already visited the University of Delaware campus in Newark, about twenty miles south of Wilmington, and has already picked out the dormitory he wants to live in and the fraternity he wants to pledge. "It's mostly dudes in engineering," he says, "and they have an awesome computer room in their house."

Robert is quite open in discussing racial issues with me. "Everybody who lives around me is black, except for a couple of old ladies who are Italian and be living there all their lives. And most of the dudes I hang with are, like, more into rap music and basketball. And they say, Robert, you go down to Newark and you probably be the only black dude in those engineering classes. See, I'm talking like them now, but that's not the way I talk in school. It's like, I know I'm black, and I'm always going to be black, but a computer don't know if you're black or white, you know what I mean?"

I ask Robert where he thinks he'll be in ten years. "Not here in Wilmington, I know that. Maybe in California. But my mom and my sister are coming with me. This really isn't a good place for them to live. It's too boring, you know. Whoever says, let's move to Wilmington, it's such a cool place?"

On September 11, 1950, Gardner Bishop led eleven black youngsters into the principal's office at John Philip Sousa Junior High School in Washington, D.C. This brand-new school was located across from a golf course and had a student body that was entirely white. Bishop knew they would be refused admission to the white school, which had several empty classrooms, but he planned to file a lawsuit against the school board and wanted to let the judge know what happened to his eleven charges. The suit was filed early in 1951, and the first plaintiff was Spottswood Bolling, Jr., a seventh-grader who had been turned away at Sousa. Spottswood spent that year at Shaw Junior High, an all-black school in a run-down neighborhood, about two miles north of the White House.

Fifty years later, the Sousa school is no longer all white and Shaw is no longer all black. In the 2000 school year, Sousa had 343 black students, 3 Hispanics, and not a single white student. Shaw Junior High had 561 black students, 25 Hispanics, 3 Asians, and just 1 white student. In fact, white children make up just 4 percent of the public school students in Washington. The District's schools have once again become segregated, by choice instead of law. For the black children in Sousa and Shaw, the legal distinction between de jure and de facto segregation is irrelevant. They are stuck by their families' poverty in Jim Crow schools, while black and white children in more affluent families attend private schools or live in the Virginia and Maryland suburbs that ring Washington.

During the five decades since the Supreme Court struck down school segregation, Washington's public schools have become educational basket cases. The schools suffered from conflicts between District officials, who often feuded with each other, and penny-pinching members of Congress, who held the purse strings. The academic performance of the District's students plunged so far that in 1997, the elected school board was stripped of its powers and re-placed by an appointed set of administrators, with a retired army general as superintendent. Not until June 2000 did a newly elected board resume control of the public schools, with calls for reform filling the air but with little substantive change taking place in the schools.

The abysmal record of the District's schools can be measured by student performance in 1999 on the Stanford Achievement Tests, popularly known as the Stanford 9. Scores on tests of reading and math proficiency are grouped in four categories: Advanced, Profi-cient, Basic, and Below Basic. Performance at the Basic level is de-fined at "partial mastery of knowledge and skills" in the subject, while Below Basic is defined as "little or no mastery of fundamental knowledge and skills." Overall, the Stanford 9 scores of the District's students fell sharply as the grade level increased. Among first-graders, only 14 percent scored in the Below Basic category in math, and 16 percent on the reading test. By the ninth grade, scores dropped in both math and reading, with 37 percent in the Below Basic category on math and 66 percent in reading. The District's eleventh-grade students did even more poorly, with 48 percent in the Below Basic category in math and 75 percent in reading.

The Stanford 9 scores at Sousa Junior High and Shaw Junior High reflect the District as a whole. On the math test, 79 percent of Sousa's students and 72 percent of Shaw's scored in the Below Basic category. Reading scores showed more promise, although 40 per-cent of Sousa's and 33 percent of Shaw's students tested at the Below Basic category. These alarming test scores also reflect the "demographic profile" of the Sousa and Shaw students. Some 85 percent at Sousa and 66 percent at Shaw live in families with in-comes below the federal poverty line, and more than two-thirds of students at both schools live in female-headed households. At the high school level, the SAT scores of the District's students are the lowest in the nation. In 1999, the average SAT score on the verbal test was 416, almost a hundred points below the national average of

505. The District average on the math test was 397, more than a hundred points below the national average of 511.

Fifty years after Spottswood Bolling was turned away from the Sousa school and was forced to attend Shaw Junior High, I spent an hour with two Shaw students. DaWon and his friend Lafayette— who prefers "Frenchie" to his given name—are both seventh-graders, as Spottswood was in 1950. Shaw now occupies a sprawling brick building with a large, black-topped playground around two sides, at Ninth Street and Rhode Island Avenue in northwest Washington. DaWon and Frenchie are high-spirited kids, one short and the other tall for his age, a natural comedy team. They are eager to tell me what they think of their school and their neighborhood.

"This school, man, it's like a jail," DaWon begins. "They got security guards and you can't see out the windows, and you can't hardly hear anything in the class, people talking and yelling so loud."

"We got books that are so old your grandma probably used them," Frenchie adds. "I mean, when we get new books, it's like they added a new century of stuff in them."

I wondered if they like anything about Shaw?

DaWon thinks for a minute. "Yeah, we got some good teachers, they say, Here's my rules: don't be rude, don't be vulgar, stay in your seat, and we get along fine. And they spend time with you, answer questions, show you how to do stuff, give you high fives when you do good." DaWon and Frenchie exchange high fives, with low fives for me.

Our talk shifts to families. The 2000 census reported that 91 percent of the families in the neighborhood around Shaw were headed by single mothers; only 47 percent of adults had high school diplomas and just 2 percent had college degrees. DaWon lives with his mother and two older sisters; one goes to Dunbar High and the other works as a security guard at a suburban mall in Maryland, just across the District line.

"My mom, she looks after this old white lady in Georgetown,

and she also works part-time as a cashier in this shoe store on M Street," DaWon says.

Frenchie is an only child and lives with both his parents in a small row house, about three blocks from Shaw. "It's like all the houses you see over there," he says with a wave at the row houses on Rhode Island Avenue. "I can reach from one side of my room to the other." Frenchie's mom is a secretary in a federal agency, although he can't recall its name, and his dad drives a delivery truck for a furniture store.

Both boys are wearing baggy pants and expensive sneakers, the standard uniform of urban kids their age. DaWon says his mom dropped out of school after the tenth grade, but adds that she reads a lot to the old lady she cares for and brings home a lot of books. "They mostly have white girls with low dresses on the cover, kissing white guys with long hair," he says.

Frenchie says both his mom and dad spend their evenings watching television, and neither of his parents pushes him very hard to do his homework. "My mom, she says it's better to have a big heart than a big head. And my dad, he don't say nothing about school."

Neither boy recognizes the name of Spottswood Bolling, nor can they identify Rosa Parks or Linda Brown. They do know that Martin Luther King, Jr., was a famous black person, but they have no idea when he lived or how he died. Dr. King gave his famous "I Have a Dream" speech at the Lincoln Memorial, just three miles from Shaw Junior High, and both boys recognize that phrase. When I asked what King's dream was, they look at each other and make exaggerated "beats me" looks. They are obviously not thrilled to get quizzed on black history.

I ask one final question: Would either boy rather attend a mostly white school in the suburbs than Shaw?

"No way," says DaWon. "This is my home school." Frenchie nods his agreement.

What if the suburban school had much better teachers and facilities, I persisted.

"No way," says DaWon again. "They going to look at me like I'm ignorant. If I was a little kid, like in first grade, maybe it would be better. But I don't want a bunch of white kids do their little 'ha, ha, ha' if I don't know the capital of some country I never heard of."

Frenchie cracks up. "Ha, ha, ha, you ignorant knee-grow," he says with an affected upper-class white accent.

On April 23, 1951, Barbara Johns started the student strike against Jim Crow schooling at Robert R. Moton High School in Farmville, Virginia, the seat of Prince Edward County in the state's tobacco-growing region. Fifty years after Barbara told her fellow students that "things will never be better until we have integration," the schools of Prince Edward County are integrated. Almost 40 percent of the public school students are white, in a county with a white population of 60 percent. Today, all three of the public schools—elementary, middle, and high school—sit on a grassy, 135-acre campus, about a mile south of Farmville's downtown area. Remarkably, even the former Prince Edward Academy, the private school into which the county's white students fled to avoid integration, is now integrated, with about ten black students among six hundred whites. The Academy has been renamed the Fuqua School after a wealthy benefactor who donated $10 million to create "a model of rural school excellence."

The leaders of both the public and private schools in Prince Edward County proudly claim to have established models for integration in a state that set the model for "massive resistance" in the decade after the *Brown* decision. There is no denying that more black and white students attend school together in Prince Edward County than in most districts, far more than in most big cities, both north and south. But have things gotten better in the schools, as Barbara Johns expressed her hopes for integration?

If we measure "better" through the test scores of the county's public school students, the answer depends on our standard of comparison. Judged against past scores, we can see remarkable progress.

In 1972, more than 90 percent of the students were black and their scores on statewide achievement tests stood near the bottom. The combined scores of the county's fourth-graders on the reading and math tests placed them at the 17th percentile of the state level; eighth-graders were at the 14th percentile, and eleventh-graders only at the 9th percentile. But the high school juniors who scored so low had been kept out of school during the two years they would have been in first and second grade, from 1962 to 1964, when the county shut down all its public schools to avoid integration. Those black children had missed the first steps in learning to read, write, and count. Their poor performance in 1972 can fairly be attributed to the hostility of the county's white racists, who robbed the black children of the education they deserved.

Three decades after white students began filtering back to the county's public schools, test scores have improved substantially. On the 1999 statewide tests, called the Standards of Learning, about half of the third-graders passed the SOL tests in four areas, with percentages of 51 in English, 54 in math, 53 in science, and 50 in history. The percentages of students in all of Virginia's third-grade classes who passed these tests ranged from 61 in English to 68 in math. The state education department did not provide a racial and ethnic breakdown of the SOL scores, so the performance of black and white children in Prince Edward County cannot be compared. Students at Prince Edward County High School, however, fell below state norms on all the SOL tests, trailing the passing rate by more than 10 percent on each test. The county's high school seniors also failed to match statewide and national norms on the SAT test; in 1998, they averaged 459 on the verbal test and 442 in math, for a combined average score of 901, more than 100 points below the state and national levels. Again, the scores of black and white students in Prince Edward cannot be compared, although teachers in the high school report that most black students receive SAT scores below those of most whites, with the highest scores almost entirely going to white students.

Another measure of whether things are better in Prince Edward County's schools, after three decades of integration, comes from the students themselves. I met recently with a tenth-grade social studies class, in which the students listened to a tape recording of oral arguments before the Supreme Court in the Little Rock school integration case, decided in 1958. The students heard Thurgood Marshall's passionate argument for Little Rock's black children. "Education is not the teaching of the three R's," Marshall told the Court. "Education is the teaching of the overall citizenship, to learn to live together with fellow citizens, and above all to learn to obey the law."

After this class, and a spirited discussion of the Little Rock case and the school-closing period in Prince Edward County, eight students skipped their lunch period to talk with me around a table in the classroom. The volunteers for this session include four boys and four girls, four blacks and four whites. They are so lively and eager to voice their opinions that I impose a "raise your hand" rule to keep order. Initially, they agree that integration was a good thing and that students of all races got along well at Prince Edward High. One white girl, Samantha, says that she had transferred to the school after five years at the private Fuqua School.

"My parents really didn't want me to come here," Samantha says. "They didn't think I could get into a good college if I came here, but I think really they didn't want me going to school with so many black kids. Now my best friends are black kids, and I'm glad I came here."

Demetrious, a tall, serious black student, speaks up. "My parents don't want me bringing home any white kids. They are very old-fashioned, and they think the races should keep to themselves. They don't mind us going to school together, but they don't want us socializing, and they don't like the idea of black boys going out with white girls." Around the table, most of the kids nod their agreement. Integration is fine inside the school, but it stops at the front door of most homes, black and white.

When I ask the group whether black and white students are

treated equally in the school, agreement begins to unravel. "You look around this classroom," a black girl says, "and you see black kids and white kids together. But you look at the honors classes, and they're almost all white. The teachers pick the white kids for those classes because they're nice and quiet, not rowdy like us black kids."

Another black girl, Calista, jumps in without raising her hand. "Some of the teachers don't call on black kids as much as white kids, and they always correct our language."

Samantha raises her hand. "It's interesting, being in a minority in this school. When I was at the Fuqua School, I never thought about what it's like to be a minority, but here, even though there's almost as many white kids as black kids, I get the feeling that the black kids run things and they have this attitude, like we're going to act like we want to."

Calista jumps in again. "Well, we have our own culture, you know, and we have a right to express it. Like, we're verbal. You go to Africa, and people are verbal there. You know, a lot of white kids just mumble and sit like totally still. We got to move around." Calista stands up and demonstrates, in a slightly exaggerated fashion, the way black students walk down the school hallways. All the kids around the table, except the very serious Demetrious, laugh. For this group of students, integration seems to work, despite the mutual awareness of racial differences in "culture" and the similar attitudes of their parents toward racial mixing outside of school.

On November 11, 1949, a stocky black minister and teacher, the Reverend J. A. DeLaine, finally secured the twentieth signature on a list that had taken him eight months to compile, visiting the homes of black families in the rural town of Summerton, South Carolina. The first name in alphabetical order was that of Harry Briggs, a navy veteran in his thirties with five children. Harry Briggs, Jr., was the oldest, and his name appeared first among the children on the lawsuit against Roderick Elliott, the white chairman of the Clarendon County school board. Thurgood Marshall had picked Summerton to launch the NAACP's crusade against Jim Crow education in the Deep South because its black schools were little more than shacks, without blackboards, desks, or running water, making a mockery of the "separate but equal" doctrine of the *Plessy* case. Although the Supreme Court put the *Brown* case from Kansas ahead of *Briggs v. Elliott* when the justices struck down school segregation in 1954, the South Carolina case struck at the foulest nest of Jim Crow education.

Two decades of litigation followed the first order that integration should begin in Clarendon County's schools. The Supreme Court's directive in 1955 that federal judges should allow southern officials to proceed with "all deliberate speed" was interpreted by the county school board as an invitation to delay and evade judicial orders. The board finally allowed token integration in the mid-1960s, but the county's "freedom of choice" plan for school assignments kept most black and white students in separate schools. In 1970, Judge Simon Sobeloff of the Fourth Circuit federal appeals court issued a biting opinion in *Brunson v. Clarendon County*, a suit filed in 1960 to force abandonment of the "freedom of choice" plan. "This case is the lineal descendent of *Briggs v. Elliott*," Sobeloff wrote. "That it is still being litigated at this date, nineteen years since *Briggs* was initiated and sixteen years after the decision in *Brown*, is a most sobering thought." Sobeloff saw in the county's evasive tactics "no less than a resurrection of the axiom of black inferiority as justification for separation of the races, and no less than a return to the spirit of *Dred Scott*."

Almost every white family in Summerton abandoned the public schools rather than consent to integration. Most sent their children to Clarendon Hall, one of the many "segregation schools" established in the South as refuges for intolerance. So few white children remained in the town's public schools that county officials persuaded the state legislature to cut the county into three districts, creating a black district in Summerton and leaving the other two districts largely white. Blacks finally controlled the new district's

schools, but they lacked the resources to build new schools to replace the old Jim Crow schools. Not until 1994 did the voters in
Summerton approve a bond issue that financed the construction of
a new high school, named Scott's Branch after the black schools
with that name, in which generations of children had been educated. Located in a rural area two miles north of town, the new
school is a rambling one-story brick complex with a state-of-the-
art computer lab, a spacious library, hallways festooned with pictures
of black leaders like Martin Luther King, Jr., and posters that exhort
students to study hard and succeed.

Summerton is now a sleepy town of one thousand residents, almost 60 percent of them black. The Piggly-Wiggly supermarket
has a black manager, and race doesn't seem to affect the casual ban-
ter of customers and clerks. But the elderly white couples who
come from church to Sunday lunch at the Summerton Diner still
bristle and glare at a black woman and her son who order a take-out
meal. And the young black men who hang out at the local gas station are loud and profane as they catcall the passing girls. Summerton has only one source of good-paying jobs, the Federal Mogul
factory, which sits across the road from Scott's Branch High and
produces oil seals and molded gaskets for the auto industry. The parent company of Federal Mogul has $6 billion in annual sales and the
Summerton plant, which opened in 1974, employs more than eight
hundred county residents, many of them graduates of Scott's
Branch High.

I recently visited a Scott's Branch social studies class taught by
Moses Levy, Jr., a short, stocky black teacher whose father was a pa-
triarch of the county's black community. On the wall behind Mr.
Levy's desk is a large picture of Christ, and a Bible sits on his desk.
Despite the Supreme Court rulings that school prayer violates the
Constitution, classes begin at Scott's Branch—and in most schools
in South Carolina—with prayer, "in the name of our Savior, Jesus
Christ." Ironically, the Constitution also hangs on the wall in Mr.

Levy's classroom, but the students seem unaware of conflicts over religion. They are very aware, however, of conflicts over race, and the role Summerton played in battles over Jim Crow schools. They know the *Briggs* case was the first to be filed and to reach the Supreme Court, and they seem annoyed that the *Brown* case was pushed ahead of the one that began in the Scott's Branch school. But this is not a lively class, and the twenty-odd students do not volunteer their opinions unless they are asked directly what they think. Scott's Branch High is a quiet, orderly school, with a burly security guard in the main hallway.

Four of Mr. Levy's students agree to meet with me during their lunch period and talk about themselves and their school. Three are black and one is from India, one of the few non-black students at Scott's Branch. About ten white students and a handful from India are among the 436 in the school. The two boys, Antonio and Rodney, are both very serious and deferential. Dhruvi, the Indian girl, is outspoken and opinionated, while Deidre is a quiet, shy black girl. I first ask about their families. Antonio's family moved to Clarendon County from Georgia, and Dhruvi's father is an engineer at the Federal Mogul plant across the road from the school. Rodney and Deidre have roots in Clarendon County going back to slavery, and their families are leaders in the black community. Both sets of their parents graduated from Scott's Branch High during the short-lived period of integration in the late 1960s, before all the white students left for Clarendon Hall and other private schools. But none of their grandparents finished high school, and they all worked as sharecroppers on farms owned by whites. Neither knows how far their great-grandparents went in school, or whether they even attended school. Back in the 1920s, more than half of Clarendon County's black adults had not gone beyond the fourth grade, and a quarter had never been inside a school.

When I ask the four young people about their future plans, they all tell me they plan on college, and have careers in mind. Not one plans to stay in Clarendon County. Antonio wants to be a graphic designer and live in California; Rodney wants to work in engineering, probably in aerospace, and live in Texas or somewhere in the Southwest; Deidre plans on becoming a special education teacher and working with handicapped children; and Dhruvi wants to design computer software. There are, in fact, no jobs in any of these fields in Clarendon County, except in special education, but Deidre wants to live in Atlanta. These kids will become part of the "brain drain" that has left much of the rural South a backwater of the elderly and the unskilled.

When the conversation turns to race, Dhruvi has the most to say. "Being born in India, where dark-skinned people are looked down on as lower-caste, even when they're not, I can see the same thing in this school," she says. "The light-skinned black kids are the most popular and get into the honors courses, and the really dark-skinned kids are looked down on, like they're dumb."

Rodney, who is very dark, takes exception. "That's true in social things," he tells Dhruvi, "but not in academics. I'm president of the One Thousand Club, and there are other dark-skinned kids in it." The One Thousand Club, he proudly tells me, is for students who have combined scores of a thousand points on the SAT test or the version given in tenth grade. This is a rather small club at Scott's Branch High, where the average combined SAT score in 2000 was 836 points, almost two hundred points below the national average for all students and a hundred below the average for college-bound blacks. Nonetheless, it is 42 points above the 1999 average of 794, one of the state's lowest scores. I ask if the school has students who have serious trouble with academic work. "Oh yeah," says Antonio, "they just sit there in class and don't say nothing. The teachers sort of leave them alone."

The students in Mr. Levy's class have given me a book called *Remembering the Past, Living in the Present, Focusing on the Future*, a collection of interviews with older black people in Clarendon County, prepared by students in the school's Gifted and Talented Program. Most of the brief interviews describe life on farms and hard work in childhood, picking cotton and weeding gardens.

Joseph Richburg, now eighty, tells about his early years in the cotton fields:"I'll tell you the truth, I didn't like picking it. That was my worst job. I would tell my mom my back hurt and she would say, 'You ain't got no back. You ain't got nothing but a gristle.' And that's how our life was."

Other stories tell about going to the black schools in the countryside. "We walked about three miles to school," Netta Watson remembers of her childhood in the 1920s. "Walking was all right on the days it didn't rain or it wasn't cold. School started at eight o'clock. If you weren't there before the door closed, you had to go back home."

In the back of the book is a drawing of Scott's Branch High, with an arrow leading to a drawing of Clarendon Hall, and another arrow leading to a drawing of a composite school, Scott's Hall? "How do you feel about the white students at Clarendon Hall?" I ask.

"I feel sorry for them," Antonio says. "We have a much better school now, but their parents are so prejudiced they keep them in that run-down school. Some of them have come over here for various programs, and a couple have said they would rather go here, but their parents won't let them."

Clarendon Hall *is* run-down, in fact, housed in a wooden building with peeling white paint and a weed-covered athletic field. Joseph Elliott, the headmaster, is the grandson of Roderick Elliott, the former county school superintendent who was the first defendant in *Briggs v. Elliott.* When I visit the school, I am struck by the ironic reversal of roles: black children attended run-down wooden schools in the Jim Crow era and now have a modern brick school; white children had a spacious brick school in Jim Crow times and now attend a run-down wooden school. Headmaster Elliott tells me that parents send their children to Clarendon Hall for its

"Christian values" and strict discipline, not because they are racially prejudiced. But he says, "I've taught in public schools in South Carolina, and their standards are so low. The public schools in this county have the lowest test scores in the state, and among the lowest in the country."

The superintendent of the Summerton school district, Dr. Elijah McCants, is a longtime school official in South Carolina. He tells me, "Joe Elliott can tell you Clarendon Hall is not a 'seg school,' but that's what it is and always has been. And it doesn't have long to last; it's losing students every year and more and more are coming back to our schools, particularly in the lower grades." Dr. McCants is frank in discussing the low performance of Scott's Branch students on standardized tests. "Most of these children come from homes where their parents didn't finish high school, and those that did went to inferior schools. A lot of parents are functionally illiterate, and they don't have any books in their homes and they just watch television. So they really can't help their children with schoolwork. We are trying to get funds for programs to get parents involved with their children's education, but it's a struggle. This is a very rural area; we don't have libraries or cultural events, and most students who are bright are going to leave the county."

Despite the economic and educational deprivation of most blacks in Clarendon County, Dr. McCants remains hopeful that the public schools will give those students who remain in the county a better education. He hands me a report of the scores of tenth-graders on statewide tests in reading, writing, and math. Between 1995 and 1999, the percentage of students meeting the state standard increased from 61 to 71 in reading, 49 to 66 in writing, and 47 to 71 in math. None of the districts in Clarendon County and surrounding areas came close to matching these increases, and for the first time, District One students posted higher scores on the writing test than tenth-graders in four other nearby districts. Dr. McCants attributes the higher scores to the improved facilities and better teachers at the new Scott's Branch High. There may be little real integration in Clarendon County, and its poverty rate remains high, but the district Thurgood Marshall picked in 1950 to lead the crusade against Jim Crow schooling is finally giving black children a better education.

"The Goal Is Quality Education"

One salient fact underscores this book's discussion of Jim Crow education over the past two centuries: there has not been a single year in American history in which at least half of the nation's black children attended schools that were largely white. To be sure, pushing school integration past this "halfway" point was never the goal of the civil rights lawyers and activists who labored for so long to end the system of de jure segregation that separated black and white students in southern and border states. Their goal was simply to make sure that school assignments were no longer based solely on race. At the same time, however, many of these lawyers and activists pursued the larger, more ambitious goal of using the courts to achieve the maximum possible racial mixture of students. They urged the courts to order school boards and officials to employ a variety of means—including busing and "metropolitan" desegregation plans—that would overcome the entrenched de facto segregation of residential areas and their neighborhood schools. The failure of those efforts, after the political backlash that ended the short-lived period of "forced busing," cannot be entirely blamed on the Supreme Court and the decisions that ended judicial supervision of schools districts that had achieved "unitary" status. Yet, the Court quite clearly yielded to political pressure, and reflected in its decisions the increasingly conservative mood of the American public, which has endorsed school integration in numerous public opinion polls but has balked at concrete plans to implement that policy in their own cities and neighborhoods. It is fair to conclude that school integration has failed, or—put more honestly—was never seriously tried.

The failure of integration over the past half-century, after the imposition by law during the previous century of inferior Jim Crow schools on the vast majority of black children, adds force to the statement of Justice John Marshall Harlan in 1896 that whites constituted the dominant race "in prestige, in achievements, in education, in wealth and in power." The historic and persisting gap between blacks and white—measured by any part of Harlan's yardstick—is largely the consequence of generations of Jim Crow education. This single factor lies at the root of the problems that afflict or touch virtually every member of America's urban black population of some 25 million people: higher rates of crime, domestic violence, drug and alcohol abuse, teen pregnancy, low-wage jobs, unemployment, infant mortality, lowered life expectancy, and many other indices of social pathology. Singling out one factor to explain a multitude of complex social problems may appear simplistic and reductionist. But there is no denying that the system of Jim Crow schooling has given millions of America's black residents inferior education as children, has consigned them to unskilled jobs as adults, and has made it difficult to escape the urban ghettos into which rural migrants were confined by poverty and white hostility.

There is also no denying that many blacks have overcome the legacy of Jim Crow education and have joined a growing black middle class. The numbers of black doctors, lawyers, engineers, managers, and other professionals have increased since the adoption of "affirmative action" plans by colleges, corporations, and government agencies. But, much like school integration imposed through busing, affirmative action plans imposed through racial "preferences" have produced their own political backlash; federal judges have struck down such programs at the University of Texas and other schools, and the Supreme Court has rejected minority "set-aside" plans designed to channel more public funds to minority-owned firms. Even the modest gains in black education and employment have been slowed, and in some cases reversed, as the economic boom of the 1990s has gone bust and given way to recession and retrenchment in recent years.

One measure of the damaging impact of school resegregation on black students can be found in the report issued in August 2001 of the federally funded National Assessment of Educational Progress on tests of math skills of students in the fourth, eighth, and twelfth grades. On the positive side, the NEAP report showed that the math scores of fourth- and eighth-graders had improved since 1990. Disturbingly, the scores of high school seniors, which had risen slightly during the past decade, dropped sharply between 1996 and 2000. Broken down by race, the NEAP figures show a huge performance gap between black and white students at every grade level. For example, the number of white eighth-graders who scored at the "proficient" or "advanced" levels in math grew from 19 percent in 1990 to 34 percent in 2000, while only 5 percent of blacks scored at those levels in both years. Educational experts attributed the decline in twelfth-grade scores of black students to the substandard schools which most attend. Ann Wilkens of the Educational Trust, a nonprofit organization that works to improve urban schools, stressed the impact of poor math skills on the job prospects of black students. Back in the 1950s, "people could go to work in factories with basic skills," she said. "But in the 1990s, you're seeing a growing gap between the races in the ability to participate at the high levels of society."

Studies like the NEAP report, and similar measures of academic performance on the SAT test, provide growing evidence that the increasing resegregation of American public schools is threatening to turn the "growing gap" between black and white students into a racial chasm. The failure of school integration, largely a consequence of the broken promise of the *Brown* decision, becomes an even more bitter pill to swallow in light of the clear evidence that integration works. More precisely, attending school with substantial numbers of white students improves the academic performance of black children. This reflects, of course, the advantages that majority-white schools have in terms of better-trained, more experienced, and more highly paid teachers, with access to better laboratory and library resources, a wider range of courses, particularly the Advanced Placement courses that challenge students and prepare them for college-level work, and a greater number and variety of extracurricular activities.

In his 2001 report, *Schools More Separate*, Gary Orfield of the Harvard Civil Rights Project summed up the demonstrated benefits of integrated schools for black students. Orfield cited "evidence that students from desegregated educational experiences benefit in terms of college going, employment, and living in integrated settings as adults." Black students who attend integrated high schools, and who then graduate from integrated colleges and universities, make up the majority of black professionals. Orfield and his colleague, Dean Whitla, released a study in 1999 on *Diversity and Legal Education*, which focused on elite laws schools and reported that "almost all of the black and Latino students who made it into those schools came from integrated educational backgrounds."

Integrated education has benefits that go beyond academic performance. A report by Michael Kurleander and John Yun of the Harvard Civil Rights Project in 2000 compiled surveys of students, concluding that "both white and minority students in integrated school districts tend to report by large majorities that they have learned to study and work together and that they are highly confident about their ability to work in such settings as adults. Students report that they have learned a lot about the other group's background and feel confident about the ability to discuss even controversial racial issues across racial lines." These studies illustrate the truth of Thurgood Marshall's statement, during his argument before the

Supreme Court of the Little Rock school case in 1958. "Education is not the teaching of the three R's. Education is the teaching of the overall citizenship, to learn to live together with fellow citizens," Marshall told the justices.

Many people, liberals and conservatives alike, believe that the Supreme Court ended the Jim Crow system with its historic *Brown* decision in 1954. Those who profess this belief also claim that black students, now able to compete with whites on a level playing field, have only themselves to blame for doing poorly in school and failing to achieve the test scores required for admission to prestigious colleges. These advocates of "blaming the victim" fail to recognize any connection between the social and economic problems that burden the black ghetto population, and the Jim Crow educational system that has created and perpetuates the urban black underclass. After all, they argue, more than two generations of blacks have gone to schools that are no longer segregated by race, and are protected from discrimination in finding jobs and places to live by federal and state civil rights laws. Consequently, those blacks who can't find decent jobs, and who live in decaying urban ghettos, cannot blame the Jim Crow schools of past generations for their problems. Nor can they blame the Supreme Court for deciding that "resegregation" based on residential housing patterns is not something that federal judges can remedy, and for allowing the number of one-race schools to increase every year.

In my opinion, those who argue that courts have no further responsibility to remedy the damaging effects of Jim Crow schooling on America's black population are either naive or callous. To assume that two generations of "desegregation" can erase the educational harm of the preceding five or six generations is simply wrong. Studies of the continuing impact of yesterday's Jim Crow schools on today's black children are persuasive. The best compilation of these studies, *The Black-White Test Score Gap*, edited in 1998 by Christopher Jencks and Meredith Phillips, argues that grandparents "pass along their advantages and disadvantages to parents, who then pass them along to the next generation of children." Pushed back several generations, this commonsense observation has a cumulative and highly damaging effect, given the very low educational levels of blacks during the century before the *Brown* decision. Even when black families match whites in years of schooling and income, "it can take more than one generation for successful families to adopt the 'middle-class' parenting practices that seem most likely to increase children's cognitive skills." Jencks and Phillips conclude that "it could take several generations before reductions in socioeconomic inequality produce their full benefits" in higher school performance by black children.

A paradox emerges from these studies. If the past effects of Jim Crow schooling have such harmful consequences on today's black students, what benefits would they obtain from greater "reintegration" of schools? Many black leaders and educators have given up on the ideal of integration and now press for improving the quality of the one-race schools that most urban black children attend. "At this political moment, integration of the schools has been an abysmal failure," Doris Y. Wilkinson wrote in 1996. A leading black sociologist at the University of Kentucky, Wilkinson argues that the "benefits gained from obligatory school integration do not outweigh the immeasurable cultural and psychological losses." These losses include the black school as a community center and resource, the leadership training of black students in their own teams, clubs, and activities, and the close involvement of black parents in their children's education. "What has been neglected in integration history" since the *Brown* decision, Wilkinson claims, "has been a rational assessment of the emotional, motivational, learning, and community impact of abolishing the black school on poor and working-class African American children."

Another black sociologist, Leslie Innis of Florida State University, was herself a "desegregation pioneer" in the 1960s. Her study of other blacks who were among the first to attend formerly white schools shows that "the pioneers generally feel they have paid too high an emotional and psychological price for what they now perceive as too little change in the whole system of race relations." The pioneers "do not seem to have fared any better in terms of objective social status criteria such as education, occupation, and income than their peers who went to segregated schools," writes Innis. She asserts that a "deepening dissatisfaction with the educational system has created feelings of alienation and anger" among many blacks. "These feelings have generated a call for new educational policies to be considered. Among these new policies are schools that are racially separate but equal in all important aspects—buildings, facilities, books, and personnel."

Given the growing chorus of black educators and activists who have literally given up on integration, would it not be more helpful to the millions of black children who now attend virtually all-black schools to abandon the futile efforts to achieve racial balance through busing and other means of moving children from their neighborhood schools? In place of these policies, for which there currently exists hardly any political clout, why not campaign for better-trained and better-paid teachers in urban schools, new buildings, more computers and science labs, and more rigorous standards in language and math skills? These are, in fact, the proposals to improve American schools that are currently fashionable. Other plans—giving vouchers for private school tuition to children from "failing" public schools, creating more "magnet" schools with specialized programs, expanding the Teacher Corps of highly motivated college graduates—have gained influential sponsors in Congress and state governments.

However laudable their goals, these and other "school reform" proposals have two major drawbacks. First, they do not address the serious problems of the "total environment" of the urban ghettos in which close to half of all black children live. This is the environment with high crime rates, low income, few cultural resources, and very high rates—more than 70 percent in most big cities—of female-headed households in which single mothers have little time or energy to help their children with homework, and most often are barely literate themselves. However good their schools and teachers, black children from this environment come to school with obstacles to effective learning that few white children must overcome.

The second drawback of current school reform proposals is that they rely largely on standardized testing to measure results. One consequence of "teaching to the test" is that school officials pressure teachers to rely on old-fashioned methods of rote learning, the mainstay of Jim Crow schools before the *Brown* decision. Creativity, curiosity, and critical thinking are stifled, and the pressure on teachers in largely black and Hispanic schools to raise test scores and avoid "failing" grades for their schools becomes intense. *The New York Times* reported in June 2001 that many fourth-grade teachers in the city's schools, the grade in which testing begins, are requesting transfers to other grades, to escape the "test pressure" that forces them to use a lockstep curriculum.

If the current push for school reforms that will not change the unbalanced racial composition of most schools means that integration has failed, is there any point in assigning the blame for this failure? We can point the finger at individuals and institutions: Justice Felix Frankfurter's insistence on the "all deliberate speed" formula in the second *Brown* decision; President Dwight Eisenhower's failure to speak out in support of court orders; the "war on the Constitution" waged by Governor Orval Faubus and other southern politicians; the Supreme Court's refusal to allow school buses to cross district lines in the *Milliken* case; and the Court's explicit approval of "one-race" schools in decisions that ended judicial oversight of desegregation orders. In a broader sense, however, the blame rests with the "dominant race" in America. Whites created the institution of slavery; whites fashioned the Jim Crow system that replaced slavery with segregation; whites spat on black children, threw rocks at buses, and shut down entire school districts to avoid integration; and white parents abandoned the cities when neighborhoods and schools passed the "tipping point" and became too black for comfort.

This is not an indictment of a race, merely an acknowledgment of reality. Many whites took part in the abolitionist crusade, fought and died in the Civil War to end slavery, campaigned to end the Jim Crow system, and kept their children in public schools that had become largely black. Most white Americans, in fact, profess their belief in school integration; two-thirds of those polled in 1994 agreed that integration has "improved the quality of education for blacks," and two-fifths said the same for white students. Belief in an ideal and support for its implementation, however, are not the same. Substantially more than two-thirds of whites oppose busing for "racial balance" in the schools, and most say they would move out of their present neighborhood if it became more than 20 percent black. The phenomenon of "white flight" shows that many people have put their attitudes into action.

Perhaps we should accept the reality that Jim Crow schools are here to stay, and make the best of the situation. Kenneth W. Jenkins, who headed the NAACP chapter in Yonkers, New York, was removed from that post by the national organization in 1996 for questioning the protracted litigation to integrate his city's segregated schools. "This thing is not working," he said. "I support integration, but I don't think integration is the goal. The goal is quality education." Even a dedicated NAACP lawyer, Ted Shaw, voiced his frustration at the futility of litigation to integrate urban schools. "You're beating your head up against the wall until it's bloody. At some point you have to ask, 'Should I continue to beat up against this wall?' To ask that question is not a terrible thing."

Perhaps the best person to answer Jenkins and Shaw, and others who share their frustration—white and black alike—is Thurgood Marshall, who put his whole life into struggling against the Jim Crow system. It is worth repeating here the words he wrote in 1974, dissenting in the *Milliken* case: "Desegregation is not and was never expected to be an easy task. Racial attitudes ingrained in our Nation's childhood and adolescence are not quickly thrown aside in its middle years." Marshall concluded: "In the short run, it may seem to be the easiest course to allow our great metropolitan areas to be divided up each into two cities—one white, the other black—but it is a course, I predict, our people will ultimately regret."

Suggested Readings and Chapter Sources

I have listed below the most important works on which this book is based. They are arranged loosely by category, although some do overlap those groupings. In the chapter sources that follow this listing, I have included citations to the books, articles, and other sources (census data, government reports, etc.) on which each chapter draws. I have not, however, included citations to page numbers for quoted material, largely in the interest of conserving space. I would be glad to supply the precise citation to any material in the book to readers who desire that information; they can reach me by E-mail at **pirons@ucsd.edu**. From my own experience, and from inquiries to students and colleagues, I feel confident that hardly anyone consults or checks the citations in book notes. A listing of chapter sources thus seems to me a good compromise between no notes and too many notes. If I am mistaken in this decision, I hope that readers will let me know.

Another difference between this book and those I have written earlier is that much of the material in this one comes from Internet sources. For example, most big-city school districts and state education departments now maintain Web sites that include data on test scores by districts and often by individual schools. I have included citations to these Web sites in the chapter sources, and readers who desire to check the data in this book or to find more can access these sites quickly and easily. The U.S. Department of Education also maintains several Web sites that contain useful information, including the Bureau of Educational Statistics. A Web site called the National School Data Bank includes demographic data on every school district in the country, based on the 1990 U.S. census reports; this data has not yet been updated to include material from the 2000 census. In addition, many newspaper and journal articles are now available through the Internet, sparing readers a trip to the library and the task of locating journal volumes on the shelves or putting microfilm or microfiche in a reader.

Most of the court decisions I have cited and discuss in this book are available on the Internet as well as in all law libraries; the most accessible Web sites are **www.findlaw.com** and the LexisNexis site. Cases can be accessed by party names, such as Brown v. Board of Education of Topeka, or by citation to the case reporter; for the Brown case that would be 347 U.S. 497 (1954), which represents volume 347 of United States Reports, page 497, with the decision handed down in 1954. The Federal Supplement, abbreviated F.Supp., contains the written opinions of federal district courts, and the Federal Reporter includes opinions of federal courts of appeals. This reporter is now in its third series, and the volumes are cited as F., F.2d, or F.3d. The opinions of state courts are available in two sets of volumes, one for each state and a second series called the regional reporters. Any reference librarian will be able to help readers locate these decisions.

Let me caution readers that the works cited below are just a small part of the voluminous and growing literature on school integration, education, and race in America. There are many books, articles, court decisions, government reports, and other sources of data that I have not included in these suggested readings and chapter sources. Even a partially complete bibliography on these topics would fill many pages. But I hope the material I cite below will help readers explore for themselves the issues raised in this book, from Jim Crow schools to the broader questions of race in American society.

SUGGESTED READINGS

There is not yet available a full historical account of the education of black Americans. No writer has tackled this important topic, and the books on the period that preceded the *Brown* cases were published many decades ago and are available only in reprint editions. Four books were extremely useful in writing the first chapters of this book: Carter G. Woodson, *The Education of the Negro Prior to 1861* (1919); Horace Mann Bond, *The Education of the Negro in the American Social Order* (1934); Henry Allen Bulloch, *A History of Negro Education in the South* (1967); and Howard K. Beale, *A History of Freedom of Teaching in American Schools* (reprint edition, 1966).

Anyone who writes about the school segregation cases, or wants to read about them, must begin with Richard Kluger's monumental and exhaustive book *Simple Justice: The History of* Brown v. Board of Education *and Black America's Struggle for Equality* (1976). Kluger based his account of the *Brown* cases on more than 130 interviews, the papers of Supreme Court justices, trial transcripts, and local newspapers. Like many others, my book is greatly indebted to Kluger's work, which ends with a postscript written in 1975. Kluger does not address the impact of Jim Crow schooling on the post-*Brown* generations of black children, but his book includes a wealth of detail on the *Brown* cases and the people involved in them. *Simple Justice*, in my opinion, is one of the five best case studies in American legal history; only its length (823 pages) has kept it from becoming an assigned text in my own courses. Hopefully, its publisher will issue an abridged version, much like the shorter version of Don Fehrenbacher's book on the *Dred Scott* case.

An excellent companion to Kluger's book is the volume edited by Leon Friedman, *Argument: The Oral Arguments Before the Supreme Court in* Brown v. Board of Education of Topeka, *1952–1955* (1969). This volume includes the verbatim transcripts of all the Supreme Court arguments in the five *Brown* cases. Another source of oral argument transcripts, and of the briefs submitted by the parties and by amicus groups in major cases (including more than half of those discussed in this book) is the series edited by Philip Kurland and Gerhard Casper, *Landmark Briefs and Arguments of the Supreme Court of the United States: Constitutional Law.* Transcripts of oral arguments are available only for cases decided since 1955, when the Supreme Court began recording arguments on audiotape; before that time, transcripts are available only for a few cases in which one or both parties hired private court reporters, and in which the transcripts were donated to the Court.

There are a number of books that deal with various aspects of the *Brown* cases and of other lawsuits that challenged school segregation. The most important is the combined history and memoir of Jack Greenberg, who served for thirty years on the NAACP legal staff and who succeeded Thurgood Marshall as general counsel. Greenberg's book, *Crusaders in the Courts: How a Dedicated Band of Lawyers Fought for the Civil Rights Revolution* (1994), also covers the NAACP's litigation in other areas, and is both engaging and insightful. Mark Tushnet, a Georgetown University law professor and former law clerk to Thurgood Marshall in the Supreme Court, has written three books that explore Marshall's roles as lawyer and justice: *The NAACP's Legal Strategy Against Segregated Education, 1925–1950* (1987); *Making Civil Rights Law: Thurgood Marshall and the Supreme Court, 1936–1961* (1994); and *Making Constitutional Law: Thurgood Marshall and the Supreme Court, 1961–1991* (1997). There is not yet a full-scale biography of Marshall that draws on the papers he donated to the Library of Congress; the best available biography so far is by Juan Williams, *Thurgood Marshall: American Revolutionary* (1998), a journalistic account for which Williams conducted more than a hundred interviews.

Several books have addressed the impact of the *Brown* decisions. They include Norman Bartley, *The Rise of Massive Resistance: Race and Politics in the South During the 1950s* (1969); Lino A. Graglia, *Disaster by Decree* (1976), a highly critical book by a highly conservative University of Texas law professor who has vigorously opposed affirmative action plans in schools and workplaces; J. Harvie Wilkinson III, *The Supreme Court from* Brown *to* Bakke (1979), by a former University of Virginia law professor who now sits on the U.S. Court of Appeals in Richmond—Wilkinson takes a moderately conservative view of the Supreme Court's civil rights decisions; and Raymond Wolters, *The Burden of* Brown: *Thirty Years of School Desegregation* (1984)—Wolters looked at the experiences with school integration in each of the five *Brown* communities, focusing on the problems in the schools, but without any analysis of the consequences of Jim Crow education in those communities. Between them, the books by Graglia, Wilkinson, and Wolters portray school integration as a failed policy that resulted from judicial overreaching, rather than judicial timidity in the face of southern resistance. David Armour took a more neutral stance in *Forced Justice: School Desegregation and the Law* (1995).

The most recent study of the *Brown* decisions is the book by James T. Patterson, a Brown University historian, Brown v. Board of Education: *A Civil Rights Milestone and Its Troubled Legacy* (2001). Patterson focuses on the political reaction to the Court's school integration rulings between 1954 and 1995, and relies largely on news accounts of the cases and events he discusses. This relatively short book (223 pages) is more a synopsis than an exhaustive study, and is part of an Oxford University Press series *Pivotal Moments in American History*.

Three books looked at the federal judges who were responsible for drafting and enforcing the desegregation decrees that followed the Supreme Court's "all deliberate speed" ruling in 1955. Jack W. Peltason, a political scientist, focused on the district court judges in southern states in *58 Lonely Men* (1961). Jack Bass, a journalist, wrote a highly sympathetic account of the judges on the Fifth Circuit Court of Appeals in *Unlikely Heroes* (1981). And Frank T. Read and Lucy S. McGough examined the Fifth Circuit school cases in *Let Them Be Judged* (1978).

Surprisingly, there are only two books that focus on individual communities that were involved in the *Brown* cases. Bob Smith, a journalism professor, wrote *They Closed Their Schools: Prince Edward County, Virginia, 1951–1964* (1965). Smith drew on interviews and the local press, and gives the flavor of events in Prince Edward County through the period of "massive resistance" in Virginia. Jeffrey A. Raffel, in *The Politics of School Desegregation: The Metropolitan Remedy in Delaware* (1980), provides an academic account of school integration in Delaware that is much less readable than Smith's book. There are no book-length studies of the school battles in Clarendon County, South Carolina, Washington, D.C., or Topeka, Kansas. One participant in the Topeka case, Paul Wilson, offers an interesting perspective as the lawyer who defended the city in the Supreme Court in *A Time to Lose: Representing Kansas in* Brown v. Board of Education (1995). As his title implies, Wilson has no regrets about losing the case.

There are a number of books that recount the battles over school desegregation in various communities. J. Anthony Lukas looked at Boston, one of the bloodiest battlegrounds in the wars over busing, in *Common Ground: A Turbulent Decade in the Lives of Three American Families* (1986). Another book about

Boston, more academic in approach, is Ronald Formisano, *Boston Against Busing: Race, Class, and Ethnicity in the 1960s and 1970s* (1991). Eleanor P. Wolf focused on Detroit in *Trial and Error: The Detroit School Segregation Case* (1981). The city of Charlotte, North Carolina, the locale of the first Supreme Court decision to approve busing as a desegregation remedy, has been the subject of three books. Bernard Schwartz, a law professor and prolific writer on legal issues, wrote *Swann's Way: The School Busing Case and the Supreme Court* (1986). Frye Gaillard, a Charlotte journalist, looked at the city's political struggles over busing in *The Dream Long Deferred* (1988). And Davison Douglas wrote a detailed academic account in *Reading, Writing, and Race: The Desegregation of the Charlotte Schools* (1995).

Three books on various aspects of racial segregation in America were of particular help in writing this book. Douglas S. Massey and Nancy A. Denton have documented the persistence of residential segregation in urban centers in *American Apartheid: Segregation and the Making of the Underclass* (1993). Christopher Jencks and Meredith Phillips edited an excellent collection of essays, several of them discussed in this book, in *The Black-White Test Score Gap* (1998). The essays in their volume examine the issue from several perspectives, and provide evidence of the deep roots of racial differences in test performance in Jim Crow education. Gary Orfield, who directs the Harvard Civil Rights Project, is the nation's leading authority on school segregation. A book by Orfield and Susan Eaton, *Dismantling Desegregation: The Quiet Reversal of Brown v. Board of Education* (1996), shows how opponents of school integration used the busing issue to inflame public opinion, despite the fact that millions of children, black and white, had taken buses to school for decades, simply as a means of transportation. The foes of "forced busing" were really fighting to keep their "neighborhood" schools largely white. The periodic reports that Orfield and his colleagues produce are the best available sources of data on the resegregation of American schools.

Two books have examined the topic of desegregation from the perspectives of social science. Nancy H. St. John looked at the effects of school desegregation in *Desegregation: Outcomes for Children* (1975); and Jennifer Hochschild, a political scientist, took a gloomy view in *The New American Dilemma: Liberal Democracy and School Desegregation* (1984).

Race relations in general have been addressed in several books over the past decade. Andrew Hacker, a sociologist, used census reports and other statistical data to document the persistence of racial disparities in *Two Nations: Black and White, Separate, Hostile, Unequal* (1992). Stephan Thernstrom and Abigail Thernstrom, a husband-and-wife team from Harvard who are closely identified with the Republican party, concluded that the status of blacks in America has never been better in *America in Black and White: One Nation, Indivisible*

(1997). Another Harvard professor, Orlando Patterson, is an African American who echoed many of the Thernstroms' views in *The Ordeal of Integration: Progress and Resentment in America's "Racial" Crisis* (1997).

In addition to the books cited above, three academic journals provide continuing coverage of issues related to school integration and the education of black children: *The Journal of Negro Education, The Negro Educational Review,* and *Equity and Excellence in Education.*

Four reference sources provide citations to hundreds of articles that have been published on various aspects of school integration over the past five decades. Articles in dozens of magazines, such as *Time, Newsweek, The New Republic,* and *National Review,* are indexed in the *Reader's Guide to Periodical Literature.* Articles in scholarly journals, including those in the fields of sociology, education, and political science, are indexed in the *Public Affairs Information Service.* Law review articles are indexed in the *Current Law Index* and the *Index to Legal Periodicals,* which largely duplicate each other. In addition, the indexes to the *New York Times* provide citations to that paper's coverage of the issues discussed in this book.

Chapter Sources

Chapter 1

The stories of former slaves are taken from a fascinating audiotape and book set, *Remembering Slavery,* edited by Ira Berlin, Marc Favreau, and Steven F. Miller (1998). The tapes in this set include recordings made in the 1930s of the reminiscences of former slaves, which had been stored in the Library of Congress. Hearing the stories of former slaves in their own words is both exciting and educational.

The material on the education of blacks during the period of slavery and through the 1930s is based on the following books: Carter G. Woodson, *The Education of the Negro Prior to 1861* (1919); Horace Mann Bond, *The Education of the Negro in the American Social Order* (1934); Henry Allen Bullock, *A History of Negro Education in the South* (1967); Howard K. Beale, *A History of Freedom of Teaching in American Schools* (1960); and Ernst W. Swanson and John A. Griffin, eds., *Public Education in the South: Today and Tomorrow* (1955).

The cases discussed in this chapter include: *Roberts v. City of Boston,* 59 Mass. 198 (1849); *State of Ohio v. McCann,* 21 Ohio St. 210 (1871); *Ward v. Flood,* 48 Cal. 36 (1874); *Bertonneau v. New Orleans,* 3 Woods 177, Fed. Cases 1, 361 (1878); *Cory v. Carter,* 48 Ind. 337 (1879); *King v. Gallagher,* 93 N.Y. 438 (1883); and *Lehew v. Brummell,* 15 S.W. 765 (Mo. 1890).

Chapter 2

The only book-length treatment of the *Plessy* case is in Charles Lofgrem, *The Plessy Case: A Legal-Historical Interpretation* (1987). This is a fairly dry and technical book, and treats the case from a narrow legal perspective.

The *Plessy* decision in the Louisiana supreme court: 11 So. 948 (La. 1892); the U.S. Supreme Court decision is *Plessy v. Ferguson*, 163 U.S. 537 (1895).

The Georgia high school case: *Cumming v. Richmond County*, 175 U.S. 529 (1899).

The quotations from Booker T. Washington and J. L. M. Curry are from the two-volume biography by Louis R. Harlan: *Booker T. Washington: The Making of a Black Leader, 1856–1901* (1972); and *Booker T. Washington: The Wizard of Tuskegee, 1901–1915* (1983). Washington's autobiography, *Up From Slavery*, is available in several editions and is sparse on the details of his career. Also see J. L. M. Curry, *A Brief Sketch of George Peabody and a History of the Peabody Educational Fund* (reprint edition, 1969).

Statistics on black literacy are compiled from numerous volumes of U.S. census data.

The report on black education in the South during the 1930s, prepared for the American Council on Education: Charles S. Johnson, *Growing Up in the Black Belt: Negro Youth in the Rural South* (1941). Anyone who is inclined to minimize the damaging effects of Jim Crow schooling on southern blacks should read this devastating report.

The material on black migration from south to north is compiled from U.S. census data from 1910 to 1960. Also see Daniel M. Johnson, *Black Migration in America* (1981); and Joe William Trotter, ed., *The Great Migration in Historical Perspective: New Dimensions of Race, Class, and Gender* (1991).

Article by Benjamin Mays: "Improving the Morale of Negro Children and Youth," *Journal of Negro Education* 19 (1950).

Material on black schools in the South: "The New South," *Life*, October 31, 1949.

Report on Clarendon County case: *Newsweek*, November 27, 1950.

Chapter 3

Story of Annie Martin Gibson: interview with author in Summerton, South Carolina, October 1999.

The history of the Scott's Branch schools: *The Growth and Development of Schools for Negroes in Clarendon County from 1670 to 1966*, prepared by the Clarendon County Teachers Association, Retired, mimeographed, 1997.

Statistics on Clarendon County: compiled from U.S. census data for South Carolina, 1950.

Reports on the Isaac Woodward case: *The Crisis* (monthly magazine of the NAACP), September 1946; see also Richard Kluger, *Simple Justice*, pp. 298–99.

Tinsley E. Yarbrough has written an excellent biography of Judge Waring, *A Passion for Jusice: J. Waties Waring and Civil Rights* (1987).

The beginnings of the Clarendon County case are chronicled in Kluger, *Simple Justice*, chs. 1 and 13.

Biographical data on Thurgood Marshall: Kluger, *Simple Justice*, chs. 8–10, and Juan Williams, *Thurgood Marshall: American Revolutionary* (1998).

The Margold Report is discussed in Mark Tushnet, *The NAACP's Legal Strategy Against Segregated Education, 1925–1950*, pp. 25–28; see also Kluger, *Simple Justice*, pp. 133–39, and Jack Greenberg, *Crusaders in the Courts*, pp. 56–62.

Supreme Court decision in *Yick Wo v. Hopkins*: 118 U.S. 356 (1886).

Supreme Court decision in *Gong Lum v. Rice*: 275 U.S. 78 (1927).

Supreme Court decision in *Missouri ex rel. Gaines v. Canada*: 305 U.S. 337 (1938).

Supreme Court decision in *Sipuel v. Oklahoma Board of Regents*: 332 U.S. 631 (1948).

Supreme Court decision in *Sweatt v. Painter*: 339 U.S. 629 (1950).

Supreme Court decision in *McLaurin v. Oklahoma State Regents*: 339 U.S. 637 (1950).

The discussion of the Clarendon County case is drawn from Kluger, *Simple Justice*, ch. 1.

Chapter 4

The account of Kenneth Clark's role in the Clarendon County case is drawn from Kluger, *Simple Justice*, chs. 14 and 15. Also see Kenneth Clark, *Prejudice and Your Child* (1955); Kenneth Clark and Mamie Clark, "Segregation as a Factor in the Racial Identification of Negro Pre-school Children: A Preliminary Report," *Journal of Experimental Education*, Spring 1940; Kenneth B. Clark, "Effect of Prejudice and Discrimination on Personality Development," Report for Mid-Century White House Conference on Children and Youth, Federal Security Agency (1950).

The trial transcript in the *Briggs* case is filed under Civil Action No. 2657 (1950), United States District Court, Charleston, S.C.

Opinions of the three-judge court in the *Briggs* case: 98 F.Supp. 529 (E.D.S.C. 1951); 103 F.Supp. 920 (E.D.S.C. 1952).

Chapter 5

For accounts of the Prince Edward County case, see Kluger, *Simple Justice*, chs. 19 and 20; and Bob Smith, *They Closed Their Schools* (1965). The files of the

Farmville *Herald* include many articles giving the segregationist view of the school segregation dispute.

The trial transcript in the *Davis* case is filed under Civil Action No. 1333 (1951), United States District Court, Richmond, Va.

Decision of the three-judge court in the *Davis* case: 103 F.Supp. 337 (E.D.Va. 1952).

Chapter 6

For an account of the District of Columbia case, see Kluger, *Simple Justice*, ch. 21; see also Constance M. Green, *The Secret City: A History of Race Relations in the Nation's Capital* (1967); and Carl F. Hansen, *Danger in Washington: The Story of My Twenty Years in the Public Schools in the Nation's Capital* (1968). Hansen was the superintendent of schools in Washington during the period of integration, and was the defendant in several lawsuits filed against the District government by civil rights activists.

Statistics on the status of blacks in the District of Columbia: compiled from U.S. census data, 1950.

Court of Appeals decision in *Carr v. Corning*: 182 F.2d 14 (D.C. Cir. 1950).

For an account of the Delaware cases, see Kluger, *Simple Justice*, ch. 18.

Statistics on the status of blacks in Delaware: compiled from U.S. census data, 1950.

The Delaware supreme court decision in *Parker v. University of Delaware*: 75 A.2d 225 (Del. 1950).

The state court decisions in *Gebhart v. Belton* and *Gebhart v. Bulah*: 87 A.2d 862 (Del. Chancery 1952); 91 A.2d 137 (Del. 1953).

Chapter 7

For an account of the Topeka case, see Kluger, *Simple Justice*, chs. 16 and 17; also see Greenberg, *Crusaders in the Courts*, ch. 10; and Paul E. Wilson, *A Time to Lose: Representing Kansas in* Brown v. Board of Education (1995).

Decision of Kansas supreme court in *Reynolds v. Board of Education of Topeka*: 66 Kan. 672 (1902).

Statistics on the status of blacks in Topeka: compiled from U.S. census data, 1950.

Transcript of trial in *Brown* case is filed in the U.S. District Court, Topeka, Kansas, trial date of October 16, 1951.

Decision of the three-judge court in the *Brown* case: 98 F. Supp. 797 (D.Kan. 1951).

Chapter 8

The brief of the U.S. government in the *Brown* case is reproduced in Kurland and Casper, eds., *Landmark Briefs and Arguments*, vol. 49, p. 113.

The oral arguments in *Brown* and the other school cases are in Leon Friedman, ed., *Argument: The Oral Argument Before the Supreme Court in* Brown v. Board of Education of Topeka, *1952–1955* (1969). They are also in *Landmark Briefs and Arguments*, vol. 49.

For accounts of the oral arguments and the Supreme Court deliberations in the school cases, see Kluger, *Simple Justice*, chs. 23 and 24; also see Greenberg, *Crusaders in the Courts*, ch. 13.

For an excellent biography of John W. Davis, see William H. Harbaugh, *Lawyer's Lawyer: The Life of John W. Davis* (1973).

The Supreme Court opinions in *Dred Scott v. Sandford* are at 60 U.S. 393 (1857). For an outstanding account of the case, see Don Fehrenbacher, *The Dred Scott Case: Its Significance in American Law and Politics* (1978).

Chapter 9

The second and third rounds of arguments in the school cases are reproduced in Friedman, *Argument*, and *Landmark Briefs and Arguments*, vols. 49 and 49A.

For accounts of the arguments, see Kluger, *Simple Justice*, chs. 25 and 26, and Greenberg, *Crusaders in the Courts*, chs. 14 and 15. Kluger also recounts the Supreme Court's deliberations in the cases.

Chapter 10

The southern reaction to the *Brown II* decision is discussed in Kluger, *Simple Justice*, ch. 26. Many other statements are quoted in articles in *Time, Newsweek, U.S. News & World Report*, and the *New York Times* and *Washington Post* in the weeks following the decision in May 1955.

Judge Parker's decision in the *Briggs* case: *Briggs v. Elliott*, 132 F.Supp. 776 (E.D.S.C. 1955).

Articles on border-state compliance with the *Brown II* ruling can be found in many articles in *Time, Newsweek*, and *U.S. News & World Report* during the months of August–October in 1955, 1956, and 1957. See, in particular, articles in *Time* in the issues of September 19, 1955, and September 23, 1957.

Reports on the violent resistance to integration in Clinton, Tennessee, Mansfield, Texas, and Sturgis, Kentucky, appeared in the September 16, 1957 issue of *Time*.

For an excellent account of the Little Rock crisis, from a legal perspective, see Tony Freyer, *The Little Rock Crisis: A Constitutional Interpretation* (1984).

Daisy Bates, the Arkansas NAACP president who shepherded the nine black students through the mobs around Central High, wrote a powerful memoir in *The Long Shadow of Little Rock* (1962). See also Greenberg, *Crusaders in the Courts*, ch. 17; and articles in *Time, Newsweek,* and *U.S. News & World Report* during 1957 and 1958.

Judge Lemley's decision in the Little Rock case: *Cooper v. Aaron,* 163 F. Supp. 13 (E.D.Ark. 1958); the Court of Appeals decision: 257 F.2d 33 (8th Cir. 1958).

The Supreme Court arguments in the Little Rock case are in *Landmark Briefs and Arguments,* vol. 54.

The Supreme Court decision in the Little Rock case: *Cooper v. Aaron,* 358 U.S. 1 (1958).

Chapter 11

A good reportorial account of the conflicts over school integration in Prince Edward County is Bob Smith, *They Closed Their Schools.*

The lower-court rulings in the Prince Edward County case: *Allen v. Prince Edward County,* 198 F.Supp. 497 (E.D.Va. 1961); 207 F.Supp. 349 (E.D.Va. 1962); *Griffin v. Prince Edward County,* 322 F.2d 332 (4th Cir. 1963).

The Supreme Court decision in the Prince Edward County case: *Griffin v. Prince Edward County,* 377 U.S. 218 (1964).

An excellent journalistic report on the role of the Fifth Circuit judges in school cases is Jack Bass, *Unlikely Heroes.*

The Fifth Circuit decision in the Jefferson County case: *United States v. Jefferson County, Alabama, Board of Education,* 372 F.2d 836 (5th Cir. 1966).

The Supreme Court arguments in the New Kent County cases are in *Landmark Briefs and Arguments,* vol. 66.

The Supreme Court decision in the New Kent County case: *Green v. New Kent County, Virginia,* 391 U.S. 420 (1968).

For accounts of the *Alexander* case, see Bass, *Unlikely Heroes,* ch. 18; and Greenberg, *Crusaders in the Courts,* ch. 28.

The Supreme Court decision in the *Alexander* case: *Alexander v. Holmes County, Mississippi, Board of Education,* 396 U.S. 19 (1969).

The Supreme Court decision in the *Carter* case: *Carter v. West Feliciana, Louisiana, Parish School Board,* 396 U.S. 290 (1970).

Chapter 12

An excellent journalistic account of the *Swann* case is in Frye Gaillard, *The Dream Long Deferred* (1968). An account from a legal perspective, which focuses on the Supreme Court case, is in Bernard Schwartz, *Swann's Way: The School Busing Case and the Supreme Court* (1986).

The lower-court opinions in the *Swann* case: *Swann v. Charlotte-Mecklenburg Board of Education*, 243 F.Supp. 667 (W.D.N.C. 1965); 369 F.2d 29 (4th Cir. 1966).

Regrettably, the Supreme Court arguments in the *Swann* case are not in the *Landmark Briefs and Arguments* series. However, a near-verbatim account is in *United States Law Week*, October 20, 1970.

For a detailed account of the Supreme Court deliberations in the *Swann* case, see Schwartz, *Swann's Way*.

The Supreme Court decision in the *Swann* case: *Swann v. Charlotte-Mecklenburg Board of Education*, 402 U.S. 1 (1971).

My account of the political controversy over the busing issue, the debates over anti-busing legislation in Congress, and the statements of President Nixon is drawn from reports in the *Congressional Quarterly Almanac*, 1971, pp. 601–18, and 1972, pp. 673–90, and the *Public Papers of the Presidents: Richard Nixon, 1969–1972*.

On the violence in Pontiac, Michigan, see *Newsweek*, September 20, 1971.

Judge Roth's decision in the Detroit busing case: *Milliken v. Bradley*, 345 F.Supp. 918 (E.D.Mich. 1972).

Chapter 13

Statistics on Detroit: compiled from U.S. census data.

Judge Roth's rulings in the Detroit case: *Milliken v. Bradley*, 338 F.Supp. 582 (E.D.Mich. 1971); 345 F. Supp. 918 (1972).

Court of Appeals ruling in the *Milliken* case: 484 F.2d 215 (6th Cir. 1973).

The Supreme Court arguments in the *Milliken* case are in *Landmark Briefs and Arguments*, vol. 80.

The Supreme Court opinion in the *Milliken* case: 418 U.S. 717 (1974).

Statistics on the academic performance of students in Detroit and suburban schools are from the Web site of the Michigan Department of Education.

For background on schools in Boston, see U.S. Commission on Civil Rights, *Hearings Held in Boston, Massachusetts, June 16–20, 1975* (1978); see also Robert Coles, *School* (1998); and Ralph Edwards, *Black Power/White Power in Public Education* (1998).

Judge Garrity's ruling in the Boston busing case: *Morgan v. Hennigan*, 379 F.Supp. 410 (D.Mass. 1974).

For accounts of ROAR's activities and the Boston busing controversy, see articles in *Time* and *Newsweek* during 1974 and 1975, especially *Newsweek*, January 20, June 9, and September 22, 1975.

Judge Garrity's second ruling in the Boston busing case: *Morgan v. Hennigan*, 401 F.Supp. 216 (D.Mass. 1975).

For an account of the beatings of Theodore Landsmark and Richard Poleet, see Ed Zuckerman, "Beaten Up in Boston," *The New Republic*, May 22, 1976.

Chapter 14

District court opinions in the Oklahoma City case: *Dowell v. Oklahoma City School Board*, 219 F.Supp. 427 (W.D.Ok. 1963); 244 F.Supp. 971 (1965); 388 F.Supp. 1256 (1972).

Court of Appeals opinions in the *Dowell* case: 485 F.2d 1012 (10th Cir. 1972).

The Supreme Court arguments in the *Dowell* case are reported in *United States Law Week*, October 9, 1970.

The Supreme Court opinion in the *Dowell* case: 498 U.S. 237 (1991).

The subsequent Court of Appeals decision in the *Dowell* case: 890 F.2d 1483 (10th Cir. 1993).

Court of Appeals decisions in the DeKalb County case: *Freeman v. Pitts*, 755 F.2d. 1423 (11th Cir. 1985) 887 F.2d 1438 (1989).

The Supreme Court arguments in the *Freeman* case are reported in *United States Law Week*, October 15, 1991.

The Supreme Court opinion in the *Freeman* case: 503 U.S. 467 (1992).

District Court opinions in the Kansas City case: *Missouri v. Jenkins*, 593 F.Supp. 1485 (W.D.Mo. 1984); 639 F.Supp. 19 (1985).

Court of Appeals opinions in *Jenkins* case: 11 F.3d 755 (8th Cir. 1993); 19 F.3d 395 (1994).

The Supreme Court arguments in the *Jenkins* case are not reported in *Landmark Briefs and Arguments* or *United States Law Week*; these quotations are drawn from articles in the *New York Times* and *Washington Post*, January 12, 1995.

The Supreme Court opinions in *Missouri v. Jenkins*: 515 U.S. 70 (1995).

Justice Thomas's opinion in *United States v. Fordice*: 505 U.S. 717 (1992).

Chapter 15

Statistics on the racial composition of American schools: compiled from data on the Web site of the Bureau of Educational Statistics, U.S. Department of Education, and from U.S. census data.

The 2001 report by Gary Orfield, *Schools More Separate: Consequences of a Decade of Resegregation*, is available on the Web site of the Harvard Civil Rights Project.

The 1997 report by Gary Orfield and John Yun, *Resegregation in American Schools*, is available on the Web site of the Harvard Civil Rights Project.

Statistics on the status of black families in various cities and nationally: compiled from U.S. census data.

The Brookings Institution report: Christopher Jencks and Meredith Phillips, eds., *The Black-White Test Score Gap* (1998).

Statistics on black-white income and education disparities: compiled from U.S. census data.

Data on parenting practices in black and white families is from the *National Household Education Survey*, National Center for Education Statistics (1991).

Richard Nisbett's rebuttal to Herrnstein and Murray: "IQ, Race, and Heredity," *Commentary*, August 1995.

Study of black single mothers by Shirley A. Hill: "African American Single Mothers," *Signs*, Spring 1999.

Study of black single women in Springfield, Illinois, by Prohanda K. Nandi and Hugh Harris: "The Social World of Female-Headed Black Families: A Study of the Quality of Life in a Marginalized Neighborhood," *International Journal of Comparative Sociology*, May 1999.

Statistics on academic performance at Lee Elementary School in Springfield, Illinois: compiled from data on the Web site of the Illinois Department of Education.

Study of black students in Stockton, California, by John Ogbu: "Low School Performance as an Adaptation: The Case of Blacks in Stockton, California," in *Minority Education and Caste: The American System in Cross-Cultural Perspective* (1978); also see Ogbu, "The Consequences of the American Caste System," in Ulrich Neisser, ed., *The School Achievement of Minority Children: New Perspectives* (1986); and Ogbu, "Racial Stratification in the United States: Why Inequality Persists," *Teachers College Record* 96 (2), 1994.

Studies by Claude Steele: "Stereotype Threat and the Test Performance of Academically Succesful African Americans," in Jencks and Phillips, *The Black-White Test Score Gap*, ch. 11; "Race and the Schooling of Black America," *Atlantic Monthly*, April 1992; "A Threat in the Air: How Stereotypes Shape the Intellectual Identities and Performance of Women and African Americans," *American Psychologist*, June 1997.

Study of Lee Jussim, Jacquelynne Eccles, and Stephanie Madon: "Social Perception, Social Stereotypes, and Teacher Expectations: Accuracy and the Quest for the Powerful Self-fulfilling Prophecy," *Advances in Experimental Social Psychology* 28 (1996). See also Ronald F. Ferguson, "Teachers' Perceptions and Expectations and the Black-White Test Score Gap," in Jencks and Phillips, eds., *The Black-White Test Score Gap*.

Study by Susan Gross: "Early Mathematics Performance and Achievement: Results of a Study Within a Large Suburban School System," *Journal of Negro Education* 62 (1993).

My discussion of the "composite" children, Kaitlin and Keisha, is based on statistics compiled from U.S. census data.

Study of black-white differnces in adult literacy: *Adult Literacy in America*, National Center for Education Statistics, September 1993.

Chapter 16

Quote from Linda Brown, now Linda Brown Smith: Timothy Phelps, "The Legacy of *Brown v. Board of Education*," a series of eight articles in *Newsday*, May 1994. Phelps visited all five of the *Brown* case communities in reporting this series of articles for the fortieth anniversary of the Supreme Court opinion in the *Brown* case.

Statistics on Topeka schools: compiled from data on the Web site of the Kansas Department of Education.

My report on classes and interviews with students at Topeka High School is based on my visit to Topeka in September 2000.

Statistics on Delaware schools: compiled from data on the Web site of the Delaware Department of Education.

My report on Howard Tech and my interview with "Robert" is based on my visit to Wilmington, Delaware, in September 2000, and from data on the Web sites of the Delaware Department of Education and of the Howard Technical School.

Statistics on Washington, D.C., schools: compiled from data on the Web site of the District of Columbia Department of Public Education.

My report on Shaw Junior High School and my interviews with "DaWon" and "Frenchie" are based on my visit to Washington, D.C., in October 1999.

Statistics on Prince Edward County schools: compiled from data provided by Margaret Blackmon, Prince Edward County superintendent of schools; the Web site of the Virginia Department of Education; and from Raymond Wolters, *The Burden of Brown*, Part Two.

My report on Prince Edward County schools and the Fuqua School and interviews with students at Prince Edward High School is based on my visit to the county in October 1999.

Judge Sobeloff's opinion in the Clarendon County school case: *Brunson v. Clarendon County*, 429 F.2d 820 (4th Cir. 1970).

Statistics on Clarendon County schools: compiled from material provided by the staff of Clarendon County School District No. 1, Summerton, S.C., and from the Web site of the South Carolina Department of Education.

My report on Clarendon County schools and Clarendon Academy, and my interviews with students at Scott's Branch High School, and with Superintendent Elijah McCants, are based on my visit to the county in October 1999.

Conclusion

Report on math scores of fourth-, eighth-, and twelfth-grade students: National Assessment of Educational Progress, report of August 2001, available on Web site of U.S. Department of Education; see also "Tests Show Students' Gains in Math Falter by Grade 12," *The New York Times*, August 3, 2001.

Studies of the benefits of integrated education: Gary Orfield, *Schools More Separate*, report of Harvard Civil Rights Project, 2001; Gary Orfield and Dean Whitla, *Diversity and Legal Education*, report of Harvard Civil Rights Project, 1999; Michael Kurleander and John Yun, "Is Diversity a Compelling Educational Interest? Evidence from Metropolitan Louisville," report of Harvard Civil Rights Project, August 2000.

Article by Doris Y. Wilkinson: "Integration Dilemmas in a Racist Culture," *Society*, March–April 1996.

For the remarks of Kenneth W. Jenkins and Ted Shaw on the merits of school integration, see article in *The New York Times*, February 19, 1996.

Index